WILLIAM W. HOLDEN

THE JAMES SPRUNT STUDIES
IN HISTORY
AND POLITICAL SCIENCE

Published under the Direction of the
Departments of History and Political Science of
The University of North Carolina at Chapel Hill

VOLUME 59

William W. Holden

North Carolina's Political Enigma

Horace W. Raper

The University of North Carolina Press
Chapel Hill and London

© 1985 The University of North Carolina Press

All rights reserved

Manufactured in the United States of America

Library of Congress Cataloging in Publication Data

Raper, Horace W., 1918–
   William W. Holden: North Carolina's political enigma.

   (The James Sprunt studies in history and political
science; v. 59)
   Bibliography: p.
   Includes index.
   1. Holden, W. W. (William Woods), 1818–1892.
2. Reconstruction—North Carolina. 3. North Carolina—
Politics and government—1865–1950. 4. North Carolina—
Governors—Biography. I. Title. II. Series.
F259.H72R36   1985   975.6′041′0924 [B]   84-2353
ISBN 0-8078-5060-8

Design by Paul Dean

To Bette
   Devoted wife and constant supporter

CONTENTS

ILLUSTRATIONS

PREFACE

With the publication of this study I am realizing two long-held objectives: first, I hope to remove the sense of enigma that has long beleaguered the Holden reputation, and, second, I can express my appreciation to the University of North Carolina and especially to Fletcher M. Green, master teacher, for affording me the inspiration to pursue an academic career specializing in southern history. The late Howard K. Beale first influenced my study of history, but it was Green who introduced me to Holden and directed my graduate studies on the subject. His relentless guidance and wise counsel not only challenged me to write this biography but also enabled me to fulfill his desire for someone to present a new view of the man and his role in North Carolina history. For this, as well as for his friendship for more than thirty years, I will always be grateful.

I have received invaluable assistance in this project from many sources. Foremost would be the directors of the manuscript collections of the Southern Historical Collection, University of North Carolina; Perkins Library, Duke University; North Carolina Department of Archives and History; and the Library of Congress. They greatly facilitated my research by their helpfulness in making available the Holden and other manuscript collections. I am also indebted to J. Isaac Copeland, longtime personal friend and former director of the Southern Historical Collection, and to two colleagues, B. F. Jones, Chairman of the Tennessee Tech History Department, and Nolan Fowler, for the many hours discussing the Holden project, reading my original manuscript, and providing much objective criticism. Research grants of release time from the Tennessee Tech Faculty Committee on Research allowed me a lighter teaching schedule, and Lois Richardson showed great patience and efficiency in typing the earlier drafts, as well as the final one. I especially wish to express appreciation to the staff of the University of North Carolina Press for their cooperation and support in the editing of this study. To my wife, Betty Brookshire Raper, must be given my deepest gratitude. Without her encouragement and assistance in every phase of this undertaking, the task would have been impossible.

INTRODUCTION

William Woods Holden was the dominant figure in mid-nineteenth-century North Carolina history; yet he has remained an enigma to most state politicians, newspapermen, and historians. In fact, he has been the most reviled and maligned person in modern state history. No doubt this is because he pursued a career at the edge of society's pale: he did not subscribe to the prevailing credo or mythology of the righteousness of the plantation system, the Confederate cause, white supremacy, or the supreme beneficence of the Democratic party—the glories of the Old South.

It can be said that Holden was a product of the times, and yet he rose beyond his illegitimate birth and lowly upbringing to become an influential newspaper editor, a leader in the formation of three successful political parties, and twice the state's chief executive. Although always a controversial political personality, he helped shape the state's history in the desperate years before, during, and after the Civil War.

Holden's career proved that he was both a visionary and a pragmatist. He understood the needs of the people and of the state usually far in advance of other leaders; yet when he attempted to translate the needed reforms into reality, he ran afoul of those who resisted change. He was an early and constant advocate of a balanced economy of both industry and agriculture, an educational system designed for all children and young people from the primary grades through the university or vocational training, and an improved transportation system connecting the state's geographic divisions. He also worked for an improvement in the welfare of the common man and a racial understanding that would guarantee equality before the law for all.

Born in Hillsborough in 1818, Holden never enjoyed the traditional family benefits or a formal education. At the age of ten he was apprenticed to the printing trade and was thus committed to a journalistic career in Hillsborough and after 1836 in Raleigh. By 1843 he had established himself well enough to be named editor of the *Raleigh North Carolina Standard*, the nearly bankrupt Democratic party organ. Under his direction the *Standard* gained a reputation for journalistic excellence, both for its contents and management, and became one of the South's most distinguished newspapers. As an editor, he was articulate with a crisp and forceful style. He realized that the *Standard* should not only be Democratically oriented and partisan in politics but should use its influence to support needed reforms within the state, especially in the area of human needs. He thus won for himself and the *Standard* the respect of readers and competitors alike. He proved fearless while directing campaigns for causes that he regarded as just, gaining popular support from people across the state in a surprising majority of such cases.

By 1858, having made governors of men less capable than himself, he determined to win election to that high post. Knowing that he had a genuine appeal to the public, he believed that if elected, as he felt he could be, not only could he serve the state well but he could also gain the social acceptability for his family which was still denied because of his lowly background. Nevertheless, he was deprived of the Democratic nomination at the Charlotte convention, causing him to seek other means of achieving the post. In 1865, President Andrew Johnson appointed him provisional governor, and in 1868 he won election by a Republican victory.

Holden the politician was unlike Holden the editor. He was a positive and farsighted leader, a crusader for ideals and principles far ahead of his time. This was the glory and tragedy of his life. Because his views were more attuned to those of the twentieth-century South, he doubtless would be looked upon today as one of the South's most progressive champions of reform. In the mid-nineteenth century, however, he was regarded as a tyrannical governor, a political demagogue, and a chameleon who changed party ties for the sake of ambition. While it is true that he was an active member of four state political parties—Whig, Democratic, Conservative, and Republican—he did not shift party allegiance merely to gain favor or popular approval. He was "for years . . . the militant champion of minorities; those who he conceived as the downtrodden, the aggrieved, the underdogs, those without votes or educational facilities . . ."* He placed principle ahead of power and believed that the role of government was to serve all mankind rather than the privileged few. Had he the tendency toward demagoguery by sacrificing principle, undoubtedly he could have gained the approbation of the ruling class and avoided most of the later abuse.

Once in office, Holden failed to live up to the promise of being a strong and popular leader. While he correctly understood the needs of his party and state, he allowed personal animosities to get in the way of political harmony. Thus he would not tolerate intellectual shallowness among officeholders; it was unheard of to support mediocrity. Nor would he approve of professional

---

*Wilson Mirror, 7 March 1892.

politicians monopolizing state offices. He preferred that officeholders represent all classes and come from all geographical sections of the state.

A major handicap to Holden the politician was his lack of oratorical ability and flair for showmanship. While recognized as a competent speaker, his straight talk and factual presentations could never hold an audience spellbound. In a state not known for its political maturity, he was never able to overcome this weakness. Another serious fault was his brusque manner of dealing with antagonists. This sometimes created the impression that he was dictatorial by nature, but those who knew the inner man recognized that he was basically gentle, considerate, and compassionate.

The Conservative refusal in 1865 to support his election as governor caused Holden to embrace Radical Republicanism in 1867. By organizing a coalition of Unionists, including representatives of the common man and the newly enfranchised blacks, he won the governorship in 1868. Yet he was not temperamentally suited to work with the northern Radicals, being more interested in state and local issues, while the Republicans were more concerned with national developments. Once in office, however, Holden acceded to the wishes of carpetbaggers and blacks, undermining his effectiveness and the general character of his administration. False charges of corruption, financial excesses, and black favoritism marred the popularity of his governorship, but accusations of dishonesty and lack of integrity were never proved. In the end, the Ku Klux Klan's fight to maintain white supremacy forced him to resort to strong measures in maintaining law and order. As a result, Holden was impeached, convicted, and forced out of office in 1870 for upholding his principles.

Upon his removal from office, Holden fled to Washington, D.C., to escape further persecution and seek employment to support his growing family. He had sold the *Standard* in 1868 after assuming the governorship, making it impossible for him to resume his earlier career. Instead, he was named political editor of the *Washington Chronicle*, which he hoped would become the official party organ of the Grant administration. Despite the journalistic and financial success of the paper, however, Holden did not enjoy the capital scene and returned to North Carolina as postmaster in Raleigh, a post he held with distinction until forced into retirement in 1883. More important, he used the intervening years to attune himself to a life of redemption and service and to regain respect for the Holden name. His home was often the gathering place for political and professional people from all political parties, enabling him to keep abreast of all issues even though he was denied state office. Death came slowly in 1892 after three major paralytic strokes.

In the past eighty years there has been no complete biographical study made of Holden, and it has been sixty-nine years since Professor Joseph Gregoire de Roulhac Hamilton published his survey of the state's Reconstruction history, *Reconstruction in North Carolina*. That work, written in a period of hot tempers and wounded feelings, presented many unfair impressions of Holden which, unfortunately, have been perpetuated by succeeding generations of historians. Recent research and the view of a different age show the need for major revisions to bring the past into proper perspective. Holden's contributions to the social, economic, and political progressivism of North Carolina are the major focus of this study.

WILLIAM W. HOLDEN

ONE

The Making of a Newspaperman

William Woods Holden was born out of wedlock in an isolated log cabin near Hillsborough in Orange County, North Carolina, 24 November 1818. His grandfather, Thomas Holden, had migrated from England, first to Massachusetts and then to Orange County, where he became a successful farmer. William's father, Thomas W. Holden, operated a gristmill near Hillsborough, while his mother, Priscilla Woods, lived with her parents and reared young Billy, as he was known throughout his youth. Priscilla later lived in Hillsborough with her mother in a house given her by William until her death after the Civil War.

A year or two after William's birth, Thomas Holden was married to Sally Nichols, also of Orange County; to this union ten children were born.[1] Sally Holden must have been a remarkable woman. In 1824, without the knowledge of her husband, she went to the Woodses' farmhouse and arranged for six-year-old Billy to live in his father's household. Thomas was so pleased by this act that, upon returning from his day's work at the mill and finding the boy safely tucked in bed, he exclaimed, "Sally, you are an angel."[2] The name of William Woods Holden was then officially entered into the Holden family Bible, and thereafter he was brought up as a member of the family.

Although his half-brothers and half-sisters did not learn his true origin until they reached maturity, William never enjoyed a close family relationship. His apprenticeship and later employment in Raleigh necessitated separation from his family during his youth, and his later political career led most of his family to sever all remaining ties. One brother, Brock, openly clashed with William during their entire adult lives. While serving as first lieutenant of Company B, Fifty-ninth Regiment of the North Carolina Troops, Brock participated in a protest meeting of North Carolina officers in August 1863 at Orange County Court House, Virginia, against Holden's newspaper, the *North Carolina Standard*, for opposing the war. In 1864 he ran for the state legislature on a ticket opposed to Holden's peace movement efforts, but was defeated. Later, in 1870, he was a member of the Ku Klux Klan in Caswell County and worked against the governor's military occupation of Yancey-ville.[3]

Young Billy was considered a willful lad by family members because he frequently insisted upon having his own way and tended to rebel against authority. Although he seemed to fear his stern and demanding father, he respected him and maintained close contact with him until Thomas's death in 1852. In reality, Billy Holden was timid and shy, even in adulthood never forcing himself upon others or offering an opinion unless asked. Sally Holden lived until 1875, and William was always attentive to her needs, as well as affording safety and comfort to his brothers and sisters during the Civil War and Reconstruction, when requested. One example is the appointment of his brother-in-law Henry Murdock, husband of his sister, Margaret, as a mail carrier at a time when jobs were scarce and living expenses high.

Yet there is a paucity of family letters or references to personal contacts in the voluminous Holden correspondence. Doubtless, his "unpretending ori-gin," to use his words, placed him under a handicap with which he struggled constantly, but there must have been something in his heritage that gave him the ability, determination, and ambition to make him a gifted and astute journalist, partymaker and strategist, and governor on two occasions. If his lowly origins elicited a disdainful attitude toward him from some, they gave him a sympathy for the common folk and affirmed his belief that he should always speak for them and work on their behalf to upgrade their place in society.

At the age of ten, Billy was apprenticed to Dennis Heartt, editor of the *Hillsborough Recorder* and one of the state's most enthusiastic Whig advo-cates. It was in the *Recorder* office that Holden's keen intellect was honed; there he gained intense determination for self-improvement and a knowledge of Whig ideals. His duties as a "printer's devil" called for him to work in the shop preparing the type, first sorting and later typesetting, and to deliver papers. Heartt used a double-pull Ramage press, with buckskin balls for inking the form. Type was extremely costly, but Heartt engraved the head of his paper and illustrated his articles and advertisements. He made his own composing sticks of walnut wood, lined with brass, and as Holden later recalled, "I remember to this day the sound made by the types as they were dropped by the left thumb into their places. The latest news from China was printed once in three months; and Northern news, brought to Hillsborough by the tri-weekly stage coach, was condensed and printed once a week." He also commented that "the best man in all respects whom I have ever known was my old master and teacher, Dennis Heartt."[4]

During William's apprenticeship an incident occurred which illustrates the lad's ambition for self-advancement. At the age of twelve, poorly clothed and barefoot, while delivering papers one cold morning in Hillsborough, he was invited into the dining room of a wealthy subscriber. Sitting at the table was a well-dressed young man, a student from the nearby University of North Carolina, who, at the insistence of the lady of the house, disdainfully passed him a hot buttered biscuit. William ate the biscuit quietly and slowly, but within him rose a wave of resentment as he realized the inequity of opportunity that faced them. William determined then, as a pledge of honor, to become a success in life and keep pace with the young man who had treated him so shabbily. And that pledge was kept, for in 1868 Holden defeated Thomas Samuel Ashe, the university-trained student, for the governorship of North Carolina.[5]

Another anecdote from Holden's apprenticeship days which he loved to relate was how he acquired his first dollar from his later nemesis William Alexander Graham. In Hillsborough, as in other small towns and communities, it was customary for friends to gather in various homes at Christmastime to visit and sing carols. Seeing this as an opportunity for his "devils" to earn extra money, editor Heartt would have the carols printed for the lads to sell. One Christmas Eve young Billy Holden returned to the print shop after experiencing no luck with his sales. Upon hearing this, Heartt inquired, "Have you tried Mister Graham?" Billy replied that he had not. The editor then suggested he try the famous, kind-hearted Graham. The young boy trudged through the snow-covered streets in the dark to the Graham residence and knocked on the door. An old servant ushered him directly into the spacious living room, where a party was in progress. The lad was so bashful that he almost forgot his mission, but Graham put him at ease as he said, "So you have brought me some Christmas carols, and they will be ten cents each, and I will take the entire set." Billy's face lit up over the sale and brightened even more as the party guests gave him candy and fruit. Graham then counted out ten dimes and walked young Holden to the door. "Merry Christmas," he said, taking the boy's hand firmly and pressing into it a flat, round object. "This is yours," Graham said, "and may you have a happy Christmas." When outside, Billy realized that the object in his hand was a silver dollar. Later Holden described the incident: "The first dollar I ever had to call my own was given me by the venerable William A. Graham, after I had sold some Christmas carols that Editor Heartt had sent me out to sell."[6]

One of the most humiliating and deeply resented experiences that Billy encountered during his apprenticeship was the flogging administered to him by an older *Recorder* worker for taking an unauthorized holiday during the 1834

Fourth of July celebration. Being fifteen years of age, possessing an independent spirit, and unwilling to take such chastisement, young Holden fled the city. According to custom, Heartt advertised in the next *Recorder* issue threatening with the penalty of law anyone who should harbor the runaway and offered a five-cent reward for Holden's apprehension. It is not known where the runaway stayed during his absence, but he obtained a copy of the paper and noted the editor's advertisement. He then secretly returned to the office and changed the *Recorder*'s notice so that the next issue notified the public that the paper and its editor were for sale, and both might be purchased for fifty cents. While changing the type, young Holden scratched on the desk, "From this day I will be a man."[7] He thus conducted himself as long as he worked for Heartt and the *Hillsborough Recorder*.

Holden seldom spoke of his apprenticeship and the hardships encountered in his youth, but these experiences led him in later years to befriend many young men who worked in his printing establishment and became successful newspapermen or literary writers. Richard H. Whitaker and John H. Boner, the Salem poet, among others, reminisced about their relationships with Holden. Whitaker wrote:

> I used to go to the *Standard* office to spend many of my leisure hours for the reason that, though boy as I was, Mr. Holden would take time to talk with me, and seemed to be pleased with my visits; always discussing such topics as, he thought, would interest and instruct a school boy. Sometimes he would say, as I would be leaving: "Here's a book perhaps you'd like to read," and sure enough, I'd find it to be a book that not only pleased but instructed.[8]

Boner later wrote,

> I remember one stormy autumnal night—I think it was in 1865—he and I sat alone by a smouldering log fire in the rear room of the old *Standard* office. We fell to talking about poetry, as was generally the case when we were alone, . . . Gov. Holden had fine poetic taste; he was a good critic, though inclined to favor religious verse. Milton was his ideal poet. He was familiar with the English Classics.[9]

Only once, at a banquet given in 1868 for all employees of the *North Carolina Standard*, did he reminisce about his early life. Even so, he revealed little that was not known except that he had not completed the required time on his apprenticeship.[10] Yet he often expressed contempt for those who ridiculed his lowly origins or "who would 'punish' me on account of my origin, and because I had the energy and the ambition to struggle upwards in life, who, if they had been born in the condition in which I was, would have been there yet."[11]

Before completing his apprenticeship contract, Holden decided to go out on his own. At sixteen, after working out agreeable terms with Heartt, he left Hillsborough for nearby Milton. He walked the thirty miles carrying a small bundle of personal belongings. He soon found employment in the office of the *Milton Spectator*, edited by Nathaniel J. Palmer, which later became known as the *Milton Chronicle*. Becoming restless, he left within four months and went to Danville, Virginia, where he went to work with a local paper edited by Gen. Joseph C. Megginson. There, working as a compositor, he wrote his first article. Like Benjamin Franklin, fearing that it would be scorned if the true authorship were discovered, he slipped it under the door of the editorial room. Two days later when the article was published, he walked the streets "the proudest boy in Danville."[12] Within a year, however, he returned to Hillsborough, "restless but not dissipated, and full of enterprise and ambition."[13]

Realizing that his only formal education had been a few months at an old field school, William decided against returning to the *Recorder*. Instead he became a clerk in a local store, hoping to have more time to pursue a course of private study. This he studiously did and within a year had laid a foundation for what biographer William Kenneth Boyd later called "that broad culture which ranks him among the best literary men the State had produced."[14] In time the young boy realized that clerking offered little challenge and no future to satisfy his ambitions, and so in the fall of 1836, when not quite eighteen years old, Holden left Hillsborough and headed for the state capital. He caught the Greensborough-Raleigh stagecoach on the night of 7 October and soon found himself in the company of a number of students from the Caldwell Institute at Hillsborough. Two of them, some thirty-five years later, took an active part in his impeachment trial—Thomas Sparrow and William John Clarke. Sparrow managed the prosecution, and Clarke was commander of state troops that Holden, as governor, would use to suppress the Ku Klux Klan. That night Holden had seven dollars and an expensive gold watch in his pockets. He later recalled going into debt $150 for the purchase of the watch and the broadcloth greatcoat he was wearing.[15] That he could obtain such credit was an indication that he had proved his reliability and that he had the promise of a bright future.

It is not known whether William made the decision to relocate in Raleigh without the prospects of a job or whether he had made previous arrangements with Thomas J. Lemay, editor of the *Raleigh Star*, but he immediately went to work for Lemay as a journeyman typesetter and compositor.[16] With the exception of an abortive attempt in the fall of 1837 to launch the *Oxford* (North Carolina) *Kaleidoscope and Republican*, he remained with the *Star* until 1841.[17] In addition to regular printer's duties there, he wrote numerous articles. He lived in a log cabin adjacent to the Lemay home and ate his meals with the family. One of Holden's later recollections was of sleeping "a whole winter in [the] log-cabin, . . . daubed with mud, without any fire, even in the coldest weather."[18]

After several years of this association he was steeped in strong Whiggish political philosophy, as Lemay and Heartt were both strong Whigs. Lemay then proposed to bring the young printer into a full partnership and suggested that he borrow the necessary funds to purchase his half of the *Star*. Unable to secure the funds locally, Holden turned to William A. Graham, the state's leading Whig politician, and was turned down.[19] One can only speculate how the state's later political history might have been affected had Graham accommodated him, binding young Holden to the Whig cause and thereby precluding his later development as a leader of the opposition.

With Lemay's encouragement, Holden began the study of law, reading privately under the direction of a Raleigh attorney, Henry Watkins Miller, who won acclaim as one of the state's most eloquent orators.[20] In spite of working a regular shift in the print shop and studying at night, Holden seemed to consume Blackstone and made such rapid progress that he soon passed the bar examination. On 1 January 1841 he received a license to practice in the county courts. Supreme Court Justice William Gaston, who was one of the examiners, commented that "the class of students who on Saturday last applied for license was a good class, and the printer was among the foremost."[21]

Holden immediately left the *Star* and entered legal practice, attending the courts of Wake, Orange, and Granville counties. Evidently he had originally planned to locate in the western part of the state, thinking that section would offer greater opportunities to a young, unknown barrister, but those expectations never materialized. Failing that, he applied to Chief Justice Thomas Ruffin for the position of supreme court reporter, promising that with printing experience he could provide prompt and proficient service.[22] Later, he opened a law office at no. 5, in the new building of B. F. Smith, where, according to his "card" in the *Raleigh Star*, he could "always be found, when not absent from the City on professional business. Collections of any amount promptly and faithfully attended to."[23]

The young lawyer immediately immersed himself in city politics and civic affairs, realizing that this was a quick and sure means of gaining a favorable reputation. In April 1842 he was appointed assignee in bankruptcy for Wake County and attended the state Whig convention as a delegate from Wake. He also maintained the close friendship with Lemay and supplemented his meager income by writing for the newspaper. Late in 1841 he took another major step that would later lead to his professional success and social acceptance. On 3 November Holden married Ann Augusta Young, daughter of John Wynne and Nancy Peace Young. Her father was a native of Baltimore, but was now living in Raleigh, where he was employed by Joseph and William Peace, leading Raleigh merchants. Ann was the granddaughter of Joseph Peace, who, in addition to his mercantile interests, had extensive landholdings in Granville County. When Peace died in 1842, Ann and another grandchild, Thomas W. Lemay, each inherited a half-interest in one of his plantations.[24]

William and Ann's wedding ceremony was quite simple, with only close friends and immediate families present. Holden's father Thomas and his sister Atelia drove over from Hillsborough and presented the young couple with a family gift.[25] From the beginning the marriage proved a happy one. Four children were born to the Holdens: Laura, Joseph William, Ida Augusta, and Henrietta Reid (Ettie). The household also included William Peace, Ann's uncle, who lived with the Holdens from their marriage until his death, 11 July 1865, despite the death of Ann on 20 June 1852 and Holden's remarriage two years later. A portrait of Peace hung prominently in the Holden residence for years until it was given to Peace Institute in 1885.[26] Ann's tragic death came in the midst of the trying gubernatorial contest between John Kerr, Jr. (Whig) and David S. Reid (Democrat). Despite his personal grief, Holden continued to work for a Reid-Democratic victory. His most immediate problem, however, concerned the well-being of his children, especially the newborn infant Henrietta Reid, who was named for Mrs. Reid. Fortunately, one of the household slaves, Sally, nurse-fed the child, who, Holden said, was never "sick an hour."[27]

Through the Peace-Young family connections, the young lawyer gained immediate social and financial respectability. It also enabled him two years later to change the course of his life and to reenter the journalistic field, the first and true love of his life. In 1840 and 1842 when the Democratic party suffered major defeats in state elections, party leaders placed the blame, first, on ineffective organization within the party and, second, on lack of cooperation from the party's political organ, the *North Carolina Standard*. Also, besides his failure to support Democratic principles and candidates, Thomas Loring, the editor, had permitted the paper to fall into financial straits.

Party leaders were convinced that a new editor must be found to turn party fortunes around and began looking for someone to take over the paper. First consideration was given to Perrin Busbee of Raleigh, who was passed over because of his "aristocratic and pretentious" nature.[28] James Biddle Shepard then suggested Holden's name, even arranging the necessary funds for Holden to assume both the ownership and editorship of the *Standard*.[29] Shepard himself loaned five hundred dollars and Duncan Cameron, president of the State Bank of North Carolina, loaned an additional two thousand dollars upon the endorsement of William Peace.[30] With the money, Cameron gave the young man some sage advice: "You will find that the surest, if not the quickest and most permanent and certain road to power in this country, is that of the press. It may not be so now, but in my judgment in future years it will be so. . . . My advice is, as you have chosen the press, to abandon all ideas of the law."

With such backing, Holden assumed his new post on 1 June 1843.[31] Some state Democrats expressed skepticism about Holden's Whiggish background, and his former mentors Heartt and Lemay were dismayed over his action, but Shepard had confidence in his journalistic abilities. For the next twenty-five years, Holden conducted the *Standard* with unparalleled success. Few newspapers, if indeed any, in the history of the state have wielded a more powerful influence. Yet the *Greensborough Patriot* greeted the editorial change in its 8 July 1843 issue with something less than open arms. "Mr. Holden is a very smart young man; but the integrity of a renegade is always more or less doubted, and the proverbially hot zeal of a proselyte is looked upon by the more sensible portions of mankind with 'many grains of allowance.' "

Many have speculated about the reasons for Holden's "heresy" in severing his previous Whig connections and turning to the *Standard* and its Democratic principles. Certainly there are puzzling aspects to the question, but considerations of personal aggrandizement, immediate financial rewards, or a sudden change of political sentiment do not offer a completely satisfying solution. As he recalled later, the undertaking posed major pitfalls for someone only twenty-five years old and with neither formal education nor editorial experience. Also he had a young family to support. The paper's financial conditon was not promising; there were only 775 subscribers—half unpaid— while twelve thousand dollars remained on the books as due. As for the Democratic party itself, Holden, writing many years later, described it as having not more than eight thousand members in the entire state, and most of those, in a social sense, were no better than "scalawags." The Whigs, he wrote, lived mainly in the towns and villages and possessed a large proportion of "the intelligence and all the decency," supporting the reforms of public education and internal improvements, while the Democrats were "ignorant, awkward, and opposed to reform."[32]

Therefore, the real reason for his decision appears to have been the major challenge that the position offered, with its chance to set forth his ideas on individual liberties, the rise of the common man, and states' rights. Holden's explanation came in an editorial published in the first issue of his paper. The Democrats, he wrote, "have always approved [*sic*] themselves the friends and supporters of equal rights; because they have ever been, and are now, the advocates of the many against the few; because whilst they yield to the Federal Government the exercises of its acknowledged and undoubted constitutional powers, they at the same time guard with peculiar vigilance the freedom, sovereignty, and independence of the respective states."[33] Prior to the purchase of the *Standard*, he had told close friends that he was not only sympathetic with the Democratic party but was an "out and out" Democrat.[34] Quite early in his editorship he adopted for the paper the slogan "The many instead of the few."

From the outset, the *Standard* set an example of journalistic excellence. Some fifteen years later the *Leisure Hour*, a literary paper published in Oxford, commented that "aside from politics, we regard it as one of the most interesting papers published in the State. . . . We remember to have heard a gentleman connected with one of the Petersburg [Virginia] dailies to say, that the *Standard* was decidedly the handsomest sheet that came to that office."[35] Holden's aggressive and provocative editorials and his brilliant literary style commanded attention. His editorials were read, not glanced at; pondered over and discussed, not forgotten; acted upon, either in rebuttal or by constructive action by those in agreement, not ignored. He constantly commanded the attention of his fellow editors, often provoking replies, for they felt it necessary to answer him when they might have ignored similar statements from another. Thus, the *Standard*'s audience was many times larger than the circulation of the paper.[36]

Holden's style was simple, straightforward, and readable. He also watched closely over the morals of his readers, never publishing vulgar or suggestive anecdotes or stories. Even the most sensitive woman could read his paper without a blush.[37] As a printer, he insisted upon correct grammar, proper punctuation, and accurate spelling. Only on the rarest of occasions did the reader find a misspelled word or an ungrammatical sentence. His editorials were generally positive, and today they command the reader's attention, even though the issues are neither timely nor familiar.

Holden was a master of sarcasm and possessed the ability to grasp a shift in a political situation and to understand its likely effect upon the common people. It was this feel for and understanding of human problems and needs that gained for Holden and the *Standard* immediate popular approval and support, which he would maintain throughout his journalistic and political career. While editor Holden was peculiarly proficient in provoking his editorial opponents, he was unusually forbearing in returning their cutting epithets. In his 1881 *Address on the History of Journalism*, Holden best summarized his theories on the duties and powers of a newspaper editor: "The Press is emphatically the power in this country. There is more potency in the click of the type in the composing stick than in the click of the musket. . . . Editors cannot create, they only collect and utter public opinion. . . . [The Press] leads by not seeming to lead. It condenses and propagates public thought."

From the very beginning of his new career, Holden realized that newspapers of his day not only served to report news and to express editorial views but also more importantly were to be organs of political parties and consistently to reflect the view of the supporting parties. Therefore, he immediately dedicated himself to rallying the disorganized Democrats of North Carolina, laying a campaign to upgrade the party image while placing the Whig party on the defensive. Writing from the Democratic point of view, he ridiculed the leaders of the opposition in a series of dramatic sketches entitled "Mysteries of Coondom Unveiled." In the sketches, George E. Badger was called "Whiskerando"; John M. Morehead, "Ajax the Second"; Weston Gales, "The Great Western"; and Thomas Lemay, "The Little Blower of the Little Whig Trumpet."[38] This campaign gained for Holden much notoriety and a reputation as one of the outstanding verbal duelists in the state. Within six months there was an upsurge in the number of *Standard* subscriptions, and the leaders of the Democratic party came to trust him as an exponent of their views.[39] This infusion of new life prompted party leaders to hold county conventions to solicit local support and challenge the Whig monopoly of offices across the state. At the 2 November meeting of the Wake County Democrats, Holden acted as secretary and served on the resolutions committee and the committee that arranged for a statewide convention to meet 14 and 15 December in Raleigh. At that meeting, attended by 146 delegates representing 31 counties, Holden served as co-secretary and was elected to the executive committee. Michael Hoke of Lincoln County was named to make the governor's race, and a new party platform was adopted which Holden announced under the heading of "Democratic Principles" in the 27 December issue of the *Standard*:

> The doctrines laid down and carried out by Thomas Jefferson—
> no bloated National Bank, . . . no Tariff for Protection, . . . no dis-

tribution of the sales of Public Lands at a time when the Treasury is empty, . . . no assumption of State Debts—the Constitution as it is, . . . the right of the States to elect their own members of Congress, . . . a strict construction of the Constitution—no Monopolies— no executive privileges—equal justice for all, . . . the greatest good of the greatest number, . . . elections free, and suffrage universal—no mysteries in government inaccessible to the public eye—Principles first—Principles last—Principles all the time.

It was upon these "Principles" that Holden built the *Standard* into the state's leading newspaper and built his own political career.

Within a year Holden and the Democrats were in a position to offer a serious challenge to the Whigs. Although unable to elect Hoke, who was defeated by the popular William A. Graham, Holden did play a major role in the outcome of the national election. The major issue in the presidential campaign of that year concerned the annexation of Texas. When Henry Clay, the Whig nominee, spoke in Raleigh in April, Holden refused to accede to the suggestion that all parties unite and extend to Clay the hospitality of the city; instead, he chided Clay for failing to give his views on the Texas question.[40] Later Clay officially proclaimed his opposition to annexation in a letter from Raleigh dated 17 April and addressed to the *Washington* (D.C.) *National Intelligencer*. This gave Holden the opportunity to lead the state Democrats in the national contest. He printed the Clay letter in the 1 May issue, commenting: "May that Providence who has watched over this country in all bouts, whether of prosperity or woe, and who preserved the garments of Washington, so that they knew no stain like this, or any stain whatever, preserve us also from so great a calamity as would befall us in the election of Henry Clay!" He then vigorously appealed to the state's voters to support James Knox Polk, the Democratic nominee and a native North Carolinian. To Holden it was a matter of defending southern rights as well as state loyalty. Many historians attribute Clay's ultimate defeat to his Raleigh speech and his statements on the Texas issue, although he was later to reverse his position in hopes of gaining southern support. If, in calling Clay out on the issue, Holden played a major role in the outcome of the national election, he also, and more importantly, emerged as one of the state's Democratic leaders.[41]

The news of congressional annexation of Texas was received in Raleigh "by all the Democrats and many of the Whigs with sincere joy"; in fact, Holden began his account by proclaiming "Joy! Joy!" and helping arrange a celebration with the firing of a cannon at the Capitol on 1 March. Another celebration with firing cannon was held on Polk's inauguration day, "once in honor of the day, once for Texas, once for Florida and Iowa, once for Oregon, and once for the Union of the States."[42] A week later, 12 March, the *Standard* claimed "for North Carolina the honor of having finalized the Democratic party, and passed the Texas resolutions."[43]

Holden's joy was soon silenced by the news of the death of Andrew Jackson, beloved leader of the Democratic party. He arranged a mass meeting in Raleigh on 20 June to honor "the hero of the common man." There Holden served as secretary, together with William J. Clarke, and helped plan a memorial procession for 12 July, from the Governor's Mansion through the business district to the Presbyterian church, where Jackson was eulogized. During the march merchants closed their shops, bells rang throughout the city, and minute guns (cannons firing at intervals of a minute) fired.[44]

After his successful start with the *Standard* (he proposed making it a semiweekly publication in 1845, but it was not until 6 November 1850 that sufficient subscriptions warranted such action) he realized that drastic measures were necessary before the Democrats could gain control of the state's political structure. The Whigs held not only the governor's office but both houses of the state legislature, the two United States senators, and a majority of the representatives, and had redrawn the state's congressional districts to their own advantage. Governor Graham had defeated Hoke by a vote of 42,486 to 39,433 and two years later was reelected by defeating James Biddle Shepard, 43,486 to 35,627.[45] To alter the situation, Holden planned a strategy for the Democrats that involved more representation in the state press (the Whigs at that time enjoyed a two-to-one advantage in the number of papers published), an appeal to the common man portraying the Whigs as members of an exclusive and aristocratic party, sponsorship of the popular issue of free suffrage, which he found in the 1848 gubernatorial candidacy of David Settle Reid abolishing voting restrictions in the election of state senators, and, finally, the shortening of the duration of campaigns. As Holden explained it, "We always lose by long campaigns. The adversary has full time to rally—to bring out his cross road politicians and merchants—to circulate his documents and 'revolutionary circulars'—and to put his papers . . . full to work. A short campaign . . . is the sort for us."[46] Thus by 1847, only twenty-nine years of age with four and a half years of editorial experience, Holden had begun to assume more and more the duties of tactician for the state Democratic party.

In 1846, Holden acquired his first taste of officeholding: along with Berry D. Sims and Gaston H. Wilder he was elected to the house of commons from Wake County. In 1843, before assuming control of the *Standard*, he had considered making the race, but as he did not own any property (a constitutional requirement), it was impossible at that time. To overcome this handicap he wrote to W. A. Jeffreys seeking to buy the required property and at the same time expressing his opinion on officeholders: "*Politicians by trade* must be put down; and the people consulted, obeyed and honored."[47] While conducting a vigorous and energetic campaign in 1846 for the house seat, he began a practice that he followed throughout his career—not permitting the *Standard* to sponsor his candidacy except to list his name along with other Democratic candidates for office.

His record in the commons was not an outstanding one, consisting largely in voting with his fellow Democrats against Whig candidates and measures.[48] The only legislation that he specifically sponsored called for the erection of a building in Raleigh for the improved care of the state's deaf mutes. This later led to a bill approving ten thousand dollars for such a building. He did learn, however, an invaluable lesson on the art of "log-rolling." "When the proposition to enclose the capitol grounds was pending and $12,000 was required to build the present iron fence around it, Colonel John A. Fagg, of Buncombe, said to me, that if I would vote $800 for the Buncombe turnpike road he would vote $12,000 to enclose the capitol square. I told him I would do it. The bill passed by Colonel Fagg's vote, and this was as far as I ever went in what is called 'log-rolling.' "[49]

Early in 1848, Holden announced in the *Standard* that he would not seek a return to the commons, although he could have easily been reelected. Perhaps he had discovered that officeholding and journalism do not mix, or it could have been that he foresaw added responsibilities in the upcoming gubernatorial race. Nevertheless, in retiring he expressed complete satisfaction about his service: "I honestly endeavored to do what was right, and at the same time to carry out the wishes and give expression to the will of those who elected me; and I have the satisfaction of believing that my course meets the approval of a majority of the people of the county."[50]

Political success came slowly to Holden and the state Democratic party. The party held an impressive convention in Raleigh in April 1848, with Stephen A. Douglas and Sam Houston the keynote speakers. Douglas gave such a stirring speech that Holden forgot his newspaper duties and failed to report it properly in the *Standard*, noting instead, "We took a few notes of this great speech, but we shall not do Mr. Douglas the injustice to attempt to report him. [He spoke] for nearly two hours, with a style and force of logic never equalled in that Hall, and with such eloquence as drew tears from the eyes of many. . . . We wish every man in North Carolina could have heard him."[51]

Yet Holden had done his homework well in planning for the convention, for he had lined up strong delegate support for the nomination of David Settle Reid, United States representative from the Third District. Reid, who was not present at the Raleigh meeting, easily won nomination, but in a letter to Holden he declined to run. Meeting in conference, Holden and other party leaders were able to convince him to accept the nomination after assuring him that "free [equal] suffrage" would be the main issue in the campaign. At that time North Carolina limited the franchise in the election of state senators to holders of fifty acres of land in the county in which one voted, and as Holden pointed out, there were at least 110,000 people in the state—30,000 industrial laborers, 60,000 nonslaveholding small farmers, and 20,000 farm wage laborers—who were unable to vote for state senators because of this requirement. Moreover, as the 1850 census later showed, 40 percent of the farms in the state contained less than fifty acres.[52] It is not known who suggested "equal suffrage" as a campaign issue—Holden, Reid, Green Caldwell (who brought the question before the 1842 General Assembly), or Stephen A. Douglas during his Raleigh convention address. Nevertheless, abolition of this class distinction became the major theme in the Democratic campaign.

A month after the Democratic convention, Holden started a new journalistic policy that greatly affected state politics. A Philadelphia correspondent had suggested that Holden issue a "cheap campaign sheet" and that the party organization distribute it across the state to acquaint the voters with the candidates and issues.[53] Thus on 17 May, Holden announced that he would forward the *Standard* to new subscribers for five months at the rate of $1.00 "to embrace all the facts and discussions of the campaign, and full results will be furnished of the State and Presidential elections."

The ensuing campaign waged by Reid and Holden was forceful and daring. Both parties had agreed to have their respective candidates open the campaign with an eastern tour, New Bern and Beaufort being the first stops. Charles Manly of Raleigh was the Whig gubernatorial choice and expected an easy election. He spoke first at New Bern on 10 May, giving his usual entertaining anecdotal speech, and was totally unprepared for the bombshell of free suffrage which Reid introduced at the close of his remarks. Although asked to give an immediate reply, Manly was unable to respond, but at Beaufort a week later, 17 May, after consulting with party leaders, he gave a negative reply. The fate of the Whig party in North Carolina was thus sealed. "So I announced in my next paper," said Holden.[54] Actually, before the *Standard* printed an account of the free suffrage discussion, Holden left on 18 May to attend the Democratic national convention in Baltimore, where he supported James Buchanan of Pennsylvania for the party's presidential candidate. After Lewis M. Cass's nomination, however, he gave full support to Cass's "popular sovereignty" concept of slavery expansion in the western territories.[55]

Upon his return from Baltimore, Holden used the *Standard* to support a vigorous campaign for Reid and free suffrage. Writing to Reid, Holden said, "The suffrage question is still working well. We continue to hear of changes in your favor, but none for Manly. . . . The truth is, the enthusiasm is all on our side."[56] Later, at Holden's instigation, the Democratic party reversed itself and made a call for an improved system of common schools for the state. As a result, the campaign, which started as a certain Whig victory, turned into an extremely close contest; Manly defeated Reid by only 894 votes. For the first time in many years the Democratic leadership was optimistic about the party's future, and this bright prospect was in large measure due to the ingenious strategy devised by Holden and enunciated in the *Standard*.

In spite of the Whig victory of 1848, Holden exuded extreme confidence over his improving financial fortunes, his secure position of leadership in the Democratic party, and the optimistic position of the *Standard* in dealing with national issues. By 1850 he had paid off the $2,000 debt from purchasing the paper, had paid $1,350 for a house and lot for his growing family, and had on deposit in the Cape Fear Bank $5,000 to build a large permanent residence at Hargett and McDowell streets. He had also bought new printing equipment for the *Standard*, including a power press run by a steam engine which he named the "Little Giant" in honor of Stephen A. Douglas.[57] Formerly he had concentrated on state and local issues, with editorials on national affairs comparatively rare and cautiously attempted except for the question of the annexation of Texas and the Mexican War.[58] During 1849 and 1850, however, the slavery expansion issue, especially the congressional attempt in the Wilmot Proviso to prohibit slavery in territory ceded by Mexico, the Nashville convention, the Compromise of 1850, and the issue of the "right of secession" led him to become the extreme voice of the state on such matters. In fact, a rival paper later accused him of having "educated the people of North Carolina in favor of the doctrine of secession" and gave him the title of "the high priest of secession."[59]

Holden began his editorial career as a Calhoun Democrat and throughout his years as a publisher maintained a strong view of states' rights—not only in the decade of the 1850s but also in his opposition to Jefferson Davis and the Confederate government. Although he was regarded as a "fire-eating secessionist," at least he was consistent. As one who has minutely studied Holden's journalistic career has pointed out, Holden always considered secession more from an academic viewpoint, as the abstract right of a state to withdraw from the Union if it had just cause and as a weapon to be used as a threat rather than as a feasible and advisable move. In spite of all the aggressions the South suffered prior to 1860, whenever the situation approached the brink of disunion he shrank back and cautioned deliberation.[60] Moreover, when the question of secession entered the state's political arena, with the Democrats usually affirming the right to secede and Whigs denying such a course, the editor of the state's leading party organ was expected to give vigorous expressions of such views. Finally, Holden was concerned over the danger to the institution of slavery from strident abolitionists and believed that the South had to speak decisively and clearly if the institution was to be preserved. The threat of secession, therefore, was to be used to unite the South so that it would speak with one voice and would gain from the North respect for the rights of the slave states. As long as the South vacillated or remained on the defensive, it would be impossible to maintain the type of federal union created by the constitutional convention of 1787. It was this constitutional union that Holden was determined to preserve, and for that reason he assured editors who criticized his policies that his stand made him a better friend of the Union than they were.[61]

It was the introduction of the Wilmot Proviso declaring that slavery was to be prohibited in the whole of the territory acquired from Mexico that first raised his ire. He feared that it would be followed by a bill abolishing slavery in the District of Columbia, and thus the whole antislavery movement would pose a threat to the South's constitutional rights.[62] Consequently, he declared the Proviso to be "treacherous and dangerous" and predicted that if it became national policy, "the Union will be destroyed as sure as God lives in Heaven!"[63] Later he warned those living in the North that there was a point beyond which Southerners "will not be driven, and at which, come weal or woe, they will take their final stand."[64]

In pursuing the matter, Holden thought that a southern convention, with delegates chosen by state action rather than by popular vote, was the proper method of handling the question. He further asserted that if the other states adopted this plan, "*we should hold it the duty of Governor Manly to convene the Legislature of this state*, with a view to appoint or to make provision for appointing Delegates to the Convention to be assembled in Nashville in June next."[65] But he also cautioned there need be no breakup of the Union if the people of the North really wanted to prevent it. "All they have to do is to repeal the laws protecting our slaves when they escape to their soil, to cease the agitation of this question in Congress, and to let us alone. Will they do it? *They are the agressors . . . not we.*"[66]

Holden further argued that North Carolina's failure to send delegates

> would expose her to the just suspicions of her sisters, and would be
> seized upon by our Northern assailants as proof positive of her indiffer-
> ence to what we all know to be her dearest interests and rights. . . .
> North Carolina will never consent to remain in the Union an inferior or
> degraded State. She will have *equality* as a sovereign in the Union, or
> independence out of it. She will yield up everything but her honor and
> her vital interests to preserve the Union; but these she will maintain "at
> all hazards and to the last extremity."[67]

With the passage of the Compromise of 1850, which North Carolina
accepted in the hope that it represented a final settlement of sectional differences, Holden wrote: "Let the question of slavery alone; take it out and keep it
out of Congress; and respect and enforce the Fugitive Slave Law as it stands. If
not, *we leave you!* Before God and man . . . if you fail in this simple act of
justice the bonds shall be dissolved!"[68] In taking this positive stand, Holden
was seeking a nationwide hearing on the issue. He had no desire to lead his
state out of the Union, and certainly North Carolinians displayed little sentiment for such drastic action.

It was on the state level in 1850, however, that Holden won his first
notable victory, one which prompted his future political course. Governor
Charles Manly was renominated by the Whigs, while David S. Reid finally
became the Democratic nominee. For months prior to the state Democratic
convention, Reid had steadfastly refused to be considered as a candidate
because of ill health. But Holden refused to give up hope and tried to persuade
Reid to change his mind, for he had complete confidence that 1850 was the
right time for a Democratic victory. Despite Holden's many pleas, Reid continued to resist almost until the last week before the state convention. Reluctantly,
Holden planned to accept Reid's refusal and to express his despair in the
Standard. But before doing so, as he later wrote to Reid,

> Mr. John Wheeden came into my office, and said, "This will never do;
> Col. Reid *must* run. Let me set the type in the galley, and let us wait
> one more week." I replied, concurring with him. I went at once to con-
> fer with Jerry Nixon. The result was he walked up Hillsborough Street
> to James B. Shepard's to consult him. He agreed with us that you must
> run. I then wrote the letter to you, . . . you accepted, came to Raleigh,
> took the field, and thus, in 1850, the State was won to the Democracy.
> But for Wheeden you would not have run, the State would have re-
> mained Whig.[69]

With Reid in the race and with Holden the party's major tactician, the outcome of the 1850 gubernatorial race was never in doubt. For two months before the campaign Holden kept out of the *Standard* all references to Manly's unpopularity in order to spring at the strategic moment the governor's opposition to the popular reform issues of that day. The strategy worked so well that the Whigs never understood how an incumbent candidate could fail in his bid for reelection. For Reid, Holden devised a three-point platform that called for a denial of the power of Congress to legislate on slavery in the western territories, a position later endorsed by the United States Supreme Court in the Dred Scott decision of 1857; universal, white, manhood suffrage; and the popular election of state judges. This platform proved to have widespread appeal; Reid was a popular candidate and a forceful speaker, and the Democrats won the election by an almost three-thousand-vote majority.

For his contribution to the Reid victory, Holden received financial rewards and opportunities for further service to the state. He was appointed state printer, a very lucrative position. As he later wrote in his memoirs, Holden cleared eight thousand dollars annually from this contract during the ten-year period that he held the office.[70] During the later administrations of governors Thomas Bragg and John Willis Ellis he served as a member of the state's Literary Board, which handled public school funds, member of the board of directors of the North Carolina Institution for the Deaf and Dumb and the Blind, and as board member of the state insane asylum. He was also a trustee of the University of North Carolina and Wake County Warden for the Poor.[71]

Not all the citizens of the state were pleased with Reid's election and reelection in 1852, fearing that the *Standard* editor would be "governor de facto."[72] Paul Cameron expressed such fears: "And poor Manly is beaten. . . . What a Governor we shall have in Reid! He will give Holden the reins of the State."[73] And the *Raleigh Register* wrote, "Some persons are malicious enough to suppose that the *Editor of the Standard* is the Governor, 'de facto,' and that he decides all points of difficulty which arise in the gubernatorial conclaves, with as much authority, as ever the Oracle of Apollo spoke."[74] Holden immediately denied these charges. Although there is no evidence that he tried to be governor, party power was centralized in Holden's hands, and for the next years he became the "drill-master" or "top-sergeant" of the Democratic party in the state.[75]

Charges of party "dictator" also came from Democratic party ranks. In the congressional race of 1853, Holden supported Augustus Marion Lewis of Franklin County rather than Abraham W. Venable of Granville. Venable had previously served three terms from the Fifth District, but because of a redistribution found himself running for the Fourth District, which included Wake County. Venable opposed Holden and other party leaders over the issue of distribution of public lands. Although he defeated Lewis, he made disparaging remarks about Holden and even arranged to start a new paper, the *Raleigh North Carolina Statesman*, under the editorship of Edward Cantwell. The paper began publication on 7 January 1854, but finding little support among the public, it ceased operations three weeks later.[76]

During this period of journalistic and political success, Holden took another step which advanced his career and guaranteed his future personal happiness. Holden's capacity for hard work was an established fact. He was a man who would devote whatever energy was required to achieve his ambitions, but he found it impossible to carry his work load alone after his wife's death in June 1852.[77] The tasks of conducting the editorial and business affairs of the *Standard*, serving as a major political adviser to Governor Reid, and maintaining a proper household for four active children approaching adolescence were beyond his capabilities. In 1854 he married Louisa Virginia Harrison, daughter of Robert Harrison, a prosperous Raleigh business leader who had extensive real estate holdings.

This proved to be one of the wisest decisions ever made by Holden. The second Mrs. Holden, known to friends as "Lu Lu," was a faithful companion and helpmate during a long and happy marriage. She became the family's bedrock, remaining steadfast when Holden later suffered his impeachment difficulties and his debilitating illnesses. Mrs. Holden's social position and personal wealth assured her husband financial independence and acceptance. William H. Harrison, Holden's brother-in-law, was active in municipal politics, serving several terms as mayor of Raleigh; the union of the two families enabled the Holdens to play a leading role in the city's social and political life for several decades.

Louisa Holden made her greatest contribution, however, as a devoted wife and mother. Immediately after their marriage she assumed control of all household duties and soon endeared herself as a gracious but unobtrusive hostess to their many guests. Moreover, she loved the Holden children and soon gained their affection and loyalty. To this family circle were added four additional children, and both groups became a close-knit unit. The children of this second marriage were Mary Eldridge, Beulah, Charles, and Lula.[78]

As was customary in that day, Holden left the personal and educational training of the children to his wife, but he was careful to leave time for the family. Whenever possible, he arranged family trips, especially vacations to the Carolina beaches or jaunts with the children to the State Fair, which they all considered the big event of the year. His political career unfolded and necessitated many absences from home, but he tried always to bring small gifts to each of the children. In his letters he would remind Louisa to give each child "a great big kiss." In some ways, Holden was probably an indulgent parent, especially in his relations with the older son, Joseph. He did not insist that "Jo" complete his education at the University of North Carolina, and unfortunately the young man developed a fondness for strong drink that he never overcame.[79] All of the children, however, received much attention and affection, and through the guidance of their parents they developed into singular individuals who took pride in their heritage and had happy and successful marriages.

By today's standards, the Holdens' marriage might be considered a formal or stylized arrangement, but actually it was a close and endearing relationship. Holden wrote long letters to his wife and children when away from home, and even though he habitually signed them "W. W. Holden," he affectionately added "Good-bye, dearest Wife" or "Your Devoted Husband." In one letter he wrote, "I think of you and my dear children *many, many* times. But words are no avail—*you know* how I love my dear wife."[80] When Laura, the eldest daughter, was attending Salem Female Academy in 1858, he reminded her frequently of his love and talked in one letter of "the depth of the interest I take in your happiness," continuing, "Rest assured that we all remember you constantly and love you, and pray for your continued health and happiness."[81] In another, Holden expressed his sentiments on religion, morality, and marriage, from which one may gain a clear insight into his own character. On religion, "It is no matter of whim or fancy, to be thought of to-day and forgotten tomorrow; but it should be a part of our daily lives, always paramount, and manifesting itself in all that we say or do." And on marriage, "Remember that those who marry are wedded for life, and that they must bear each other's foibles and infirmities." He then concluded: "I desire most ardently to see all my children happy here and saved hereafter. I may not have much to give them; but if they should be well educated and should be moral, just, courteous, honest, industrious, gentle and yet spirited when occasion really requires it, I will esteem this as infinitely better for them than dollars and cents."[82]

Holden expected 1854 to be a banner year for him personally, professionally, and politically. His courtship and marriage to Lu Lu Harrison made for marital and family bliss, while increased subscriptions to the *Standard* allowed him to employ Frank I. Wilson, former editor of the *Rutherfordton Mountain Banner*, as his associate editor and business manager.[83] Since the

Compromise of 1850 had failed, he and other North Carolinians looked to the passage of the Kansas-Nebraska Act in the hope that it might end the slavery agitation. Instead it led to the disintegration of the Whig party and the election of Thomas Bragg as governor. Incumbent David S. Reid was ineligible for reelection, and Holden and other Democratic state leaders turned to Warren County native Bragg. During the winter months of 1853–54 he contacted Bragg and secured his consent to be the party's candidate. He also engineered resolutions of endorsement of Bragg's candidacy in various counties across the state and published them in the *Standard*, thereby placing him in the forefront as the "popular" nominee well before the party's convention. Then once again Holden and the *Standard* orchestrated the Bragg campaign in opposition to Alfred Dockery, the Whig–Know-Nothing nominee, stressing the Democratic party's support of an improved common school system, expanded internal improvements, and free suffrage for all. The result of these efforts brought victory to Bragg by a 2,061-vote margin.

Also during 1854 Holden traveled to the North, via Portsmouth, Virginia, Baltimore, and New York, a trip which convinced him of the soundness of the Democratic party and its principles. Thereafter he was determined "to abate no efforts which Providence may enable him to put forth *to unite the South* as one man in defense of Southern institutions."[84] As for the emerging Know-Nothing party, Holden later wrote,

> When Know Nothingism first made its appearance in the South, at least when it first began to be talked about, it was regarded as a sort of myth, a joke, a hoax, or a harmless order of fanatics, or something of that kind. Curiosity was excited, the scheme was deeply laid, and not being open opposition it sprang up rapidly. It arrived, too, just at a time when the Whig party was gasping its last breath over the defeat of its last principle; and the transmigration of its soul into the body of Know Nothingism was easy and natural, as soon as it felt the attraction of politics therein, and such politics as were hostile to the Democratic administration. Thus at one gulp down went the Whig party, while curiosity and false pretences swallowed some good Democrats and a large number of bad ones. Unscrupulous Whig leaders seized upon it as their last chance of riding it into power—the Whig press wheeled into rank.[85]

Holden was amazed to learn in May 1855 that James B. Shepard, his former mentor, would run for the Fourth Congressional District seat on the Know-Nothing ticket; during the campaign Shepard would ask, "Who made the Editor of the *Standard*?" But Holden would not forsake the Democratic party or its principles; instead, he supported Lawrence O'B. Branch and called the new party a "cabal of proscription, intolerance and vengeance."[86] With the *Standard*'s unfailing support, Branch defeated Shepard by a majority of 1,591 votes, and Democrats won five of the eight congressional seats in the state.

With the 1855 victories, Holden was so firmly entrenched in state politics that he made full use of his paper and personal influence to get involved in national affairs. He publicly condemned Harvard University for rejecting Judge Ellis G. Loring as a member of its law faculty for his enforcement of the Fugitive Slave Law and returning Anthony Burns to his former masters.[87] He also wrote a congratulatory note to a young student who withdrew from Harvard to pursue his studies in North Carolina because of the incident. In the *Standard* he commented,

> This course does him honor. It furnishes evidence that his heart is in the right place—that it beats in unison with those among whom Providence has cast his lot, and is true to the institutions of his native land. We concur with him, that since the extraordinary proceedings against Judge Loring, it is time all Southern students "should seek knowledge outside the walls of Harvard." . . . The people of Massachusetts will have it so. Alienation of feeling, distrust, hatreds and revilings— whose fault is it? When have we done it? Were we to shirk and cower under their aggressions, insults, the manhood of their own region would despise us.
>
> This incident is one among many, going to show that the chain of intercourse and affection between the two sections, is growing weaker and weaker.[88]

North Carolina was more concerned with the national election of 1856 than with its own gubernatorial contest. Governor Bragg was renominated by the Democratic party and won reelection easily, defeating John Gilmer, the American or Know-Nothing candidate from Guilford County, by 12,000 votes. The presidential contest was a triangular one, with James Buchanan as the Democratic candidate, Millard Fillmore as the nominee of the American party, and John Charles Frémont as the nominee of the newly emerged anti-slavery Republican party. Holden did not attend the Cincinnati Democratic national convention, choosing to remain in Raleigh to supervise the installation of a new cash subscription policy for the *Standard* (the first newspaper in the state to do so, although soon afterwards the *Fayetteville Observer* and other state papers followed) and to prepare for his Fourth of July oration to be given in Raleigh.[89] While he confined his remarks primarily to national issues, he did give in the speech a harbinger of things to come. Having "made" Democratic governors, he was now placing himself in line to become the next Democratic governor of North Carolina.[90]

There was little doubt of an overwhelming Democratic victory in the national presidential election. Holden thought a Frémont election would "inevitably lead to a separation of the States. Even if no overt or indirect act of dissolution should take place, we could not carry on the government. No true or decent Southern man would accept office under him, and our people would never submit to have their post offices, custom houses and the like filled with Fremont's Yankee Abolitionists."[91] Former president Fillmore, in a letter to William A. Graham, recognized his inevitable defeat: "Your letter has prepared me for probable defeat in your State, which, from the partial returns, seems likely to prove true. . . . Brook's [*sic*] attack upon Sumner has done more for Fremont, than any 20 of his warmest friends North have been able to accomplish. If Fremont is elected, he will owe his election entirely to the troubles in Kansas, and the martyrdom of Sumner; and the Republicans ought to pension Brooks for life."[92]

One of the major controversies of the campaign was the Hedrick case at the university in Chapel Hill, and here Holden was the chief instigator. Benjamin Sherwood Hedrick, professor of agricultural chemistry and editor of the *Carolina Cultivator*, was a native of Davidson County. Although by no means a militant abolitionist, he had from birth been sympathetic to the western small farmers in their opposition to slavery.[93] In August rumors began to circulate that Hedrick favored the candidacy of Frémont and that he planned to vote accordingly in the November election. Upon hearing the rumor, Holden published an editorial in which he expressed the opinion that the university should be scrutinized and if a "Black Republican" were found teaching there he should be driven out, since such a person would be neither "a fit nor safe instructor of our young men."[94] This was followed two weeks later by the publication of a letter under the signature of "an Alumnus," but written by John A. Englehard, a law student, which claimed to furnish proof that there was such a professor who was an "open and avowed supporter" of the Republican ticket.[95] Hedrick's name was not mentioned, but students and faculty knew his identity. Hedrick defended his position in a forceful reply, which Holden published. In his rebuttal, entitled "Defense," Hedrick spoke of his political beliefs and his attitudes on slavery and decried the publicity given the issue. He denied also the accusation that faculty members were attempting to influence the political opinion of the students.[96]

Indignant outbursts followed throughout the state. The university faculty met in an attempt to prevent the question from erupting into a statewide issue, and a resolution was adopted stating that Hedrick's "political opinions expressed are not those entertained by any other member of this body."[97] But this did nothing to suppress the issue, for student mass meetings were held and Hedrick burned in effigy. Finally, the trustees forced Hedrick to resign, and two weeks later in Salisbury, where he was attending an educational meeting, he barely escaped tar and feathers.[98]

Fortunately for Holden, the state, the South, and the nation escaped the prospects of disunion when James Buchanan defeated Frémont for the presidency. At the time, however, Holden was of the opinion that had Frémont and the Republicans won, nothing could have prevented the separation of the states. Prior to the election, Governor Bragg had extended an invitation to southern governors to attend the North Carolina State Fair in October, the real purpose of his invitation being a proposed conference to discuss southern strategy in the event of a Frémont victory. Only two governors, Henry A. Wise of Virginia and James Adams of South Carolina, attended, but prominent state Democrats were present, among them being Holden, Moses A. Bledsoe, and Lawrence O'Bryan Branch. With Frémont's defeat, the question became moot and no action was taken.[99]

TWO

Journalist Turned Politician

The turning point of Holden's career came in 1858. Whereas he had achieved success and fame by becoming the state's outstanding newspaperman and political strategist, he now sought to become the state's chief Democratic politician as well. Having clearly demonstrated his political acumen in leading his party to victory in the elections of David S. Reid and Thomas Bragg, he now felt that he was entitled to more than mere influence in party affairs and in the choice of governors. He wanted not only to elect but to be elected himself.

In his own mind, Holden never doubted that he was equal to the task, for he knew his talents and abilities compared favorably with those of his contemporaries. Certainly no one had a better understanding of the major issues facing the state, or better ability to plan progressive reforms. He also knew how to generate popular support for the success of such programs. Holden never seemed to doubt that, once given the opportunity to seek the governorship, he would be elected, since he had the support of the people. But aside from the desire to exercise the power of the governor, he coveted the office for its social prestige—not for himself but for his family, especially the children.[1]

In every sense, by 1858 Holden had reached that point in life that entitled him to seek the governorship. Financial independence, as well as political success, made him a highly respected and public-spirited citizen. He had also become a large slaveholder with important family connections through his two marriages.[2] Yet his humble origins and lack of formal education left a social chasm between his family and the state's elite that he thought could be bridged only through election to high office, and he was determined that nothing would stop him from achieving that acceptance.

Friend and foe alike regarded him as a sensitive and proud gentleman, both in appearance and in the conduct of his personal life. Of medium build— one editorial critic put his height at five feet, six inches, which would be considered small by modern standards—his was a good figure which he never allowed to grow fat or flabby. His dark blue eyes were his dominating feature, kindly and steady, but able to penetrate the mind of any antagonist. Dark hair and eyebrows, long nose, long upper lip, with the lower face covered with a closely trimmed beard—such was the physical man. He was regarded as a genial and entertaining conversationalist, but he had a weak and ineffective voice for public speaking.[3]

From his earlier political campaigns, Holden knew the popular issues of the day, and he had aligned himself on them so that his candidacy would have the endorsement of the common people. He advocated full manhood suffrage, improved transportation that would connect all sections of the state and expand industrial and agricultural development,[4] the erection of a state penitentiary to alleviate overcrowding in the local jails and promote the rehabilitation of criminals,[5] the elimination of social distinctions and class interests, and the improvement of the state's public school system.

Holden was especially interested in changing the status of labor. For too long, many in North Carolina and the South had accepted the aristocratic notion that manual labor was undignified; this attitude was the prime villain in the lack of economic development in the state and region. Now Holden sought to change southern thinking, both in precept and by example, as he had done in his own print shop.

> When will the days of sentimentality be over in North Carolina? When will those of our young men who are now fashionable idlers, cease to be so, and turn their hands either to farming or to some useful branch of the mechanics? . . . The truth is, many of our young men have been ruined perhaps for life, by the mistaken kindness of parents, and by the false and pernicious notion that labor is dishonorable. . . . Let the truth be taught to our children as a house-hold word, that labor is honorable—labor of the hands, as well as of the head.[6]

In his advocacy of public education, Holden joined forces with Calvin H. Wiley, North Carolina's outstanding superintendent of common schools. Through their public addresses and the columns of the *Standard*, the two of them were responsible for much of the progress made in the state school system in the years prior to 1860. Holden was an active participant in local and state educational conventions and made every effort to see that all educational activities were given full report in his paper. This was true not only for matters affecting the primary grades but also for issues that involved the state university, which he recognized as the state's major source for trained leaders in the decades ahead.

It is impossible to pinpoint the exact date when Holden decided to seek the governorship, but addresses such as his 4 July 1856 speech in Raleigh, his address before the North Carolina Educational Association at Warrenton, 1 July 1857, and the one before the Duplin County Agricultural Society, 6 November 1857, spread his name before the public long before the 1858 contest. All three speeches were printed in the *Standard* and sent to all other newspapers in the state.[7] Other names then under consideration, and given trial runs to test their popularity, included Lawrence O'B. Branch of Wake County, John W. Ellis of Rowan, William W. Avery of Burke, Judge Samuel J. Person of Moore, and Daniel W. Courts, state treasurer, of Rockingham.[8] Also, early in 1858 the *Fayetteville Observer* reported that key Democratic leaders were working out a plan that would have guaranteed Holden's election to the governorship. According to the *Observer*, Senator Asa Biggs would resign his post to become United States district judge: he would be replaced by Thomas L. Clingman, allowing Governor Bragg to assume the other senatorship by defeating the incumbent, David S. Reid; Holden would then be elected governor.[9]

Holden's Warrenton address before the North Carolina Educational Association, delivered in the local Methodist church rather than in the convention site, the Warren County courthouse, because the audience was exceedingly large, gave him much favorable statewide publicity, since it was one of the best ever delivered to that organization up to that time.[10] He proposed five basic reforms to upgrade the educational system in the state. First, he called for more and better-trained teachers, educated through the establishment of state-supported normal schools. Until this could be accomplished, short-term teacher institutes should be conducted throughout the state as a means of improving the quality of instruction. Second, he proposed the establishment of school libraries and uniform textbooks published and distributed by the state, thereby realizing substantial savings. Third, Holden urged state citizens, and especially parents, to demonstrate an awakened interest in education. Fourth, he urged that the subscription schools (where tuition fees were paid by students) and common, or public, schools unite their financial efforts and thereby provide a standard school term of five to eight months duration. Finally, Holden called for the establishment of an institution that would offer technical and military training, supplying the state with professionally trained leaders. Throughout the speech, Holden reiterated his belief in the importance of a public educational program available to all children in the state regardless of class or locality in which they lived; such a strong school system, he said, was essential to the state's future growth and progress.

On 7 January 1858, Holden went to Winston and met with supporters to plan his future strategy, and the next day the *Western Sentinel* endorsed his nomination, the first paper to do so. Holden's name was not formally recommended to the Democratic party, however, until 15 February at a Wake County party meeting.[11] The day following his Winston meeting he returned to Raleigh to chair a Democratic executive committee meeting,[12] at which time the site and date for the state party convention was determined, 14 April in Charlotte.[13] Formerly, Raleigh had always been the convention site, but Holden realized that if it were held there again, it would appear that he might have an unfair advantage; therefore he acquiesced to the advice of his supporters, as well as the insistence of his opponents, and consented to the selection of a neutral site. Thus, as Holden wrote in the *Standard* on 13 January, Charlotte was selected because of the "urgent invitation" of the city and in recognition of the "gallant Democracy of the West." Some thought, however, that the western site was designed to keep eastern delegates away because of high travel costs, and it was from that section of the state that Ellis expected most of his support. From early January 1858, it was generally considered to be a two-man contest between Holden and Ellis for the nomination.

Holden began the race as the party's favorite, but as the opposition coalesced behind Ellis, his chances declined. Since none of the candidates actively campaigned prior to the convention, Holden's *Standard* maintained a discreet silence. At no time were the readers informed of his candidacy or subjected to campaign rhetoric. In fact, the general public did not learn of his candidacy until the convention met.[14] Nevertheless, the convention attracted the largest number of delegates ever assembled in the state up to that time, with 427 present representing seventy-two counties (only twelve not represented), although twelve were by proxies.

As the delegates gathered in Charlotte, the *Raleigh Register* expressed an opinion shared by a vast number of North Carolinians. "The lawyers and upper crust generally are for Ellis, while the unwashed multitude are for Holden. Although not entitled to a seat in a Democratic pew, we have all along been a strong Holden man. We think he is entitled to the nomination, and are of the opinion that it would be a burning shame, if one who has spent his life making great men out of the very smallest sort of materials, should be refused the reasonable reward which he so urgently seeks."[15]

From the opening session, the Ellis forces, endorsed by the eastern planter aristocracy, controlled the convention. This became evident when W. J. Houston of Duplin County, a strong Holden supporter, offered a proposal making the nomination dependent on a two-thirds majority vote.[16] The Houston proposal was defeated, and the convention adopted instead a plan originally suggested by the *Wilmington Journal* in February that allotted votes to each county based on the number of Democratic votes in the 1856 gubernatorial election.[17] Holden's fate and defeat were thus sealed, for now the eastern counties were in control and able to dilute the western vote, which contained the state's greatest population and Holden's strength.[18] The Houston motion was tabled by a vote of thirty-eight counties (representing 26,766 voters) to thirty counties (24,276) for Holden.

The convention began the nominating process on the second day of the meeting, 15 April. Avery withdrew his name from consideration, whereupon Capt. John Walker of Mecklenburg nominated Holden and paid him a glowing tribute.

[I] knew him when the Democratic party was in adversity—when the flag was low, dragging in the very dust. It was a time of despondency and gloom. The darkness of night was upon our cause—no star—no ray of hope! It was a time, Mr. President, when we needed a leader—a man of nerve and daring. That was the time, sir, when W. W. Holden, of Wake, sprang to our dismayed front; and seizing our flag, resisted by a most arrogant opposition, he gave it to the breeze, high before men's eyes. And he stood firm, in that desperate onslaught which he was assailed. His voice could be distinctly heard above the roar and din of battle, as he hurled defiance in the teeth of his arrogant enemies, or as he cheered, by his encouraging shouts, the drooping hearts of his dispirited forces. At that day, Mr. President, it was not respectable to be a Democrat. But men took heart. . . . The hope was realized—he did lead them on to victory![19]

Ellis's name was then placed in nomination by William Lander of Lincoln County without a formal speech, since "he needed no eulogy." The convention immediately proceeded to ballot under a simple majority rule, not by individual delegates but by county allotment according to the 1856 vote. Ellis emerged the decisive victor, 25,051 to 21,594, forty counties casting their votes to Ellis and twenty-seven to Holden. Even though Holden was apparently the choice of the rank and file of the Democratic party, he had failed to gain the support of the upper-class party leaders, men who not only scorned him because of his humble origins but who feared him because of his influence over the state's masses. They realized that if Holden had been elected governor, their power and that of the vested interests would be substantially curtailed; the man whom they would be dealing with was totally independent.

Holden accepted his defeat without visible resentment and supported

Ellis wholeheartedly in his victorious campaign against Duncan McRae, an independent. Upon his return to Raleigh, Holden praised both the party and the nominee in the 16 April issue of the *Standard*.

> It is a good nomination, and will receive my cordial and active support. Such an appeal, I feel sure, is not necessary; but as I was voted for in that Convention, and lest my position and feelings should be misunderstood and misconstrued, I appeal to all my friends, in every portion of the State, to go as I did, heartily and entirely for this nomination. The nominee is worthy; and besides, brother Democrats, we owe it to ourselves, to our principles, and to the cause of Constitutional Union, to present a solid front to the common adversary.[20]

Nevertheless, he always felt that his defeat was due to unfair methods used by his political enemies and especially the open support given by Governor Bragg to Ellis. This he did not quickly forget or easily forgive. But at the moment he refused to express resentment against any of the responsible parties. "Next to the loss of the hopes of heaven. . . , next to the loss of 'wife, children, and friends,' is that feeling of desolation and loneliness which comes over the bosom of the faithful public servant, when he thinks he has reason to conclude that the people have abandoned him without cause. . . . But the people have not abandoned me . . . and so help me God, I will never abandon the people, nor their cause, nor the Democratic party of the country."[21] Ultimately, however, his rejection caused him to leave the party and cost the state and Democratic party his valuable leadership.

Despite Ellis's overwhelming victory over McRae, the summer months of 1858 marked a trying time for North Carolina Democrats, for personality conflicts and smoldering animosities flared openly throughout the state. It did not take long for Holden's enemies to realize that the Charlotte defeat had not crushed his political aspirations. Many assumed that he would seek election to the United States Senate, not realizing that he had little interest in a federal office, but preferred to work at the state level where his talents could be used best. When the *Warrenton News* criticized Governor Bragg for giving state and federal appointments to recently converted Whigs, many persons thought that Holden was the culprit behind the articles. Holden promptly denied authorship or that he was trying to disrupt party harmony. The *Standard*, he said, could be searched in vain for any word in condemnation of Ellis—"I have no resentments of this kind to gratify."[22] Actually, he sought to forestall party rupture in the fall session of the state legislature, saying that all should "unite in causes, and adhere with an iron will to caucus action and party organization."[23]

Holden suffered a second defeat in 1858 during the November session of the state legislature. While there was no proof that a cabal of state leaders had schemed to have Clingman succeed Biggs in the United States Senate and Bragg replace Reid, part of the plan was carried out. Biggs did resign his post in May, and Governor Bragg appointed Clingman to take his seat. But when Bragg sought to defeat Reid, Holden's friends, convinced that his initial defeat could be laid at Bragg's doorstep, urged him to fight back by contesting Bragg's election. Holden finally agreed to have his name placed in nomination; the contest for this second senatorship became, therefore, a three-man race between Bragg, Reid, and Holden. After much behind-the-scenes politicking, the senate cast forty votes for Bragg, thirty-six for Holden, and eighteen for Reid. Reid was accordingly eliminated from further consideration, and on the second ballot Bragg won an overwhelming victory, fifty-eight to thirty-six. One of the ironies of this defeat was that Reid and Holden, the two men most responsible for putting the Democrats in control of North Carolina's government, were defeated. For many, Edward J. Hale said it best: "As to Gov. Bragg, we are disappointed. We regard him as inferior in all respects to Mr. Holden, and especially are we amazed that the party overlooked, in his favor, Mr. Holden's talents and service."[24]

Once again Holden had suffered defeat by Democratic party leaders without having the opportunity to take his case to the people. Even though he displayed no show of emotion, Holden was forced to rethink his role in the party, especially when the *Raleigh Democratic Press* was started by Richard H. Whitaker but financed by leaders of the opposing faction. This was the first serious invasion of Holden's domain since 1843, and it brought into question whether he was spokesman for the party.[25] He openly accused the paper of being a plot by the aristocratic leaders to ruin him politically and to drive him out of journalism.[26] That plot failed. Within a year, however, editor Whitaker was forced to sell the paper to John Spelman and retire from the political arena. Meanwhile, the *Standard* increased its circulation to over twenty-five hundred for its weekly edition and four hundred semiweekly by 1860.[27]

Holden continued to play a prominent role in state affairs during the summer of 1859, despite growing friction with party leaders. In June, President James Buchanan visited the state and addressed the graduating class of the University of North Carolina at Chapel Hill. Holden was on the welcoming committee that met his train at Weldon and conducted him to Raleigh, where he spent the night, and then to Chapel Hill.[28] A few days later, Holden attended the North Carolina Educational Association meeting at New Bern and was elected president for the ensuing year. Governor Ellis was also present and was called upon to accompany him to the chair.[29]

But a new issue, the ad valorem taxation of slaves, created a strained

relationship between Holden and Governor Ellis. The idea had been introduced in state politics as early as 1856 by Moses A. Bledsoe of Wake County,
and while Holden had allowed the *Standard* to act as a forum in its discussion,
he declined to take a definite stand on the issue. Such silence infuriated Ellis,
for he actively opposed the tax as being detrimental to the slave interests of the
state.[30]

National developments in 1859 and 1860 alienated Holden from Democratic party leaders and ultimately led him to desert the party. The John Brown
insurrection at Harpers Ferry,[31] the publication of Hinton Rowan Helper's
book *The Impending Crisis*,[32] and the speech by William L. Seward, one of
the aspiring Republican presidential candidates, on 25 October 1859, in which
he spoke of the "irrepressible conflict," all combined to create ill will and a
spirit of unrest in the state. In December, Holden warned, "The people of the
South will not submit to Black Republican rule. They will sunder the bonds in
1860, in 1864, in 1868, or in 1872 before they will do it. We mean precisely
what we say, and ninety-nine hundredths of those who may read this article
will agree with us."[33]

But Holden was unwilling to take any action that would precipitate North
Carolina's secession from the Union, even though for the previous ten years he
had supported the southern states in their claim to this right. His shift from a
militant stand to a policy of moderation, even of opposition, was primarily
because of his growing dissatisfaction with the slaveholding aristocracy of
North Carolina and his genuine love for the nation. Furthermore, Holden had
long prided himself on publishing the only newspaper in the state which
actually expressed the thinking of a majority of the state's citizens instead of
that of the vested interests. Therefore, in January 1860 he asked to "hear from
the people without regard to party" on the chief issues facing the state at the
time: (1) Should the state remain in the Union if a "Black Republican" were
elected president? (2) If not, should it await an overt act against the institution
of slavery? (3) What would be the best time and best plan, if the first question
was answered negatively, for putting the state in armor and preparing an
adequate defense? (4) What would be the best plan for cutting off trade and
intercourse with the abolitionist states, and so enhance the state's own ability
in manufacturing or in obtaining foreign goods? and (5) Should North Carolina
and the other southern states propose a constitutional convention to reconcile
conflicting interests and protect future rights—and reestablish the Union on a
more enduring basis—or, failing this, to make provision for a peaceable
separation?[34] A political realist, Holden refused to advance a cause that the
people would not follow, and although he never published a tabulation of the

replies sent in, he was convinced that North Carolinians were opposed to secession in early 1860.

In March 1860, Holden endorsed and strongly supported Governor Ellis in his successful bid for reelection. He was rewarded by being selected a delegate-at-large to the national Democratic convention in Charleston, where he refused to join the ranks of the radical proslavery advocates, or "Fire-eaters." They were threatening to bolt the party should it nominate Stephen A. Douglas of Illinois or should the platform fail to contain a straightforward statement guaranteeing the protection of slavery in the western territories. His stand placed him alongside Bedford Brown of Caswell County, Robert Paine Dick of Guilford, John William Bryan Watson of Johnston, and others who wanted to prevent "precipitate or hasty action." Holden's views were emphatically stated in a speech to the convention delegates: "I could not be a party to any steps looking to disunion; that my party had sent me to maintain and preserve, and not destroy, the bonds of the Union; that by an immense majority the people of my State with George Washington the Father of the Country, 'would frown indignantly on the first drawing of every attempt to alienate any portion of our Country from the rest, or to enfeeble the sacred ties which line together the various parts.' "[35]

Had the North Carolina delegation joined the withdrawal movement, the convention might well have broken into sectional groups and the "party would have gone to pieces . . . having no common basis on which to reconstruct or reunite its disjointed parts. By her firm stand, North Carolina saved the party, and to that extent contributed to save the Union."[36] But the effect of this action was short-lived, since the Democrats failed to nominate a presidential candidate, and a second convention was called to meet in Baltimore in June.[37] Holden appealed to his readers for calmness during the crisis; they should not lose sight, he said, of the most important issue facing the state and nation—the question was "not slavery in the territories—not squatter sovereignty—not ad valorem taxation, but whether the Union is to continue in peace and harmony, without convulsions and bloodshed, or whether it is to rock to its foundations and be broken up by abolition rule."[38]

When the Democrats reconvened in Baltimore, Holden once again was a state delegate, and he joined with other conservative party leaders who were hopeful that some compromise on party platform and candidates could be arranged. Dissension immediately arose over the seating of delegates who had bolted from the Charleston meeting, however. The Fire-eaters promptly led a withdrawal of southern delegates to Richmond, Virginia, where they nominated John C. Breckinridge of Kentucky and Joseph Lane of Oregon for president and vice-president. Holden, with two other North Carolinians, Robert P. Dick and J. W. B. Watson, refused to join them, choosing instead to remain in Baltimore and continue to participate in the convention proceedings. Realizing that Stephen A. Douglas, who ultimately was nominated by the northern wing of the Democratic party, would not have the support of the North Carolina Democrats, Holden supported the candidacy of Robert M. T. Hunter of Virginia. This decision was made in the best interests of the party as he viewed the situation, even though he considered Douglas the ablest of the candidates.[39]

Thus Holden viewed the November presidential campaign without enthusiasm. Formerly he had been the happy warrior, eager for the battle and always the optimist as to the outcome. Now, with the Democratic split a reality, he reasoned that the election of the Republican candidate, Abraham Lincoln, would likely break up the Union, with a devastating war to follow. With a sense of loyalty he supported Breckinridge and Lane, but this support was conditioned on the understanding that the state's presidential electors would vote for the stronger of the two Democratic candidates, Breckinridge or Douglas. Should the state's vote be insufficient to elect either candidate or to throw the election into the House of Representatives, the electors would then be free to vote their own choice.[40] But Holden's feelings can best be seen in an editorial written for the *Standard* in July.

In a word, no reason exists why North Carolina should contemplate at this time a dissolution of the Union. While we would surrender no right of our State, and while we would preserve her honor untarnished among her sisters, yet disunion is one of the last things to be thought of. Disunion would be fraternal strife, civil and servile war, murder, arson, pillage, robbery, and fire and blood through long and cruel years. It would unsettle all business, diminish the value of all property, put the lives of both sexes and all ages in peril, and launch the States on a sea of scenes which no eye has scanned and no navigator sounded. It would bring debt, and misrule, and oppressive taxes, to be followed, perhaps, by the military rule of titled tyrants. It would wrench apart the tenderly entwined affections of millions of hearts, making it a crime in the North to have been born in the South, and a crime in the South to have been born in the North. It would convert the great body of the conservative men of the North, who are now our friends, into either deadly enemies or indifferent spectators of our intestine struggles, which would increase in intensity until law, order, justice, and civil rule would be forgotten or unknown. We repeat, there is no good cause *now* for dissolving the Union. The cause may arise, but let us not hasten to make or meet it.[41]

By the fall of 1860 North Carolinians were far from united on a course of action. Some favored immediate secession, others acquiesced, while the majority favored a policy of careful waiting. Few felt that the election of Lincoln would warrant disunion; they reasoned that his power to attack southern institutions would be limited in view of the Democratic majority in Congress. Holden was of this opinion and cautioned North Carolinians to "watch and wait." Even after South Carolina's secession in December, he called upon North Carolinians to act with the "border states" as peacemakers, thereby preventing a crisis in the national government. After the secession of the Gulf States many North Carolinians still envisioned the formation of a great middle confederacy, composed of border, slave, and free states.[42]

Holden's pro-Union stand brought immediate retribution upon him, for when the state legislature convened in November, it replaced him as state printer with John Spelman.[43] Spelman purchased the old equipment of the *Democratic Press* and established the *State Journal* as the official state Democratic administrative journal. Holden gave his version of his ouster in an article published in the *Charlotte Democrat*, 11 February 1881. On the first day of the legislative session, Capt. John Walker of Mecklenburg and James H. White of Gaston visited the *Standard* office.

> [Walker] told me that he and other friends were anxious to support me again for the office, but, with his usual candor, he asked me to say whether I would continue to act with the Democratic party. I replied that the question of the Union was above party; that even so momentous a question as that of peace or war should not be allowed to distract or divide the party; but that if the issue should be finally pressed, my mind was made up to stand by the Union without regard to consequences. Capt. Walker nominated me in the caucus that night for State Printer, and I was defeated by 5 votes. That evening I learned from a mutual friend directly from Gov. Ellis, that he would take ground for disunion in his message to be sent the next day, and I told that friend if Gov. Ellis should do that, I would certainly assail and denounce the message.

The defeat was a hard blow for Holden personally and financially. He interpreted it not only as punishment but, more significantly, as indicative of the course of action that the Democratic leaders planned to pursue: "A bare majority of the party has solemnly declared, . . . that no man is to be recognized as a true Democrat or friend of his country, who is opposed to disunion. . . . We denounce the disunionists, and we appeal to the people against them."[44]

Ever the fighter, Holden retaliated. On 30 November the local Union men conducted a rally in front of the Yarborough House, with Zebulon Vance of Buncombe County as speaker. Later, a committee chaired by Holden drafted resolutions for adoption at a meeting the next night. Holden not only presented the resolutions but declared that the election of a sectional president was insufficient cause for destroying the Union. The *Standard* then encouraged the people across the state to hold similar meetings and "to speak out against disunion." Holden spoke during the next several weeks at such meetings, claiming that he had not changed his views, but party leaders had: "The truth is, it is our secession assailants who have changed."[45] He also ran a regular column, "The Voice of the People," in which he published letters of those approving his stand. "Prepare, and then Watch and Wait" became his motto. "Beware of panics and false dreams. Sift every rumor to the bottom."[46]

To allay the pressure on the state to join its sister states in secession, the pro-Union element agreed on 29 January 1861 to permit the General Assembly to hold a statewide election on 28 February to decide whether a state convention should be held and determine the question of union or secession. The call for the February election also designated that delegates to the proposed convention should be elected at the same time. The unionists felt that a convention allowing open discussion might calm the public mind and were convinced that they could elect a majority of those who would oppose secession. Both unionist and secessionist forces launched campaigns to win control of the proposed convention, with Holden as the leader of the prounionist forces. Through the *Standard* he sought to alert the entire population, impressing upon them the seriousness of the issue. There was, he said, only one question—"Union or Disunion." He warned, "Nominate no man—vote for no man who will not pledge himself against secession and disunion. Be sure that you know your men before you commit yourselves to their support."[47] So effective was the strategy that the proposed convention call was defeated 47,323 to 46,672, while unionist delegates won election over secessionist delegates, 83 to 37.[48]

Even so, tempers flared and Holden was publicly attacked by Spelman. Early in February a group of men were conversing in front of Yarborough House, the political and social center of Raleigh. Both Holden and Spelman were present, but talking with different groups. Governor Ellis passed by, and

Holden supposedly remarked loudly enough to be heard by all—"There goes the meanest man in North Carolina except John Spelman." The latter immediately approached Holden and demanded he repeat his remark. Whereupon, according to one version of the story, Holden began striking Spelman with his cane, one blow causing blood "to flow very freely" from Spelman's head. Spelman drew his pistol and fired, the shot hitting an upper-story window of the hotel. He fired a second time but again missed. Then a *State Journal* clerk, W. H. Laugter, drew a pistol, but a bystander told Laugter that "if he did not put up his pistol he would knock his d..d head off." Laugter complied immediately.[49] The two contestants were hauled to court the next day and each put under five hundred dollar bond. Evidently, no action was ever taken on the matter; at least no record was noted in any of the state papers. While the above statement was out of harmony with Holden's character, three years later he did say that "under much provocation, we on one occasion caned him publicly."[50]

At another time Holden was challenged to a duel by John W. Syme, editor of the *Raleigh Register*, who claimed that Holden had held the South culpable for beginning the war. Holden denied having made the statement, but when J. W. Cameron handed him a written challenge, he promptly declined, saying that he regarded the code of dueling as "barbarous and unchristian."[51]

Neither North Carolina nor Holden could stop the flow of history, and in April, when news arrived of the Fort Sumter bombardment and President Lincoln's call for troops, Union sentiment was virtually destroyed.[52] Holden remained loyal to the Union cause, but he supported Governor Ellis in summoning a special session of the General Assembly, which, in turn, called for the election of delegates for a convention to meet in Raleigh on 20 May 1861, with the express purpose of taking North Carolina out of the Union. By this time, differences among the state's leaders had vanished, and no attempt was made to submit the question of secession to a popular vote. It was generally agreed that there was no alternative but to work with the other southern states to achieve independence.

The convention assembled in Raleigh with 112 delegates present, including Holden. It was a remarkable body of men, perhaps as able a political body as had assembled in the state's history. The group included those representing almost every walk of life and every political faction.[53] Unionist strategy was formulated in two closed-door meetings presided over by former governor Graham, the first in the Holden residence and the other in the home of Henry Watkins Miller. The convention members quickly adopted an ordinance of secession by unanimous vote. This news was received with wild excitement in Raleigh and throughout the state. In writing later, Holden recalled, "I remember well, that when the act of secession was consummated, the body looked like a sea partly in storm, partly calm, the secessionists shouting and throwing up their hats and rejoicing, the Conservatives sitting quietly, calm and depressed."[54] One writer reported that Holden purchased a gold pen for the occasion and as he signed the documents said, "This is the greatest act of my life."[55] He even expressed sympathy for the Confederate cause, pledging "the last dollar and the last man" in the state.[56] As events unfolded, however, he was to regret making such an enthusiastic outburst, since his heart was never with the Confederates.[57] As he so well knew, and previously warned, secession would result in a defeat at the hands of federal forces—and the economic and political devastation of the South.

North Carolina's entry into the war propelled Holden into a new and enigmatic, almost destructive, phase of his political career. While there is some justification for the belief that Holden had signed the secession ordinance in an attempt to regain his position of leadership within the Democratic party, it was not his destiny to be part of the southern war effort for long. He broke with the state administration (Henry Toole Clark served as governor after John Willis Ellis died in office in July 1861), but that mattered little. The Democratic leadership never forgave him for having deserted their cause in 1858 and 1860, while the old Whig element distrusted him in view of his separation from the principles of their party in the 1840s. Nevertheless, neither group could deny him the opportunity of assuming the leadership of a new political force within the state.

Contemporary political leaders, and later historians, bitterly rebuked Holden for his denunciation of secession and his persistent opposition to the Confederate administration of Jefferson Davis, and for his involvement in the formation of a "Peace" party. His critics declared his activities ignoble and detrimental to the Confederate cause, especially when he pointed out the North's military superiority. But his motives, as well as his activities, need to be restudied, particularly in view of his fight for individual liberty. Holden was a Union supporter and a man of peace because he saw the futility of the long war before anyone else did. He considered it far wiser to negotiate an honorable peace while terms could be arranged than to wait for an unconditional surrender. He further held that North Carolina and the other southern states should overthrow their existing political, social, and economic order; then they should build anew, creating a society based upon industrialism and the welfare of the masses rather than the maintenance of a planter aristocracy for the privileged few. In this he was ahead of his time by at least ten years. One can only speculate on how much better North Carolina would have fared throughout the last quarter of the nineteenth century, and even today, had the state's political leaders listened to and been willing to follow his sage advice.[58]

In the early months of the war, North Carolina approved the cause and supported the Confederacy through its manpower and materials.[59] But it was not long before criticism and opposition began to develop, and Holden found himself the focus for such opposition. In the summer of 1861, Holden expressed concern over what he called the inadequate defense of the North Carolina coastline. "We never expect Lincoln to fight his way through Virginia to the North Carolina line," but a "point of easy access to the enemy, without a sufficient force to repel him at the offset, is the seacoast."[60] He was openly critical of Governor Ellis, as well as the Confederate government, for the "inefficient and dilatory preparations" and for the partisan basis of appointments (both military and political). Ability and qualification were ignored, while the selections seemed to be based on whether or not the applicant was a Democrat.[61]

At the same time, the *Standard* expressed solicitude for the home-front conditions and the welfare of the common foot soldier. Holden's concern was genuine, not an attempt to exploit an explosive issue for his own political benefit. In fact, he contributed much of his own wealth to provide much-needed relief. By 1862 he was openly demanding relief for the privates whose "pitiful pay brought them and their families to the door of starvation."[62] Also, the *Standard* published numerous accounts of the volunteer efforts made to send clothing, food, blankets, and other such items to the men in service.

Editor John Spelman of the *State Journal* suggested that the state's newspapers be placed under tight censorship to prevent military secrets falling into Union hands. Holden joined with most other state editors in opposition. "The Constitutional right, purchased with the blood of our fathers, will be maintained by members of the press in this state at all hazards and to the last extremity." Another time he shouted: "Muzzle the Press in North Carolina! Why just as soon attempt to chain the lightning."[63] Tempers flared once again, and he was faced with another personal confrontation. On 27 November he fought with William Robinson, assistant editor of the *State Journal*, on Fayetteville Street.[64] Holden was not usually a violent man, however, as attested by John H. Boner:

> He was a brave man. First of all, he was a gentleman. Personal assaults upon him were not infrequent, but he was never harmed. He never carried a weapon. I was once with him on Fayetteville Street when a malignant man leveled a pistol at his breast. The Governor was always

alert. Quick as a flash he struck the pistol from the gentleman's hand with his cane. Instead of following up his advantage with a blow, the Governor, apparently without loss of temper or composure, said to him: "Shame on you, sir." There was no further trouble. I never heard Gov. Holden use an oath of any kind, and I am sure no one ever heard him indulge in the slightest colloquial vulgarity.[65]

Working slowly and quietly, Holden assumed leadership of the discontented elements. By 1862, with the help of other "Union men," he had organized a new party, generally referred to as the Conservative party, which wrested political control of the state by winning the gubernatorial contest. Many political leaders were convinced that North Carolina had been slighted by the Davis administration's failure to give the state a fair share of the top military and cabinet appointments, particularly in view of the number of troops and the amount of equipment the state had supplied for the war effort. Also, because of the Conscription Act of April 1862, some alleged that the Richmond government was guilty of despotism, raising the question of whether the war was actually being fought to preserve states' rights.[66] Furthermore, Holden realized that the responsibility for military defeats and economic hardships would be placed on the government in power, and he took advantage of ill feelings generated by the Davis administration's failure to prevent the loss of Hatteras Inlet in August 1861 and the capture of Roanoke Island in February 1862 and Elizabeth City and New Bern in March 1862. In the first of these military defeats he had a very real interest since his son Joseph was among those taken prisoner.

The governor's race in 1862 was hotly contested. The Democratic party leaders, believing that the people were overwhelmingly enthusiastic in their support of the Clark administration and the Confederacy, ignored the strategy of the Conservatives aimed at winning control of state affairs. After realizing too late the strength of the movement orchestrated by Holden and the *Standard*, they abandoned the Democratic party label and began to call themselves "Confederates." At the same time they urged the people to retain the incumbent government as a means of quelling partisan strife and avoiding interference in the state's participation in the war. Failing to win popular support for this plan, the Confederates next proposed that the state forgo a statewide election, a new governor to be selected by a state convention instead.[67] This was totally unacceptable to the Conservatives, who replied that a governor's race would not interfere with the state's war efforts but would give the people an opportunity to express their thoughts on the issues. In the end, the Conservatives won their demands. The "Secession Convention" (the body which was to act in lieu of the General Assembly until May 1862) ordered that an election be held and that the newly elected governor assume office in September rather than in January.[68]

The Confederate and Conservative parties entered the governor's race with keen anticipation, both hoping to control the state's future course. The incumbent, Clark, was rejected because of his unpopularity and political ineptness; instead the Confederate party endorsed William Johnston, president of the Charlotte and South Carolina Railroad Company, a former Whig who had been one of the original secessionists.[69] The Conservatives had hoped to nominate William A. Graham. When he declined, other names were proposed to test public opinion: Holden, John A. Gilmer, Bedford Brown, Edwin G. Reade, and Col. Zebulon B. Vance. Had the reaction to Holden's name been favorable, there is no doubt that he would have accepted the nomination. But lingering fears caused party leaders to look elsewhere for one with more popular appeal who could unify the party. Through the influence of Augustus S. Merrimon, the *Fayetteville Observer* placed Vance's name before the public, ultimately bringing about his nomination.[70] Then Holden and Edward Hale, editor of the *Observer*, warmly and enthusiastically endorsed the Vance candidacy. It was through the efforts of these editors that Vance was persuaded to accept the nomination while yet stationed with his North Carolina troops at Kinston. Vance was still of the opinion that there was greater need for fighting men than politicians, but after much persuasion he consented to resign his military post to head the Conservative party ticket.[71]

The Vance campaign was managed entirely by Holden and Hale, with the colonel taking no part other than making a few speeches to groups of servicemen. Throughout the campaign, Holden charged in the *Standard* that Johnston's military title had been gained through the "pork and beans" of the Commissary General's Department, while at the same time he drew compensation as a member of the Secession Convention.[72] Holden further attacked the inefficiency and corruption of the Confederate party in state affairs, noting its failure to clothe the soldiers properly and its use of government offices for selfish purposes.

> Those who have been in power for the last twelve months have shown themselves utterly incompetent to manage our public affairs; or, if competent, they have been so occupied in parcelling out offices among themselves, and in proscribing the conservatives or late Union men, that they have not devoted their time and their thoughts, as they should

have done, to the duties assigned them. Besides, . . . [they] are unfit for office. Impulsive, passionate, inveterate prejudice, and a want of judgment and forecast, seem to be natural to them; and it is on that account, as well as because of their selfishness and greed for place, that they have shown themselves so unequal to the crisis and so unworthy of the popular confidence.[73]

The Conservatives capitalized on the growing dissatisfaction with the war's progress as evidenced by the increasing disloyalty to the Confederacy throughout the state. The Conscription Act of 1862, which drafted white men between eighteen and thirty-five (later extended to males between seventeen and fifty) for three years' service but permitted the hiring of substitutes or exempted plantation owners owning twenty or more slaves, drew much opposition. It stirred up such latent class antagonisms and dissension that large numbers of troops deserted and returned to their homes. Particularly in the middle and western counties, the presence of so many deserters threatened political stability; for example, Gen. E. Kirby-Smith was forced to send a detachment of troops to Madison County to maintain law and order.[74] All this, as Tatum has written, raised the cry of "a rich man's war and a poor man's fight." Holden "advocated repeal of both the substitute clause and the 'twenty-negro law,' . . . as a proof that the war was not being fought by the poor for the rich. Holden's criticisms were difficult to meet."[75] In such a climate, the outcome of the 1862 election was never in doubt. Vance was elected by a popular vote twice as large as that of his Confederate opponent, and a large majority of "peace men" were elected to the General Assembly.

There is little doubt that Holden, more than anyone else, was responsible for Vance's election. His success with the Conservative party had demonstrated once again his political acumen as well as his ability to lead. Moreover, the outcome demonstrated the state's lack of enthusiasm for the Confederacy; the stage was being set for the peace movement that Holden hoped would take North Carolina out of the war.

THREE

Peace Leader: Agitator or Dreamer?

In the early days of the Vance administration the relationship between the new governor and Holden was a close one. The *Standard* supported administrative policy, and Holden served as an adviser whose counsel Vance sought on all major issues.[1] To be sure, Vance's popularity and early political successes were not due solely to Holden, but his support made the transitional period easier. The accord between these men was demonstrated by the election of Holden as state printer in November 1862, upon the insistence of Vance.[2] Also, the Conservatives, having majority control in the General Assembly, implemented a plan devised by Holden to replace all non-Conservative state officials.[3] But this friendship was not destined to last.

There are many explanations for the break between these two Conservative leaders, but it developed primarily because of an irrepressible conflict between two politicians. In his attempt to reassert his former role of "party boss," Holden failed to realize that Vance could not be controlled by anyone. When the governor discovered that he could administer the state without the Holden touch, strained relationships ensued. However, the final breach was the result of the ensuing peace movement and their differing viewpoints. For the first part of Vance's administration both were advocates of peace but differed on objectives and goals. Seeing the futility of war, Holden sought to convince Vance that he should support the peace movement, not only as a means of ending the state's participation in the war but also as an instrument to secure better treatment for the state from Confederate authorities. He was satisfied that either result could work to North Carolina's advantage. Vance, on the other hand, believed that the movement for peace should be undertaken jointly and in complete cooperation with the other Confederate states. He agreed with Holden that peace negotiations would offer a quick solution to the war, yet was unwilling for North Carolina to act alone. Vance's thoughts were, of course, impractical because in 1862–63 the other states of the Confederacy had no intention of quitting the war except on their own terms. When Holden failed to gain Vance's acceptance of his ideas, he turned his thoughts to ways of ending Vance's career and replacing him with someone who would be more amenable to his own plans.

Holden proposed that, if necessary, North Carolina should act alone in seeking a negotiated peace, even should secession from the Confederacy be required. If a state had the right to secede from the United States, as Calhoun had argued, it also had the right to leave the Confederacy, Holden said. It was on this point, however, that he lost the backing of many state and southern leaders. They considered the idea treasonable and never forgave him. Holden did seem to have support from large segments of the state's population, but there is some question whether this was popular support or support made by the *Standard*. Nevertheless, Governor Vance decided not to back the Holden plan and instead to give full military aid to Jefferson Davis and to fight to the finish. Now determined to prevent Vance's reelection, Holden began to make plans accordingly.

By the spring of 1863, rumors of a possible peace became more than gossip; it was a subject for open talk on the streets in cities and towns throughout the state. Soon, with Holden as one of the leaders, an organized movement for peace materialized—this despite his insistence that the people's wishes were merely being followed. His statements went so far as to claim that four-fifths of the people in the state were ready to return to the Union but their wishes had been thwarted. If Governor Vance was not totally convinced by the Holden claims, he agreed in principle that the state troops would fight better if they knew that friends at home were preparing the way for negotiating an honorable peace. "After a careful consideration of all the sources of discontent in North Carolina, I have concluded that it will be perhaps impossible to remove it except by making some efforts at negotiation with the enemy. . . . If fair terms are rejected [by the North] it will . . . rally [our people]. . . . I have not suggested the method of these negotiations or their terms; the effort to obtain peace is the principal matter."[4]

There is no question, then, that resentment against the authorities in Richmond had begun, and Holden hoped to use it to advantage. Desertion had become a major problem; many North Carolina soldiers were leaving their military posts in Virginia, hoping to escape the hardships of war and ready to join their families in promoting the peace movement. While it is impossible to measure the total number of such desertions, newspaper advertisements offering rewards for the retention of the miscreants give an indication of the extent and seriousness of the problem. Some named as many as 42 from a single company as absentees, while others listed 66, 125, and even 188 from regiments whose full muster was less than 1,000.[5] Numerous public meetings were held across the state, mainly in the Piedmont and the western counties, and resolutions were adopted demanding that authorities negotiate a quick settlement of the war.[6] Holden published such resolutions in the *Standard* and proposed state conventions aimed at securing an "honorable peace." Always, however, he denied encouraging desertions. "We have never written, or uttered, or printed a word designed or calculated to cause desertion. On the contrary, we have written and printed more, perhaps, to discourage desertions and to encourage volunteering than any Editor in the State."[7]

There was a larger question—the concentration and centralization of power in the Confederate government. On this issue, Vance, who was most assertive on states' rights, supported the opposition. When the Confederate government enacted the impressment and tithing laws in 1863, Vance joined with Holden and other Unionists in crying aloud in protest, "The Central Government takes our fighting men with one hand and a tenth of our substance with the other."[8]

Not only had dissatisfaction with and disloyalty to the Confederate cause increased within the state during 1863 but knowledge of such had spread beyond North Carolina's borders. Charles Dana, assistant United States secretary of war, talked with Andrew Johnson, governor of Tennessee, and wrote that North Carolinians "will seize the first opportunity to free themselves from the Confederate Government."[9] Major General John G. Foster, writing to Secretary of War Edwin M. Stanton, informed him that he had sufficient information from private sources to cause him to hope that North Carolina Unionists were ready to act "on certain contingencies," and to move toward severance.[10]

Meanwhile, Vance realized the serious nature of the problem. On 5 January 1863, he wrote James A. Seddon, the Confederate secretary of war, that "the impunity which the deserters enjoy and the contagion of their example is operating most ruinously upon the efficiency of the army, to say nothing of the injury to property and citizens."[11] This was followed on 26 January by a proclamation to the absentee soldiers asking that they return to their posts and promising to "share the last bushel of meal and pound of meat in the State" with the army and homefolk. But these actions failed to end desertions, and reports on the situation together with reports on peace agitation within the state soon reached Washington and Richmond. President Davis became so alarmed that he wrote Vance to ask if Holden's "treasonable action" warranted criminal prosecution. It was later disclosed that he was prepared to have him arrested for disloyalty, along with Bartholomew F. Moore and Richard S. Donnell.[12]

The governor quickly replied that there was no cause to fear North Carolina action and that "it would be impolitic in the very highest degree to interfere with Holden or his paper."[13]

The number of peace meetings, which grew more quickly in 1863, undoubtedly served to give Holden some sense of the feeling across the state, although he may have encouraged them as a means of showing Governor Vance that it would be wise for him to give open support to the peace drive. After a visit to Richmond in August 1863, however, Vance returned home convinced that a "split with Holden is decreed by God. I have made up my mind to it and prepared for it any day, [though] I did nothing to 'precipitate' it." He reasoned that Holden by this time stood for surrender, "reconstruction or anything else that [would] put him under Lincoln, and stop the war—and I might add—punish his old friends and collaborators—the Secessionists."[14] Vance also feared that the North would gain an erroneous opinion of the southern war effort, thus defeating all efforts for peace except on the basis of absolute submission. While one could argue that the governor was still a peace man, it is evident that he was for peace only as a basis of separation and independence. On the other hand, the motto of the peace men remained, "Let us fight and talk peace at the same time."[15]

In July and August 1863, the Heroes of America (also known as the "Red Strings" because members wore such badges in their coat lapels), a secret society devoted to returning the state to the Union and whose work was conducted primarily by ministers and noncombatants, held more than one hundred meetings throughout the state, with sixty reported in the *Standard* alone.[16] Bitter protests were immediately forthcoming, especially from the armed services. Over thirty state regiments passed resolutions denouncing Holden, the peace meetings, and especially the actions of the "Red Strings." On 12 August delegates from each of the state's regiments met in convention in Orange Court House, Virginia, and issued a formal protest, urging the people to support the Confederacy.[17]

Confederate leaders demanded that Holden's activities be stopped, while Vance sought the help of William A. Graham and Edward J. Hale to dissuade Holden from further participation in the movement. When this failed, he drew up a public statement concerning the role of the peace movement. Upon seeing this, Holden advised the administration to give more consideration to the issue and specifically to consult other state citizens before publication. Accordingly, former governors William A. Graham and John A. Gilmer, Edwin G. Reade, and Edward J. Hale, along with Holden, were invited to a meeting in Raleigh on 2 September to discuss the controversy. There, Holden insisted upon the right to hold public meetings without interference from the state, while the governor responded with an offer to withhold publication of the document if Holden would give his word that future meetings would be discouraged. When the offer was refused, Vance prepared a more denunciatory proclamation, which he toned down upon the advice of former governor Graham. The final version was issued on 7 September; it urged the people of North Carolina to cease such activities in view of the fact that they "were endangering the public peace and tranquility, as well as the common cause of independence." It closed with the comment, "Surely, you will not seek to cure the evils of one revolution by plunging the country into another."[18] Holden's reply was simple and direct: "Let the people speak, it is refreshing to hear them."

Two days later, Holden was made aware of the maxim "those who sow the wind must reap the whirlwind." Troops from Gen. Henry Benning's Georgia Brigade were passing through Raleigh, and one of the regiments—that of Colonel Wright—decided that Holden's peace activities had exceeded the limits of patience and that they should administer a proper lesson. Marching in a body, the Georgia troops went to his residence and, not finding him there, proceeded to the *Standard* office, which they found closed. They then crushed the heavy doors and destroyed nearly everything: cases of type were emptied on the floor or flung into the street; the massive marble slabs with set type were turned over; the type was thrown into a huge heap upon the floor; and, finally, kegs of ink were emptied over the entire lot. For some reason, the valuable press escaped injury, probably because it was in another part of the building.

Warned of the possible assault, Holden had gone to the Governor's Mansion to seek help. Vance went to the scene and called for an immediate end to the violence, whereupon the soldiers promptly returned to their bivouac. The governor demanded that those responsible should be punished by the Confederate authorities, for he was convinced that the incident had been planned well before the troops' arrival in Raleigh. The officers in the brigade had given encouragement to the outrage by failure to take necessary action to prevent it. Furthermore, General Benning himself had known of the plan and condoned it, or so Vance believed. Unfortunately, before Vance could lodge an official protest, a group of some forty citizens of Raleigh, led by Mark Williams, who was a strong Unionist, formed a retaliatory mob. They attacked the office of the *State Journal*, the pro-Confederate paper, destroying its presses and ruining the type and other office materials.[19]

The two demonstrations had an immediate impact on Governor Vance and his administration. No longer was Vance a partial supporter of the peace movement; he became one of its active opponents. While he never believed that Holden's actions had been treasonable, he was quite willing to protect the civil rights of all citizens. Now he was convinced that continued rebellion would lead to an end of state government, with resulting anarchy or despotism. Accordingly, Vance telegraphed President Davis requesting that permission be refused for troops to pass through the capital city; added to the request was a threat to recall state troops if future outrages upon the dignity of North Carolina were not checked. When another demonstration occurred a few days later involving troops of the Fourth Alabama Regiment, Vance appeared promptly, and his presence, along with that of troops from nearby Camp Gilmer, prevented the *Standard* office from being sacked again.[20]

At the time of the second mob scare, Holden fled to the countryside, not for fear of his own safety but rather to spare his family and residence, located on a lot adjoining the *Standard* office. Once peace and quiet were restored, he returned to the city, showing neither fear nor remorse. Refusing to take the incidents as a warning to alter his views or to change his course of action, he resumed publication of the *Standard* within a month and capitalized on the disturbances as a means of justifying his peace activities. And the elections of the fall of 1863 emboldened him even further. Of the ten Confederate elected congressmen, eight were new to their posts and five were pledged to work toward obtaining an honorable peace.[21] Holden and the *Standard* had played a major role in the election and bore a large measure of responsibility for the composition of the state's delegation.

By late 1863, Holden was convinced that peace would come not through the Confederate government but rather by individual state action. Lincoln had announced that the Union would accept only unconditional surrender, while Davis had sworn never to yield unless absolute independence were granted to the southern states. Peace, Holden maintained, should be made while the South was in a position to bargain for terms. Otherwise the remaining states would face a fate similar to that of Mississippi and Louisiana, where military rule reigned. Vance realized the validity of such an argument; in December he wrote Davis stating that it would be impossible to remove the sources of discontent in the state unless the Confederate government made reasonable efforts to negotiate. The Davis reply, "We have made three distinct efforts to communicate with the authorities at Washington, and have been invariably unsuccessful," was not satisfactory to either Vance or Holden.[22]

Early in 1864 peace agitation reached its height. On 19 January, Holden editorialized in the *Standard* not only his views on the necessity for peace but also his reasons justifying such action. North Carolina, he wrote, had the right to call a convention and to hold it without being responsible to any power on earth. Should "the war be continued twelve months longer Negro slavery will be utterly and finally destroyed. . . . Its sudden destruction would involve the whole social structure in ruin." He further declared:

> Peace can never be obtained as long as we contend for Maryland, Kentucky, Missouri, and West Virginia; and that in all probability, it can be obtained only by the sovereign states cooperating with the common government. We are, therefore, for a Convention, and for a cooperation with our sister States of the South in obtaining an armistice, so that negotiations may be commenced. . . . Is there any treason in these propositions? . . . We wish, first, to save human life and to prevent the impoverishment and ruin of our people; secondly, to prevent the sudden abolition of slavery, the blighting effect of which would be seen on this continent for generations; and thirdly, to prevent the extinction of the State sovereignties, which if it should take place, would reduce us to the condition of territorial dependents on the favor of some great, central, despotic government. But why delegates to a Convention now? Because the State may be so occupied by the enemy as to render the election, at some future day . . . impossible.

Because of Holden's influence, the General Assembly reputedly adjourned its 1863 legislative session earlier than planned in order that its members might be out among the state's citizens agitating for a convention that would remove North Carolina from the Confederacy. A proposal to this effect was prepared by Holden and introduced by James Thomas Leach as a resolution at a peace rally in Johnston County.[23] This was followed by a series of such meetings throughout the state where similar proposals were made. John Pool, a state senator, and Jonathan Worth, a member of the Vance administration, served as the two principal Holden followers in the movement. Worth believed that Governor Vance would cooperate if the people would only make known their strong desires.[24]

Holden warned the governor that by not joining the movement and by failing to call a state convention in May, he was inviting an opponent in the upcoming election. Vance's reaction was definite and immediate; he broke completely with Holden and thereafter pursued a vigorous prosecution of the war in every way. Writing to William A. Graham, he commented, "I will see the Conservative party blown into a thousand atoms and Holden and his understrappers in hell . . . before I will consent to a course which I think would bring dishonor and ruin upon both State and Confederacy."[25] Nevertheless, Vance was fearful that his decision might not meet popular approval; in fact, his fears were so strong that he considered declining renomination. Holden, on the other hand, continued to maintain a friendly relationship with the governor, even intending to endorse Vance's reelection should he support the Conservative party's principles and its peace policy.

The growing fear of peace agitation and the defeats suffered on the battlefronts caused the Confederate Congress, upon President Davis's request, to suspend the writ of habeas corpus, an action contrary to civil law and an infringement of civil liberties of the worst sort. Without this safeguard, after consulting with close friends Holden felt compelled to suspend publication of the *Standard*. "I felt that if I could not continue to print as a free man," Holden wrote, "I would not print at all, and I could not bear the idea of lowering or changing my tone"[26]

Once having decided to seek reelection, Vance began his campaign early in the year by invading the heart of "peace country," the western portion of the state. On 22 February 1864 he spoke at Wilkesboro, a mountain village where desertion and resistance to the Confederate cause had run extremely high, using as his theme the claim that southern independence could be gained only if all southern states solidly supported the Confederate government. He followed this address with a speaking tour of army camps in Virginia, where again he strongly allied himself with the war party.

Such a bold and energetic start placed the peace advocates in dire straits. They feared that the popular governor had left the Conservatives and given his allegiance to the "Destructives."[27] In so doing, he would demoralize their party in the same manner that John Tyler might have destroyed the Whig party in 1842 had not Henry Clay intervened.[28] Not to oppose Vance would be the same as abandoning their cause. They reasoned, therefore, that a peace candidate, even if he had to run on an independent ticket, must oppose the governor.

Vance, by process of reasoning, sought to establish a list of his probable opponents; after eliminating Judge Edwin G. Reade, Daniel G. Fowle, and then Holden (for the obvious reason that his candidacy would create party disunion), he concluded that the peace candidate would have to be Gen. Alfred Dockery, Edward J. Warren, or Judge Thomas Settle.[29] Yet despite strong pleas from peace leaders, none of these men would consent to campaign against the governor. Holden, on the other hand, was unafraid to fight for a cause in which he thoroughly believed. So against his wishes and probably against his better judgment, since he had hoped that someone else would run, he announced his candidacy on 3 March in a special issue of the *Standard*.

> To the People of North Carolina
>
> In compliance with the wishes of many friends, I announce myself a candidate for the office of Governor of North Carolina, at the election to be held on the first Thursday in August next.

My principles and views, as Conservative "after the straightest sect," are well known to the people of the state. Those principles and views are what they have been. They will not be changed.

I am not disposed, at a time like this, to invite the people from their employments, and add to the excitement which prevails in the public mind, by haranguing them for their votes. We need all our energies to meet the common enemy, and to provide means of subsistence for our troops in the field and the people at home. Let the people go calmly and firmly to the polls and vote for the man of their choice. I will cheerfully abide their decision, whatever it may be.

If elected I will do everything in my power to promote the interests, the honor, and glory of North Carolina, and to secure an honorable peace.[30]

Thus the stage was set for an all-out battle, with the peace issue as the dominant question. Vance had earlier planned his strategy in a letter to Edward J. Hale.

The convention question is to be my test and I am to be beaten if I oppose it. . . . My desire is to make a record showing every desire for peace except at the expense of my country's ruin and dishonor; and I want the question narrowed down to *Lincoln or no Lincoln*, and I don't intend to fritter away my strength on any minor issue. I advise you therefore to make no fight on the substitute questions—the country will settle that—on taxation, schools, or anything of that kind.[31]

Vance carried his campaign to the people in an extensive tour, while Holden remained in Raleigh, true to his promise to wage neither a sensational nor a broad campaign. He was handicapped by the fact that not until May could he feel himself sufficiently safe from prosecution to resume publication of the *Standard* and use its broad appeal as his main campaign instrument. Vance and his supporters were confident of reelection because their party was well organized and disciplined, and the governor's record had been a successful one with full support from the "war party." Moreover, they knew that Holden lacked an effective organization and would not have time in the short campaign to coordinate his supporters. The major concern of the Vance supporters was the lack of a strong supporting newspaper in Raleigh to offset the *Standard*'s prestige. This was solved quickly by the establishment of the *Raleigh Conservative*.

Other Conservative leaders were not as confident as Vance about the election's outcome, for they refused to underestimate the popularity of the peace issue or Holden's ability to wage a campaign. Duncan K. McRae, writing to Edward J. Hale of the *Fayetteville Observer*, disclosed some of their fears in saying that

> Holden and his friends are working slyly, industriously, meanly to carry him through; and we tell you worriedly there is danger of their success, unless the most harmonious and hearty cooperation of all opposed to him can be effected. Governor Vance seems not to be aware of this— he is exuberant in confidence of his own strength, and seems to be more regardful of winning over Holden's friends, than of securing those for himself who differ with him on many points.[32]

In the pages of the *Standard*, Holden expressed confidence, yet he realized that there was little hope of his defeating Vance. As a political pro, he realized that he had insufficient time to build an effective organization and that the very nature of the times precluded a hard-hitting, derogatory campaign that would create disruption. Still, despite some efforts in May to force him from the race in the interest of harmony, Holden refused to withdraw and accelerated his efforts in the hopes of carrying to the people his message of peace.[33] Perhaps this was foolish pride or perhaps he had permitted himself to be convinced that the people truly wanted peace with secession from the Confederacy. In any event, his entire campaign was based on the belief that the growing opposition to the war, especially among the state troops, could turn the tide of the campaign and result in his election. In a letter to Calvin J. Cowles, who became his son-in-law in 1868, he commented that "the intelligence I receive continues to be of the most cheering character. I feel sure of a decided majority in the army. The minds of the people and soldiers are made up, and nothing will change them."[34]

As the campaign unfolded, there were developments that worked to Holden's disadvantage. The first was the exposure of the Heroes of America. Early in the campaign there were rumors that Holden was connected with a "treasonable organization." Since such had been a common campaign practice in the state, little thought was given to the matter until 6 July, when Vance supporters published a full account of the Heroes of America, with the signed confession of the Reverend Orrin Churchill of Caswell County. The society, originally started in the North working for peace and union, had by 1864 established many branches in the state and was ardently supporting the Holden candidacy. J. F. Johnson, a society member from Forsyth County, purportedly went to Washington and initiated President Lincoln, Benjamin S. Hedrick, and others into the state organization. This disclosure led some Holden critics to believe that not only was he an active member but he was also in the pay of the federal government.[35] Many came to believe the latter accusation because of publicity in the state press. There was no truth to the charge, but because he was unable to refute it adequately, it cost him many votes.[36]

The other development involved campaign rhetoric about "treason" to the Confederate cause. At the height of the campaign the General Assembly met for a two-week session, which Holden and his peace supporters hoped to use to their political advantage. They planned to force the legislature to adopt a resolution calling for a special state convention that would take the initiative in making a separate peace. Instead of adopting Holden's peace proposal, though, the General Assembly passed resolutions declaring that the Confederate government had the sole power to negotiate for peace and then only on the basis of independence. It was thus made to appear that the convention scheme was designed to remove North Carolina further from the Confederacy and that Holden was planning a treasonable act. Robert P. Dick of Guilford County, a lifetime Unionist, vehemently denied the accusation and stated that the sole purpose of the convention plan was to permit negotiations with other southern states and to invalidate any acts of the Confederate Congress that might be unconstitutional.[37]

Voting among the state's armed forces was conducted on 29 July, some two weeks prior to the regular state election. The result was an overwhelming majority for Vance, a strong indication of the ultimate outcome. Holden had not counted on a vote of 13,209 for Vance out of 15,033 cast. He immediately protested, claiming that fraud, despotism, and intimidation were used to prevent a free vote. But it was all to no avail. Writing to Calvin J. Cowles the day after the voting and before he knew the final results, Holden said,

> You have no doubt seen or heard before this letter reaches you of the wonderful excesses of Governor Vance in the Army. My heart sickens at the memory of what occurred yesterday. Never before in the annals of American history did such voting take place. The Provost Guard of this place was marched up and voted under orders, and beneath the supervision of Confederate officials. All Holden men were summarily disposed of, in guarding the bridges in many instances. The Hospitals were filled with women who in some instances maligned the soldiers bitterly, snatching the tickets from their hands, tearing them up and stomping upon the remnants. They then gave them Vance tickets. The surgeons also browbeat and abused the privates. There was no withstanding such censure. So the Holden men generally refused to

vote, and some timid ones were forced to vote the other way. Colonel George Settle of Vance's staff engineered the whole matter. We have the proof. . . . How has the balance of the Army gone? If they voted freely, we have no fears, if tyranny has been put upon them also, God only knows. . . . It is fraud and despotism. Where are our liberties?[38]

And such charges were not without foundation, for similar accounts appeared in both the *Standard* and the *Raleigh Progress* indicating that a free election had not been allowed by the authorities. Two soldiers later explained their desertion on grounds that they had not been permitted to vote for Holden.[39] Gen. Robert D. Johnston informed the governor that he originally planned to allow no one under his command to vote for Holden, yet later had permitted oral voting only.[40]

Even without such acts of intimidation in the army vote, it is likely that Vance would have been victorious, but the race would have been more interesting. The final election vote showed Vance with a total of 43,579 against 28,982 for Holden.[41] If Holden had received half of the army vote, and he had expected more than half, the outcome would have been close. In fact, Holden and the peace movement might well have carried the day.[42]

Although shocked and hurt, Holden did not press charges of fraud, realizing that he had no chance for redress.[43] Instead, he resumed the editorship of the *Standard*, endeavoring to "render it a more welcome and entertaining vehicle of news, literature, and science." He further proclaimed his friendship to both the Confederate and state governments, denying that he had counseled the withdrawal of North Carolina from the Confederacy, the submission of the state to federal authority, and the reconstruction of the Union.

> On the contrary, I have uniformly maintained, as I do now, that the war must be prosecuted in self-defense, but that at the same time the President, the Congress, the Governors of the States, and the States themselves should resort to every means in their power to obtain an armistice, so as to transfer the great question in dispute between the two sections from the smoke of the battlefield to the calm, clear atmosphere of reason, and diplomacy in civil councils, where alone, in the end, these questions must be settled.[44]

Throughout the remainder of 1864 and into 1865, Holden pressed for peace while preparing for the ultimate and unquestionable defeat of the Confederacy. Conditions were depressingly bleak, for military defeats were announced daily and desertions were rampant. Not only in the western counties but in all the unoccupied sections of the state economic depression and suffering were all too evident, and the people's morale had reached a staggering low. Even Governor Vance was convinced that the war could not last through 1864, and accordingly he began preparations for the end. In October he requested from the Council of State authority to call a special session of the General Assembly, a request unwisely denied. Vance then sought a conference of southern governors to meet in Augusta, Georgia, and devise a uniform plan of action. But the governors found themselves so divided in opinion that no plans could be agreed upon.[45]

Meanwhile, the General Assembly conducted a session, lasting from 21 November to 23 December and reassembling in January, which was unable to agree upon future plans. It did defeat resolutions calling for peace negotiations, however. Senator John Pool, of Bertie County, proposed that five commissioners be elected by the legislature to join commissioners from the other southern states, with the authority to conduct such negotiations. The senate rejected the proposal by a close vote of 24 to 20.[46] In the lower house a resolution was offered by J. T. Leach proposing that President Davis appoint peace commissioners empowered to negotiate directly with President Lincoln. This was rejected when members of the commons realized that Lincoln could not receive commissioners without recognizing the validity of the Confederacy.[47]

The peace movement in North Carolina did not abate during the remainder of the war. On 24 February 1865, Holden reported:

> The latest news may be given in a few words. Charleston, Wilmington, and Columbia are in the hands of the enemy. . . . The prospect is gloomy. We can see no blessed star pointing to peace, but on every side the clouds of war, tipped with the fires of battle, are rolling and surging. How many more widows and orphans, how much more suffering, and how many more of the true and brave of our veteran troops must be slaughtered before the end shall come? Oh, if the people of the two sections could only take all these troubles in hand, and settle them according to justice, truth, and humanity!—but the people have long since ceased to rule, and everything precious must be sacrificed to the vague hopes or the inveterate passions of our rulers.

On 17 April 1865, Holden resumed publication of the *Standard* on a daily basis. It had been suspended in part for fear of censorship and in part because of the scarcity of newsprint. Now he could say,

The contest is now over, and it is the duty of every good citizen of this State to do all in his power to reestablish and strengthen the national authority. Davis has fled, Vance has fled, [E. Kirby-]Smith has fled, secession is dead, treason has been extinguished in its own blood, and Thank God for it. The period so long looked for and labored for by the true men of this State has at last arrived. Let those who are the authors of all horrors through which we have passed, and those who during the last two years have identified themselves with the Davis and Vance despotism, make up their minds to retire to private life. The people have no use for them.[48]

FOUR

Provisional Governorship:
A Revolutionary Concept Rejected

The Civil War was over at last, but North Carolinians were in no mood to think beyond the necessity for survival. The shocking news of President Lincoln's assassination profoundly alarmed Holden. Yet he would not permit the news to dim his hope that the state would have a quick return to the Union. If he had fears that northern resentment might turn against the South and delay North Carolina's reentry, he also knew Andrew Johnson and felt confident that if permitted by the Republican leaders, he would continue the Lincoln policy of reconciliation. As Holden told his *Standard* readers, Johnson was

> a native of this City, and under the blessings of Providence, eminently a self-made man. We know him well. He is a man of first rate ability, possessed of an iron will, and enthusiastically devoted, as his whole public life shows, to the rights and interests of the people. We believe he will make a safe and able President. He will have the warm sympathies of the people of his native state, and their earnest prayers that his administration may promote the happiness of the whole American people.[1]

In his eagerness for restoration and unity, Holden immediately pressed for administrative action. "Our people want to commence de novo," he wrote. "They desire to have restored to them once more the right to govern themselves."[2] As so often before, he was a step ahead of his time, for he was prepared to suggest a solution to the problems of reconstruction. In April he advocated a general plan for reconstruction of the entire South that proved to be almost identical to the formal statement of policy issued by Johnson on 29 May 1865, when he appointed Holden provisional governor of the state. This plan called for the appointment of a military governor "whose duty it shall be, in cooperation with the regular military power, to restore order among the people, to enforce the laws, and to suppress that terrible guerrilla warfare which is already afflicting the State." The governor should then call a convention which would revise the state constitution, order an election of state officials, and provide for the election of congressmen. "By this mode order will be maintained, the people will be consulted, the institution of slavery will be promptly disposed of, a new State government will be established deriving its existence immediately from a Union people, and the State will have her members of Congress in readiness to take their seats even before that body shall meet in December, 1865."[3]

President Johnson's idea, however, was that state reorganization should be the work of the people, acting in their sovereign capacity without military supervision. Even so, Holden realized that restoration to the Union would be under the jurisdiction and sympathetic eye of a native son, and this engendered hope. Johnson selected North Carolina, rather than Virginia, as the state to begin reconstruction. In formulating his plans he sought the advice of the state's strongest Union leaders.[4] He telegraphed Holden on 9 May, asking him to report to Washington at government expense, bringing with him any persons he might desire. Holden made plans accordingly, arranging for William Mason, Robert P. Dick, John H. P. Russ, John C. Williams, and W. R. Richardson to travel with him from Raleigh, the group to arrive in the capital on 18 May. In Washington they were to be met by John Hill Wheeler and Dr. Robert J. Powell, both North Carolinians and federal employees, and by George W. Jones, who would make the trip directly from Charlotte. He wanted Judge Edwin G. Reade of Roxboro to accompany the group, but the uncertainty of mail made it impossible to get in touch with him. Transportation being secured by Gen. John M. Schofield, the Holden party traveled from Raleigh to Norfolk by way of the Chesapeake and Albemarle Canal, then by boat to Baltimore, and finally by train to Washington.[5] Another group, composed of three former governors, David L. Swain, William A. Graham, and John A. Gilmer; Bartholomew F. Moore; Bedford Brown; and William Eaton, Jr., had requested permission to join the discussions. The president at first rejected their request completely, but, with Holden's consent, later permitted Swain, Moore, and Eaton to join the talks. These men were all loyal Unionists; yet they represented a shade of political opinion different from that of the Holden followers. Acting as the official spokesman for his group, Swain expressed the idea that the proper course of action would be to retain the incumbent state officials and, through a state constitutional convention called by the General Assembly, have a reconstruction program drafted.[6]

The two delegations held several conferences with Johnson and General

Schofield, the president's military adviser, during which they discussed the possible terms of reconstruction and drafted a list of names for consideration as nominees eligible for the chief executive post. Although convinced that he was the logical choice for the position, Holden had planned to ask President Johnson to appoint someone else, hoping that it might bring harmony to the Union factions within the state. Looking forward to this end, he requested and secured an interview to take place in the president's private quarters. Before Holden could broach the subject, however, the president was called to review troops parading outside the White House, thus denying Holden the opportunity to present his ideas. Subsequently, his friends, knowing his intentions, urged him "in the most earnest terms not to decline the appointment."[7]

At a final meeting of the delegations, President Johnson presented his own reconstruction plans, including his proposed North Carolina proclamation. He left blank the space for the naming of a governor, saying only that he would appoint whomever the delegates selected, and then he left the room. Swain declined to involve himself in the selection proceedings and also left the conference. Holden, who had not participated in that day's discussions for fear that he might be accused of seeking the appointment, arose and joined Swain outside. The two men walked from the White House to a point overlooking the Andrew Jackson statue in Lafayette Square, where Swain suggested that if the appointment were tendered, Holden should refuse. Swain added that he offered this advice in the name of harmony, but thinking that Swain might have apprehensions about the future of the university, Holden replied: "Governor, I have always been a firm friend to the University, though myself not a graduate as you were not. I am not assured of my appointment. I may be, or I may not be, but in any event I am your friend, and the friend of Chapel Hill."[8] Meanwhile, the remaining delegates, except for Moore and Eaton, inserted Holden's name in the blank space on the proclamation. Upon his return, Johnson expressed extreme pleasure with the choice. On 29 May he made the formal announcement, naming Holden as the provisional governor of North Carolina.[9]

The president's appointment should not have surprised North Carolinians, for Holden was the logical choice. His efforts toward peace and the restoration of federal authority had attracted attention throughout the nation and offered convincing proof that he was the leader of Unionism in the state. Further, his denunciations of the Confederacy as being despotic indicated that he would insist upon the protection of individual liberties, while his background and his record certainly made him a "people's representative." Thus it was thought that through his contacts with the common folk he would be better able to express their wishes than any of the state's political leaders. This was important to the administration, since Johnson hoped to create a new "classless" society within the South and to develop a balanced economy by upgrading industry and improving the status of labor. Both Johnson and Holden had achieved success by overcoming the prejudices of the aristocracy, resulting in a friendship that generated mutual respect. Above all, no one in the state was more highly regarded by federal authorities than Holden, and it was thought that his appointment would bring close cooperation between the state and the federal governments.

It was not until 8 June that Holden formally occupied the governor's office.[10] In his proclamation, Johnson had enumerated the powers and duties of the state's new governor and at the same time outlined a plan of reconstruction for North Carolina. This plan would, in turn, become the basis for the reconstruction of the other states. The governor's first duty was to restore order and make preparations for calling a constitutional convention, the first step toward readmission to the Union. After the convention completed its work and the constitution was approved by the voters, the provisional governor would then call for an election of state officials and representatives to Congress; when the congressmen were seated, this would indicate that the process of state reorganization had been completed and the state had been restored to the Union. Two qualifications for participation in the new state government were established. First, no person who had been engaged in the rebellion could qualify as an elector or officeholder without subscribing to the amnesty oath based on a promise of future loyalty, and individuals falling into any one of fourteen listed categories were excluded from amnesty except by first receiving a pardon issued from the president's office.[11] Second, one might qualify as a voter only in accordance with the state laws and constitution as they existed prior to 20 May 1861, the date of North Carolina's secession. The latter would prevent members of the former free black community, who had been denied suffrage in the antebellum era, from qualifying. Secretary of State William H. Seward, in a letter to Holden accompanying the proclamation, added two provisions. First, the new governor would hold office at the pleasure of the president, and the term of office would terminate when the conditions for reorganization had been met. Second, the governor's compensation would be three thousand dollars per year.[12]

Upon assuming office, Holden realized that local government, municipal as well as county, had ceased to exist, and that there were no officials to assume the responsibility for administering local affairs or maintaining law and order.[13] The state was occupied by federal troops, the civil rights of its citizens no longer protected. The administration was without funds, and the state's economy lay in complete ruin with little prospect for recovery except by federal aid. The governor's office was deluged by those seeking presidential pardons, by applicants for federal and state positions, and by urgent requests for the release of state troops detained in federal prisons. The situation was further complicated by growing racial tensions. This was particularly true in the eastern counties; there former slaves began to congregate in areas where they sometimes attempted to exert control over entire communities. Wilmington and New Bern soon erupted into open violence, but racial problems were not confined to those cities, for many freedmen had been led to believe they would be given "forty acres and a mule."

On 12 June, Holden presented his plan for state reorganization, though two days previously he had appointed Jonathan Worth to serve as state treasurer and Charles R. Thomas, secretary of state.[14] Having served in the Vance administration in similar capacities, both men were familiar with their duties, but the Worth appointment was an exceptionally wise choice. Not only did Worth know the state's financial conditions, but he was scrupulously honest; also he was a devout Unionist and had been a close associate of Holden in the peace movement. Though he had supported Vance in 1864, he felt earlier that Holden's views were more acceptable to the people.[15]

The proclamation of 12 June had called for the creation of a permanent state government through a state convention that would alter or amend the constitution to make it compatible with federal requirements. Meanwhile, the governor proposed to appoint temporary officers to county and municipal governments. Justices of the peace would have authority to transact county business and would be responsible for the election of other county officials. They would be prohibited, however, from conducting any trials that under the constitution required trial by jury. Mayors and commissioners would perform in like manner for city governments. Superior courts of oyer and terminer would be created and judges duly appointed. Directors and proxies in corporations in which the state was a stockholder or held financial interest would be appointed by the governor; this would enable banks, railroads, and other corporations to continue operation.

The reorganization of the eighty-seven county governments, and innumerable municipal governments, was a monumental task, but Holden was equal to it. Inviting the leading Union men to confer with him in Raleigh, he requested their nominations for officeholders. Those unable to attend the party caucus were asked to submit individual recommendations; in some instances the local military commanders had previously submitted lists, which were incorporated with the others.[16] In cases where conflicting recommendations were received, Holden made the final decision, and it was here that his contacts from his previous party work and on the *Standard* stood him in good stead. He possessed a wide knowledge of local leaders upon whom he could rely. Disregarding previous party affiliation, Holden insisted only upon a true and binding allegiance to the Union from those he would appoint. The next step was to select key men in each county to serve as commissioners, whose duty it would be to qualify and organize the new appointees to county courts.[17]

Throughout the summer, Holden was criticized for his plan; he was assailed for delay in completing some of the county organizations, and the quality of some of his appointments came under attack.[18] Such criticism was unwarranted, for a study of the approximately four thousand appointments demonstrates that he used caution, and in most cases his appointees were worthy of the office. Had he not attempted reorganization of local governments and merely reappointed incumbents (as his critics preferred), he would not have interrupted state services but he would have violated the instructions imposed upon him by Johnson, as well as the president's trust.

It is true that some counties experienced long delays before they had working governments, but Holden acted as soon as loyal citizens displayed an interest in the matter, made recommendations to him, and notified him of their action. Never did he impose his will upon the people; rather he preferred that they take the initiative as long as they proved their allegiance to the Union. This would explain why Sampson County was reorganized by 22 June, while McDowell remained unorganized until 21 August. Had Holden taken time personally to check the qualifications of each appointee, months, rather than weeks, would have been required to complete the job. The almost complete disruption of the state's transportation system was enough in itself to cause frustrating delays. Holden's judgments were, therefore, chiefly based on local recommendations, which were rendered in contexts of subjective local and personal issues. At times, of course, he received bad advice. Even so, when error was demonstrated, Holden sought to make immediate amends; for example, he invalidated his appointive lists for Cleveland and Washington counties when he discovered that the lists were not trustworthy. Undoubtedly, the rejected appointees held this against the governor.

The task of reorganizing local units of government across the state was not easy, yet by the end of the summer of 1865 the work was completed. But the most pressing problem remained: adequate funds for the operation of these state and local agencies had to be secured. The problem concerning Sheriff Richard J. Jones of New Hanover County was typical. He inquired of Holden if he, as sheriff, was authorized or required to collect taxes to fund the local government, to which Holden replied that taxes were to be "authorized by the Convention or General Assembly," and that county courts might borrow money for support of the poor, or they might borrow provisions.[19] Given the bankrupt condition of the state and the uncertainty of federal assistance, local officials could only hope to provide the minimum of necessities for those in need and to lay the foundation for a permanent system of government after the state had gained readmission to the Union. Furthermore, antagonism between the former Confederates and Unionists, each seeking control of the local governments, created dissension within the local citizenry and greatly increased Holden's problems.

Moreover, racial difficulties between freedmen and officials of the white-dominated governments became so heated that both Holden's provisional policies and those of the local governments were severely strained. Holden attempted to overcome the racial problems by establishing a system of county police in cases where immediate action was required. Companies of approximately seventy-five men were formed, with local citizens serving as officers and operating under the supervision of the occupying military forces. This system, with the cooperation of federal troops, was somewhat effective in maintaining peace between the races, for no mob violence was committed by either race. An election day episode in the town of Concord proved the exception and offered ample proof of the effectiveness of Holden's policy. When a group of rowdies there attacked several Negroes, the local police were powerless to suppress the riot; in fact, a few of the policemen joined the fray. But the disorder was immediately quelled by a company of the county police force.[20]

Holden sought to perform his administrative duties with a reduced staff, believing it wiser to operate within his financial limitations.[21] Those whom he did select were carefully chosen for their abilities and political considerations, with no attempt to achieve a geographic balance. The offices of controller, auditor, and superintendent of common schools were left vacant, while the Council of State, Literary Board, Internal Improvements Board, and Sinking Fund Board awaited permanent reorganization of the state government. Realizing the necessity for a reputable and honorable court system, however, Holden made outstanding appointments to the supreme court and the superior courts. For the supreme court he selected Chief Justice Richmond M. Pearson, William H. Battle, and Matthias E. Manly, and his superior court appointees consisted of David A. Barnes, Edward J. Warren, Daniel G. Fowle, Robert B. Gilliam, Ralph P. Buxton, Anderson Mitchell, Robert P. Dick, and Edwin G. Reade.[22]

The provisional government quickly ran into trouble over the jurisdiction of the courts, for Holden thought that their reestablishment would give them control over all civil and criminal cases. The military authorities, though, refused to give them jurisdiction over cases involving blacks. The problem was further complicated by a state law that would not admit the testimony of blacks against whites, while military authorities on the other hand refused to allow Negroes to be tried in courts that would not permit their testimony. The result was that all cases involving blacks were tried in Freedmen's Bureau courts, which functioned without juries. Whites thought this violated their constitutional rights. In one case, when William A. Marcom of Chatham County was charged with killing a freedman, to which he admitted when he surrendered voluntarily to local authorities, Holden requested a civil trial, but this was denied by the commander of the Department of North Carolina, Gen. Thomas H. Ruger. The governor appealed to President Johnson, but the appeal was denied.[23]

Later, Ruger and Holden reached an agreement on this question, which was approved by Gen. George W. Meade, commander of the Department of the South. All cases of misdemeanors or violations of law involving only whites were to be tried in the provisional courts, with those involving blacks remaining under military jurisdiction. General Meade assured Holden that when the military authorities felt a black would receive justice in state courts, they would discontinue military interference.[24] In the western counties beyond the Blue Ridge, no military forces existed; accordingly, General Ruger allowed superior court judges to arrest and bind over all persons involved in criminal action, regardless of race. The justices could set bail in cases in which it was permitted by law; if not, they were to lodge the offender in the county jail, subject to the order of the district military commander.[25]

Holden was conscientious in the performance of his duties and in general received favorable comments. Kenneth Rayner, reporting to President Johnson, praised his work. "Gov. Holden is progressing successfully in the reorganization of the state government. In the discharge of his duties, he is giving general satisfaction; and I think the common sentiment of our people is, that all loyal and conservative men should rally around and sustain him in his laborious duties, towards the restoration of law and order."[26] Henry M. Watterson, acting as Johnson's personal observer in the South, was of the same opinion.

> Governor Holden is progressing with the great work before him about as rapidly and as satisfactorily as any mortal man could well do. He is a calm, clearheaded, systematic, laborious gentleman. . . . These admi-

rable traits in his character are fast removing any prejudices that may have been engendered against him by the terrible conflict through which we have just passed. The general idea prevailing here is—and in that idea I fully concur—that you could not have made a better selection. . . . I doubt, all things considered, whether you could have made as good.[27]

At the war's end North Carolina held large quantities of cotton and rosin, as well as other extractive products. By far the largest amounts, however, had been seized by federal troops and Treasury Department agents, who classed them as "rebel" property; in fact, several hundred bales of captured cotton had been shipped to New York for sale by Treasury agents. Realizing the unfairness, if not illegality, of such seizures, Holden dispatched Jonathan Worth to Washington in an attempt to persuade the president to permit the reclaiming of the property and the using of the revenue to liquidate state debts. Worth was only partially successful, for he obtained permission to collect only such property as not previously seized by the federal agents; from this source alone, however, the Holden administration brought to the state treasury approximately $150,000—a sum sufficient not only to defray the entire cost of the constitutional convention but to leave a cash balance of $40,000 at the end of Holden's provisional governorship. In addition, Holden sought to improve the economy by using his influence with the president to have the 25 percent tax on the sale of cotton remitted and to have other federal taxes postponed. In this last category was the 8 percent tax on all lands as valued for the year 1861, which was tax money the government had not collected at the time of North Carolina's secession. He succeeded in both instances. Had the property owners been forced to pay the land tax for 1861, the majority of North Carolinians would have been forced to default; they simply did not have the money to make payment. By his foresight in securing tax relief, Holden had prevented the collapse of the state's economy.[28]

By late summer conditions were almost stable. The military authorities made it possible for countless citizens to borrow army horses and mules for use in planting and harvesting crops. Through federal funds and army aid, the governor was able to operate the state humane institutions, although only the most minimal of care and relief was provided to the state's blind, deaf and dumb, and insane. The problem of local relief, however, was not so easily resolved. Poor relief was regarded as a local responsibility, financially and administratively, and Holden agreed with this concept. But many communities felt that they had neither the power nor financial resources to meet the problem, and since the state was under provisional rule, they felt that the federal government should assume responsibility for dispensing all relief. In spite of this difference of opinion, Holden authorized county magistrates to make financial arrangements to provide for their poor, and by the end of the year the counties were handling the problem.[29]

The most criticized aspect of Holden's administration was the matter of presidential pardons. In his proclamation of 29 May, President Johnson had issued general amnesty to all who had engaged in rebellion except those in the fourteen classes that would be required to apply for individual pardons. Thus from the beginning of his term the governor's office was filled with applicants seeking such pardons—a matter that was time consuming for both the governor and his staff. Before being sent to Washington for final review, all applications for pardon had to be routed through his office, where he marked them granted, postponed, or rejected.

Holden was to answer three questions: (1) Was the petitioner likely to be a useful and peaceful citizen? (2) Had any proceedings been instituted against his property under the Confiscation Acts? and (3) Was any of the applicant's property in the possession of the federal authorities as "abandoned property"? To assist with this operation, Holden appointed Robert J. Powell as state agent in Washington to supervise the handling of all applications.[30] But pressed with other duties, plus a prolonged illness in the summer of 1865, President Johnson often delayed signing the individual requests. These delays brought considerable criticism of Holden, who was accused of personally and whimsically delaying the applications. These charges came especially from former political enemies and those who felt that he acted vindictively toward those whom he disliked.

It was not unusual for Holden, when pressed, to write Powell and request speedy action on the pardons. On one such occasion, Powell replied: "The President is thronged continually—when I ask him to sign pardons for our people—unless it be such as are here in person—he replied he will do so as soon as he can."[31] There were many North Carolinians who soon learned that they might expedite the process by going to Washington, sometimes even receiving favorable action against Holden's recommendation.[32]

Of the 1,555 applications that passed through Holden's office, he forwarded 1,451 with recommendations for approval, temporarily suspended action on 100, and rejected only 4 outright.[33] Those rejected were Theophilus Holmes, William T. Dortch, Duncan K. McRae, and James R. McLean; Holden opposed their pardons because he questioned whether they would ever willingly submit to Union rule.

In his memoirs he later recalled what happend to the applications of four other prominent state citizens, William A. Graham, Josiah Turner, Jr., Thomas Bragg, and Paul C. Cameron. Graham filed his application in August, when Holden was out of his office confined to his house by illness. Upon his return, he read the document carefully and was pleased with it. "It was an able and truthful paper." He then instructed the pardon clerk, William H. Bagley, to endorse the application, for "his pardon is to be granted by the President at once." Whereupon, his aide Joseph S. Cannon said, "Governor, have you seen the *New York Herald* of this morning?" Holden replied that he had not. Cannon continued, "The *Herald* says, 'Gov. Graham has been pardoned already, and you are engaged in pardoning a great many distinguished unpardoned rebels.' I would advise you to send on the paper, and mark it continued, and in a few weeks write to the President and ask him to send the pardon." Holden took the advice and continued the case, "lest the radicals North should complain and lose confidence in the President."[34]

Meanwhile, Josiah Turner, Jr., consulted Holden on the status of his and Graham's pardons, and when the governor refused to specify what his recommendation had been, Turner left the office unhappy. He then arranged a public meeting in Raleigh and delivered a very critical speech against Holden and his reconstruction policies. Consequently, Holden refused to recommend that Turner receive his pardon.[35] On the other hand, he approved Josiah Turner, Sr.'s pardon.[36]

With former governor Bragg, Holden demonstrated a pettiness which further strained their personal relationship. Holden had recommended to President Johnson that Bragg's application be suspended, and he therefore refused to deliver it in spite of the fact that the president had granted it. Perhaps his action was owing to his belief that Bragg had primarily been responsible for his gubernatorial defeat in 1858. Another possible explanation was that he considered Bragg's refusal to pay a courtesy visit to the governor's office a personal insult. Accordingly, he told his aides to inform Bragg that if he would call at the office the last day of Holden's tenure, he would turn over the pardon personally. This was done on 29 December 1865.[37] As for Paul C. Cameron, reputedly the wealthiest man in the state in 1861, Holden was inclined to withhold his pardon, but when Cameron was in Raleigh for the Forty-ninth Episcopal Convention and called upon Holden, they reached an understanding and his pardon was granted.[38] In general, Holden aided most citizens to secure their pardons, even the "original secessionists," but he distrusted the "Vance Destructives." The Vance men had not accepted defeat, and "to pardon such men . . . would be to open . . . bitter discussion, and . . . strengthen the factions now being secretly organized against the administration."[39]

North Carolina was not the only southern state in which presidential policies received criticism; the northern press circulated statements by Southerners which implied that whites were determined to reenslave blacks as soon as federal troops were withdrawn and that Confederate war debts would be assumed by the states. Johnson realized that untold harm would result from such rumors and accordingly telegraphed all southern provisional governors, ordering them to check these rumors immediately. When the president's telegram arrived, Holden was away, having gone to Kittrell Springs for a brief respite from the summer's heat.[40] Upon reading the telegram after his return to the city, Holden concluded that the president's message was an attack upon his administration, and he replied immediately, stating that he had been careful in carrying out the instructions given him and that "I am sure there are no grounds for apprehending that North Carolina will not present an acceptable constitution. The great body of her people are loyal and submissive to national authority. I know there are malcontents, radicals, and not good men who are engaged in misrepresenting facts, and fermenting strife for certain purposes; but none of these things move me in the performance of duty."[41] Johnson sought promptly to assure Holden that his original telegram intended no criticism but was merely to call the governors' attention to erroneous charges being leveled by certain elements in the North and to remind the governors of the necessity of counteracting them.

The status of the former slaves, both legal and real, had during the summer months become an increasingly controversial issue. Gen. John Schofield, commander of the Department of North Carolina, had issued a general order on 27 April, proclaiming that all former slaves were free, that former owners should employ them as hired workers at reasonable wages, and that the military would not tolerate idleness or the congregating of freedmen in towns or army camps.[42] But such orders were not acceptable to either whites or blacks. Conflict seemed inevitable. Many freedmen left their homes and congregated in towns, where they expected to have food, clothing, and shelter provided. Some of the more outspoken ones demanded full economic and political equality immediately. The presence of black soldiers complicated the matter, since they possessed arms and whites did not. Clashes between armed rioters took place in New Bern, Wilmington, Beaufort, Kinston, and other eastern towns.

Almost to a man, political leaders agreed that the freedmen's status could legitimately be redefined only by the people acting through constitutional amendments or legislative action. The majority of the citizens agreed with Holden that there was nothing to fear in placing the alphabet, the Bible, or school books in the hands of blacks, and they approved of the marriages of blacks being on the same civil basis as those of whites.[43] The extension of the right to vote, though, caused consternation and wild discussion. Chief Justice Salmon P. Chase visited Wilmington and urged the state's citizens to extend full suffrage rights to freedmen, at which point J. L. Pennington, editor of the *Raleigh Progress*, replied: "We told him that our people would be opposed to giving the right of suffrage to the freed negro, and that should the general government attempt to force it upon them, they would feel aggrieved and mortified."[44] Later, the *Raleigh Sentinel* stated that if the whites ever consented to suffrage for blacks voluntarily, it would be only after they were convinced that blacks merited the right and were capable of exercising it, making it beneficial to both races.[45]

As adamant as this sounds, a remarkable feature of the issue was the openness and calmness with which the subject was discussed throughout the state; yet a year later it raised great bitterness. This was indicative of the freedom of discussion that Holden encouraged throughout his provisional governorship. David L. Swain stated that if the freehold qualifications for voting for state senators should be restored, he would favor restricted Negro suffrage for the house of commons. Alfred M. Waddell advocated limited suffrage to qualified blacks, but Victor C. and Rufus Barringer took a stronger stance, supporting the idea that voting rights should be applied equally to both whites and blacks. It was their contention that the privilege should be extended to the blacks voluntarily to offset the growing Radical Republican demand that expansion of the electorate be imposed on the South. In fact, the Barringers predicted that unless the South acted, black suffrage would be imposed as a requirement for southern states to reenter the Union.[46]

In late summer, Negroes, anxious to press the subject, began to hold mass meetings in the eastern part of the state. John P. Sampson, a native of New Hanover County but at that time the editor of the *Cincinnati Colored Citizen*, returned to the state to become a leader of the movement. At a Wilmington meeting it was decided that blacks should hold a statewide convention to agitate for suffrage. Thus, the first freedmen's convention held in the South assembled in Raleigh's Methodist African church on 29 September 1865. Some 117 delegates, representing forty-two of the state's eighty-seven counties, were present for the opening session. The majority were newly freed; they were farm laborers, and less than one-fourth could read and write.[47] Still, the delegates comprised a surprisingly able group, and from this date the state's political leaders could not ignore blacks or their political activities.

The convention's major accomplishment was the preparation of an address to the state's constitutional convention, which would meet shortly. The document summarized the status of blacks in the state and specifically asked for full citizenship rights. It also requested adequate educational opportunities, including facilities; the removal of discriminatory laws; the protection of the sanctity of families and the care of orphaned children; the encouragement of Negro industry; and protection against cruel employers. Finally, the freedmen asked for shelter and subsistence during this period of change.[48] Several speakers, as well as letters read from William M. Coleman of Cabarrus County and Horace Greeley of New York, demanded immediate suffrage rights, but the leadership studiously avoided mention of that touchy issue in the final draft.

While the convention was in session, the campaign for freedmen's rights received further encouragement by the establishment of the Equal Rights League, with headquarters in New Bern, and a newspaper in Raleigh primarily designed to sponsor black suffrage. The *Journal of Freedom* began its publication on 1 October 1865, with J. T. A. Crane as publisher and Edward P. Brooks as editor. Neither the paper nor the league proved successful, both ceasing their operations within a year.

As he had known from his first day in office, Holden had the primary task of preparing North Carolina for readmission to the Union, a task which could be achieved only by an acceptable revision of the state's constitution. Realizing the importance of this act, Holden made mention of it in his first proclamation, dated 12 June, even though he waited until 8 August to issue a call for the election of delegates to the proposed convention. Holden was sharply criticized for the delay, particularly since other governors, some whose appointments were made after his and in states where Union sentiment was believed to be weaker, had already started the reconstruction process.

Holden had moved cautiously, though, for several reasons. First, he wanted as many of the state's citizens as possible to participate in the reorganization. Had he called an early convention, as did William Sharkey, governor of Mississippi, many voters would have failed to qualify either because of inability to take the amnesty oath or lack of time to receive individual pardons. The *Standard* estimated that fully one-third of the Mississippians who might have participated in their state's election were unable to do so because of insufficient time to secure pardons. Second, Holden wanted to have the public clearly informed on the issues of the day, including the repeal of the secession ordinance, black suffrage, the status of wartime judicial proceedings and contracts signed during the war, and, especially important, the question of the legality of Confederate debts. Third, excessive heat and humidity made the capital city an unfavorable convention site during the summer. Fourth, the state had been in no position at an earlier date to pay the cost of a meeting, since Treasurer Worth was only then beginning to place the state once more on a solvent basis. Fifth, ever the politician, Holden hoped that during this temporary appointment he might build a party following sufficiently strong to return him to office. Finally, the illness of both Johnson and Holden caused at least a two-week delay. Holden notified the president on 17 July that he was ready to act, but illness prevented him from completing the plans and submitting them to Johnson until 26 July. Even so, the president did not study Holden's plan until 7 August, when he telegraphed his approval. One day later, 8 August, Holden made the official announcement for a convention.[49]

In his proclamation, Holden designated 2 October as the date for the opening session of the constitutional convention, while 21 September was the date for the election of county delegates. Membership (120 delegates) was apportioned on the same ratio as membership in the house of commons, and justices of the peace, who were to supervise the local elections, were charged with administering presidential amnesty oaths to those who could qualify. The campaign for delegate elections generated little excitement, since Union sentiment generally prevailed across the state. It was agreed that the convention should confine its attention to constitutional questions and that the discussion of war debts should be left to the General Assembly.

The one controversy that did evolve was whether unpardoned persons could legally participate in the convention. The question was raised when former governor William A. Graham of Orange County, while refusing to be a candidate himself since he had not been pardoned by President Johnson, maintained that unpardoned persons had the right to serve as delegates. Holden insisted that unpardoned persons were ineligible and promptly appealed to the president for a decision on the matter. Johnson sustained Holden's position with the statement that "if the party comes within any of the exceptions, they must obtain a pardon before voting or sitting as a member."[50] The president also said that should any unpardoned person be elected to the convention, he would grant an immediate pardon upon Holden's favorable recommendation.[51]

The results of the election were favorable to Holden and to Union men generally. Only two of his preferred candidates, Chief Justice Richmond M. Pearson and Dr. James T. Leach, failed to be elected. The latter was probably defeated because of poor health which prevented his waging an effective campaign, while Pearson's defeat might be attributed to his being away from his native county too long and losing touch with local conditions, or perhaps because many voters thought it impolitic for the chief justice to seek any elective post. The majority of the victorious candidates were former Whigs who had acquiesced in secession instead of favoring it and who collectively were sincere in their efforts to restore the state to the Union. On the whole, the delegates possessed considerable ability and were broadly experienced in state politics; this was true even though many well-known names of the antebellum period were conspicuous by their absence. Among the convention's leaders were Bartholomew F. Moore, Edwin G. Reade, Lewis Thompson, Nathaniel Boyden, Bedford Brown, John Pool, Dennis Ferrebee, Edward Conigland, William A. Wright, Alfred Dockery, and Matthias E. Manly. Also there were new names making their debut to state politics: Calvin J. Cowles, Ceburn L. Harris, John B. Odom, and Churchill Perkins.

Holden secured permission from General Ruger for the use of the Capitol, and the furniture that had been removed during the federal occupation was returned; the convention then assembled on 2 October in the hall of the house of commons. Edwin G. Reade was selected presiding officer, and once the convention's organization had been completed, Holden submitted a message in which he outlined work to be performed by the convention. On 4 October an agenda was prepared which designated the following matters for consideration: (1) setting of the number of justices of the peace in each county; (2) revision of the state constitution to bring it in line with federal requirements; (3) repeal of the state's secession ordinance; (4) abolition of slavery; (5) redistricting of congressional districts; (6) deciding which acts of state government since 20 May 1861 should be validated; (7) amnesty for all persons who had participated in the war; and (8) consideration of appropriate action concerning constitutional changes not referred to the people for ratification.[52]

Two days later, the committee on agenda submitted additional recommendations: (1) a committee should be appointed to study amendments to the constitution necessary to limit the power of the General Assembly to increase the state's indebtedness; (2) a committee should determine what proposals coming from the convention should be submitted to the voters for their approval; and (3) a committee should be appointed to study the treasurer's report and to determine what action, if any, the convention should take.

Holden had no direct part in the convention proceedings; yet he kept in constant touch with all of its deliberations through friends. Little action was taken without his consent or approval. Reade, president of the convention, took great care in making committee assignments, and controversial subjects were entrusted either to Holden supporters or "true Union" men.

The convention first considered the abrogation of the secession ordinance, and although virtually all members realized the necessity of conforming to President Johnson's demands that the ordinance be repealed, they differed greatly as to the manner in which it should be done. Nathaniel Boyden was chairman of the committee responsible for making the recommendation, but before his committee could act, J. W. Jones of Rowan County had introduced a bill which, though it would repeal the 1861 ordinance, was phrased in an exceedingly apologetic tone. Jones's bill passed first reading on the same day that Boyden submitted his committee report, which declared with finality that the ordinance was repealed, rescinded, and abrogated and had, in fact, been at all times null and void. This led to tabling the Jones proposal.

On the following day Dennis Ferrebee offered a compromise proposal that would not have annulled legislation enacted by the state or invalidated legal actions such as marriages performed during the war years. Judge George Howard of Edgecombe County, an "original secessionist," led the fight in opposition to the committee resolution. He stated that he was not against the state's restoration to the Union, but he felt the 1861 ordinance was the basis for the state government during the war years. Any attempt to abrogate it would nullify all subsequent state actions. Howard was joined by two groups: one felt that adopting the committee's proposal would reflect badly upon the 1861 convention, while the other group maintained that the convention, a legislative body and not a judicial one, was not qualified to discuss the question at all. Bartholomew F. Moore led the fight to abrogate the 1861 ordinance on the ground that it was the one guarantee of restoration to the Union and that anything apologetic in tone might not be acceptable. Edward J. Warren of Beaufort County supported Moore by declaring that Ferrebee's resolution was an attempt to "hoodwink" the convention into an endorsement of secession. Samuel F. Phillips of Orange County expressed what was perhaps the general sentiment of the convention, saying that since the convention had equal rank with the 1861 assembly, it had the power to declare null and void acts of the former body. The Moore strategy prevailed; on 7 October the convention, by a 94–20 vote, adopted the measure that declared the ordinance of secession "repealed, rescinded, and abrogated; and the said supposed ordinance is now and had been at all times, null and void."[53]

On 5 October, the fourth day of the session, Holden forwarded the memorial from the Raleigh black convention, which was immediately referred to a committee headed by John Pool. After six days of consideration the committee submitted its report, adopting the position that the question of the legal status of the freedmen was one upon which the General Assembly could more appropriately act, and recommended that the provisional governor appoint a commission of qualified jurists to prepare a code of laws on the subject and report to the next session of the legislature.[54] Holden acted immediately by appointing to the commission B. F. Moore, William S. Mason, and Richard S. Donnell. This commission completed its work and reported to the General Assembly in January 1866.

The second issue, the abolition of slavery, did not precipitate as sharp a debate as had the secession issue. Slavery was no longer controversial since the adoption of the Thirteenth Amendment. Accordingly, Thomas Settle, chairman of the committee on slavery, reported a bill prohibiting slavery within the state, which, two days later, John Odom of Northampton County attempted to amend and show that abolition was involuntary. His resolution was promptly rejected, and the convention proceeded to adopt the original measure: "That slavery and involuntary servitude, otherwise for crime, . . . shall be and is hereby forever prohibited in this state."[55]

After passage of the resolutions dealing with secession and slavery, Holden telegraphed President Johnson to report the convention's action. In reply, Dr. Robert Powell, the state's agent in Washington, wrote: "The President is very much gratified with the action of the convention. I write this in his office, and he tells me the Convention has done what is right, and that such action adds greatly to our strength here."[56]

The convention next turned its attention to providing a permanent government for the state. It was decided that the General Assembly should convene on the fourth Monday of November 1865, with the governor authorized to issue writs of election for the second Thursday of November to each sheriff in the state, who in turn would plan for and oversee the local elections. At the same time, an election for members of Congress and for a governor was scheduled. The latter's term of office was contingent upon the expiration of the provisional government upon restoration of the state to the Union; the provisional government would lapse automatically on 1 January 1866. The assembly members would hold their seats until the next election, scheduled for the first Thursday in August 1866.[57] An attempt to create the office of lieutenant governor failed, the convention members seeing no need for it at the time.[58]

In regard to local government, they decided that both county and municipal governments should continue relatively unchanged in form. Local elections would be scheduled at the same time as state elections, and the elected officials would assume office at the expiration of the provisional government. The exact terms of office, however, would be decided by a later session of the General Assembly.[59]

At the beginning of the convention's second week the committee charged with the responsibility of determining those ordinances that should be ratified by the voters recommended only those treating secession and slavery. Although the report was adopted, acrimonious debate erupted concerning the wording of the ratification referendum. For political reasons, Tod R. Caldwell of Burke County sought to have it read "Secession" or "No Secession" and "Slavery" or "No Slavery." His proposal was bitterly attacked by those who had opposed the stronger wording for the bill to abrogate the secession ordinance, especially by Judge Howard. In his argument, Howard directed his remarks specifically at several members who had never supported the Union movement until after the fall of the Confederacy and had then become most caustic and vindictive in their remarks.[60] Northern journalist Sidney Andrews declared that he found in the convention much hatred for secession which was primarily caused by political factors rather than by any love for the Union.[61] The Caldwell proposal failed, and the resolutions were submitted to the voters simply on a ratification or rejection basis and with the understanding that the outcome of the vote would carry the effect of law.

The convention was occupied for the better part of two days in settling doubts regarding the validity of post-secession legislation and judicial proceedings. It was eventually decided that all laws passed after 20 May 1861 consistent with the federal and state constitutions would continue in full force unless repealed or modified; that all judicial proceedings were valid regardless of the state's attempted secession; that all contracts executed and all marriages solemnized were binding on both parties; that to protect state officials of the war years no person would be held liable for any act done in the proper execution of duties imposed upon him by lawful authority;[62] that the General Assembly should provide a scale of depreciation for Confederate currency and that all contracts were in money of the value determined; and, finally, that all acts of the provisional governor and his appointed agents were valid, but all appointments should terminate at the close of the first session of the next General Assembly unless the assembly should direct otherwise.[63]

The judges of courts of oyer and terminer appointed by the provisional governor were invested with those powers conferred upon regular superior court judges, and their terms of office would cease with the restoration of the superior courts. The provisional courts of pleas and quarter session were given the same criminal jurisdiction as their regular counterparts, but appeals from such courts would await the regular term of the superior courts.[64]

Having been selected by presiding officer Reade, Judge Daniel Fowle of Wake County was appointed by the convention to determine state claims to property. He would hold hearings to receive complaints from the state treasury against all persons who had detained, used, sold, destroyed, or unlawfully converted state money or property for their own use. The ordinance was to be administered within its own right; Judge Fowle could deputize ministerial officers and issue writs of injunction, sequestration, or attachment for the protection of such money or property. Also, he might order the sale of property, and he had, in general, the powers of a court of equity.[65]

The most difficult convention issue involved state finances. Treasurer Worth had prepared a complete financial report for Governor Holden, showing how the state could raise necessary revenue to support itself and to provide future stability. Holden submitted the report to the convention, which readily adopted it, and then levied fifteen new taxes as a means of supporting it.[66] But the convention was then thrown into a major furor concerning the question of repudiating the state's war debts. Despite the president's insistence that southern states must repudiate all such debts, the general consensus in North Carolina was that it was a legislative issue and the convention should not consider it. The *Wilmington Herald* pronounced that delay was merely evasive and that such a policy was a "grand scheme . . . to fasten the rebel debt upon the people of the state."[67]

The problem involved more than the principle of repudiation: the question of the legality of all state debts was inseparably tied to the legality of secession. It involved the financial interests of all citizens in the state. Should state bonds be repudiated, individuals would obviously lose their investments.[68] Even worse, state banks would be ruined, affecting the economy of the entire state; the endowments of the common school system and the university would be wiped out. Should the state assume debts, the expense would be distributed among the entire population, but it would mean also that North Carolina would not be permitted to reenter the Union. This had been made quite clear by President Johnson.

Convention sentiment was divided three ways: between those who wanted repudiation, those who wanted assumption, and those who wanted postponement of the question. The last group hoped to delay until restoration into the Union had taken place, after which the state could act as it pleased.[69] At first, Holden was inclined to support the idea of postponement, but on 17 October he wired President Johnson asking for advice on the subject and stated the following:

> Contrary to my expectation, the convention has involved itself in a bitter discussion on the State debt made in aid of the rebellion. A continuance of this discussion will greatly excite the people and retard the work of reconstruction. Our people are believed to be against assuming the debt by a large majority. Is it not advisable that our conven-

tion, like that of Alabama, should positively ignore this debt now and forever? Please answer at once.[70]

The president's answer was immediate and emphatic: "Every dollar of the debt created to aid the rebellion against the United States should be repudiated finally and forever."[71]

Holden then transmitted the president's telegram to the convention, with the desired effect. On 20 October the convention adopted a resolution of repudiation.[72] Holden had shifted to a position favoring immediate repudiation not only because he knew that repudiation was one of the president's "musts" for reentry into the Union but also because he had an eye on the impending gubernatorial election.

As noted previously, Holden desired above all else to be the duly elected governor of his state. His former private secretary Lewis Hanes once said, "I believe that in everything he did, he kept constantly in view no object but his own political advancement."[73] Many of the state's political leaders believed that Holden's excellent provisional administration entitled him to the office without opposition; others thought that his election would ensure the state's reentry into the Union and that, because of his close relationship with the Johnson administration, the state would receive generous financial aid in overcoming the depressed economic conditions.[74] In fact, on 14 October fifty-three convention members signed a petition requesting him to become a candidate in order that the state's restoration might be completed by one "under whose guidance it . . . [was] so auspiciously begun."[75] Holden accepted the petition as a formal nomination and immediately announced his intention to seek the governor's post in the upcoming election. Furthermore, he was optimistic about his chances.

Other state political leaders, however, refused to support Holden's candidacy, or even to acquiesce in his ever being governor, provisional or otherwise. As early as July 1865, there were rumors that the former "Secession" party leaders were organizing opposition and urging Bartholomew F. Moore of Raleigh to enter the contest. When that move failed, with Moore refusing to permit his name to be placed in nomination, other names began to surface as the convention continued. Among those suggested by the state press were Edwin G. Reade, Alfred Dockery, Bedford Brown, John Pool, Lewis Thompson, Nathaniel Boyden, and Richard S. Donnell. But all declined, either for fear of stirring up disunity or from the belief that Holden was President Johnson's candidate and, should he be opposed, North Carolina would not receive favorable consideration for restoration to the Union.

In desperation, opposition leaders, including former Governor William

A. Graham, Josiah Turner, Jr., Charles C. Clark, and Patrick H. Winston, persuaded Jonathan Worth to announce his candidacy on 16 October.[76] Just prior to his announcement, Worth had been in "painful uncertitude" as to whether or not he should allow his name to be submitted.[77] Holden always believed that Worth was, in effect, forced into the race by the leaders of the old plantation aristocracy, Graham in particular, who sought to prevent a change in the economic or political control of the state. In fact, Holden declared that Worth had proposed—through friends, but with Worth's knowledge and approval—that if he would not run for election in 1866, Worth would not become a candidate in 1865. Naturally Holden refused the proposition.[78] "Indeed," Holden wrote President Johnson, "it is known that [Worth] had agreed to disentangle himself from the secessionists and retire, but another letter from Gov. Graham determined him to be a candidate."[79]

The two candidates did not conduct extensive campaigns. Holden remained in Raleigh attending to his administrative duties and supervising the successful conclusion of the constitutional convention, while Worth was permitted by Holden to continue in his treasury post. Instead, the campaign was conducted by the state press and by the twenty-three aspirants to the seven congressional seats. The people had little choice between the candidates concerning political philosophy. Both were strong Unionists, both had been original "peace men," and both were strong advocates of a speedy restoration to the Union. Worth had supported Holden in his earlier political endeavors, but when Holden had broken with Vance over the peace movement issue, Worth had retained the treasury post he held under Vance, officially supporting administrative policy while remaining on close and friendly terms with Holden. It was in matters of personality and ability that the men differed. Cornelia Phillips Spencer, the old-line Chapel Hill aristocrat, expressed this better than others when she wrote in her diary, "I see very little to choose between them except that Worth is probably the honestest [sic] of the two, while Holden is the ablest."[80]

Holden launched his campaign with great optimism, for early indications pointed to an easy victory. As the campaign progressed, however, and the Worth forces organized themselves into a viable political machine, Holden's assurance gave way to personal abuse of Worth and finally to an inflated appeal to "save the state for the Union." Holden's supporters asserted that a Holden victory was the only way to regain statehood, and many northern papers undertook to show that Worth was destroying the political harmony within the state and was actually hostile to the president's plan for restoration. As expected, Holden used the *Standard* to take his message to the people and attempted to win popular approval by using the following motto on its mast-head: "W. W. Holden and Go Back to the Union, or Jonathan Worth and Stay Out of the Union."[81]

The Worth campaign was managed by Josiah Turner, Jr., and William Pell, the editor of the *Raleigh Sentinel*. Turner, who was seeking the congressional seat from the Fourth District, deeply resented Holden's refusal to endorse his application for pardon. The Worth forces circulated two campaign documents throughout the state which proved to be most effective propaganda. One was a reprint of a speech by Turner defending his own political record, while the other, a full-page circular, was entitled "Facts for the People: Record of W. W. Holden." The latter reviewed Holden's public career and attempted to show, by quotations from his newspaper editorials, the shifting course of his policies—from his advocacy to the right of secession to his pro-Union stand, and from his support of the Confederacy to his peace movement activities. The circular also stressed attacks that Holden had made on Governor Vance in 1864.[82]

On 27 October an article in the *Standard*, no doubt edited, if not written, by Holden, attempted to answer the circulars.

> Mr. Jo Turner, who does the dirty work for Mr. Worth and Brother Pell, has much to say about "Holden's Record." The disunionists of Wake, in February, 1861, sang the same tune. . . .
>
> For more than five years Gov. Holden has been one of the best Union men in the South. He never was a secessionist—that is, he never held that a State had the right to secede at will from the Federal Government. . . .
>
> But there is one feature in "Holden's Record" of which his friends are proud; and that is, *he has always, on all questions, been the advocate of popular rights*. That is what galls the oligarchs.[83]

The central issue of the election clearly was William W. Holden—not his success or failure as provisional governor, his ability to govern the state, or his popularity with the people of the state but the probability that if elected in his own right, he would build a political following that would bring a new order contrary to the vested interests of the landed gentry class that had ruled the state for so long. In no previous state campaign had there been more money spent, or more falsehoods circulated, than in the campaign against Holden in 1865.[84]

While Worth defeated Holden by a margin of 5,939 out of a total vote of 57,616, the Holden forces elected four of the seven congressmen.[85] Before the

results were officially tallied, Holden's secretary wrote the president expressing fear of defeat and informing him of William A. Graham's election to the
state senate, Rufus Y. McAden to the house of commons, and Josiah Turner,
Jr., to Congress.

> Governor Graham is the originator and leader of all the disaffec-
> tion in North Carolina. His great desire is to unite enough of the old
> Whigs, to the Secessionists, the advocates of the payment of the Rebel
> debt, and disaffected men, to break down the National Union party.
> His opposition to you is as strong as it is to Governor Holden. Jonathan
> Worth, Josiah Turner, and Rufus Y. McAden were put forward at his in-
> stance against the repeated remonstrances of all the leading Union men
> in the State.
> Josiah Turner canvassed . . . [by] speeches of ridicule and slan-
> der. He declared "he would not vote for you to save your life." . . .
> The Union men . . . believe that if Your Excellency will refuse to
> pardon these men, disaffection will be struck a death blow in North
> Carolina, and will not be able to rise again.[86]

The surprising news of Worth's election caused great alarm in the North.
The *New York Tribune* declared that North Carolina was not ready for statehood on a footing of genuine, hearty loyalty. In a private letter to a friend in
Annapolis, Maryland, governor-elect Worth expressed his own uneasiness
saying, "I fear the North will deprive me of all but the honor of the approbation
of my State. A strange illusion prevails in the North. My election is regarded
as indicative hostility to Prest. Johnson's plan of reconstruction."[87]

In the final analysis, the real loser was North Carolina. Had Holden been
accepted by the old plantation aristocracy and elected without opposition, he
might well have done much to lead the state into an improved relationship with
the federal government. By defeating him, the Graham-Worth forces had lost
his valuable influence with the people of the state; in the long run, they set into
motion the events that created the racial tensions of 1868–72.

Certainly the defeat was a disappointment to President Johnson, who had
formed a close friendship with Holden. Two days after the election he instructed Holden to continue to exercise the duties of his office until personally
relieved. And Secretary of State William H. Seward assured Holden "that your
efforts to sustain the administration of the government and give effect to its
policy are fully appreciated and that they will in no case be forgotten."[88] Later,
the president wrote, "Accept my thanks for the noble and efficient manner in
which you have discharged your duty as provisional governor. . . . The results

of the recent election in North Carolina have greatly damaged the prospects of the State in the restoration of its governmental relations. Should the action and spirit of the legislature be in the same direction, it will greatly increase the mischief already done and might be fatal."[89]

Despite his election defeat, Holden did not expect his term of office to terminate quickly. Indications are that he thought the provisional government would continue until Congress recognized the new state government by the admission of its representatives. His decision to replace Worth with William Sloan as treasurer, his preparations to rejuvenate the judicial machinery at all levels, and his preparation of legislative recommendations for the meeting of the General Assembly support this view. Even as late as 6 December he wrote, "If the Provisional Government is to be continued it will be indispensible that the Courts of the State shall be put in full operation . . . I will have sufficient means to support a Provisional Government, and to put the entire machinery in full operation."[90]

When the General Assembly met on 27 November, Holden and his supporters were in firm control. Thomas Settle was elected president of the senate, defeating Dennis Ferrebee, a Worth supporter, and Samuel F. Phillips of Orange County was elected speaker of the house of commons. Although Phillips was a strong Holden man, in this instance he was considered a compromise choice. Holden sent a brief message to the assembly on 30 November which stressed the absolute necessity of harmony if restoration to the Union was to be accomplished. He said, "Let the divisions and differences which exist among us disappear under the influence of a more intense and devoted patriotism." The last obstacle was ratification of the Thirteenth Amendment, and for this he advocated immediate acceptance. The following day both houses approved ratification, despite strong opposition in the senate by John M. Morehead and Ferrebee. Both protested, declaring that under the amendment Congress would be given unlimited power; the freedmen might be given the right to bear arms, give testimony in courts, intermarry with whites, and vote; and the Union would be taking unfair advantage of the South by forcing it to take action that would otherwise be rejected.[91]

The assembly began its work amicably enough. Resolutions were adopted setting forth the per diem and mileage rates for members, state officers,[92] and court members.[93] On the matter of the election of two United States senators, however, controversy arose. Two vacancies existed, one complete six-year term and the unexpired portion of the term scheduled to have begun on 4 March 1861. William A. Graham was elected to the complete term, while John Pool was elected to the short term.[94] Privately, the short-term senatorship had been offered to Holden, who refused it because it was tendered "by authority" of former governor Graham.[95] A condition of the offer was that Holden intercede with the president for Graham's pardon, thereby permitting him to assume a seat in the Senate. At first, Holden had accepted the proposal, but he had later countered with his own condition that upon their election both men would resign immediately. When Graham turned down his proposal, Holden declined the post outright.[96]

Except for the selection of senators the General Assembly made no attempt to deal with serious matters or to enact legislation of a permanent nature, since there was little assurance that action taken would be considered valid when North Carolina's civil government had been recognized by Congress. Furthermore, by common consent, the assembly agreed to recess on 18 December and meet again in February 1866. This proved most unfortunate. The constitutional convention had declared that all provisional appointments would automatically expire at the termination of such government, yet the new legislature had made no provision for justices of the peace in the various counties. Consequently, when Holden's provisional government ended, the newly elected county officials were unable to qualify and the state was left without municipal or county governments. This oversight required correction by a special legislative session.

The assembly refused to establish the legal status of the freedmen. When it finally did in 1866, the harshness of the "Black Codes" that it enacted served as ample warning that the Worth administration and the citizens in general were unrepentant and determined to withhold full civil rights from blacks. There is no doubt that such attitudes caused the Republican party to change its strategy, resulting in the adoption of the Fourteenth Amendment and the move toward "Radical Reconstruction," both serving to enforce loyalty to the federal government and protect Negro rights.

Though the provisional government had not officially ended, Jonathan Worth was sworn into office by Justice Daniel G. Fowle on 15 December. The ceremony took place in the house of commons, and the new governor pledged the state's loyalty to the national government. Yet he warned that if the steps taken by the state to meet readmission plans were not "sufficient to entitle us to confidence, we can scarcely hope to do anything which will be held satisfactory."[97] In an address to the people of the state, delivered 30 December, Worth congratulated the people for "the restoration of Civil Government. . . . We are now under laws of our own enactment."[98]

The governor's willingness to cooperate with the national government on

North Carolina's own terms represented a major change of attitudes. Discounting his prejudices, Holden was correct when he wrote,

> I regret to say that there is much of a rebellious spirit in this State. . . . In May and June last these rebellious spirits would not have dared to show their heads even for the office of constable; but leniency had emboldened them, and the copperhead now shows his fangs. If these men had supreme power . . . the condition of the real Union men and of the freedmen would be exceedingly disagreeable. . . . It may be that the policy of the government has been too lenient; or it may be that I have seriously erred in the discharge of duty.[99]

While there is no doubt that Holden would have preferred for the provisional government to continue until the new year, he made no strong effort to have the president set aside the Worth election and confirm him in office.[100] It was rumored that Johnson had told Kenneth Rayner that federal troops would not be removed from the state during Worth's administration; this may have led some to believe that a return to martial law was imminent.[101] Holden made it clear to the president that he would relinquish state control whenever requested: "My chief wish is to be of benefit to my afflicted State, and to see your administration successful."[102]

On 23 December, President Johnson was ready to end Holden's provisional government, and Secretary of State Seward telegraphed Holden:

> The time has arrived, when, . . . the care and conduct of the proper affairs of the State . . . may be remitted to the constitutional authorities chosen by the people. . . .
>
> By direction of the President, therefore, you are relieved from the trust . . . as Provisional Governor. . . .
>
> It gives me especial pleasure to convey to you the President's acknowledgment of the fidelity, the loyalty and the discretion which have marked your administration.[103]

Accordingly, Holden transferred the Great Seal of the State to Worth on 28 December 1865, and his provisional government officially came to an end.

FIVE

Governor at Last!

On 26 January 1866, after an extended holiday, Holden resumed the editorship of the *Standard*, determined as ever to continue the fight for restoration of the state to the Union. Early in the new year, however, Holden detected a marked decline in Union sentiment and immediately placed responsibility for this on the Worth administration. Worth had steadily replaced Union men with "leading war men" or "rebels" and had little interest in restoring the state to the Union. Confident that he had the support of President Johnson in most matters relating to the state, Holden decided that it would be in the state's best interest, and his own, if he could wrest control from the Worth-Graham faction. The *Standard* declared, therefore, that if disparagement of Holden and praise of former governor Vance by the state's press did not cease, the paper would request that the president return Vance to prison, even though Holden had interceded for his earlier release from prison.[1] In March, Holden openly declared war on his opponents.

> We know that the true Unionists are depressed at the prospect before them, and feel they have a right to look to Washington for sympathy and for such practicable aid as will enable them to put the enemies of the Union where they ought to be—under their feet. And we now give notice that we have commenced this warfare on traitors, not without having counted the cost, and we intend to continue it until they are driven from every office of importance in the State. Nothing shall divert us from our purpose.[2]

As summer came, Holden perceived Johnson's waning strength, his inability to complete the restoration of the southern states, and the ascendance of Radical Republicans and their demands for a congressional plan of reconstruction.[3] He also realized it was unlikely that the Worth-Graham leadership would gain northern acceptance as long as the state's leaders were bent upon returning the former ruling class to power. At this point, Holden began to reason that if North Carolina's restoration could not be effected by President Johnson and Governor Worth, then the alternative was to work with the group in the North that could produce that result. In doing so, he realized that it would require his changing party affiliations for the fourth time in his career, leaving himself open to the charge of being a political opportunist. Yet his unyielding devotion to both Union and state caused him to accept such risk and challenge, for he knew that the only solution to the state's problems was in an early return to the Union.[4]

In June 1866, Holden was nominated as minister to San Salvador,[5] but he failed to win approval because he was unable to subscribe to the ironclad oath requirement then being advocated by congressional leaders. As enacted into law later by the Reconstruction Acts of 1867, no person could hold public office who had held administrative office or given aid or comfort to the Confederate cause. After all, Holden had served in the Raleigh Home Guard, contributed much of his personal wealth to alleviate suffering within the state, and acted as state printer and adviser to Governor Vance. In all probability the appointment was urged on President Johnson by the Worth forces, who hoped to silence Holden by removing him from the state.[6] It is possible, however, that it was tendered as deserved compensation for services rendered and because of his friendship with the president. Holden went to Washington in July to press his claim to the position (although he stated later that he intended to decline), hoping thereby to use its influence to regain his place in state politics. During his visit to the capital, he was able to talk with the president and give his views of the Worth administration. He hoped that this would convince the president that he should be restored to the governorship, even if by military occupation. The president listened, but rather than granting Holden's wish for a full endorsement of the Holden administration and condemnation of Worth's, he instructed Holden to put his thoughts in writing, implying that he would endorse the same. The statement would then be published in the *Standard*. Holden wrote two documents, the first his own evaluation of the political situation in the state and a second one that he intended for Johnson's endorsement. The latter began,

> I have heard with concern of the condition of things in North Carolina. Your administration as Provisional Governor had my entire approval. I so telegraphed you last November. It was, and is my wish that the same means and instrumentalities that commenced, should complete the work of restoration. . . . Unpardoned persons, and persons who cannot take the prescribed oath, cannot expect to be ad-

mitted. . . . [States] are entitled to representation; but in order to secure it, and to sustain my plan of restoration, they should send men
who can successfully stand any existing Constitutional or legal test.[7]

This statement the president refused to endorse, thereby indicating to
Holden that he could no longer count on his support. Holden, therefore, gave
up any thought of opposing Worth's reelection in 1866, though he did lead the
fight in the adjourned session of the state's constitutional convention to seek
greater representation in the legislature for western counties, where his support
lay.[8]

Governor Worth publicly joined Holden in endorsing ratification in a 2
August vote, but failed to provide strong leadership. Thomas Ruffin, Matthias
E. Manly, and William A. Graham, among others, opposed the constitution.
Some based their opposition on their doubts concerning the authority of the
convention to draft the document. Others opposed it because they saw eastern
supremacy threatened with abrogation of the three-fifths count. Others were
disappointed because the new constitution had not expressly permitted the
assumption of the state's war debts. And, finally, there were those who indicated their intention of contesting the legality of the abolition of slavery
without compensation, basing their argument on the claim that the state accepted the Thirteenth Amendment under duress.[9] Despite Holden's best efforts, the proposed constitution failed ratification by 1,982 votes out of a total
of 41,122 votes. It was obvious by this action that the followers of Worth and
Graham, now in control, were not willing to face the reality of racial equality,
nor were they willing to accept any major economic or social reforms.

Before September 1866 the Republican party had neither organization nor
many followers in North Carolina. The defeat of the constitution by the Worth
forces and the refusal of the president to repudiate Worth convinced the state's
loyalist leaders that the only hope for the state's return to the Union would be to
accept the Radical Republican way. On 31 August a meeting of New Bern
citizens, under the chairmanship of Charles R. Thomas, called for a statewide
convention of all who were dissatisfied with the Worth administration to meet
in Raleigh and set in motion the steps necessary to organize a Republican
party. The meeting, open to all who had the time and means, would permit all
such persons to take counsel with other "unmistakable loyal men."

The convention met in Raleigh on 20 September, with thirteen counties
represented and Holden as chairman.[10] No attempt was made at party organization; rather, the gathering served as a vehicle to oppose the state administration. A committee on resolutions brought forth the following: that only loyal

men, regardless of their antecedents, should be elected or appointed to office; that the legislature should ratify the Fourteenth Amendment; and that North Carolinians generally desired to cooperate with President Johnson's reconstruction policies, policies that Governor Worth was hindering by his dilatory action. In a message to the delegates, Holden made clear his opinion that southern states must accept the political reality of congressional control, warning that if the state procrastinated or insisted upon dictating its own terms, such as those expressed in the Black Codes, it must suffer the consequences.[11]

The convention's major decision was that Worth should be opposed in his reelection bid, and Alfred Dockery of Richmond County was selected as his opponent. But Dockery, a former Whig and a true Unionist, declined to enter the race.[12] He did not feel that the convention was sufficiently representative of the state's citizens to reflect the will of the electorate. Also, since the election would take place within thirty days, there would not be time to organize a party strong enough to canvass the state. Worth was therefore reelected without opposition, though Holden urged people to vote for Dockery so as to make the "office seek the man."

The fundamental issue of the 1866 election was the ratification of the Fourteenth Amendment, at times referred to as the Howard Amendment. Worth opposed ratification, saying that since North Carolina was not represented in Congress and had no part in drafting the amendment, it should not vote. He was supported in this by the unofficial organ of his party, the *Raleigh Sentinel*, which used as its slogan the words "For the Constitution of the United States, AS IT IS, and the UNION AS IT WAS. No further Amendments." While this argument was popular throughout the state, its proponents failed to recognize the change in the national temper. Therein lay a weakness of the Worth-Graham forces in their concept of state government.

Before the September convention adjourned, Holden appointed a steering committee to promote the Union cause, but its members soon realized that political power could not be wrested from their opponents without a strong statewide party.[13] They also realized that the Republican party was the logical instrument to secure the power needed to guarantee the state's return to the Union. Thus, the committee, under Holden's guidance, began a campaign to organize a party. Petitions were sent to Washington from all sections of the state asking "protection from Rebel persecution." One from the western counties with five thousand signatures petitioned the House to create a new state in the mountain region (no doubt following the pattern of West Virginia, which left Virginia during the Civil War) or, if that were impossible, to reorganize North Carolina on a "Union basis."[14] Final proof of the necessity of forming a new party came when the General Assembly rejected ratification of the Fourteenth Amendment by 45 to 1 in the senate and 93 to 10 in the house of commons. This led Gen. Ulysses S. Grant to comment that "if the Southern States had accepted the amendment instead of rejecting it so hastily, they would have been admitted by Congress in December, but now I think they will have to take the amendment, and manhood suffrage. Congress will insist on this."[15]

In December 1866, Holden headed a delegation to Washington composed of John Pool, Ceburn L. Harris, and David A. Jenkins to consult with the Radical Republicans on plans for the formation of a state Republican party and drafting of legislation that would end the Worth administration and quickly return the state to the Union. On 13 December, the same day on which the General Assembly rejected the Fourteenth Amendment, Thaddeus Stevens of Pennsylvania introduced the North Carolina Enabling Act, which provided for the reestablishment of civil government in the state, the first step toward readmission. Holden, Pool, Stevens, and Nelson T. Taylor of New York were the chief authors of the bill, which was quite similar to the first Reconstruction Act of 2 March 1867, the exception being that it did not call for the complete enfranchisement of the Negro.[16]

Northern reaction was favorable. The *New York Times* stated that it had "not a single characteristic which may justly be called ferocious," and in its issue for 20 December *The Nation* declared it to be "the most sensible and conservative plan yet submitted to the public—and, . . . it, or something like it, is pretty sure in the end to be adopted not for North Carolina only, but for all the States." Alphonse B. Miller in his biography of Stevens declared the bill of utmost significance because it revealed quite accurately what Stevens had in mind concerning local government, once he was convinced that the southern states were submissive.[17] If this is correct, then Stevens was driven to propose harsher measures in 1867 by the contumacy of the South.

While Holden and his delegation were active, Worth appointed a "bipartisan" delegation composed of Bedford Brown, Patrick H. Winston, Augustus S. Merrimon, Lewis Hanes, Nathaniel Boyden, and James T. Leach to proceed to Washington and present evidence to counter the "misrepresentation" of the Holden group and to express opposition to the North Carolina Enabling Act. Governors James Orr of South Carolina and William L. Sharkey of Mississippi, former governors William Marvin of Florida and Lewis Parsons of Alabama, Judge J. T. James of Arkansas, several members of Congress, and President Johnson worked with the members of this delegation in January and early February 1867, drafting compromise legislation known as the North

Carolina Plan. It had two major parts: first, a constitutional amendment resembling the proposed Howard Amendment, but without the disqualification provision for those who participated in the rebellion, plus a clause which declared the Union perpetual; and, second, an amendment to each state constitution that would call for a suffrage requirement, strictly qualified by property and educational requirements, yet excluding no one who previously had the right to vote.[18]

The plan was immediately rejected by Congress, since it did not have the endorsement of southern leaders generally. The Reconstruction Act of 1867, passed a short time later, was a sharp rebuff to states that were formerly members of the Confederacy for their refusal to prove submissive and to accept the inevitability of Negro suffrage.[19] To Thad Stevens this simply meant:

> Go home! Governor Holden, and rule your state, as you see fit; but waste no time sending delegates to this body. We have whipped the South to the door of the Union, and there we mean to keep her! Yes, Sir, by God, Sir, she shall knuckle on her marrowbones for ten years to come! Ten years, Sir, before she shall have any voice in this House, Sir! It will do her good! It will take pride out of her! And furthermore you may tell your people they shall have no peace until a negro is free as a white man, votes like a white man, and is treated as a white man! Hark what I say—we mean it.[20]

Meanwhile, Holden worked in full cooperation with the Radicals. In January he had declared himself in favor of unqualified Negro suffrage and had introduced to a meeting of Raleigh Negroes a resolution requesting Congress to reorganize the state government on the basis of "loyal white and black suffrage." Later, he charged that "obstructionist" state leaders were "bent on mischief": "The people of this State have at length reached a point when they must act and restore the State to the Union, or incur the hazards of anarchy and civil war. The Union people . . . have borne as much and as long as they intend to bear. All honest, thoughtful, decent citizens will either unite with them in the work of restoration or retire and remain quiet. *Traitors must* take back seats and keep silent. . . . The issue is Union or Disunion."[21]

Republican leaders joined Holden in opposing Johnson's North Carolina Plan, arguing that it would be to the state's advantage to submit to the inevitable and to accept congressional rule. A letter from Holden to Senator John Sherman, Republican from Ohio, indicates what they had in mind.

As the bill recently passed to reconstruct the Southern States is likely
to become a law, . . . the present State governments are, I take it, illegal and can have no binding effect on the people. Do they cease to
exist, or are they simply tolerated, the military commander "allowing"
their local civil tribunals to take Jurisdiction, &c? The loyal people of
this State desire to act immediately. They believe they can call a Convention, frame a Constitution, and elect members of Congress in time
to be admitted next December.[22]

When Johnson vetoed the first Reconstruction Act, later overridden by
Congress, Holden said that the president had defied the will of the people and,
rather than yield gracefully to public opinion, had encouraged "rebels and
traitors." "It is a sad reflection that a public man with so noble a Union record
should have staked and lost himself for Rebels and Rebellion."[23] Under the 2
March act, legal government was ended in all southern states except Tennessee
and the South was divided into five military districts with each under the
command of a Union general. As the price for readmission to the Union, the
states were required to call new constitutional conventions, chosen by universal male suffrage, white and Negro, to draw up new constitutions and organize
their governments (subject to congressional approval) guaranteeing to blacks
the right to vote and hold office. A further requirement was the ratification of
the Fourteenth Amendment. When accomplished, the states could then apply
for readmission, with Congress having sole authority for ending military rule,
withdrawing Federal troops, and seating the newly elected congressional
members.

With this action, Holden broke completely with Johnson's moderate
supporters and began the formation of a Republican party that would carry out
the edicts of the Radical Republican reconstruction plans. The party leaders
held a caucus in early March while the General Assembly was in session;
Ceburn L. Harris presided, and the group decided to hold a convention on 27
March, its purpose being to finalize the formation of a state Republican party
and plan a new constitutional convention. A new constitution, they hoped,
would prepare the state for readmission to the Union under the congressional
plan. Writing to the *Standard*, Robert P. Dick saw this as a necessity, since the
Unionists "must show Congress and the Northern people that there is a strong
loyal element in our State, which, if sustained and encouraged, can and will
overcome disloyalty and treason."[24] The *Salem Observer* went a step farther,
suggesting the adoption of the name and organization of the Republican
party.[25] This met with the hearty approbation of Holden, who wrote, "While

we do not presume to dictate, we would respectfully advise our friends to at once accommodate their political language to this important change. The Republican party of the United States of America! It is an honorable name; and history will record that through its efforts the federal government was preserved, and the integrity of the nation maintained."[26]

State Unionist leaders, acting under the guidelines set down by the Reconstruction Act of 2 March, pressed forward with their plans for a statewide Republican convention. One hundred and fifty-six carefully selected delegates were invited to attend.[27] As one examines the list, it is interesting to note that no black was included; however, this was soon corrected. Holden, through the *Standard*, issued an open invitation to interested blacks and assured them that every loyal Unionist who came to the meeting would receive a cordial reception. This was no doubt brought about by pressure from meetings of blacks in Raleigh and Fayetteville. In both instances delegates were appointed to the 27 March convention, even though they had no formal invitations.[28]

The convention met in the House of Commons Hall in the Capitol, with the delegates being called by the ringing of the Capitol bell. A total of 147 delegates attended, 101 whites and 46 blacks. This was the first racially mixed convention of any size in the history of the South, and the *Standard* headlined its account of the first day: "THE LOYAL REPUBLICANS OF THE STATE OF BOTH RACES IN COUNCIL!!! HARMONY AND ENTHUSIASM!!! THE FIRST STEP TO 'THE MUSIC OF THE UNION'!!!"[29] Ceburn L. Harris, chairman of the General Assembly caucus that summoned the convention, called the session to order, and Alfred Dockery was elected temporary chairman. Alexander H. Jones of Hendersonville was chosen permanent president.[30] Appointments to other permanent offices were shared by members of both races. David Heaton of Craven and Dr. O. P. Hadley of Richmond, both white, served as vice-presidents, with James H. Harris of Wake and J. R. Goode of Craven who were black. Henry J. Menninger, a white citizen of Craven, shared the duties of secretary with J. E. O'Hara, a black resident of Wayne.

Following the election of convention officials, Robert P. Dick, according to prearranged plans, moved that the convention form a Republican party. Daniel R. Goodloe immediately opposed the use of the name "Republican," saying that it was odious to Southerners; Benjamin S. Hedrick urged instead the adoption of the name "Union party."[31] Goodloe's objection was overruled by Holden and his friends, and the name "Republican" officially adopted. As Thomas Settle commented, "Republican was the choice for party name by all loyalists."[32]

The meeting's major work was the adoption of a platform and the creation of a statewide party organization. The latter was particularly important if the party was to become sufficiently strong to win control within the state. Actually, though, its later success was primarily the result of Holden's strategies and organizational abilities. David Heaton prepared the draft of the platform. He included a statement accepting the congressional plan of reconstruction, with complete equality for Negroes. Future party planning and organization were placed in the hands of an executive committee composed of twenty-three whites and sixteen blacks, with Holden as chairman.[33] Twice before in organizing state parties, he had succeeded in leading the new party to administrative power, but this time the problems he faced were more difficult.

The convention and the newly organized Republican party were bitterly criticized by the opposition press. The *Raleigh Sentinel* deemed the convention of so little significance that no reporter was sent to cover it. It merely editorialized: "Look at the material at this meeting! Old party hacks, broken down, spavined demagogues, mere seekers of office."[34] The *Greensboro Union Banner* wrote, "A part of its members were honest, genuine men, who were bamboozled into the affair to give it *eclat*. The remainder were shams, perfect political mushrooms."[35] The *Weldon State* spoke of the "cowards who will go down to posterity with the finger of scorn pointing at them as the wretches who gave the last stab to the hopes of the State."[36] The *Wilmington Dispatch* referred to the convention as the "Holden miscegenationists." Northern reaction, however, was favorable, and the *Nation* probably expressed the feeling best in saying, "[It] seems to have been a body eminently respectable for numbers, for honesty of purpose, and for ability. . . . We are glad to see this movement begun; in North Carolina we suppose nearly half of the vote of the State can be controlled by it."[37]

Holden and the executive committee immediately began planning for a statewide organization. Party members in each county would select their own delegates and develop the strategy most likely to win popular support. Mass meetings were planned to highlight Independence Day celebrations. In Raleigh more than five thousand persons witnessed a parade of blacks and Union League members and heard orations by various Republican leaders of both races.[38] The party received considerable aid from northern friends. The Union Republican Congressional Committee, headed by Thomas L. Tullock, probably contributed the largest sum, but state organizations, such as the Massachusetts Reconstruction Association, were also helpful with contributions of money and campaign literature. The Republican Executive Committee supplied large amounts of literature, twenty thousand dollars in cash, unstinted use of franking privileges, and more than seventy full-time speakers and organizers.[39]

The introduction of the Union League, and its control of the Negro vote, was probably the most notable feature of the Republican party's development in North Carolina. Albion W. Tourgée is generally credited with organizing the state's first League chapter in Guilford and surrounding counties in 1866, and by the summer of the following year the League had spread statewide.[40] Virtually every black male was a League member, and those few who declined to join tended to follow the League's dictates. Freedmen's Bureau agents, northern carpetbaggers, and native white Republicans all joined to attest party loyalty, but it was among blacks that it concentrated its activities. After the League had grown into a statewide organization, Holden was designated head, and the *Standard*, quite logically, served as its official organ. The League brought with it considerable political benefit, and there is little doubt that it contributed to the successful rise to power of the Republican party in North Carolina.

The failure of Congress to abolish the Worth government greatly annoyed the Republican leaders. It had been generally assumed that the state would resist the enforcement of the 1867 reconstruction act, resulting in the removal of civil officers and resumption of complete military rule. As a matter of fact, Governor Worth contemplated such an idea and had even instructed Reverdy Johnson of Maryland to prepare a case that he hoped would lead ultimately to a Supreme Court decision,[41] thereby testing the power of Congress to reorganize the southern states.[42] But Worth failed to follow through with such plans. Meanwhile, a committee of twenty-six Republican leaders was instructed to proceed to Washington (but only David Heaton, John T. Deweese, Calvin J. Cowles, and James T. Harris actually went) to petition Congress for the removal of the Worth administration—an effort that proved unsuccessful. Holden expressed his thoughts very bluntly: "All we ask is fair play under the Sherman Act. Give us that, and we can restore the state. To do this, the rebel State Governments must be swept 'from turret to foundation stone.' They are nests of treason. Give us a military government pure and simple, and military Government of our own. Do this for us, and the Old North State will cast her nine Electoral votes for the candidate of the Radical party."[43]

The most discussed issues of the summer of 1867 were black suffrage and the threat of property confiscation. Northern Radicals had determined that civil rights for blacks must include the franchise, thereby guaranteeing Republican rule, and as Governor Worth wrote, "They [the blacks] are carried away with the idea."[44] Although disapproving of the idea of black suffrage, the Conservatives realistically accepted it on a limited basis. However, they bitterly opposed the future possibility of black officeholders in the state.

The threat of confiscation alarmed white Conservative leaders even more. Since the war's end there had been vague promises to the freedmen of a "mule and forty acres," which meant a redistribution of southern lands. No doubt some promises of this nature were made to win black support for the Republican cause and, perhaps, to induce cooperation or acquiescence from reluctant Southerners. The *Charlotte News*, however, hinted that such rumors were designed to stampede landowners into selling their property at ridiculously low prices to northern investment associations.[45] Certainly, if the choice had belonged to Thad Stevens, the rumors would have been translated into law. In a speech before the House of Representatives in the spring of 1865 he had urged confiscation, which he repeated in September when speaking in Lancaster, Pennsylvania.[46] In March 1867 he introduced legislation to this effect, but his bill was never passed; Congress evidently felt that restrictions already imposed were sufficient.[47]

Despite these developments, Conservative leaders were lethargic. Either they did not realize the growing influence of the state Republican party or they were too stunned by congressional reconstruction to make serious efforts to maintain favorable public opinion. There had been earlier efforts to win the black voters with mass meetings in Raleigh and Governor Worth as speaker, but by summer the disposition was to forgo any interracial alliance. There was talk, also, of having the governor convene the assembly and of issuing a call for a constitutional convention, thereby circumscribing the authority of the military commander. This idea was short-lived, however, for Gen. Daniel E. Sickles, commander of the Second Military District, postponed the upcoming session of the assembly. The *Standard* expressed deep gratification for his action.[48]

The building of a state Republican party was not without incident. Loyalty and support were divided among party leaders along sectional lines, native whites versus northern "carpetbaggers." Efforts were soon made to transfer leadership from Holden and his supporters to the northern faction and its black backers. In an attempt to prevent a breach, Holden called a meeting of the party's executive committee in Raleigh on 5 June. There the decision was made to hold another state convention on 4 September, with each county permitted to send as many delegates as desired, but the official vote would be limited to the county's representation in the house of commons. Also, it was recommended that councils of the Union League should act through county party organizations rather than through separate delegations.[49]

The Republican convention assembled on 4 September; 286 delegates were present, with seventy-two of the state's counties represented. Unhappily, dissension began with the first session. This was evidenced by the election of

Joseph C. Abbott as permanent presiding officer instead of Alfred Dockery, who had been led to expect the position, and a fierce fight over the party platform.[50] Holden preferred Dockery, but he supported Abbott's nomination in order that he might retain his chairmanship of the executive committee. The Negro vote, plus that of the northern carpetbaggers, proved to be the decisive factor, for together they greatly outnumbered native white delegates.

On another issue, this group was not as successful. John Pool was chairman of the committee on platform and resolutions, and his group reported that confiscation of private property for political offenses was repugnant to the state Republicans, that free and unlimited suffrage should be granted to every male citizen above the age of twenty-one, and that Congress should remove all suffrage disabilities from true Unionists. The black members were upset by the confiscation resolution and tried to defeat it, failing by a vote of 53–47. Later, David Heaton submitted a substitute proposal which committed the party to abide by whatever plan of reconstruction Congress adopted. Holden endorsed this proposal and declared: "I commit myself neither for nor against confiscation for the present. . . . Sir, if, in the sequel, as the result of any threatened disorganization of the Republican party, or if obstructions to reconstruction measures should be perverted,—and if, in the end, it is necessary to do it in order to insure reconstruction on a loyal basis, then I say let confiscation come."[51]

His speech appeared to satisfy the warring groups, for it brought about a unanimous acceptance of the Heaton amendment, and the resolutions on suffrage and removal of disabilities were tabled. The convention closed with a request to the military commander for an early election and suggested another constitutional convention; these actions, it was hoped, would gain for North Carolina readmission to the Union. A new executive committee was selected; although Holden remained chairman, only eight of the original twenty-one members retained their seats. By this action, control of the North Carolina Republican party passed over to Northerners.

On 18 October 1867, Gen. Edward R. S. Canby, who had succeeded Sickles as military commander of North Carolina on 26 August, concluded that the state was sufficiently reconstructed to begin anew the process of reunion.[52] He ordered an election be held on 19–20 November to determine whether to hold a constitutional convention and, simultaneously, to elect convention delegates. The approval for the convention was taken for granted, and the Republican party lost no time spreading the news and lining up organizational strength. The Conservative opposition split three ways. The *Raleigh Sentinel*, the Conservative party organ, supported the call for a convention and advised that a strong effort be made to secure the black votes in order to control the convention. This idea was opposed by those who felt that the entire congressional plan was unconstitutional, and therefore the idea of a convention should be defeated. A third group opposed the Republicans on a strictly racial basis by opposing black suffrage. Although Governor Worth urged citizens to vote for delegates, he dared not tell supporters how to vote for fear he would be removed from office and replaced by a Republican. Actually, Worth opposed the called convention and agreed with Graham that the congressional plan was unconstitutional.[53] The Conservatives, despite their public meetings in Raleigh, failed to inaugurate a vigorous campaign, thereby insuring a victory for the convention and for Republican control.

The election was conducted peaceably, with only scattered reports of violence or disorder. The call for a convention carried by a majority of three to one—93,006 to 32,961—and the Republicans elected 107 of the 120 delegates.[54] Of this number 94 were white, while 13 were black. Throughout the campaign the *Standard* took the lead in boosting popular support for the convention and Republican candidates, but in the final analysis the party's success was largely the result of the heavy black vote in the eastern counties, the strong Unionist sentiment in the west, and failure of whites to vote in the middle counties. The outcome was proof that the Republican party was a formidable organization in state politics and would have to be reckoned with. It was also a foregone conclusion that Holden intended to use the party's success in gaining control of the state's government to place himself once again in the governor's chair.

During the winter months of 1867–68, Governor Worth found it increasingly difficult to work with General Canby. He charged Canby with maintaining a military despotism in North Carolina, and in January he sent a forty-page letter to President Johnson by W. G. Moore, his Washington agent, describing the conflicts between the two and asserting that the removal of Canby was justified.[55] The president sided with Canby. As scheduled, the constitutional convention met in Raleigh on 14 January 1868.

Calvin J. Cowles was the convention's president, and under his guidance an entirely new constitution was slowly written.[56] The so-called carpetbagger members of the convention exercised considerable influence in the preparation of a document that represented a major step toward self-government.[57] Some of its significant provisions were: abolition of slavery; a provision for universal manhood suffrage; elimination of all property and religious qualifications for voting and officeholding; popular election of state and county officials; abolition of the county court system and adoption of the township–county commission form of local government; provision for a board of charities and public welfare; provision for a general and uniform system of public schools to be open "for at least four months in every year";[58] expansion of higher education to include agricultural, mechanical, mining, and normal school instruction, as a part of the free public school system; creation of four new elective administrative offices—lieutenant governor, auditor, superintendent of public instruction, and superintendent of public works; alteration of the two-year term for the governor to a term of four years; redesignation of the house of commons as the house of representatives; and reduction of the number of capital offenses to four—murder, arson, burglary, and rape—with the purpose of punishment to be "not only to satisfy justice, but also to reform the offender, and thus prevent crime."[59] The convention completed its work, ordering a vote for or against ratification to take place on 21–23 April; on the same ballot state officials for the new government would be chosen.

The "Conservative Union Party," as the Conservatives renamed themselves in a convention on 6 February, was the first to start the 1868 political campaign. Its members hoped to defeat the new constitution, thereby remaining in power. But they had difficulty in finding an acceptable slate of candidates. Former governor Zebulon Vance was the popular choice, though Worth declared that he himself would accept if renominated. The party's executive committee ignored Worth's suggestion and tendered the nomination to Vance. When he declined, the nomination was successively offered to Thomas Bragg, Daniel G. Fowle, Augustus S. Merrimon, and at last to Thomas Samuel Ashe, a former Democrat.

The Republicans held their convention in Raleigh on 26 February, with Holden presiding. The majority of their delegates were serving in the constitutional convention, which was in session; in fact, the work of writing a constitution virtually ceased for the duration of the Republican convention. Benjamin S. Hedrick, with Holden especially in mind, proposed that no one should receive a party nomination who was disqualified from holding office under the 1867 Reconstruction Acts or the Fourteenth Amendment, but this proposal was immediately rejected. As expected, Holden was nominated for governor without opposition. Alfred Dockery was twice offered the nomination for the office of lieutenant governor, but he declined, being unwilling to accept the second position. Tod R. Caldwell was finally nominated. Native Southerners were nominated by the Republicans to all but five of the major posts in the executive, judicial, and congressional offices; the exceptions were secretary of state, superintendent of public instruction, and congressmen from the First, Second, and Fourth districts.[60]

The ensuing campaign was a bitter one. The Conservative Unionists campaigned on three major issues—opposition to ratification of the constitution, the unfitness of Holden to serve as governor, and the doubtful character of other Republican candidates.[61] Their campaign technique is shown in these questions which they kept before the public:

> The great paramount issue is: shall negroes or whites rule North Carolina? All other issues are secondary and subordinate, and should be kept so.
> Shall white children be compelled to go to the same schools with negroes?
> Shall marriage between negroes and whites—amalgamation—be allowed?
> Shall negro guardians be appointed for white wards? Convention didn't prohibit it.[62]

Hardie H. Helper, brother of Hinton Rowan Helper, author of *The Impending Crisis of the South: How to Meet It*, stopped publication of the *Raleigh Register* so that he might bring out a campaign sheet, *The Holden Record*, and give his support to Daniel R. Goodloe, who was running as an independent. In Charlotte, Salisbury, and Raleigh, the Conservatives were responsible for mass meetings where Holden was hanged in effigy. During the campaign also the Ku Klux Klan first made its appearance in the state. In Warren County, Klansmen, garbed in their white sheets, dug graves along the roads that led to Warrenton as a warning to the blacks. In Raleigh and Wilmington placards were posted on city streets which read:

> K.K.K.
> Attention! First Hour! In the Mist!
> At the Flash! Come. Come. Come!!!
> Retribution is impatient! The grave yawns!
> The sceptre bones rattle!
> Let the doomed quake!
> > It is commanded.
> > 2nd G. C. or BL. HOST.[63]

Republicans, in the meantime, organized a campaign that covered the entire state. On 10 March, Holden launched a far-reaching canvass, addressing large biracial crowds of supporters in all of the major cities. Hoarseness and a severe cold prevented his making appearances in Wilmington and the northwest portion of the state, but other orators took to the stump. Hardly a town of any size was ignored. Once again the Union League was pressed into service to combat the Ku Klux Klan, and special efforts were made to secure the support of the poor whites and working men. To the latter, a circular was widely distributed, showing how they had been stigmatized by the southern aristocracy, now members of the Conservative Union party, as "poor white trash" or "greasy mechanics." The Republican party, the circular assured them, was working for their interests by its advocacy of civil, political, and religious liberty and by its denunciation of class legislation.[64]

In the closing days of the campaign the *Register* suggested to its readers that the Congressional Executive Committee of the Republican party had considered forcing Holden to withdraw from the race because of certain defeat. Even if elected, it claimed, he would not be pardoned; therefore, any vote cast for him was a lost vote. The *Standard*, being edited by Joseph W. Holden and William M. Coleman, replied with a statement from Robert C. Schenck, chairman of the National Republican party, who assured Holden that his services were appreciated by the party and that no objection had been made to his candidacy by any Union member of the House or Senate.[65] In addition to this communication from Schenck, the national party reportedly sent flocks of Howard University students to make speeches in the South and added an extra two hundred thousand dollars to the party's campaign fund in North Carolina.

The election resulted in a resounding Republican victory. The constitution was ratified by a 93,084 to 74,015 vote, while Holden was elected by a vote of 92,235 to 73,594.[66] The Republicans also elected 6 of the 7 congressmen and all of the executive and judicial officers except one judge and one solicitor.[67] Furthermore, the party carried 58 of the 89 counties and secured majorities of 38 to 12 in the senate and 80 to 40 in the house of representatives. At last Holden had fulfilled his boyhood pledge to surpass his student adversary and had finally achieved his ambition to be governor.[68]

Holden began his gubernatorial career under ominous circumstances, despite his overwhelming victory. For example, he knew that Governor Worth bitterly disapproved the "Canby Constitution" and would resist, if at all possible, turning the state government over to a Republican administration. For this reason he urged congressional leaders to arrange for the military removal of Worth and the immediate installation of his own administration. Plans were also made to call a special session of the General Assembly in order that the newly elected members could cast a favorable vote on the requirements for statehood. But two major problems confronted him: on the one hand, congressional approval had to be secured for the newly ratified constitution; on the other, a majority of the newly elected state and local officials were disqualified from holding office by the Reconstruction Acts. General Canby required that all officers installed prior to the restoration of the state must take the "ironclad" oath in addition to meeting the requirements imposed by the Fourteenth Amendment. This meant that several members of Holden's administration could not assume their positions without congressional dispensation. Congress, though, was deeply involved in the impeachment trial of the president and was slow in attending to any of its legislative duties. Meanwhile, Holden was forced to wait, and he was not a patient man.

Local Republicans encouraged Holden to take the initiative and, as governor-elect, to call the legislature into session on a provisional basis. Bryon Laflin, newly elected member of the House of Representatives from Pitt County, telegraphed Holden from Washington: "Senators and General Rawlings advise you as Gov-Elect to issue call for Legislature to convene on June 29th."[69] And General Canby telegraphed from Charleston, "I would suggest that the call be made conditional to meet the possible contingency of a delay in the final passage of the bill if it should be vetoed."[70] Holden decided against taking the initiative, but he was not above trying to speed up congressional action by advocating the conviction of President Johnson: "The salvation of the South depends on the conviction of Andrew Johnson."[71] He wired several northern newspapers urging conviction and removal, even stating that if Johnson were acquitted before North Carolina's new government had been installed and the state had representation in Congress, war would resume in the state.[72] No doubt Holden was encouraged to take this strong position by the advice of friends such as John Pool:

> Allow me to say, . . . that we must all now see that no reliance can be placed upon the words, the honor or the position of any man thoroughly imbued with the fanaticism of sectionalism. . . . They must be made to feel that loyal men *will* be the masters in this State. Your only reliable friends look to you to hold a strong & unflinching hand. If you do, your administration will be sustained by us to the last extremity.[73]

Governor Worth expressed concern over the possibility that his administration might be ended by military edict. Writing to former governor Graham, he sought advice should Holden ask him to vacate his office.

> What remedy is there for the villainous government imposed on us? . . . Personally I prefer to retire, but I shrink from no responsibility which duty imposes. When Holden shall demand of me to vacate, would you advise that I yield to the demand, with or without protest— or that I refuse to yield to it with the view of raising the question as to the constitutionality of the law under which he claims to be elected?

Could I get up the question by such refusal? If put under arrest I have no idea that any of our judiciary would relieve me on habeas corpus.[74]

On 25 June, Congress passed the act providing for readmission to Congress for North Carolina's representatives, along with those of five other states, the readmission to take effect when the state legislature had ratified the Fourteenth Amendment. Johnson vetoed the bill, which was nevertheless promptly enacted into law. At the same time Congress removed disabilities from approximately seven hundred North Carolina citizens, thus permitting the duly elected officials to assume office without subscribing to the ironclad oath. Through this action, Holden was able to begin his administration without further opposition.

Without waiting for final congressional action, Holden issued a proclamation on 25 June summoning the General Assembly into session on 1 July.[75] On 29 June, General Canby instructed Chief Justice Pearson to take the oath of office from a United States commissioner, thereby qualifying himself, and then to administer the oaths to other newly elected officials. Accordingly, Pearson notified Governor Worth that he would administer the oaths and install the new administration on 1 July, and at ten o'clock that day Holden took the oath and began performance of his duties as governor. Worth surrendered his office quietly, but only after writing Holden a strong protest in which he questioned the validity of the April elections and concluded by saying that he regarded "all of you, as, in effect, appointees of the Military power of the United States, and not as 'deserving your powers from the consent of those you claim to govern.' "[76] Holden recalled his reaction to this in his memoirs, written many years later.

> He had taken my place in December, 1865, just as cheerfully and as
> promptly as I had retired from it. Suppose for example, the Hon.
> Thomas S. Ashe had been elected Governor in my place, would not
> Governor Worth have yielded to him at once? Would not his Demo-
> cratic friends have required it of him? But instead of this, he took a po-
> sition in his protest that rather than have a Governor chosen by the Re-
> publican vote, he would have no Governor at all. . . . His protest was
> hailed and approved throughout the State by his partisan friends and to
> this day there has been no condemnation of it in so many words.[77]

On 4 July, before a packed General Assembly, Governor Holden delivered his inaugural address, laying down the principles his administration would follow.

The unity of government, which constitutes us one people, has been restored. The Great Rebellion is suppressed. The will of the majority, from which there is no further appeal, has been pronounced. . . . The Union has been preserved. It has been preserved not only on its former basis of liberty for one race, but its foundations are now broad enough for the whole people, of whatever origin, color, or former condition.

He then reviewed the new constitution, explaining that the state's laws would operate equally for all and that every citizen would enjoy equal protection of the courts. He also pointed out the need for a genuine state-supported (but segregated) educational system. He promised the reorganization of the state militia in order that peace could be preserved fearlessly and firmly. He reaffirmed to the Negroes the right of suffrage, declaring that it would never be taken from them again: "The repugnance of Negro suffrage, which exists among many of our people, will gradually subside when they shall be convinced by actual experience that none of the evils they anticipated have resulted from it." In closing, Holden declared:

Cherishing neither malice nor resentment for anything that had occurred in the past, I shall endeavor to do my duty. . . . I love the Union, because it is the first, and last, the only hope of my State; and I love my State, because her people have been good and kind to me, and because her sky is above my home, as it will be above my grave. If I have enemies, that does not make me an enemy of my State, nor move me to a course of action based on resentment or revenge. I follow the principles of Washington, who founded, and of Lincoln, who saved the Republic; and when these principles cease to lead, I shall cease to follow.[78]

On 2 July the Fourteenth Amendment was ratified following a vote of 34 to 2 in the senate and 82 to 19 in the house, whereupon General Canby ordered all military interference with civil functions to cease immediately. On 6 July five of the state's seven congressional representatives (John R. French, David Heaton, John T. Deweese, Israel G. Lash, and Alexander H. Jones) were admitted to their seats in the United States House of Representatives, while Nathaniel Boyden and Oliver H. Dockery were forced to wait until 20 July, when their disability of subscribing to the ironclad oath was removed. Senators John Pool and Joseph C. Abbott were sworn into office on 13 July, having no difficulty in signing the required loyalty oaths. Thus, North Carolina was once again restored to the Union and congressional reconstruction had come to an end.

SIX

The Republican Regime, 1868–1870

As he had in 1865 during his provisional governorship, Holden chose to remain in his own home rather than move into the Governor's Mansion, which was still in a deplorable condition from the abuse by federal troops who had occupied it during and after the war. The Holden two-story colonial house was built in 1852 at the corner of Hargett and McDowell streets at a cost of five thousand dollars. It contained four rooms on the first floor with a hall extending through the center. A spiral stairway, located near the front, led to the second floor, which duplicated the downstairs arrangement. The home was considered one of the finest in Raleigh; it probably had the first bathtub in the city, the waterworks being connected to a tank on top of the house. Behind the home was a sunken garden, filled with boxwoods, blooming flowers, and towering trees. One, a weeping elm, was the only one of its kind in the city. A long porch extended along one side of the house on McDowell Street, and here the governor would pace back and forth taking his exercise, composing speeches and editorials, and playing with his children. Not only did he find pleasure in the house's spacious accommodations but he also enjoyed entertaining with genuine southern hospitality his many guests. The holiday seasons always afforded Governor and Mrs. Holden an opportunity to spread a bounteous table—a dinner that usually included roast pig complete with red apple in its mouth, a large turkey, along with vegetables, relishes, and desserts as was customary in the South at that time. The Holdens were well known as congenial hosts, and they seemed always pleased to share the house with family and friends.[1]

A lengthy controversy later developed over Holden's use of some of the furniture from the Governor's Mansion that he had obtained in 1865 and kept until 1877. When Mrs. Zebulon Vance fled to Statesville in 1865, she carried most of the valuable mansion pieces with her, and Holden did not ask the Vances to return such furniture. He did recover some pieces from R. H. Bradley, keeper of the Capitol, but turned them over in 1866 to Governor

Worth. Like Holden, Worth had also chosen to live in his own home and returned the articles to Holden in 1868. After leaving office in 1871, Holden notified Governor Tod R. Caldwell that he was prepared to return the furniture, but since Caldwell was single and not keeping house, he asked the former governor to retain possession. Later, in 1874, Holden informed Governor Curtis H. Brogden of the furniture, but was again told to retain possession until it was called for.[2] When Vance occupied the Governor's Mansion in 1877, the first governor to do so since the Civil War, Holden turned over to him all the state furniture that had been in his possession since 1865.

For the use of his residence and for repair of the mansion's furniture, Holden was paid $5,000, although the dated receipts show only $3,500 and $941.44 actually paid.[3] The legislature had appropriated $10,000 for these expenses, which Holden did not choose to make full use of.[4] In spite of this, Holden was accused of using state funds for his private benefit when he made large purchases in New York and other cities of furniture for his own house; the money thus spent had actually come from the $30,000 received from his sale of the *Standard* when he assumed the office of governor.[5] The largest portion of the *Standard* money was placed in Mrs. Holden's name in 1869, which proved to be a wise decision since his political enemies attempted to confiscate his wealth.[6]

In getting his administration under way, Holden was faced with two major problems. The first was the filling of vacant state offices. According to article 14, section 5, of the constitution of 1868, the governor was empowered, "in the absence of any contrary provision," to appoint all officers in the state whether previously appointed by the governor or elected by the people, "until their successors shall have been chosen and duly qualified according to the provisions of this Constitution." Holden wrote General Canby that the framers of this provision had as their objective the prompt removal of all officers holding posts under Worth; they had intended to give the new governor temporary power to operate until such time as the General Assembly could provide for popular elections.[7]

Thus, as in 1865, Holden began the arduous task of appointing county and municipal officials, complicated by the fact that many incumbents refused to vacate their posts until the General Assembly declared on 24 July that all previous offices be vacant.[8] But this time, Holden did not make his mistake of 1865 by seeking to placate his former opponents. He filled the offices with loyal Republicans, who held their posts until the first Monday of January 1869, when elections were held and their successors were named.

Holden's second problem was the organization of a state militia for the maintenance of law and order. He sent a special message to the assembly on 17

July, calling for immediate action in order that the government could be "a terror to evil-doers, and a friend to them that do well." After considerable delay, the legislature passed a militia law on 13 August, even though twenty-nine house members signed a protest, charging that it was unconstitutional, subversive of the rights and liberties of the people, and calculated to invoke a disastrous civil war. The new law provided that every male citizen between the ages of twenty-one and forty was subject to serve in the militia, unless exempted by a physician's certificate or payment of an annual contribution of two dollars; that the governor was authorized to organize six regiments of infantry, three battalions of cavalry, and one battery of artillery for each of the three geographical divisions of the state; that the governor was empowered to call the militia into service upon the request of any five county magistrates; that white and black militiamen were not to be compelled to serve in the same units; and that if the militia was ever called into duty to preserve peace during an election, it was not to use any influence over voters.[9]

By 1 September, Holden had completed the militia organization and begun the necessary arrangements for obtaining equipment. Abial W. Fisher of Bladen County was appointed adjutant general; Franklin G. Martindale, a carpetbagger from Martin County, J. Q. A. Bryan of Wilkes County, a Union ranger during the Civil War, and Willie D. Jones of Wake were appointed commanders of the eastern, middle, and western divisions. Commanding officers were appointed also for each of the counties. The securing of arms and other military supplies was considerably more difficult, since the state treasury had no funds to make such purchases. By November, however, Holden could report that sufficient quantities of arms, ammunition, and equipment had been obtained without cost to the state other than for transportation. No doubt most of this was "on loan" from Republican-controlled states of the Northeast, such as the large quantity of Springfield rifles received from Governor John B. Page of Vermont.[10]

From its beginning the administration was accused of nepotism and criticized for high administrative costs. The first charge is legitimate, for Holden's son, Joseph, served as speaker of the house of representatives, though only twenty-four years of age and without previous legislative experience, and was appointed state director for two railroad companies; Holden's son-in-law Calvin J. Cowles presided over the 1868 constitutional convention and was appointed a state railroad director; another Holden son-in-law, Lewis P. Olds, served as a railroad director, as special legal adviser to the state, and as attorney general; and Holden's brother-in-law, Robert Harrison, served as mayor of Raleigh throughout the years of the administration.[11]

The other accusation was primarily "politicking" by the opposition. By law, Holden was entitled to three clerks and two messengers, but he employed only one secretary, one clerk, and one messenger—the same number that Governor Worth had employed. Furthermore, since the war only one additional laborer had been employed in the upkeep of the Capitol, even though the building was badly deteriorated when the new administration took over. The condition was so bad that Governor Holden would have been justified in putting several carpenters and grounds keepers to work restoring the building and its grounds to their former well-kept condition. As he had done with his newspaper, Holden kept a tight rein on expenditures to make certain that the public's money was not wasted.

In other ways, though, state operating costs increased tremendously during the two years of Holden's tenure. Most of this can be accounted for by the high rate of inflation experienced by the nation during the postwar years, by the new programs and services initiated by both the 1868 constitutional convention and the General Assembly, and by the general malfeasance of the Republican leadership. A code commission was created by the constitution of 1868 to prepare a Code of Practice and Procedure and to draft legislative bills for the General Assembly, but Conservative opposition was quick to claim that each of the commissioners—Albion W. Tourgée, William B. Rodman, and Victor Barringer—was paid $200 a month mainly to copy the New York code.[12] Eleven lawyers were paid a total of $5,400 during 1869–70 to assist the state in the prosecution of murder cases and revenue matters. (In retrospect, this sum is quite small when compared with the fees paid to the prosecution team during Holden's impeachment trial.)[13]

One expenditure arousing particular criticism was the governor's use of a detective force in his effort to ferret out the illegal activities of the Ku Klux Klan. Sixteen detectives were employed at various times at a cost of $3,646.32 in salaries and $6,539.27 in expenses.[14] For these efforts to maintain law and order and to guarantee equal protection of the law for all citizens, Holden should have been praised; instead the most virulent aspersions were made against him. Another expenditure that raised criticism was the cost of official stationery; in a two-year period, 1868–70, the state spent $37,718.83 for this purpose, or about twice the amount of the previous administrations. Inflation offers a partial explanation, but it is also true that some of the stationery was sold for private gain. As a result of this, fraud charges were levied against Secretary of State Henry J. Menninger.[15]

At the same time all governmental costs rose generally and dramatically. Compensation for members of the legislature was set at $7 per day, with presiding officials granted $10 per day, and $.20 per mile was allowed for travel. Salaries of county sheriffs, previously ranging from $500 to $3,000 per year, rose to a scale of $2,000 to $15,000, while superior court clerks, who were making from $800 to $3,000, soon began to earn as much as $15,000. Also, writ and suit costs rose from the $6-to-$8 range to $20. It is interesting to note, however, that the assembly refused to adopt a resolution that would provide franking privileges.[16]

The presidential campaign of 1868 was of special concern to North Carolinians; a Republican victory would insure the continuation of the party's rule, while a defeat would inevitably end "Radical Reconstruction." Holden was confident that he could carry the state for the party, even before the Grant-Colfax ticket was selected, but he felt even more assured after the slate had been nominated by the national party. Some of the state's leaders, including those outside the Republican party, believed it was in the state's interest to work with the party in power in an effort to gain peace and national unity; this made Holden's task of getting a large vote for Grant much easier. As examples, Sixth District Congressman Nathaniel Boyden, the only Democrat, endorsed the Grant ticket, thereby winning for himself the Republican nomination, and Chief Justice Richmond M. Pearson announced his support for Grant, saying that it was the only means of averting another civil war. Writing to a Republican friend, Pearson commented that he was supporting Grant in order to "avert a civil war; for to my mind, the war clouds are as dark now, as in the winter of 1860. Some gentlemen have said to me—'rather than permit free negroes to vote and hold office, we are ready for another war.' I tell them, 'No.' Let us have peace, the war nearly ruined us—another war will finish the job. Let us try to make the most of a bad bargain, and not make bad worse."[17]

Pearson published an address to the Conservative party in which he accused its leaders of agitating the Negro issue and of attempting to nullify the Reconstruction Acts. He justified this partisan role by saying that "silence would be criminal" and that he hoped this would not draw him into the vortex of politics. Pearson concluded his address with a warning to the Conservatives, urging them to cease their resistance that might well result in war. "Let us have peace. This is the point on which my opinion rests."[18]

The Holden administration conducted an effective campaign for the Republican ticket in both the state and national races. The Union League was once again active among the blacks, although Holden had severed his official relationship with the organization, believing that a public officer should not belong to a secret society. The national Republican party's office sent $4,500 to help in the local contests, and the Union Republican National Committee made available 9,900 campaign badges for voters in the state.[19] The Republican executive committee for North Carolina distributed some fifty thousand copies of the Pearson address.[20]

In all probability, the most effective Republican weapon was the action of the Conservative leaders themselves. Their aggressive support for the Democratic ticket of Seymour and Blair convinced blacks, even more than did Republican oratory, that they must vote, and vote the Republican ticket. They knew well that a defeat for Grant would mean the loss of their newly acquired political power. And when former governor Vance went north with Howell Cobb and John B. Gordon of Georgia to explain southern views, the northern press quickly attacked their stand as "reactionary." The *New York Evening Post* flatly stated: "What the Confederacy fought for would be won by Seymour and Blair."[21]

The North Carolina Conservatives concentrated their campaign on state congressional races; in this way they could stress local issues and focus their major attack on the Holden administration. However, they suffered from a lack of funds.[22] Many of their leaders, including Vance, were unable to mount statewide canvasses, yet whenever possible they stressed the extravagance and inefficiency of the Republican administration.[23]

The party also resorted to new schemes to win the election. For example, in the hope of confusing illiterate voters, a group of five Raleigh lawyers proposed that separate ballot boxes be used for each congressional contest, for presidential electors, and for vacancies in the General Assembly; if any ballot was found in an improper box, it would not be counted.[24] Holden asked his attorney general, William M. Coleman, for an opinion on the legality of such procedure. Coleman told him that since one ballot would be used in the election, only one box was necessary.[25] Also, the Conservatives planned to print a ballot under the heading of "National Republican Ticket," bearing the names of Grant and Colfax in large type but with the names of Democratic presidential electors printed beneath.[26] This scheme was discovered long before the election, enabling Republican leaders to forewarn their supporters.

While the campaign was bitterly contested, the election itself was surprisingly peaceful. The only reported disturbance occurred in Asheville, where a race riot resulted in the death of one Negro.[27] The dispatch of United States troops to all parts of the state may explain the calm. To be sure, the Conservatives claimed much fraud had taken place among black voters, but in view of threats from the Ku Klux Klan against blacks it is surprising that there were not more charges and countercharges.

The Republican victory was overwhelming; it won the presidential contest by a 96,226 to 84,090 vote and elected six of the seven congressmen.[28]

Several of the Republican candidates had won their party nomination only after bitterly contested races, resulting in rancor and enmity among Republican leaders, but Holden welded the party into an effective unit which paid returns in an ultimate victory.[29] Two congressional contests ended in confusion. Plato Durham, Democrat, was at first certified as the victor in the Seventh District, but after a three-month delay the seat was awarded to his Republican opponent, Alexander H. Jones. In the Sixth District, Francis Shober defeated incumbent Nathaniel Boyden, who was running as a Republican, but Boyden contested the outcome on the grounds that Shober was unable to take the ironclad oath. Shober was seated after Congress altered the law requiring the oath.

On 6 November the Republicans conducted a victory celebration in Raleigh. The townspeople were awakened by the sounds of artillery, as one hundred guns were fired from dawn until dusk. Later, a large crowd of blacks paraded through the city, stopping in front of the governor's house. There, from his large porch, Holden spoke briefly. He congratulated party leaders and voters for their work, but he focused most of his remarks on a criticism of Klan activities during the election, which he claimed attempted to prevent a Republican victory and to agitate for another rebellion. Warning that the law would be enforced, he concluded his remarks by saying:

> These people, who advise lynch law, and who speak of "organizations" and "State delegates" to effect any change not warranted by the Constitution and the laws will be made to respect the Courts and to obey the law. This law is as much for the colored man as the white man. . . . There is no appeal from it but to the sword, and they who advise appeal from it advise the sword. . . . What has been the lesson taught you since you became men? It is, that your salvation as a self-governing people in common with the white race, depends not partly, but entirely on your standing together as one man. Your advancement in education, in manhood, in material strength, in good citizenship, is involved in this. . . . You owe everything under Providence to the Republican Party.[30]

As a result of his leadership during the 1868 campaign, Holden was given some support on the national level for an appointment to the president's cabinet; this, it was hoped, would be another step leading to national unity. Raleigh's *New York Times* correspondent reported that one of the state's congressmen had been assured by Vice-President Colfax that Holden would receive such an appointment. But Senator John Pool told Holden that he was doubtful that the state would be given such recognition; he also warned, "The present pay is not sufficient to support the Cabinet officers in the style they are required to maintain." Holden, realizing that his forte was politics at the state level, did not press for an appointment. He would not have sold the *Standard* had he expected to return to the editorial field at the end of his administration. He must have considered the possibility of national office, though, as one means of gaining relief from his radical associates. Already he was increasingly afraid of the consequences of growing charges of corruption within the Republican party. Senator Pool commented on such developments:

> If possible, stop the progress of certain parties in North Carolina who are reported to be putting in jeopardy the interests of the State and life of our party, for their private, pecuniary gains. . . . I fear much injury & perplexity to some of our party friends. . . . Try to prevent the necessity for such things, hereafter. I feel that you can do much to check the wrongs, if any has been done, & to save the disgrace to man & injury to the State. I hope . . . that no corruption has existed, & none contemplated. But active & acute minds are upon the subject, & facts are known that need explanation. I hope you will act in the whole matter, so as to command the approbation of all good men, & give our enemies no advantage over you. If you find friends involved, do not compromise your administration, with their defense.[31]

From the beginning of his administration, Holden had hoped to lead the state into an era of economic progress and long-needed social reforms. From a reading of his Inaugural Address of 4 July and one sent to the General Assembly, 17 November, one can ascertain that his goals included putting the state on a sound financial basis, guaranteeing racial equality before the law, developing a balanced economy between industry and agriculture, elevating the position of labor, accomplishing extensive internal improvements that would tie the three geographic divisions together and promote economic growth, expanding state aid for the state's unfortunates and handicapped, building a state penitentiary that would work for prisoner rehabilitation, and alleviating human want and misery. In short, he hoped to leave his mark on state politics by creating a more democratic society with a flourishing economy.

He was unable to achieve these goals, however, in large part due to the instability of the national government, compounded by the harassment at home by political enemies and his weakness as an administrator. He had demonstrated that he understood how to engender and control public opinion for the purposes of organizing political parties and conducting successful campaigns, but he did not have the temperament that characterizes a successful administrator. In his desire to be popular, Holden often made compromises in appointments and policies that characterized him as a weak executive, giving opponents grounds for personal criticism. In turn, Holden frequently allowed personal animosities to influence his decisions, thus interfering with political harmony within the state and denying him bipartisan support. In addition, his abilities as an orator were not sufficient to move his followers; in fact, his brusque manner toward his antagonists evoked fears that he might become an autocratic "dictator." If the governor himself had no such ideas, his opponents, to whom the fears were real, felt justified in their efforts to remove him from office by whatever means available. Holden thought he knew what was best for North Carolina, but he lacked the ability to carry his ideas and programs to fruition. As had been true for much of his life, his thinking placed him ahead of the times, but his leadership skills were sadly lagging.

The Republican party had gained complete control of state politics by the time the General Assembly met for its adjourned session on 16 November 1868. Governor Holden, however, was not in charge of affairs of state, and his administrative success, or lack of it, must be studied with this in mind. Party leaders, especially those in the General Assembly, began to invoke policies that often conflicted with the governor's. Holden found himself increasingly at odds even with his own party. On the second day of the assembly's session, he delivered his annual message, at which time he announced completion of the state's reconstruction and reentry into the Union. Despite the state's bleak financial future, Holden proposed the adoption of an extensive program for internal improvements, which included railroad construction, building a state penitentiary, and public education for both Negroes and whites. The major portion of his message, however, was devoted to protection for the laboring classes. He proposed that written contracts be encouraged which both parties should be made to fulfill. He also recommended the repeal of stay laws in order that creditors and debtors might be on a footing similar to that prior to 1860. He next discussed the question of civil disobedience within the state and the role of the state militia. He declared that the present situation did not call for the drilling of troops, yet he proposed to have troops in readiness should they be needed. Very clearly he expressed his hopes that the Ku Klux Klan be disbanded and warned that he would not hesitate to use the militia to give protection to all citizens. He also indicated that should the Klan cease its activities, he would use his influence to end the activities of the Union League. Last, he urged the importance of economy in public expenditures.[32]

An examination of the state's financial status illustrates how conditions were beyond Holden's control. Well before the legislature began its sessions, rumors were circulating that the Bank of North Carolina was threatened with bankruptcy, which meant that the state would lose $503,700 of its Literary Fund and $125,000 in university funds. During Holden's previous tenure, the bank was considered the best managed in the state, but because of poor management or Conservative political manipulations during the intervening years, its officials were forced to declare bankruptcy on 30 October 1868. George W. Mordecai, the bank's president, stated the action was taken to prevent Robert Y. McAden, a collaborator of George W. Swepson, one of the state's leading financiers and later railroad entrepreneur, from collecting on a suit against the bank to the amount of $40,000.[33]

McAden replied by pointing out that in 1865 the bank possessed nearly $400,000 in gold, yet had not sold it when gold would have brought a 50 percent profit but instead had held it until 1868, when it was sold in New York at a greatly reduced price. McAden also charged that the bank had allowed friendly groups to use the gold reserve for their personal gain without paying interest. He also charged that the bank directors had approved $20,000 to $30,000 in expense money which could not be substantiated and had paid themselves at par on a deposit of $60,000 while refusing to pay other depositors more than $.25 on the dollar. Finally, McAden charged the bank had been placed in bankruptcy in order to tax the stockholders with enormous fees for assignees and attorneys that would amount to $30,000 to $40,000, then throw these fees into the hands of the same parties that had grown fat from the bank since 1865.[34]

Later, the assembly established a committee composed of O. S. Hayes, J. B. Respass, and George W. Gahagan to investigate the charges; its report was critical of the directors, stating that they had acted without the consent of the stockholders and had taken inadequate measures for the protection of state monies.[35] The bank's bankruptcy resulted in the loss of over $675,000, which partially explains the Holden administration's handicap in organizing an effective public school system. It also illustrates the graft and corruption engaged in by both Conservative-Democrats and Republicans.

As of 1 October 1868, the state's cash balance stood at $50,035.84. By 1 December another $148,793.07 was received in taxes, but the treasurer was faced with paying the expenses of the assembly, estimated at $130,000, and government operating costs approximating $375,320, plus interest of $1,032,596 on the state's debt of $19,209,945. To meet the emergency, the administration proposed the sale of $180,000 of North Carolina Railroad bonds, but Treasurer David A. Jenkins advised that on the New York market the bonds would bring only $.50 on the dollar. He then tried to dispose of them through a private sale, but this failed to attract bidders. Later, he advertised in the Raleigh papers inviting sealed bids. Bids were submitted by W. H. Jones and Company, offering to pay 80 percent of par value for $4,000 of the bonds, by George W. Swepson, who proposed to pay 65 percent for $176,000 of the bonds, and J. M. Heck, who placed a 60 percent bid for the entire $180,000.[36] After consultation with Holden, Jenkins accepted the two highest bids, receiving for the state $117,000 for bonds worth $180,000 on 11 December 1868.

Rumors circulated immediately that a deal had been made by Swepson and Holden, for it was speculated that the former made approximately $68,000 from resale of the bonds and Holden was given $30,000 as his share of the profits.[37] These allegations were inspired by the fact that Holden had spent a large sum on new furniture for his home while on a visit to New York City. Josiah Turner, Jr., made this purchase the basis for the suits brought later against Holden and his estate, but neither Turner nor anyone else could prove that Holden was involved. His furniture purchases were made with money from his sale of the *Standard* and were made many months prior to the Swepson transactions. Also, a senate investigation accepted the administration's explanation that the exigency of the treasury did not permit any other action than to sell the bonds on the best terms possible and raise cash to cover governmental expenses.[38]

Meanwhile, the construction of a state penitentiary had begun. During the Worth administration, General Sickles had directed the governor to consider building such an institution and asked that the state take into consideration the possible employment of the prisoners in mining, quarrying marble, making brick, or manufacturing so that a penitentiary could be self-supporting.[39] A site on the Deep River in Chatham County was selected, but before construction began, Sickles was replaced and the matter was dropped until the General Assembly resumed consideration on 12 August 1868. A legislative committee met with the Council of State on 23 November and selected Thomas H. Coates, a Raleigh architect and engineer, to head the planning and construction of a building that would accommodate one hundred convicts.[40] At the same time, Coates and a committee of three were authorized to make a tour of northern prisons to gain ideas for the best possible design. Various sites in Wake, Orange, Johnston, and Guilford counties were considered, but the state purchased 125 acres at the Deep River location for $100,000, as it had abundant minerals (iron, coal, and stone) for mining purposes, timber for building materials, and facilities for transporting agricultural and manufactured products from the institution.[41] Later it was disclosed that pecuniary influences had been exerted on the selection committee and that the land had been purchased sight unseen.[42] In January 1869 the legislature created an investigating committee, chaired by George W. Welker, Republican from Guilford County, which reported the Deep River site was not well suited for a penitentiary and that fraud had unmistakably been involved.[43]

In all fairness, the Deep River locality had much to offer had there been an interest in developing its potential resources. Committee member Silas Burns had written to Salmon Adams, superintendent of the Tredegar Iron Works in Richmond, Virginia, describing the commercial possibilities of the Deep River project, to which Adams replied that from his personal knowledge the iron was soft, easily worked, and remarkably strong and cohesive, and was equal, if not superior, to any iron in the United States "for car wheels, or for any other purpose where great resistance or strength is required."[44] Adams also stated that the coal was superior, although mining costs might be high. With an abundance of lumber nearby, however, a blast furnace could be worked successfully. Adams even began negotiations with Governor Holden and Superintendent of Public Works Ceburn L. Harris for the manufacture of iron products by penitentiary inmates for the Tredegar Company or for the purchase of nearby iron mines and charcoal lands for $100,000. In fact, Adams offered to do either or both, and backed his proposal by making arrangement with Raleigh banker John G. Williams for the deposit of $50,000 and expressed his willingness to deposit the other half as well.[45] Meanwhile, since no one was authorized to sell the land, the offer was dropped.

The General Assembly nullified the Deep River proposal and created another commission under the chairmanship of Alfred Dockery to select a penitentiary site elsewhere. Holden was relieved to have the episode cleared of further charges of corruption. Hence he readily endorsed Dockery's selection, knowing him to be a capable official and one who would be above bribery charges. During the summer of 1869 a Wake County site of twenty-two acres was purchased at a cost of $4,468.75, and in the following year construction contracts were let. Consequently, the Holden administration could look forward to having solved one of the state's most pressing problems, prison reform. Not all state citizens thought the project necessary, however; some considered it a waste of tax monies and another example of bad judgment on the part of the governor. Some members of the public were particularly disturbed when they learned that all construction contracts were awarded to out-of-state companies, $493,451.83 going to Ohio bidders and $116,143.35 to bidders from Maryland and Pennsylvania.[46]

One of the brighter aspects of Holden's administration, although an extremely controversial one, was the effort made to promote an effective public school system. From his earliest days as a newspaperman, Holden had

been convinced that liberty and free government were endangered by ignorance; indeed, he envisioned the state's future as dependent on enlightened
citizens and educated leaders. Furthermore, only by implementing a school
program open to children of all races could he achieve his major goal of a
democratic government for the state.

The story of Governor Holden's efforts to establish a state-supported
school system begins with the postwar period. Prior to 1860 North Carolina
had made creditable progress under Calvin Henderson Wiley, the first superintendent of public instruction, who maintained the schools even during the war
years (though on a much reduced basis).[47] With the collapse of armed resistance in 1865 all government agencies ceased to function, and Holden as
provisional governor refused to reappoint Wiley in view of the oath he had
taken to support the Confederacy.[48] Also the financial exigencies of the time
made it impossible to reestablish all state agencies; the public school super-
intendency was one of several that Holden left unfilled.

During the difficult times of 1866, the Worth administration failed to
support a movement calling for the reestablishment of public schools and the
reappointment of Wiley as state superintendent, or to provide any public
funding. The confused political situation and lack of funds undoubtedly account for some of the reasoning behind such decisions, but one must wonder if
the primary reason was not the fear of integrated schools. However, by 1867
the Conservative leaders were forced to modify their stand. By this time
Holden and western newspaper editors had generated sufficient pressure for
public education that the legislature passed two laws to meet the growing
demand for schools, at least in part. The first act authorized towns and cities to
vote on a tax which would be used for school support.[49] By establishing local
schools only, the Worth administration avoided the problem of integration and
placed the responsibility on local authorities to decide whether there should be
any schools. In the rural communities little or no attempt was made to conduct
schools. The second law required the county courts to appoint school superin-
tendents who were to serve under the same rules as in prewar years. This was
merely gesture because the law was silent on the subject of county taxation for
education purposes. Thus, most North Carolina counties did not reestablish
schools.

In 1867, with the rise of the Republican party, education became an
important political issue and a major reason for the widespread acceptance of
the Republicans by the voters of the state. As head of the party, Holden knew
not only how to use the issue effectively but also how to demonstrate the
Conservative's lack of sensitivity for the well-being of the masses—both white
and black. While promoting educational improvement, he was not prepared to

work for integrated education. He thought, as did the majority of the native Republican leaders, that blacks should first secure permanent homes and employment, then seek schooling for their children.

Holden's philosophy of the state's educational needs was best stated in his commencement address delivered at the university in 1869.

> We may say, indeed, that those who were selected at former periods to control the operations of the institution were not called to the assumption of responsibilities and duties equal to those that have been imposed upon us; for the University is now a *popular* institution; it is held to an inseparable connection with the free public schools. . . . It is now the people's University. . . . Education knows no color or condition of mankind. It should be free, like the air we breathe, and as pervading and as universal.
>
> The chief want of our people is education. . . . We have the means to sustain this University, and to establish good public schools in every township in the State. We must do it. If we fail in this we shall have failed in the work of self-government.[50]

The Republican-dominated constitutional convention of 1868 provided the real basis for a state-supported system. Under the chairmanship of Samuel Stanford Ashley, the convention's educational committee laid the groundwork for a progressive school system.[51] The constitution, as enacted, required the General Assembly to "provide by taxation or otherwise for a general and uniform system of public schools, wherein tuition shall be free of charge to all the children of the State between the ages of six and twenty-one years." The office of state superintendent was restored. Counties were to be divided into convenient districts, "in which one or more public schools [were to] be maintained, at least four months in every year"; if the commissioners failed to provide for sufficient tax revenue to operate the schools, they were "liable to indictment." A board of education consisting of the governor, lieutenant governor, secretary of state, treasurer, auditor, superintendent of public works, superintendent of public instruction, and attorney general was created to replace the old Literary Board, even though the Literary Fund was left intact. The university was made part of the public school system, and compulsory attendance was authorized. The General Assembly was then empowered to require the attendance of children from six to eighteen years of age, totaling no less than sixteen months unless educated by other means.[52]

The chief contribution of the new constitution lay in its provision for financial support. First, it called for revenues from the sale of state-owned swamp lands, receipts from fines, forfeitures, penalties, and other funds to be invested in an irreducible fund, the interest of which was to be used solely for schools. Second, it authorized taxation for school support, contemplating, no doubt, a state property tax. Third, it provided that the "proceeds of the state and county capitation tax shall be applied to the purposes of education and the support of the poor, but in no one year shall more than twenty-five per cent thereof be apportioned to the latter purpose."[53]

The Conservatives made repeated attempts to amend the constitution in an effort to require separate schools for the two races, but the Republicans were determined to keep all such references from the document.[54] The Conservatives feared that without a clear statement in the constitution regarding race, an attempt would later be made to impose integration. Actually, the Republican's refusal to include such a clause led directly to some of the racial difficulties of Holden's administration. Many lukewarm supporters of the party turned away and swung to the opposition, especially when violent disagreements developed between the Union League and the Klan over control of the state. At least some of the strife might have been prevented had the educational issue been settled earlier.[55]

Nevertheless, once elected to office, Holden was determined to carry out the provisions of the new constitution. In his inaugural address he declared:

> The injunction of the Constitution regarding education should be faithfully observed. Colleges, high schools, Normal schools for the education of teachers, and public schools for all, should be established at the earliest practicable period, and liberally sustained from the public treasury. We should so conduct our public schools as to render them superior to all others of a similar kind in the State, and thus make it the interest, as well as the duty of parents to regard them as common to all, the rich and the middle class—as well as the poor. The first duty of a free State is to educate its children.[56]

But implementation of the mandated school system proved difficult. Holden was forced to accept Samuel S. Ashley as superintendent of education in order to gain the support of the carpetbaggers for his own candidacy. And while the new superintendent assumed his position with energy and hope, believing that the educational zeal of the 1868 constitution could be translated into a full-blown system of public schools, it soon became apparent that his was an impossible task, calculated to create enemies rather than friends. In his 1868 report to the General Assembly, Ashley directed attention to the fact that the total income from the investments held by his department was a mere

$32,982.70—a pathetic figure which revealed that most of the school funds were invested in defaulted bonds. Sadly, he warned, "A state can afford to be poor, but cannot afford to be ignorant."[57]

With Holden's endorsement, Ashley secured passage by the General Assembly of "An Act to Provide for a System of Public Instruction." The bill, introduced in the senate by George W. Welker, Republican chairman of the senate's committee of education, passed final reading on 12 April 1869. The law fixed the local township as the unit for school control, and three committeemen were empowered to establish and maintain, for at least four months in each school year, a sufficient number of schools at convenient locations. A county examiner was given control over teacher certificates, and no one could teach without certification. The prescribed course of study included reading, writing, arithmetic, English grammar, geography, and other courses deemed necessary by the local committee. The law also provided that should the local trustees fail to provide the necessary revenue, the committeemen should levy taxes to support the schools.[58]

Since public support did not materialize, Ashley was unable to develop the system he envisioned. The majority of the counties were unwilling to levy the necessary taxes, or the residents were unable to pay them if levied; therefore the superintendent was blocked from carrying out the duties of his office. Even though the legislature appropriated $100,000 to inaugurate the program, it was an empty gesture, since the state was without funds.[59] This failure led the General Assembly in 1870 to adopt a property tax for school support. In March, a levy of one-twelfth of 1 percent was adopted. While it represented only a small beginning, it set a precedent for the state's present tax-supported system.

The Holden years set an impressive record for the education of blacks, although private philanthropy deserves most of the credit. James Walker Hood, who was later bishop of the Methodist Episcopal Zion church and president of Livingston College, served as the assistant superintendent of public instruction. In 1869 he made a study of the number and condition of schools for black children. By his estimate there were 347 private and public schools for blacks, 372 teachers, and 23,419 students. The Freedmen's Bureau provided additional aid; by then it had established 431 schools for blacks, with 439 teachers and more than 20,000 students.[60] The bureau teachers were chiefly white, many of them from New England, who in their zeal created antagonisms that persisted long after the bureau had completed its work. As a result many whites opposed any further educational opportunities for blacks.[61]

Holden played a more direct role in university affairs than he did in establishing a system of public schools. He had long been interested in making the institution more democratic, always feeling that it was the state's hope for future development. He had regarded his election to the board of trustees in 1857 as a highlight of his career, but until elected governor he was not in a position to affect its basic philosophy. Prior to 1865, like most southern institutions of higher learning, the university's program was designed to serve chiefly the sons of landowners and professional men. And this the University of North Carolina did very well. After the war, neither David Lowry Swain, the elderly but able president, nor the trustees realized the extent of the social and economic revolution that had occurred. Now that the masses had the right to a college education, the Swain administration not only failed to anticipate the changing mood, but resisted when it became apparent. As a result, the university, the Holden administration, and the state at large were forced to pass through difficult times that might have been avoided.

In the postwar period the university was unable to regain its position of respectability in the eyes of many state citizens. Chapel Hill, the home of the university, had been thrown into consternation when Union Gen. Smith B. Atkins encamped with a brigade of federal troops in the little village from 17 April to 3 May 1865. Officers were quartered in university buildings, while horses were allowed to graze on the campus lawn.[62] The village was further scandalized when Eleanor Swain, the daughter of President Swain, was married to General Atkins and went to live in Illinois. Cornelia Phillips Spencer, a village matriarch and staunch supporter of the university, described the occasion as follows:

> This marriage was of ill omen to Governor Swain. The blight that
> immediately fell upon the University was directly attributable to the
> fact that he not only permitted his daughter to marry an invader, but
> that he gave her a fine wedding. It was told from mouth to mouth and
> believed all over North Carolina that Ellie Swain went to Illinois
> loaded with finery and jewels stolen from the women of states further
> south, and given to her by her husband.[63]

Matters went from bad to worse after the university's debts had mounted to more than $100,000, not including arrears of faculty salaries. In late summer 1865, Swain went north seeking loans to keep the university open; but the institution was a poor risk, and interest charges would have been 12 percent. Thus, he was forced to return empty handed. Swain later confessed that ill-feeling toward the university had also hampered his efforts.[64]

In 1866 the General Assembly appropriated $7,000 for university operating expenses, but it was evident that the institution could not continue with such inadequate support. Campus buildings and equipment were improperly maintained, while student enrollment was too small to finance faculty salaries and other related expenses. In fact, there were only three students in the 1866 graduating class. As long as there were prospects of future appropriations, President Swain remained entrenched in his post; but by the year's end, many educators, as well as Raleigh's political leaders of both parties, began to suggest that he be replaced by a younger administrator who could better cope with the university's staggering problems. In October, the Right Reverend William Mercer Green, Episcopal bishop for Mississippi, visited the campus and, after surveying the problems, said publicly what others had been thinking—Swain must be replaced.[65]

Early in 1867 the university received a land grant of 240,000 acres under the terms of the Morrill Act of 1862. The land was sold by the trustees to G. G. Lewis and his associates, Fisher, Boothe and Company, for fifty cents an acre, $10,000 being paid at the time and the remainder to be paid after recognition of statehood. These funds enabled the university to operate for a short while.[66]

During the same year Conservative leaders, hoping to strengthen their political fortunes with the national administration while also winning support for the university, invited President Johnson to visit Raleigh on 4 June to assist in the unveiling of a monument honoring his father, Jacob Johnson, and to deliver the commencement address at the university. Both invitations were accepted, and Johnson traveled to Raleigh in the company of Secretary of State William H. Seward, Postmaster General Alexander W. Randall, and Gen. Daniel Sickles. There, the presidential party was joined by Governor Worth and members of his staff, and the two groups traveled together to Chapel Hill in special cars. Conspicuously absent was Holden. Although he had then broken with the president, he nevertheless resented not being invited to join the presidential party; to him it was nothing less than a personal attack. Later, when the president returned to Raleigh for the unveiling ceremony, where President Swain gave the principal address, Holden was not invited to sit with the distinguished guests. Consequently, he refused to attend the affair at all. A staff reporter covered the event for the *Standard*. This intentional oversight hurt the Conservative party and the university as well, for it made Holden more determined than ever to prove his political prowess and social position. He neither forgave nor forgot the discourteous treatment; one of his first official acts in 1868 was to end the aristocratic control of the board of trustees. In 1870 he dispatched a detachment of black militiamen to guard the university campus against Klan activities; the unit remained encamped for some time, much to the disgust of local citizens.

In the summer of 1867 it became apparent that the university could not continue operations without an administrative change. Kemp P. Battle, state treasurer, and Professor Charles Phillips, secretary of the faculty, secured the resignation of President Swain and all faculty members in order that reorganization might take place. It was understood, however, that the faculty would continue at their posts until the reorganization was completed. While cooperating, President Swain never believed that he would be asked to resign. Battle's next move was to have Governor Worth appoint a study committee, composed of William A. Graham, Thomas Settle, Thomas S. Ashe, Kemp Battle, and Samuel F. Phillips. These men gave their report in December, recommending that the course of study place more emphasis on science and mathematics, that the admission requirements be standardized, and that requirements for graduation be more stringent. But the report did not address itself to the problems of finance or service to the people of North Carolina. Before the recommendation could be put into effect, the election of 1868 swept the Republicans into power and a thorough housecleaning ensued. Holden commented that it was "time to clean out the rickety old concern."[67]

Early in 1868, Holden and his allies determined to effect a complete reconstruction of the university and the public school system. Their justification was for both political and social reasons. Under the 1868 constitution the university trustees were to be replaced by appointees selected by the newly established board of education. Since members of the board were predominantly Republican and owed their position to the governor, Holden had complete freedom to choose the new trustees. Contrary to expectation, the new board was an able one; among its members were eighteen alumni and five former trustees—the Reverend Neill McKay, Thomas Settle, John Pool, Montfort McGehee, and Holden. The greatest flaw of its composition was the requirement that each county be represented by at least one trustee. As numerous and scattered as the counties were, it was difficult to secure any continuity of board membership. The first meeting was held 22 July, at which time former governor Manly, present by invitation, read the secretary's report for the old board. The following day the resignations of President Swain and the faculty were accepted. Swain was unprepared for this action and bitterly protested, but to no avail. He died in August, the result of a fall from his horse, and all college activities were suspended for the remainder of the year.[68]

Meanwhile, Holden's Council of State gave serious consideration to the university's future. John Pool, who was acting as educational counselor to the governor, sent his brother Solomon to Chapel Hill to study the situation. Later, Solomon advised the university to remain closed to avoid the issue of desegregation, or co-racial education (as it was referred to).[69] Holden agreed. During the fall of 1868, the board of trustees tendered the presidency to Lewis P. Olds, Holden's son-in-law, who seriously considered accepting and even gave thought to a new curriculum and operation plans. Later, however, he decided that acceptance was politically inexpedient and declined.[70]

The Conservative press planted a rumor that blacks would be admitted to the university, and when the trustees met in November, the *Raleigh Sentinel* reported that they had committed themselves to such a policy.[71] The board minutes do not corroborate the *Sentinel*'s claim; instead, Victor C. Barringer moved that a school for blacks be established in or near Raleigh to fulfill the Republican pledge of equal educational opportunity. The Barringer motion was amended by a proposal of Judge Albion W. Tourgée that an institution for blacks would be a branch of the university; it was adopted in that form. The proposal was never put into effect, however, for the board later specifically prohibited "persons of color" from entering the university at Chapel Hill.[72] (Today, more than a century later, there is still a myth circulating that black students attended the university and that a black was a member of the faculty during the Reconstruction period. There is no evidence to support such a claim.)

On 2 January 1869, the university trustees began reorganization in anticipation of reopening for a spring term. Solomon Pool was elected as the new president,[73] and an entirely new faculty was chosen, including Fisk P. Brewer, Alexander McIver, David Settle Patrick, James A. Martling, and George Dixon.[74] On the whole, the new professors were professionally competent but unable to win support for themselves or the institution.

The university reopened on 3 March 1869, but from the beginning there were insurmountable difficulties to be faced. Former supporters of the university resisted the Republican-oriented administration at every turn. Local citizens, particularly Mrs. Spencer, refused social recognition to the faculty and their families, while local merchants declined credit to faculty and students. In fact, some Chapel Hillians threatened withdrawal of their church memberships rather than associate with the newcomers. Writing to Mrs. Swain, Cornelia Spencer stated her views explicitly: "Our Sunday School Superintendent has got Mrs. Brewer as one of the teachers. I did not like it, but said nothing, but when last Sunday in came Professor Brewer, affable, distributing papers, I said if he ever came there in any official capacity, I would withdraw. *I cannot help it!*"[75]

Elsewhere public opinion was against the institution. Critics advised students against enrolling or threatened social ostracism against parents who permitted their sons to enroll. In the election of 1870 a spirited controversy occurred when some of the state's religious newspapers proposed that the university be abolished in favor of denominational institutions.[76]

Although the university had been in session less than an academic year, a decision was made to hold commencement exercises on 10 June in an effort to build public support. The Republican papers made full use of the fact that President U. S. Grant would be the speaker, no doubt as a counter to Andrew Johnson's address of the previous year, but in the end it was Governor Holden who spoke. Arrangements were made for a special train to take the governor, major administration officials, and Republican leaders from across the state from Raleigh to Durham, and from there horses and carriages transported them to Chapel Hill.[77]

In his address, Holden reasserted his conviction that the university was "the people's University," and he promised full support, morally and financially. "If parents and guardians who possess the means will not send their sons here, because of prejudice, or from resentment towards those who now control the institution, the people of the state will fill these halls with meritorious poor young men, and will maintain and educate them at the public charge." As for the race issue, the governor called attention to the fact that the trustees had made the commitment to blacks for the establishment of their school elsewhere, but "it will be *one* University, the University of North Carolina. Education knows no color or condition of mankind."[78] Such remarks served to further the Conservative fears that the Republican administration would use the university as a political tool and ultimately inflict racial integration upon the state. Thus passions engendered by war, combined with loyalty to the old order, doomed the new administration to failure.

It needs to be reasserted, however, that Holden was sincere in his desire that the university become "the people's University." During the summer of 1869, he asked President Pool to supply him with the number of applicants for the fall school term and the average number of students admitted to the university since 1860. Pool replied that he had expected between sixty and eighty students for the fall, but that only thirty-five had appeared, a majority of them preparatory students. Still, this compared favorably with previous enrollments: forty-four in 1861, forty-one in 1862, twenty-three in 1863, twenty-four in 1864, seven in 1865, fifty in 1866, twenty-eight in 1867, none in 1868, and fifty-two in 1869.[79] Accordingly, Holden recommended to the General Assembly that state funds be appropriated to create sufficient endowment for free tuition for one hundred and seventy students; this proposal, however, fell on deaf ears.[80] By 1870 the legislature was more interested in cutting expenses than in supporting the university.

Though showing signs of collapse, the university operated throughout the academic year of 1869–70. The General Assembly refused to provide funds for faculty salaries or other expenses; in fact, had it not been for Superintendent Ashley's extending aid from his public school fund, the university could not have completed the year. Even with this aid, faculty members were not paid their promised salaries, and there were only 103 persons at the commencement exercises. Two of the three honorary degree recipients declined their awards.[81]

During these troubled years, another threat to the university's future developed in the form of the Klan. Locals were organized in Orange and adjacent counties to intimidate the Chapel Hill citizenry and to prevent them from fraternizing with university officials, and specifically to force the resignation of President Pool. The threat of violence became so serious that Governor Holden requested federal troops to occupy the village and safeguard university personnel. In the fall of 1869, Gen. Alfred H. Terry, commander of the Department of the South, dispatched a company of troops to Chapel Hill; the soldiers remained there, maintaining peace and quiet, until removed in the spring of 1870.

But peace was short-lived for the village. After a second Klan episode, Pool again requested protection. This time Holden advised him to have the Orange County magistrates request the aid of the state militia, since the General Assembly had passed the Shoffner Militia Act by which the Republican administration hoped to maintain law and order within the state. But Pool was unable to secure aid from county officials, no doubt due to the influence of Josiah Turner and William Graham, who still controlled the county's affairs from their Hillsborough residences. Nevertheless, through the intercession of Senator Pool, the governor was persuaded to send a detachment of black militia, who remained in control of affairs throughout the "Kirk-Holden War."

In late summer of 1870, Pool attempted to continue university operations, but only fifteen students enrolled for the new term. By December the student body had all but disappeared. The board of trustees was compelled to close the university, which remained closed until the autumn of 1875. All of the professors, without pay or jobs, left Chapel Hill within the year. In 1871, Professor Alexander McIver succeeded Ashley as superintendent of public instruction and was instrumental in the reopening of the university.

Despite Holden's failure to "reconstruct" the university, a number of Republican ideas were incorporated into the 1875 plan. In spite of its numerous tribulations, the new and a more democratic University of North Carolina eventually became one of the leading institutions of higher learning in the nation.

SEVEN

Caught in a Web of Corruption

Holden's greatest mistake as governor was his failure to maintain firm control over state finances. Consequently, his administration fell prey to schemers and manipulators who saddled the state with a huge indebtedness and provoked charges of fraud even against the governor. Despite many investigations by political opponents, however, there was no evidence proving him to be involved in any of the schemes. The perpetrators of the frauds transcended party lines and included members of North Carolina's best families. Nevertheless, the Republican failure to improve the state's economic condition caused Holden to lose popular support, and this partially explains his later impeachment and removal from office.

North Carolina's prewar economic development was achieved largely through generous financial aid to internal improvements—railroads, plank roads, and canals—but it resulted in an indebtedness of $8,761,245 as of 20 May 1861. The state incurred further debts of $3,015,000 during 1866 and 1867,[1] with the accrued interest on the two debts, amounting to $2,131,315 in 1868, totaling $14,907,460.[2] Yet by 1868, with the coming of a Republican administration, citizens of all political factions hoped to see the state resume railroad construction, which was vital to commerce and industry all across the state. Certainly Holden, a supporter of internal improvements, hoped that a wise policy of development would be a means of overcoming the state's depressed condition.

The constitutional convention of 1868, which had internal improvements as one of its major priorities, adopted seven ordinances affecting railroad legislation. The bonds of the Wilmington, Charlotte, and Rutherford Railroad were given official state endorsement. The Northwestern North Carolina Railroad Company was chartered to run from Greensboro to Salem and from there to some point on the northwestern boundary of the state. The state treasurer was authorized to lend the company $50,000 for every section of five miles of track laid between Greensboro and Salem upon completion of the road. The treasurer was directed to exchange a maximum of $1,200,000 of bonds for the same amount of bonds of the Chatham Railroad Company, and $150,000 was authorized as a loan to the Williamston and Tarboro Railroad Company. The Western Railroad Company was directed to return $500,000 in bonds of the Wilmington, Charlotte, and Rutherford Railroad, which it had been paid by the state, and would receive in exchange the same amount of new bonds. The convention directed the next legislature to fund the interest of the valid debts of the state in bonds and to pay cash for the interest falling due on 1 January 1869, or thereafter. Finally, the Chatham Railroad Company was given the state's interest in the Cape Fear and Deep River Navigation Company, hoping to insure adequate railroad facilities for the proposed penitentiary to be located on the Deep River site.[3]

Holden was in complete accord with the work of the 1868 constitutional convention. In his inaugural address of 4 July 1868 he called for further expansion of internal improvement projects. Money thus expended, and money expended for education, would "constitute the best investment the state could make."[4] As governor, however, he was unable to cope with the activities of the "Ring" headed by Gen. Milton S. Littlefield and George W. Swepson. From 1868 to 1870 it is estimated that Swepson paid $241,713.39 to influence state legislation and that General Littlefield, the chief lobbyist, received a commission of 10 percent on all bonds appropriated.[5] Among the Republicans whose votes were bought were Joseph C. Abbott, Bryon Laflin, L. G. Estes, F. W. Foster, John Hyman, James Sinclair, James H. Harris, Hugh Downing, and John W. Stephens.[6]

Large sums were paid to Conservatives as well to secure their support in legislative matters. The list of these men includes such prominent figures as Kemp P. Battle, Edward Graham Haywood, Thomas L. Clingman, Daniel G. Fowle, and Richard C. Badger. Payment to the members of this group was always in railroad bonds. Interestingly, these were the same men who later charged the Holden administration with fraud and corruption. They were all too ready to share the spoils, but when the frauds were exposed, the Conservatives proclaimed their righteousness and turned their indignation on all participants in the scandals, with the notable exception of the chief Conservative, Swepson, and his close compatriots. They instead attributed fraud to Republicans and carpetbaggers.

Josiah Turner, Jr., Holden's chief critic, could not escape involvement, however. In December 1868, Turner assumed editorship of the *Raleigh Sentinel*, which promptly became the political voice of the Conservative-Democratic party. From the beginning, Turner was hostile to the Holden administration and did everything within his power to discredit its program. His hostility became so virulent that an open feud developed between the two men, which led directly to increased Klan activities and, ultimately, to Holden's impeachment. Probably no man was more bitterly hated by the Republicans than Turner, who was portrayed as "cunning as a serpent, writing with a pen that seemed dipped in gall, he relentlessly pursued what now became the chief aim of his existence, the overthrow of the Republican party of the state."[7]

Turner was particularly critical of the Ring and its railroad frauds, though he was not always the true spokesman for his party. The more moderate Conservatives were unwilling to endorse his bitter and vindictive comments.[8] At no time, however, did Turner print a word of criticism against Swepson, the man chiefly responsible for the frauds.[9] As was learned later, Swepson was Turner's financial benefactor and supporter, and this may account for the blind eye Turner turned on his activities.

While it has been generally assumed that Swepson's financial support was prompted by his thirty-year acquaintance with the Turner family, father and son, that hardly seems a valid answer. Perhaps Swepson thought that by financing Turner's purchase of the *Sentinel* he could gain control of both parties. Another explanation could be Swepson's fear that Holden would repudiate all those involved in the railroad manipulations. Many friends advised Holden to do this, but, perhaps unwisely, he failed to take this action. It was not until 1873 that the public learned of Turner's involvement with Swepson, but by then it was too late to help Holden clear his name and remain in politics.[10]

From the beginning of his administration, Holden saw in internal improvements, particularly railroad construction, the panacea for the state's economic problems. Along with prominent business and political leaders across the state, he had faith in the integrity and judgment of Swepson and felt that whatever Swepson did would be for the ultimate benefit of the state. The special session of the 1868 legislature adopted several important acts affecting railroad construction. The state treasurer was authorized to issue to the Chatham Railroad Company, in exchange for company bonds, state bonds amounting to $2,000,000. A similar act authorized $300,000 for the Williamston and Tarboro Railroad. The Western North Carolina Railroad Company was divided into two parts, the Eastern Division to run from Salisbury to the French Broad River, and the Western Division to run from the French Broad to the Tennessee border, where, it was hoped, it would connect with other lines from Georgia and Tennessee. Already Tennessee had constructed a road from Morristown to Paint Rock, sixteen miles from Marshall, North Carolina. The capital stock of the Western Division was increased to $10,000,000 and $4,000,000 was actually issued; the stock of the Eastern Division was increased to $6,500,000. The charter of the Northwestern North Carolina Railroad was amended to allow the laying of track between Salem and Mount Airy and to permit the state to subscribe $100,000 additional stock in the company.[11]

In obedience to instructions from the constitutional convention to fund the interest due on the state debt, the legislature passed the Funding Act, which greatly benefited Swepson and his Ring. By an arrangement between Swepson and Treasurer David A. Jenkins, the October interest was to be paid by the sale of dividends from the North Carolina Railroad, which were paid in bonds of the road in the amount of $180,000. The deal was kept secret until the last possible moment to allow Swepson to speculate on the state bonds. On 19 September, Samuel McDowell Tate wrote Swepson: "When I telegraph you to do so then let the notices [of funding the interest] come out at Raleigh and here [Charlotte]; *but be sure to have Battle write the notice so as to cover all the ground.*"[12] Two days later, Tate wrote Swepson that he had bought $125,000 state bonds; later he purchased another $225,000 for $167,550, while selling $155,000 state bonds for $117,925—this one transaction profited him $3,135. Swepson also bought $176,000 of state bonds for $.65 on the dollar (Tate and W. J. Hawkins, president of the Williamston and Tarboro Railroad, were also involved in the purchase) and then sold them for $.75 to $.90. Swepson also offered Holden $25,000 in the bonds at cost and Jenkins $10,000, but both declined.[13]

By the spring of 1869 the legislature had fallen under the control of the Ring, and to maintain control of the Republican party and his administration Holden apparently had to go along with their schemes. Contrary to tradition, the Ring was not composed merely of scalawags and carpetbaggers, terms that still evoke derision today. It is a matter of record that a majority of the so-called scalawags had been strong Unionists and many could be classified as having a "Whig residue." Also, among those who came to be called carpetbaggers were prominent business entrepreneurs, farmers, and trained professionals. While no one would deny or try to condone the large-scale Reconstruction frauds perpetrated by the members of the Ring and their carpetbagger cohorts, it is apparent that Conservative-Democrats, especially the legal community and businessmen, cooperated in their schemes and oftentimes profited the most from them.

The first charge of corruption developed when William Robbins, senator from Rowan County, demanded an investigation of Treasurer David A. Jenkins, although Senator William Sweet, a carpetbagger from Craven County, was the instigator of the move.[14] Jenkins was charged with refusing to pay mileage and per diem to assembly members, delivering the Deep River penitentiary bonds without authority, accepting an unstamped mortgage from the Williamston and Tarboro Railroad Company, and accepting the Chatham Railroad mortgage securing $2,000,000 of company bonds without proper security.[15] A joint legislative investigating committee, composed of Curtis H. Brogden, Willie D. Jones, Joshua Barnes, W. G. Candler, R. D. Whitley, and George W. Gahagan, was created by the General Assembly. After holding a thorough hearing, the committee found that the treasurer had acted within the law in each instance.[16]

The investigation was an initial setback for the Conservatives and won a temporary reprieve for the administration. It was disclosed that Robbins, the leader of the investigation, had accepted a twenty-dollar fee from John W. Stephens for assistance in obtaining money for expenses and mileage in 1868 while contesting the seat of Bedford Brown. Robbins frankly acknowledged his role, and while it was not generally believed that he had acted dishonestly, he requested and received censure by the senate. Senator Sweet was also unable to prove his charges against Jenkins. He had expected a Mrs. Cavalry to testify against the treasurer and the Ring, but she had been hurried out of town by General Littlefield. Thus, the Sweet charges went unsubstantiated. The *Standard* promptly demanded that Sweet be expelled from the senate for injuring the reputation of the assembly and the credit of the state by the charges to which his rumors gave occasion.[17] This effort failed, along with the one to censure Sweet, but the suspicion of Ring involvement remained ever present in the minds of the people.

Holden's administration continued to promote the building of railroads, since the General Assembly authorized four new roads in February 1869: the University (Chapel Hill) Railroad Company; the Oxford Branch of the Raleigh and Gaston Road; an extension of the Williamston and Tarboro Railroad by a branch road to Plymouth, Washington, and Wilmington; and the Eastern and Western Railroad through Granville, Person, Caswell, Rockingham, Stokes, and Surry counties.[18] A total of $18,996,000 in bonds were authorized for the state railroads; if all had been completed, North Carolina would have had one of the finest systems in the nation.

Holden and the men appointed to head the new companies were sincerely interested in having the roads constructed and in operation in the shortest possible time.[19] But unknown to the governor, Swepson and his associates wanted the new roads built with mortgage bonds in order to force them into debt and eventual bankruptcy. This would give the Ring the opportunity to purchase them at less than true value and insure handsome profits when the roads resumed operation.

Despite the intentions of Governor Holden the railroads were not constructed, resulting in the state being saddled with an indebtedness of millions of dollars. Speculation and mismanagement on the part of railroad officials were primarily responsible for the failure, but the large amount of bonds sold in New York flooded the market and resulted in devaluation of the bonds. Thus, the state never benefited from the full amount appropriated. Also, the year 1869 was not a good one for ambitious construction programs; the gold panic brought financial ruin not only to North Carolina roads but to national roads as well.

The experience of the Western North Carolina Road's Western Division was typical. Its president, Swepson, ranked high in public esteem, while the directors associated with him were representative of the state's leading economic and social interests.[20] Swepson, with full support from his board, employed Thomas L. Clingman as chief lobbyist, who worked three months with prominent leaders of both parties—Judge Augustus S. Merrimon, Kemp P. Battle, Samuel F. Phillips, and Bartholomew F. Moore among them—to secure the passage of legislation necessary to create the new company.[21] This being accomplished, Swepson advised his board that he could not construct the road unless he could sell the state bonds, and that he could not sell the bonds unless given full authority not only to sell but also to apply the proceeds as he saw fit. This authority was willingly given in good faith in hopes of speeding construction of a road badly needed in the mountain area of the state.[22] When Swepson failed to push forward the construction program, he thereby entangled himself, the railroad, and the state with fraudulent debts.

The Williamston and Tarboro Railroad, with Jesse R. Stubbs president, is another example of manipulation and fraud on the part of both Swepson's Ring and the Conservative-Democrats. In 1868, Stubbs sent his chief engineer, W. G. Lewis, to Raleigh to secure legislation for his road, and Lewis employed Littlefield as lobbyist. The 1868 constitutional convention authorized a $150,000 loan to the company, payable in state bonds. The special session of the General Assembly later authorized an additional $300,000 to construct a branch line to Plymouth, Washington, and Wilmington. Stubbs then arranged with John F. Pickerell of New York for sale of the bonds at 65⅔ cents on the dollar and for Pickerell to build the new line—complete with depots and water stations and ready for the rolling stock—for $11,000 per mile. For this arrangement, Pickerell agreed to give a bonus of $15,000, with $10,000 going to Littlefield but endorsed to Swepson, and $5,000 to Stubbs, also endorsed to

Swepson.[23] Pickerell failed to fulfill his contract, and later when the validity of the bonds was questioned, Stubbs and Kemp P. Battle, the company's attorney, were forced to sell the bonds with a face value of $450,000 at the prevailing market price of $165,948.47, thereby ending the plans of completing the extension of the Williamston and Tarboro Road.[24]

In 1869 the Ring reasoned that the people of North Carolina were so desirous of adequate railroad transportation that they would show little concern for the means used in getting it. Henry E. Colton, a native North Carolinian living in New York City, expressed such sentiment in a letter to Swepson:

> In my opinion in years from now the people of North Carolina will see so clearly the vast benefit of the present proposed Railroads that they will care very little how or by what means they will be built. For instance your own Road will increase from 100 to 1000 per cent the value of land now perfectly unmarketable and I know one tract of land through which Dr. Hawkin's R.R. must pass which will bring him or others $5 cash the moment the R.R. touches it. The day of old fogyism is past in N.C. and people must and will rapidly learn to appreciate the end without caring for the means.[25]

The University Railroad was the special project of Solomon Pool, president of the university, who hoped to use the road to end the school's isolation and make it possible for students to travel by rail. He also hoped to extend Republican influence in Orange County, and thereby undermine the influence of William Graham and Josiah Turner. The 1869 incorporation act empowered the governor to appoint a board of directors, which Holden did; but at the same time the attorney general, William M. Coleman, was asked to furnish an opinion on the constitutionality of the act, since the governor lacked veto power over legislation. Coleman replied that he considered it invalid since it was contrary to the state requirement that state bonds could not be issued for new roads, and that, while the act contemplated action, no corporation was established by the law.[26] With this advice, Holden refused to permit the issuance of state bonds to begin construction, even though the board of directors sought a writ of mandamus to force his approval. The case was appealed to the North Carolina Supreme Court, which unanimously ruled that the incorporation act was invalid.[27]

While the court was discussing the legal issues of the case, Col. William Johnston, president of the Atlantic, Tennessee, and Ohio Railroad and a former law student of Chief Justice Pearson, called upon Pearson to learn the court's decision. Pearson supposedly informed Johnston that the University

Road bonds were invalid and that as far as he was concerned this applied to all other special railroad tax issues. Johnston informed Swepson of this threat to all railroad bonds, and also Kemp Battle, who telegraphed his friend T. H. Porter of Soutter and Company, the New York financial agent for several of the North Carolina roads.[28]

Swepson immediately went to New York and consulted with Porter and Judge Samuel Person, attorney for the Wilmington, Charlotte, and Rutherford Railroad. Person wired the court for a rehearing, and when this was granted, the Soutter Company employed Daniel G. Fowle, Richard C. Badger, Edward G. Haywood, and Judge Person as counsel in the case. Fowle was paid $2,500 for introducing the motion for a rehearing, although Judge Person had already telegraphed such a message for his client, who might well have saved this expenditure. For their services in the University Railroad case, the attorneys were paid $15,000 in cash and $75,000 in state railroad bonds by the Western North Carolina Railroad and the Wilmington, Charlotte, and Rutherford Road.[29] Most of the attorneys involved were well-known Conservative-Democratic party leaders.

The supreme court returned its decision on 21 July 1869, declaring the act incorporating the University Railroad Company unconstitutional. Chief Justice Pearson considered all of the new railroad bonds void for the same reason. The other justices refused to be as sweeping in their opinions, but chose instead to decide the merits of each case. But on the basis of the Pearson verdict in this case, the governor refused to permit the treasurer to issue bonds to the Oxford Branch of the Raleigh and Gaston Road, the Williamston and Tarboro Road, the Eastern and Western Railroad, and the Edenton and Suffolk Railroad Company.

Upon authorization by either the 1868 constitutional convention or the General Assembly in 1868–69, the state's railroad companies began actual construction programs with the bond money issued by the state. Some, however, deposited the greater part of their bonds with Soutter and Company as collateral for other types of loans. Swepson, for example, along with Bryon Laflin, Franklin G. Martindale, W. A. Moore, and Judge William B. Rodman, used the Western Division bonds to speculate in state bonds, with disastrous results. Swepson also used Western Division bonds to obtain control of the Florida Central Railroad and the Jacksonville, Pensacola, and Mobile Railroad. William Sloan, president of the Wilmington, Charlotte, and Rutherford Road, hypothecated 1,700 bonds with J. F. Pickerell, another New York broker, for a loan of $391,026.62 and $600,000 in company bonds for a loan of $272,000. Andrew J. Jones of the Western Railroad also deposited most of his 1,320 bonds with Soutter and Company for hypothecation or collateral for later loans. Owing to the large amounts of North Carolina bonds thrown upon the New York money market and the state's defaulting on the interest payments, the value of all state railroad bonds declined steadily. Without revenue the roads were forced to halt their construction programs.[30]

In the summer of 1869 two incidents occurred which prevented the Ring from being successful in their financial manipulations. The first involved a dispute between Governor Holden and his superintendent of public works, Ceburn L. Harris, concerning which official had the vested authority to appoint directors and proxies for those railroad companies in which the state had a financial interest. The question became a public issue when the Raleigh and Gaston Railroad sought to buy control of the North Carolina Railroad to make a through line across the state. As the *Raleigh Sentinel* stated it, Harris wanted to make his brother-in-law, Judge George W. Logan, president of the road.[31]

At first Holden favored the consolidation, but changed his mind when Swepson and his cohorts convinced him that such a move would be detrimental to other state roads. Accordingly, Bryon Laflin, state proxy to the Raleigh and Gaston Road, was instructed to block any consolidation move. Harris then secured an injunction from Judge Logan temporarily nullifying Laflin's acting as state proxy, and, in so doing, made the public aware of the dispute between the two men. Meanwhile, Holden replaced Laflin with William J. Clarke as the state's proxy on the Atlantic and North Carolina Railroad. When Clarke presented himself to the board of directors, Harris, acting in his ex-officio capacity, voiced opposition and by a vote of stockholders succeeded in keeping him from serving, at least temporarily. In the end, the governor retained his right to appoint proxies, but at the cost of splitting the Republican party ranks. The Harris-Logan forces controlled the political situation in Cleveland, Rutherford, and nearby counties; together with the *Rutherford Star*, which was controlled by Logan, they turned that section of the state into a region actively hostile to Holden.[32]

The other incident involved the Atlantic, Tennessee, and Ohio Railroad Company, a rail line designed to connect western North Carolina with Cincinnati, Ohio, by way of Tennessee. The state's share of the road's cost was to be financed by state appropriations to the amount of $2,000,000. William Johnston served as the road president and Rufus McAden as financial agent; both men were partners with Swepson in his many ventures. While the General Assembly was debating the appropriation, Johnston promised payment to Littlefield and John T. Deweese of the regular 10 percent commission for lobbying fees. But before collecting his fee, Littlefield fled the state, and

Johnston refused payment to Deweese. When the 1869 assembly appropriated the two million dollars, in exchange for bonds of the company to the same amount, President Johnston appealed to Treasurer Jenkins to issue the state bonds to him.[33] Jenkins refused, on the grounds that the company had not begun construction and therefore had not fulfilled its contract. Realizing that the steady decline of the North Carolina bonds could result in the total loss of the road's appropriation, Johnston, in McAden's name, negotiated a contract with Swepson for the sale of company stock, with the agreement that McAden build the road within a designated time. McAden then went to Raleigh to claim the bonds, only to be confronted with an injunction obtained by Edward G. Haywood for Deweese, forbidding the treasurer to issue the bonds.[34] Haywood took the case, knowing that it was a case of blackmail to enable Deweese to claim his lobbying fee of $20,000. It is most unlikely that Haywood had any intention of protecting the state's taxpayers from a fraudulent bond issue.

Haywood advised Deweese to secure the injunction in someone else's name, in view of the fact that he was not a taxpayer on either real or personal property. Robert C. Kehoe of New Bern was therefore asked to fill the role of plaintiff. Application was made to Judge Samuel Watts, who went to Haywood's law office to discuss the entire matter. Especially noted were the salient points of a similar case, *Galloway v. Jenkins*, in which the state supreme court had declared null and void the Chatham Railroad Act.[35] Haywood urged the immediate granting of an injunction, but Judge Watts delayed until the next day, and Deweese later claimed that the judge was paid $5,000 to speed his decision. Haywood then engaged the law firm of Fowle and Badger to assist him in prosecuting the case, but Fowle reported later to the Bragg Investigating Committee that Haywood had tricked him into believing the Johnston (McAden)–Swepson contract had called for the purchase of $2,000,000 of state bonds from the railroad at a price equal to the New York market price on a specified day; consequently the company then refused to fulfill the contract because of the declining price. Fowle claimed that when he learned the true story, he refused to file an appeal to the supreme court.[36]

Meanwhile, the Atlantic, Tennessee, and Ohio Road officials, realizing the intent of Deweese to blackmail them, sought a compromise, rather than prolong the issue and witness a future decline in value of the bonds. McAden employed Littlefield to make the best possible arrangements and was told by Haywood that settlement was possible for 163 bonds valued at $1,000 each, most of which would go to the Ring. The company offered fifty bonds, but Haywood demanded seventy-five, using the market value of $49 per $100 as a basis for Deweese withdrawing his suit, or in all amounting to approximately

$36,750. At this point, Kemp Battle, acting as company attorney, approached Judge Fowle concerning the possibility of expediting the trial, but he was reminded of the high costs of a lengthy trial and the expense of bringing witnesses from the western part of the state to testify that the road was actually a new road, thus making the act establishing it invalid. Later, Haywood informed Fowle that a settlement had been arranged by Badger, obviously against Fowle's wishes, with Badger procuring from Judge Watts a dissolution of the Kehoe injunction and seventy-seven bonds delivered to Haywood for compensation. The remaining ones were awarded to Haywood because of decreased value.[37]

When the Haywood settlement had been completed, Governor Holden had Jenkins summon Battle to the treasurer's office to determine whether issuing of the bonds was legal for the state. Battle advised that the act creating the railroad company was legal and that the issuance of bonds, as provided for in the appropriation, could proceed. Whereupon the bonds were promptly signed by the state officials and turned over to McAden, who took them immediately to New York. By this time, however, the price of North Carolina bonds had declined below $30, and William Johnston, as company president, instructed him not to sell. In 1870 the bonds were returned when the legislature called in all unsold bonds. This episode illustrates that the railroad scandals were unmistakably not confined to Republicans and carpetbaggers. In this instance the Democratic legal counsel profited most from the irregularities.[38]

In September 1869, Holden and Jenkins agreed to the formation of a pool and to go along with its plans to raise the value of the state bonds on the New York money market.[39] Swepson convinced the governor that as long as the bonds were selling at low rates, their sale would not be profitable for the state's construction program; however, should there be a rise in bond prices and a profit for their sale, the proceeds could advance construction when the economy so desperately needed it. The pool proposed to purchase state bonds on the open market using the bonds on hand as collateral, thereby creating a demand and raising the value of all North Carolina bonds. Accordingly, the pool bought $1,800,000 of the state bonds, and the price moved quickly from $50 to $56. This aroused hopes that the price would go as high as $75, assuring the state ample revenue to complete the road construction.

Serious problems soon developed, however. First, New York speculators were not misled by the scheme.[40] Second, the January and April nonpayment of interest on the state's debt created fear that North Carolina bonds were poor financial risks. Third, questions concerning the constitutionality of the tax bonds were raised by legal experts, especially after the rulings by Judge

Pearson and the North Carolina Supreme Court.[41] Finally, a "bear party" was formed in New York to counter the "bullish" North Carolina pool.

To offset this last tactic, McAden suggested to Swepson that North Carolina should pay the interest on its state debt. Swepson, with President Jones of the Western Road, advanced the funds to the state treasurer, and Jenkins advertised that not only the earlier interest but also the interest due in October would be paid. Thomas L. Clingman, Swepson's attorney, was then persuaded to write a letter to Henry Clews and Company, successors to Soutter and Company in the handling of the affairs of the pool, in which he upheld the validity of the state bonds. Clingman even concluded, "I regard the special tax bonds of the State especially as a safe investment for such persons as are seeking that class of securities."[42] This was then published in the New York papers as an open letter, whereupon Governor Holden wrote to Clews, promising that the state would pay its debts, particularly the special tax bonds.[43] This was the moment that Holden consented to have the state enter into the pool arrangement through the treasurer. Jenkins sold the railroad stock owned by the North Carolina Board of Education and used the $150,000 received, with an additional $125,000 obtained from the sale of land script for an agricultural college,[44] to buy state bonds on the open market.

Just as the speculation was beginning to have the desired effects, the gold panic of 1869 destroyed the nation's money market.[45] The North Carolina bonds (those deposited in the New York brokerage firms as collateral for future transactions) were sold at prices as low as $21 and after May 1870 were dropped from the New York Exchange listing. Thus, Black Friday not only ruined the pool's speculations but left the North Carolina railroads without revenue for their construction programs. Moreover, the various railroad presidents had heavy personal losses, with some $300,000 of the loss borne chiefly by Swepson, Sloan, and Jones. Jones failed to pay his promised share into the pool, though he later suffered considerable gambling losses. It was reported that on one occasion he was seen in New York with a pile of state bonds serving as chips, and before the evening's end he had lost sixty bonds. And then Josie Mansfield, a well-known New York courtesan, got her share; in fact, rumors were that North Carolina railroad bonds circulated widely in the demimonde.[46]

Despite this tragic turn of events, Holden continued to maintain complete confidence in Swepson and in his ability ultimately to find some way to save the state's railroads. In late November, Holden wrote Swepson: "I sincerely trust that your affairs are not seriously embarrassed. I have the greatest confidence in your wisdom and energy, and feel sure that you will extricate yourself from any troubles that may surround [you]. Happen what may I am your friend, and will never desert you."[47]

When the General Assembly opened its session in November 1869, demands were made for a thorough investigation of the railroad problems, and there was even talk of the state repudiating all railroad bonds. In the senate, John W. Graham, son of William Graham, called for a detailed examination of the Western North Carolina Road, with a special inquiry into Swepson's transactions. George W. Welker of Guilford County introduced resolutions relative to the sale of Western Road bonds. John B. Respass of Beaufort proposed legislation that would call for quarterly reports by railroad presidents showing the number of bonds possessed by each road or the amount of money raised from the sale of such bonds. These three resolutions were made the special order of the day, but instead of proceeding in order of introduction, the clerk called first for the Respass resolution.

While the senate heatedly discussed that measure, Holden, Littlefield, and Victor C. Barringer appeared in the Capitol lobby. Almost immediately, Robert W. Lassiter introduced an amendment to the Respass bill authorizing an investigation of the railroad problems that would employ a commission appointed by the governor to inquire into all state railroad affairs.[48] This threw the senate into a period of temporary indecision. Senator Graham attempted to have all 1868–69 railroad appropriations repealed, a measure too drastic for any hopes of adoption. Samuel Forkner of Surry proposed an amendment to the Lassiter bill which would take the power to appoint the commission from the governor and place it under the superintendent of public works, Ceburn L. Harris. This too was unacceptable to administration forces. At this point a compromise was agreed upon, the matter to be resolved by a select committee composed of three senators, Joseph W. Etheridge, Respass, and W. L. Love, the only Conservative member.

Meanwhile the house moved to call General Littlefield to testify, but before the summons could be delivered, he left Raleigh.[49] When Plato Durham proposed that the house send a commission to New York to ferret out fraudulent acts, the house accepted the idea. On 4 December, Speaker Joseph W. Holden announced that Durham, David Hodgin, and William A. Moore had been appointed to this commission. Although apprehensive over the possible findings in New York, the Holden forces made certain that they controlled the commission, since Durham was the only Conservative member. Later, after Hodgin was excused from serving, the proposal was reconsidered by the house, and the idea was tabled by a vote of 52 to 40.

During the Christmas recess, rumors were current that a sufficient portion of the misapplied bonds were to be adjusted to allow Littlefield to return to Raleigh and testify before a committee of the whole. Jenkins, as treasurer, even went to New York and made the necessary arrangements with the general. On 18 January 1870, the rumor became a reality; the house passed a resolution instructing the treasurer to pay no more interest on the special tax bonds. It was believed that the news of this action would deflate the price of the bonds to a price of perhaps five or ten cents on the dollar, thereby allowing the Ring to purchase enough bonds at this price to make up for those bonds unaccountable by the roads.

Littlefield did return, he did testify, and despite all attempts of Plato Durham, John W. Graham, and other Conservatives, he cleared himself of fraud charges and made a farce of the entire investigative proceedings. Littlefield even had the house believing that he had never cheated the state of a single dollar, and by intimidating the house he turned his examination into a laughing matter.[50] Such was the extent of the Ring's political control over the General Assembly and Holden's failure to take the lead in pressing for a thorough investigation.

Early in 1870, North Carolinians, having been sufficiently alerted to the immensity and seriousness of the Ring's financial activities, demanded not only a thorough investigation of its manipulations but also the passage of measures to prevent any future transgressions. On 5 February the General Assembly passed "An Act to restore the Credit of the State, and facilitate the construction of our unfinished Rail Roads."[51] Governor Holden was required to submit to the legislature the following information from each railroad: amount of bonds received by the railroad and date of receipt; amount of bonds sold, or hypothecated, price received, and where marketed; and amount of bonds unsold and on hand.[52] Swepson and Littlefield were reluctant to file such reports, but Holden had given them no alternative. Writing to them both, as he did other railroad company presidents, Holden said: "I have no discretion. You must file your accounts in accordance with the law within twenty days from 12th February, or action will be taken in the Superior Court of Wake County. Come to Raleigh in person and file your accounts."[53]

The house of representatives launched another investigation into Ring activities by creating an investigation commission in January 1870, though it did not start work until February. Since it was chaired by former governor Thomas Bragg, it was generally referred to as the Bragg Commission and consisted of Bragg, Samuel F. Phillips, and William L. Scott. Thomas L. Clingman was originally appointed to the commission, but since his whereabouts were unknown—no doubt he was attending to Swepson's many legal problems throughout the nation—he was replaced first by Rufus Barringer (who declined to serve) and finally by Scott. The commission's power of investigation was confined to only three areas—the issuance of bonds, the disposal of bonds, and the amount received by the railroads through their sale or hypothecation.

The Ring attempted to thwart the Bragg investigation, although the various railroads generally cooperated. Of all persons summoned by the commission, only Swepson, Robert W. Pulliam, and Goodson M. Roberts failed to appear.[54] Swepson was summoned for an appearance on 3 March. His summons was given to Wake County Sheriff Tim Lee on 22 February, but Lee did not serve the writ until 1 March.[55] On 2 March, Swepson left town. Before leaving, he and the governor talked for three hours, and then by means of a special train provided by the president of the North Carolina Railroad, William A. Smith, he fled the city and thereby escaped testifying.[56]

On 4 March the house directed the commission to submit its report on 11 March, making it impossible to conduct a thorough investigation. The following day, when Littlefield appeared before the commission, the house weakened the commission's power by resolving that the general not be required to testify regarding any transaction of his that involved members of the General Assembly. On 8 March, Plato Durham tried to force Littlefield to disclose the names of all legislative members to whom he had made "loans," but his motion was defeated 47 to 45.[57]

Nevertheless, members of the Ring were apprehensive that Republican solidarity might be broken and further disclosures made, and so on 11 March Littlefield hosted an oyster supper at the Yarborough House, Raleigh's finest hotel, for a number of the Republican legislators. Liquor and cigars were generously provided, and speeches were made by the general and other party leaders pointing to the necessity of discharging the Bragg Commission, whose findings were being used by the Conservative opposition. After the party had been properly roused, Littlefield struck the keynote for the evening, saying: "If [you] knew as much about the Bragg Commission as [I do], [you] would vote to repeal it [tomorrow]."[58] His argument was persuasive, for the following day, after a preliminary report from the commission, the assembly voted to discharge it.[59]

In general the Conservative press was quick to criticize the assembly's failure to press for a thorough investigation, but William L. Scott, one of the Bragg Commission members, defended the work of the commission: "I strove to discharge my duty faithfully, fearlessly and without regard to party. If there are men in Raleigh, or elsewhere, who could have furnished us evidence . . .

they ought to have done it while we were in session. . . . Had angels composed that commission, there would have been grumblers and faultfinders."[60] Josiah Turner's *Sentinel*, however, remained comparatively quiet. It printed no editorial; nor did it raise the kind of charges that characteristically would appear in its columns. It called attention to the corruption of the Holden administration, stressing that Littlefield had given watches, jewelry, and overcoats to members of the assembly and had won favor for himself by the payment of members' hotel bills and the presentation to one member's wife of a fine carriage horse.[61] As to the subject of the Bragg Commission, it remained almost silent. When the house ended the investigation, the *Sentinel* placed the blame on General Littlefield, with no mention of Swepson, Turner's financial angel.[62]

The discharge of the Bragg Commission temporarily stymied investigations into railroad frauds, although the assembly later passed a measure creating the Woodfin Commission, which attempted to recover funds for the Western Division of the Western North Carolina Railroad.[63] Woodfin and his legal staff followed Swepson and Littlefield, for both had fled the state, to New York, Baltimore, Washington, D.C., Florida, London, and Brussels;[64] but despite three settlements, they were unable to recover any more than $295,878.26 for the road.[65] From this, approximately $47,170.72 was expended in legal fees and travel expenses, causing Governor Tod R. Caldwell in 1872 to comment in his message to the General Assembly: "It appears to me that the finances of the Company have not been managed with a proper regard to economy, more especially in the item of attorney's fees and in the expense of the Commissioners."[66] A Buncombe County grand jury did report a true bill against Swepson and Littlefield, charging them with conspiracy to defraud the state. In January 1871 a joint resolution was passed by the house and senate requesting the governor to offer a $5,000 reward for the return of Littlefield to North Carolina. But nothing came of the indictment or the reward; Swepson's attorneys were able to effect a partial settlement of his Western Division account,[67] while Governor Harrison Reed of Florida refused to extradite Littlefield to the state.[68]

During the 1870–71 session of the General Assembly another commission was created to investigate corruption in the Holden administration. William Shipp, J. G. Martin, and J. B. Batchelor were the commission members, generally referred to by the name of its chairman, Shipp.[69] After a thorough examination, however, the commission was never able to place on Holden the blame for misdeeds, or even entirely on the Republican party.[70] The Shipp report did arouse fear that North Carolina would be forced to pay for the depreciated railroad bonds at face value, which by this date were being quoted at three cents on the dollar. The fear was further increased when bondholders brought charges in federal courts against the state, but all such suits were decided adversely to the bondholders.[71]

The Conservative-Democratic party gained control of the General Assembly in 1870 and attempted to solve the state's staggering financial problem by repudiating most of the state debt of $30,000,000, upon which interest charges had been defaulted. The latter consisted of $3,000,000 on prewar debts and about $13,000,000 of the special tax railroad bonds. Holden tried to prevent repudiation, knowing all too well that it would lead to financial ruin, and thus advised the assembly in his message of 22 November 1870:

> If I were disposed to court popularity at the expense of duty, or if I feared the consequences of stating plainly what I know to be the feelings of our people, I would have avoided the expression of these views to your honorable body; but the question must be met, and the longer its settlement is postponed the greater will be the difficulties that will surround it. The interest on the bonds is constantly accumulating. . . . Promptitude in the payment is indispensable to credit.[72]

In the end, a constitutional amendment ratified during the 1880 general election was North Carolina's final answer—complete repudiation of the special tax railroad bonds. The General Assembly was prohibited from ever authorizing payment of the special tax bonds or any interest thereon unless the question had been first ratified by a majority of qualified voters in a regular election. The people had spoken, but to the detriment of the state's financial creditability.

W. W. Holden, governor, 1868–1870.
(Courtesy of Department of Cultural Resources, Division of Archives and History.)

W. W. Holden, 1865, while serving as provisional governor.
(Courtesy of Department of Cultural Resources, Division of Archives and History.)

Mrs. Louisa Harrison Holden, believed to have been painted
by William Garle Brown.
(Courtesy of Perkins Library, Duke University.)

Joseph W. Holden, in Confederate uniform.
(Courtesy of Perkins Library, Duke University.)

Joseph W. Holden, 1874, when he was mayor of Raleigh.
(Courtesy of Department of Cultural Resources, Division of Archives and History.)

Laura Holden Olds.
(Courtesy of Perkins Library, Duke University.)

Henrietta (Ettie) Reid Holden Mahler.
(Courtesy of Perkins Library, Duke University.)

Mary Eldridge Holden Sherwood.
(Courtesy of Perkins Library, Duke University.)

Charles (Charlie) C. Holden, 1867.
(Courtesy of Perkins Library, Duke University.)

Holden Residence, corner of Hargett and McDowell streets, Raleigh. The house was completed in 1852, but this picture is from a much later date.
(Courtesy of Department of Cultural Resources, Division of Archives and History.)

Raleigh Post Office constructed while Holden served as postmaster. Photograph taken ca. 1905.
(Courtesy of Department of Cultural Resources, Division of Archives and History.)

EIGHT

Racial Confrontation:
Holden Opposes the Klan

Holden's greatest difficulties and, in fact, his undoing arose from racial and political problems encountered within three months of taking office. Political enemies looked upon his administration as one imposed upon the state by the national government and therefore not representative of North Carolina; not only were Republican leaders considered obnoxious but the policies of the party were unacceptable. The party's plan to guarantee political and legal equality to blacks was considered by many as an attempt to force social equality on the whites, and they absolutely refused to accept such a radical concept. Prior to his election, Holden had not been an outspoken advocate of civil rights for blacks, but he was a political realist, and by 1868 he had realized that the Republican party would insist upon full and equal rights for blacks as a requirement for North Carolina's reentry into the Union. He accepted such requirements, but he always insisted that blacks live up to their responsibilities as citizens.

> I have never advocated "social equality," as it is called, among the whites or the blacks, or between the two races. There is no equality of a social character among the whites, and there is no equality of a social character among the colored people. Each race has its own distinct and separate society. There is no trace of "social" or "negro equality" in things purely social in the reconstruction acts or in the Federal constitution. If the white people of North Carolina are suffering "socially" because the white man and the colored man stand on the same footing politically and civilly, the fault is with themselves. . . . Therefore, political and civil equality constitute one thing and social equality another.[1]

Intent on preventing a social revolution from materializing and blocking other democratic reforms contemplated by the Holden administration, the

Conservatives used every means available to overthrow his regime and reassert white supremacy. They kept the charge of corruption constantly before the people, despite the fact that their own politicians were profiting from the fraudulent deals. They also successfully turned the state away from its planned program for public schools and refused to support an economic program that might have kept the state from bankruptcy. Worst of all, they turned, as did their counterparts in other southern states, to the Ku Klux Klan as a proper tool for accomplishing their goals.

Started in Tennessee by the former Confederate general Nathan Bedford Forrest, the Klan had spread to North Carolina by late 1867 or early 1868. It consisted of three organizations: the White Brotherhood, the Constitutional Union Guard, and the Invisible Empire. Although created for the purpose of local protection, each of the Klans soon became involved in the issue of white supremacy. As Nathaniel Boyden explained in Holden's impeachment trial, the major object of the White Brotherhood was to annul all legislation giving equal rights to blacks.[2] Members of the Constitutional Union Guard were sworn to support the federal and state constitutions as they existed prior to Reconstruction, thereby denying the legitimacy of the Fourteenth Amendment. The Invisible Empire resisted Reconstruction legislation by intimidation, force, and violence if necessary.[3]

Some have excused Klan activities on the grounds that it was best for the South that the Republican regimes be overthrown and the old order reinstated. Others have used the "right of revolution" to justify the Klan, believing that there was no legal means to rid the state of Republican oppression. This rationale has caused some to place responsibility for the Klans upon those who planned and put Radical Reconstruction into effect instead of upon those who committed the acts of depredation. In the words of a participant, "The Ku Klux Klan was a gigantic conspiracy of lawless night riders who saved the civilization of the South and bequeathed it a priceless heritage to the nation."[4]

The Klan movement in North Carolina supposedly originated in Orange County and from there spread rapidly. William L. Saunders of Chapel Hill headed the Invisible Empire, although he never took the prescribed oath and therefore was not officially a member, and Edward Graham Haywood of Raleigh was the reputed head of North Carolina's Constitutional Union Guard.[5] Although many did not approve of the violence exercised by their fellow klansmen, others spoke of the necessity "to keep down the style of the niggers and to increase the Conservative party." As one of the leaders in the western part of the state noted, the Klan was formed not to achieve "a white man's government only, but—mark the phrase—an *intelligent* white man's government."[6]

Holden had been in office for three months when the Klans began operations, chiefly in the counties of Alamance, Caswell, Orange, Jones, Lenoir, and Chatham. Threats of violence and outlawry, however, occurred throughout the state. In Fayetteville, Republican judge Ralph Buxton was assailed and maligned in the public press, the doors of Christ Church were closed to his family, and some of them were even threatened with death. In Robeson County, armed bands of outlaws roamed the countryside, robbing and plundering. In Carteret, Mrs. H. J. Moore, a native of Boston, was attacked for her supposed aid to blacks in her community.[7] Conservative leaders and press explained Klan activities as being designed to regulate public conduct by spreading a salutary terror among evildoers. Yet no serious steps were taken to halt the movement.

Undoubtedly anticipating Conservative opposition and trying to forestall the rise of the Klan, Governor Holden asked in his inaugural address for the immediate reorganization of the state militia in order that the state might enforce law and order for the benefit of all citizens. He followed this with a special message to the legislature on 17 July. Meanwhile, Republicans increased the work of the Union League, particularly among the blacks. By August, membership in the League was estimated at seventy thousand in North Carolina. When the Klan began its acts of violence, the League members struck back with the weapons they knew best—setting the torch to mills, barns, and homes of their former masters. Racial discord was further created by an incendiary address prepared in the hopes of suppressing Klan activities and signed by eighty-six Republican legislators; it had, however, the opposite effect. The address read in part:

> Did it never occur to you, ye gentlemen of property, education, and character—to you, ye men, and especially ye women, who never received anything from these colored people but services, kindness, and protection—did it never occur to you that these same people who are so very bad, will not be willing to sleep in the cold when your houses are denied them, merely because they will not vote as you do; that they may not be willing to starve, while they are willing to work for bread? Did it never occur to you that revenge which is sweet to you, may be sweet to them? Hear us, if nothing else you will hear; did it never occur to you that if you kill their children with hunger they will kill your children with fear? Did it never occur to you that if you good people maliciously determine that they shall have no shelter, they may determine that you shall have no shelter?[8]

Holden's hopes for peace through the Republican strategy were doomed to failure, for Klan activities soon accelerated. As an example, Edward Mallory of Granville County reported to the governor that on 8 October 1868 a group of armed white men had entered his home in the Tally Ho community and severely whipped him and his wife, one of the men mutilating his right ear. The same night these hoodlums dragged a black woman from her bed, but when she broke loose, they fired and seriously wounded her in the head and shoulders. Mallory had earlier reported the violence to a justice of the peace, who declined to take action but rather had referred him to the governor. When Mallory showed the governor his lacerations and the mutilated ear, Holden immediately ordered the sheriff of Granville County, James Moore, to conduct an investigation and make arrests of those responsible, adding that if any magistrate failed to do his duty his commission would be revoked. "It is unnecessary to remind you that the colored people have the right to be as secure in their houses as the white people, and that the law protects them equally with the whites. . . . I will not sit here unmoved and inactive when they cry for justice and protection against men whose treatment, as in the case of Edward Mallory, is a disgrace to civilization."[9]

On 12 October 1868, Holden issued the first of four proclamations expressing hope for a peaceful solution to the state's racial problems; at the same time he indicated his determination to provide equal justice to all citizens. Holden was a peaceful man and desired to maintain civil government by peaceful means. He abhorred violence of all kinds. He realized, however, that neither his administration nor any government could long survive without law and order. His appeal read as follows:

> The object of the persons thus engaged [armed outlaws and Klan members] must be either to subvert the government, to resist the constituted authorities, or to prevent a free election in the state. . . .
>
> If it be the purpose of any portion of the people in any event to resist the laws or to subvert the government, they should bear in mind that Treason is the highest crime that can be committed; that they are liable to arrest and punishment under the "Act to punish conspiracy, sedition, and rebellion," which should reflect that the magnanimity of the government which spared the lives and estates of those who engaged in the late rebellion, may not be extended a second time to save them from the consequences of their crimes.[10]

But the proclamation did not deter the Klan; in fact, outrages by the organization increased during the remainder of 1868 and throughout the following year. In March 1869, Holden was compelled to dispatch a company of militia to Alamance County in a futile attempt to curb Klan action. This led the *Sentinel* to accuse Holden, in its issue of 25 March, of sending the militia to inflict "negro malish" rule upon the county. However, the General Assembly, sensing the growing danger from the Klan, passed legislation empowering the governor to employ a detective force to apprehend fugitives from justice.[11] On 12 April 1869 it went further by passing an act making it a felony to go masked, disguised, or painted. In announcing the passage of this new law, Holden again expressed hope that resistance would cease; if not, though, he was determined to enforce the law.

> Public opinion properly embodied and expressed will be more effectual in repressing these evils, and in promoting the general good . . . than the execution of the law itself against offenders in a few individual cases. I respectfully and earnestly invoke this public opinion. . . . I call upon every citizen to unite with me in discountenancing disorders and violence of all kinds, and fostering and promoting confidence, peace and good will among the whole people of the State.[12]

But the Conservative leadership played by neither state nor national rules, and Klan activities rapidly increased, causing the Union League to seek retaliations. Had it not been for the advice of Holden's spokesmen, such as Senator John Pool, the blacks might have resorted to widespread violence. As might have been expected, Holden acted in a spirit of forebearance, hoping that the Klan would cease its depredations.[13] Soon Klan outrages in North Carolina and throughout the South shocked the nation. Bankers in New York and other financial centers, already hesitant to extend credit, now refused to invest in the South's rebuilding programs and placed their money in the newly opened western states. In like manner, the efforts of the Republican administrations in the South failed to attract immigrants from abroad or from the more populous New England and Middle Atlantic states. It had been hoped that immigration might bring some industrialization to a region so basically agricultural. In addition, labor became disaffected; working men wondered if they would ever enjoy the fruits of their labor. In short, Klan outrages paralyzed the energy of the southern people and helped to prolong the poverty of the South.

Despite his determination to maintain order, Holden increasingly found himself in an awkward and embarrassing position. By the summer of 1869 he found it impossible to eradicate the Klan by ordinary governmental procedures. In case after case he had been unable to bring guilty parties to justice. In many instances, sheriffs themselves were Klan members, and in other cases grand juries refused to return indictments. In Alamance County not only the sheriff but also his deputies were Klan leaders. When bills of indictment were returned and parties arraigned for trial, juries frequently failed to convict, owing to sympathy for the accused or fear of retribution or because the Klan's use of disguises prevented proper identification.

If Holden had not attempted to suppress the Klan, he probably would not have provoked his opponents to demand his removal. Still, he had to act or admit the incompetence of his administration and dereliction in his duty as chief executive of the state. Either might have brought the intervention of the federal government and the reestablishment of military rule in the state.

Superior court judge Albion W. Tourgée, whose judicial district was the site of the most notorious Klan outrages, made an effort to stop the Klan, but failed. In a letter to Holden he commented upon the problems involved and the difficulty of securing convictions.

> Several bills including some twenty or more persons were found by the Grand Jury. In those cases the identification, in spite of masks, was sufficient to satisfy the Grand Jury. Many cases of very serious outrages were, however, brought to the attention of the Grand Jury, and the Court in which the connection between the act and any identified persons could not be clearly, and in some of them, not at all established. In some cases the disguise was perfect, or the acts of violence were performed by strangers, so that identification was utterly impossible. In some cases the commission of the acts of violence was only revealed by accident; and in others the parties were so fearful of their lives that they begged to be permitted to refrain from testifying and in yet other circumstances they fled the country lest they should be compelled to testify and then murdered in revenge for having done so. The acts are of almost every degree of atrocity; burning houses, whipping men and women, beating with clubs, shooting, cutting, and other methods of injuring and insult. . . . I think about twenty *known* instances of such outrages have occurred in the County. One of the parties indicted was tried and though his identification by the party beaten was most complete and positive, he proved a *perfect alibi* without a particle of trouble. The jury very properly rendered a verdict of "Not Guilty." . . . I have no idea that one of these men can be legally convicted of the crime. I believe that any one of these men can prove himself to have been just where he chooses at the time of the commission of the act with which he is charged.[14]

Since the Klan was avowedly formed to protect white society, one might suppose that its area of greatest activity would have been in districts with the heaviest concentrations of blacks, but such was not the case. In 1870 in the ninety counties in the state, sixteen had a larger black population than white, yet of these only three—Caswell, Craven, and Jones—reported Klan operations. In Alamance, where the worst of the crimes occurred, whites outnumbered blacks by almost three to one. It is useless, therefore, to maintain that there was any necessity for the formation of such a secret association.

Some newspapers in the state condoned Klan activities on the grounds that the Holden administration, by use of pardons and commutations, showed undue favoritism to blacks. An analysis of 127 pardons and commutations made prior to 1870, however, shows that, while sympathetic to the underprivileged, Holden was apparently not partial to blacks. In fact, he acted only after proper investigations by legal authorities had been conducted. Decisions were based on justice, not race. Moreover, in Alamance and Caswell, the scenes of the worst Klan activities, no pardon was granted in one county, while in the other the one pardon granted had the full endorsement of the Conservatives.[15]

During the autumn of 1869, H. C. Vogel, superintendent of the Bureau of Refugees, Freedmen, and Abandoned Lands for North Carolina, inspected western North Carolina and found substantial evidence that the Klan was concentrating its attention on the bureau, especially on its schoolteachers. One case in particular disturbed him. Alonzo Corliss, a white, conducted a school for blacks under the auspices of the Friends' Society (Quaker) and, as head of the local Union League, insisted that blacks had the right to attend church and sit among white worshipers. He immediately became a marked man. He was seized by night and taken to a nearby woods and whipped thirty lashes, one-half of his head was shaved, and one side of his face was painted black. He was told that unless he left the community within ten days, additional punishment would be administered. Further, the owner of the house in which Corliss and his wife lived refused to permit them to stay; nor would the local hotel operator rent rooms to them. Corliss fled the state.[16]

Vogel then suggested to Gen. Oliver O. Howard, the head of the Freedmen's Bureau, that the United States government should use force to protect its agents. Later, Eliphalet Whittlesay, assistant North Carolina Freedmen's Bureau commissioner, wrote Governor Holden that General Howard would join with him in requesting that President Grant furnish protection to the teachers in the discharge of their duties.[17] Holden mistakenly did not pursue federal intervention, for had he done so, it is likely that his opposition would have been less bold in their attacks. At the time, however, the governor felt confident that he had sufficient popular support. In a letter to his friend and former employer Dennis Heartt he said, "If the leaders of the Democracy would meet me half way, we would have peace in a very short while."[18]

On 20 October 1869, Holden issued a second proclamation to the people, restating his determination to protect the citizens without regard to antecedents, color, or political opinion. At the same time he pointed out that in Lenoir, Jones, Orange, and Alamance counties a state of insubordination or actual insurrection existed. He warned that if the Klan did not cease its outrages, he would invoke martial law. He declared:

> I now call upon every citizen in the Counties aforesaid to aid the civil power in a fearless enforcement of the laws. No set of men can take the law into their own hands. Every citizen, however humble, or whatever his color, has a right to be at peace in his own house, and cannot be taken thence except by due process, and cannot be punished save by the law. If there be those who counsel resistance to established authority, such persons are traitors, and should be punished accordingly; if there be those who, disguised and masked, enter the dwellings of others by force and commit acts of violence, such persons are guilty of felony, and should be punished by hard labor in the Penitentiary; if there be those who without precept or order, hang, or shoot, or otherwise deprive anyone of life, such persons are murderers, and should be punished accordingly.[19]

This second appeal also failed to rid the state of the Klan's violence, owing in large measure to the law regulating the militia. Holden could not send the state's militia into a county unless he had a request from local authorities, and the above-named counties were controlled by a Conservative-Democratic coalition sympathetic to the Ku Klux Klan; therefore, the county magistrates took no action. Furthermore, Holden found it almost impossible to obtain white militiamen. If he used black militiamen, local whites would be infuriated and probably would commit more violence.

As the Klan outrages multiplied, Holden felt compelled to appeal for a stronger militia law. Therefore, a subservient legislature passed the famous Shoffner Act, or "An Act to Secure the Better Protection of Life and Property." Holden had made his appeal to the assembly on 16 December, and the bill was immediately introduced by Alamance County senator T. M. Shoffner. It passed all three readings on the day of introduction, but the house did not act until after a Christmas recess. John Pool was the author of the bill, although

Shoffner was reportedly paid $1,200 for its sponsorship.[20] Under the terms of the law, the governor was authorized and empowered, whenever in his judgment local authorities were unable to provide adequate protection of life and property, to declare such county in a state of insurrection and to call into service the state militia to suppress such insurrection. He was further authorized to call upon the federal government for any needed assistance. All expenses for militia action would be paid by the state, but each county declared in insurrection would have to repay the cost of state services within one year.[21]

This act precipitated heated discussion throughout the state, particularly in the Conservative press. Many accused the Republicans of giving the governor despotic powers or, as the *Weldon News* termed it, "a damnable military bill." The *Sentinel* charged it as striking at the foundation of civil liberty, since "it takes away the protection which the constitution and the laws throw around the citizen, and places his life, his property and his liberty within the control, and subject to the partisan whims of one man."[22] To this the *Standard* replied that the times demanded such powers since offenders went undetected and unpunished because of the impotency, secret sympathy, or inefficiency of local authorities.[23] In private, the chief defender of the legislation, Augustus Seymour, legislator from Craven County, admitted that the adoption of this law was the only sure way for Republicans to retain political control of the state.[24]

Despite his newly won power, Holden was unwilling to exercise it, hoping desperately that a peaceful solution could be found. In conversation with John Norwood of Orange County, he remarked that if a number of local citizens would recommend an influential person to canvass the county in the interest of law and order and thereby persuade the Klan to disband and cease its crimes, he would support that person and also appoint him a representative of the law.[25] Accordingly, a petition was presented to the governor asking that Dr. Pride Jones, a highly respected citizen, former member of the house of commons, and lieutenant colonel in the Confederate Army, be appointed the county's agent to work for the suppression of the Klan. The petition was speedily accepted by Holden, and on 7 March, Jones, a Conservative, received a captain's commission in the Orange County militia. Shortly afterwards, Nathan A. Ramsey was given a similar commission for Chatham County.[26]

The directives Holden gave to Jones and Ramsey are significant. Not only do they show the governor's grasp of the problems but they also indicate the nature of the man—his wish to restore order without force and his willingness to cooperate with his Conservative opposition. He made it clear to both men that their primary objective was to restore peace and order and that their power was in strict subordination to civil authority. In so doing, he recognized the

inexpediency of both the Union League and the Klan, ordering the disband-
ment of both. Later, Holden proudly announced that both men had been
successful in their efforts to end violence in their counties.[27]

Since the Ku Klux activities in Alamance and Caswell counties were far
more extensive, Governor Holden found himself unable to use the strategy
employed in Orange and Chatham. Complicating the situation, sheriffs and
other major civil officials in both counties were known members of the Klan.
Consequently, Holden solicited the help of a volunteer to restore peace, but
without success. Writing to Thomas A. Donaho, a highly respected Republican in Yanceyville, Holden said: "I appeal to you and other gentlemen of
character and standing to interpose and arrest these violations of law. . . . It is
important to check these acts of violence at once, and before the excitement of
the campaign begins."[28]

When peaceful means failed, on 7 March, Holden declared Alamance to
be in a state of insurrection, and then Caswell on 8 July. Still, he made no
attempt to replace the civil governments, and he immediately informed President Grant and the state's congressmen of his action. Holden wrote to President Grant: "I cannot rely upon the militia to repress these outrages, for the
reason that . . . white militia of the proper character cannot be obtained, and it
would but aggravate the evil to employ colored militia. Besides, the expense
of calling out the militia would be greater than our people could well bear in
their present impoverished condition." He further observed that federal troops
would restore order, having inspired terror among the evildoers and being
respected by a majority of the local citizens. The governor then added that
there was another remedy available, namely, that Congress might authorize the
president to suspend the writ of habeas corpus. "If Congress would authorize
the suspension, by the President, of the writ of *habeas corpus* in certain
localities, and if criminals could be arrested and tried before military tribunals,
and shot, we would soon have peace and order throughout all this country. The
remedy would be a sharp and bloody one, but it is as indispensable as was the
suppression of the rebellion."[29]

In writing to the congressmen, Holden was more direct: "We want military tribunals by which assassins and murderers can be summarily tried and
shot." When action was not immediately forthcoming, he telegraphed Senator
Joseph C. Abbott: "What is being done to protect the good citizens of
Alamance County? We have federal troops, but we want power to act. Is it
possible the Government will abandon its loyal people to be whipped and
hanged?"[30]

Meanwhile, trouble continued to increase in Caswell County, where the

Republicans, under the leadership of John W. "Chicken" Stephens, attempted to resist the Klan with their Union League. Often depicted as one of the most unsavory Republicans, Stephens had been a successful harnessmaker and tobacco trader in Wentworth prior to the Civil War. He had escaped military service and once was accused of stealing his neighbor's chickens, probably accounting for his nickname. His failure to support the Confederacy no doubt provided the real basis for his unpopularity. After the war he became active in Freedmen's Bureau work and later joined the Republican party. He successfully completed the study of law and received his license from Judge Tourgée; consequently he began a successful career in law and politics. In 1868 he helped quell threatened racial violence in Caswell County and thereafter was recognized as the Republican leader in the county.

Although he pursued a policy of moderation and cooperation with some Conservative leaders, Stephens's defeat of the popular Bedford Brown for the state senate left a residue of resentment and distrust toward himself and Republican policies generally. Thomas A. Donaho, who had turned down Holden's plea to serve as a local volunteer to suppress the Klan, expressed such sentiment: "I do not think there would have been any violent antagonism between a respectable portion of the white people of the county and a *liberal* Republican, but for this misrepresentation of Republicanism. But the good people of Caswell cannot be expected to affiliate with a party whose recognized standard bearer sustains such a character at home, as does the individual alluded to."[31] Nevertheless, Stephens's two brothers, both Confederate veterans, declared him a good and honest man whose courage and ability were recognized by all. In early 1870 he began to receive threats on his life. He chose to ignore these, but armed himself with three pistols, fortified his home against attack, purchased insurance to provide for his wife and two children, and even prepared his last will and testament.[32]

On Saturday, 21 May, the Conservative-Democrats held a rally at the Caswell County courthouse in Yanceyville, which Stephens was reckless enough to attend. In fact, he occupied a seat in the front row and proceeded to take notes on the day's activities. This action, plus the fact that he had been employed by Governor Holden as a detective to ferret out Klan membership, confirmed him as one who should be eliminated from local politics. His time came during a speech by Judge John Kerr when Frank Wiley, a respected friend whom Stephens was urging to run for sheriff, suggested to Stephens that they go to a room in the courthouse for private consultation on Wiley's candidacy.[33] Entering a supposedly vacant office, Stephens was seized. The original plan was to keep Stephens locked in the courthouse until nighttime, then take him to the town square for a public hanging; but fear of discovery by Stephens's friends caused the assassins to perform their act at once. Thus he was taken to the clerk's office and hanged, his throat cut in two places, and knife wounds made on his chest; afterwards his body was thrown on a wood-pile in the dark basement. When Stephens failed to return that evening, family and friends became alarmed and organized a search party, but they were unable to secure keys to the locked courthouse rooms. Consequently, it was not until the following day that his brother discovered Stephens's body. Terror immediately spread through the black community, causing Wilson Carey, a black member of the house of representatives, to flee the county. No arrests were made, although several prominent whites were accused of complicity in the murder. Sheriff Jesse C. Griffith made no serious attempt to solve the crime, and not surprisingly since, as was later learned, he was a member of the Caswell County Klan. It was not until sixty-five years later, after the death of all participants, that the truth was known. Only then did John G. Lea, Klan leader in Caswell, confess that G. T. Mitchell placed the noose around Stephens's neck and Tom Oliver stabbed him.[34]

With state elections approaching in August and Klan violence increasing, Republican leaders were concerned whether control of the state could be maintained unless more drastic action were taken to suppress the Klan. The *Standard* reported on 14 June 1870 that during the preceding twelve months no less than five hundred peaceful citizens had been whipped by the Ku Klux Klan, no less than twenty-five murdered, no less than twenty women raped, and no less than two men castrated. This did not include other barbarities against innocent men, women, and children. Certainly the kluxers were intimidating the blacks sufficiently to frighten them away from the polls. Republicans knew that if few blacks voted, the Conservative-Democrats would gain political control and return the state to a policy of white supremacy.

The Conservative press became quite vocal in its opposition to Holden policies regarding the Klan, and William A. Hearne, editor of the *Tarboro North Carolinian*, even called indirectly for Holden's assassination.[35] Josiah Turner, Jr., strident and eccentric editor of the *Raleigh Sentinel*, openly defied Holden, daring the governor to arrest him for his defense of the Klan and saying that Holden's "want of pluck" prevented him from making such an arrest.[36]

The die had been cast! During a Republican caucus in his office, Holden, meeting with John Pool, James H. Harris, Isaac Young, Willie D. Jones, William J. Clarke, William F. Henderson, Richard C. Badger, Abial W. Fisher, S. T. Carrow, Henderson Adams, David A. Jenkins, and J. W. Hood, decided that the use of military troops was the only means of crushing the Ku Klux Klan. Holden always maintained that this decision was necessary. Even though he had the final authority to approve it, it is doubtful that he originated the plan. Richard C. Badger later claimed that the suggestion was first made by Pool and then agreed upon by the others.[37] At first, Holden opposed the use of the state militia, claiming that it was untrustworthy. Thereupon, Pool suggested the use of two regiments of white state troops as the best means of preserving civil government. Badger violently opposed this idea, but consented when he learned that Governor Powell Clayton of Arkansas was using such forces effectively to political advantage.

Still, Holden was apprehensive over possible violations of civil rights and wanted reassurance from President Grant and other federal authorities. He also knew that the state would not endorse this action without support from Washington. Thus, Thomas Settle was dispatched to the White House for a consultation with Grant, during which the president inquired why Holden had not put himself at the head of an armed force and used direct means to suppress the Klan. The president further commented that he had examined the state's constitution and was convinced that the governor was empowered to do this and to suppress all disorders. He concluded the interview by saying that if such actions produced an insurrection, he would then aid Holden with all the military power of the United States government. This was the assurance that was needed, and Settle promptly notified senators Pool and Abbott, who hurried to Raleigh to call another caucus. It was then that the administration made final plans for the use of military force.[38]

Governor Holden was thus faced with a dilemma. The majority of his advisers were determined to use military force to protect the lives, property, and voting rights of black citizens, and coincidentally protect their chances in the 1870 elections. With assurance from the president they had reason to feel confident, but Holden was concerned with protecting the civil rights of all. He had opposed the tyrannical tendencies of Jefferson Davis during the war, but he was now confronted with a similar problem. He had to decide whether to use force to secure law and order, risking open warfare. In the end he decided he had no other choice and justified the validity of such a policy in his memoirs: "I was fully aware of the great responsibility, but human life was above all price. As I said to Mr. [W. A.] Albright of Alamance, I did not care how the election of 1870 went if by what I did saved one human life. The civil and military are alike in constitutional powers; the civil to protect life and property when it can, and the military when the former has failed."[39] Later, he added: "And I again declare that all I did in that movement was done with a purpose to protect the weak and unoffending of both races, to maintain and restore the majesty of the civil law, and not to gratify personal feeling on my part, or to promote party interests or party ascendency."[40]

Having decided to use the troops, Holden issued orders to Maj. Gen. Willie D. Jones to raise the regiments of white troops for immediate active service. He also ordered that a number of "minute men" be set apart in each regiment for reserves. Col. William J. Clarke, New Bern and Raleigh lawyer and businessman, was placed in command of the first regiment, with headquarters in Raleigh. Clarke's appointment is indicative of the type of person Holden preferred to head his military force. Not only was Clarke successful in private life but he had been state comptroller, 1851–55, and had served as colonel in the Twenty-fourth North Carolina Troops during the Civil War. Ironically, Mrs. Clarke, Mary Bayard Devereux Clarke, was not only a member of a planter family but also a sister of Sophia Devereux Turner (Mrs. Josiah Turner, Jr.), whose husband was a leader of those opposing Holden and largely responsible for the Klan's organization. Mary Bayard Clarke not only followed her husband to the Virginia battlefields but broke with her family by becoming friendly with leading Republicans, even serving as secretary to Judge Edwin G. Reade.[41]

Governor Holden asked W. W. Rollins, a former Unionist from Marshall in Madison County, to command the second regiment, believing that Rollins could easily recruit the pro-Union men of the mountain region. This would strike fear among Klan members and hasten the state's return to peace. Rollins received notice of his appointment while in Washington and declined after careful consideration. In turn, he recommended George W. Kirk, a Tennessean who had lived briefly in western North Carolina, choosing him because of his notorious Civil War reputation, and because "the name which Kirk bore . . . would prevent resistance and bloodshed."[42] As commander of the Third North Carolina Volunteers, United States Army, Kirk had led a successful raid on Camp Vance near Morganton, 13–15 June 1864, destroying one locomotive and three cars; the depot and commissary buildings; 1,200 small arms, with ammunition; and 3,000 bushels of grain. One officer and ten enlisted men were killed, and 132 prisoners were captured. Later he organized scouting parties in various western counties that interrupted Confederate communications, destroying supply depots and gathering valuable military information for the Union forces.[43] Holden then telegraphed Rollins to send Kirk, who was also in Washington, for consultation. Accompanied by Tennessean George B. Bergen (ofttimes spelled Bergin), a strong Unionist supporter whom Kirk wanted as his assistant commander, he arrived in Raleigh on 20 June. After being interviewed by the governor and other Republican leaders, Kirk convinced them that he was the right man for the job. He was then appointed commander of the second regiment.

Meanwhile, Colonel Clarke was dispatched to Washington to secure the necessary supplies and equipment. In company with senators Pool and Abbott, on 17 June he called at the White House, where he promptly received the president's complete endorsement for the state's request. In fact, Grant spoke of his willingness to send four companies of troops until they could be replaced by state troops. Clarke advised Governor Holden to place an immediate call for their services, but Holden, unfortunately, decided that this would not be necessary. Clarke later reported to Holden that the president had never been "so talkative, or to talk so well," and in his own handwriting Grant wrote a letter to the acting secretary of war, William T. Sherman, saying that while the North Carolina request was irregular, it was absolutely necessary and that he (Grant) would sign any paper to validate it. Grant also expressed regrets that Governor Holden had not led the delegation and said that he would be happy to see him at an early date in Washington. Clarke closed his report with a hope for the success of the venture, saying, "Heaven seems to smile on us, and I trust that the undertaking will end as auspiciously as it has begun." Afterwards, Sherman endorsed the president's letter and informed Clarke that the governor would have to sign a bond to the United States government to pay for the supplies, but, as he noted, "it will, in effect, be payable at the day of judgment."[44] Later in the day, Clarke called on Gen. M. C. Meigs, quartermaster general of the army, presented him with Grant's letter, and drew from Fort Monroe equipment, uniforms, and supplies for a full regiment.[45]

After receiving his commission, Kirk left Raleigh for Asheville to begin the recruitment of troops, primarily among former Union veterans. Before his departure, however, he had the *Standard* print five hundred handbills for his recruitment drive. The handbill read in part:

> The horrible murders and other atrocities committed by rebel K.K.K. and "Southern chivalry," on grayhaired men and helpless women, call in thunder tones on all loyal men to rally in defense of their state. The uplifted hand of justice must overtake these outlaws. . . . 1000 Recruits are wanted immediately, to serve six months unless sooner discharged. These troops will receive the same pay, clothing and rations as United States regulars.[46]

On 22 June, Kirk wrote Holden that he had already started to form his companies, one at Marshall and the other at Marion, despite constant interference from the Klan. He added that he was leaving for Greasy Cove in East Tennessee, where many former North Carolinians were living, undoubtedly because of Union sentiments, who would gladly return to enlist with the North Carolina troops. He promised to post no handbills out of the state and to have his troops ready by 4 July for action at any designated place.[47]

Also on 22 June, Adjutant General A. W. Fisher announced the complete reorganization of the state militia. Most of the officers were strong Unionists and prominent native sons, including such names as Curtis H. Brogden, Clinton L. Cobb, Richard T. Berry, Edwin R. Brink, John Norfleet, John McL. Harrington, Oliver H. Dockery, C. S. Moring, J. J. Mott, A. C. Bryan, C. L. S. Corpening, W. W. Rollins, and E. R. Hampton.[48] Holden was quite careful in selecting the officers, hoping that a respected group of leaders would allay criticism for the use of the troops and that the public would support his administration's efforts to restore tranquility.

Contrary to charges made in the 27 June edition of the *Raleigh Sentinel*, Governor Holden made no hurried decision for use of military force and had no intention of creating a dictatorship; nor did he intend to provoke conflict between the Klan and the state's citizens in order to cancel the August elections or to place the state under martial law. In fact, no one was more determined than Holden to use peaceful means and civil authority to maintain order. Before making the decision to use troops, he had, if anything, been overly cautious. That his administration was being severely tested by Klan violence cannot be denied, and when his efforts to stop the Klan through appeals to reason failed, he had no other alternative.

John Pool, on the other hand, wanted to rush the troops into action even should open warfare result. The *New York Tribune* quoted Pool as saying: "We intend to use the military in the election and must get these statements [of Klan outrages] disseminated throughout the North."[49] From Washington, Pool wrote Holden that he had heard that Nathan Bedford Forrest, generally thought of as heading the Klan movement in the South, had been in Alamance and Caswell counties prior to recent crimes committed there. Moreover, Pool suggested that the governor investigate the situation and take whatever steps were necessary to stop Forrest and the spreading Klan movement:

> Surely Mr. Turner cannot be ignorant of the fact of Genl. Forrest's visit, if it be a fact. . . . If there is good reason to believe it true, Mr. Turner, & eight or ten other prominent men should be examined in regard to it, & made to answer. The greater the number of such men who knew it, & who have kept it secret, the more important it becomes. I

suggest Judge [Daniel L.] Russell as the most efficient Judge to be sent. Mr. [William H.] Bailey, of Salisbury, seems to be the proper lawyer, if he can be induced to undertake it.[50]

Governor Holden, ever cautious, led a delegation to Washington on 28 June to make certain that federal authorities, the president in particular, approved of the state's strategy. In the delegation were those primarily responsible for maintaining civil government: Col. Isaac J. Young of the North Carolina Military; Alexander Jones, Republican congressional candidate from the Seventh District; Samuel T. Carrow, United States marshal in the state; and Stephen A. Douglas, Jr., Holden's aide. The governor and Senator Pool had a long and satisfactory interview with Grant on 30 June, at which time the president approved the state's plan and promised the full support of the United States government if necessary. "Let those men [Conservative leaders or Ku Kluxers] resist you, Governor, and I will move with all my power against them."[51] The president sent two additional companies of troops to North Carolina to assist the state troops should Klan violence continue to get out of hand. "They will be used to suppress violence and to maintain the law if other means should fail."[52] The *Standard* expressed the hope that they would be cavalry companies armed with the "best fast-shooting guns" available, so as to better contain the Ku Kluxes.[53]

Holden's confidence was buoyed when Robert M. Douglas, the president's private secretary, spoke in Smithfield on 12 July, saying,

I speak what I know in stating that the President will give a firm support to Gov. Holden in his efforts to suppress the disorders that exist in this State. We do not wish to interfere with any man in the lawful exercise of his rights. We do not desire to prevent the polling of a single Conservative vote by any means, save legitimate argument, at the coming election. But we know our rights as free men and will assert and maintain them.

Douglas then read from the act passed 21 May 1870, entitled "An Act to Enforce the Rights of Citizens of the United States to Vote in the Several States of the Union," and concluded with the comment: "If the military forces of the United States are not sufficient, the President is empowered to call upon the militia; and it would not take long to rally round our glorious flag an army of gallant men."[54]

Meanwhile, Kirk had assembled his volunteers and left by train for Raleigh, where the men were to be mustered into service ready for action. On

6 July nine companies, a total of 670 men, left Morganton amid reports of rowdyism and disorder.[55] Professor Hamilton described them as being "utterly undisciplined." "At Newton they left the train and forced bystanders to do their bidding" under the threat of pistol shots. Continuing, he wrote, "When they reached Salisbury, they made threats of burning the town and, pretending that they had been fired upon from the hotel, they ran to the windows of the dining-room and made a demonstration against women and children with muskets, bayonets, and pistols."[56] For authority, Hamilton cited a letter from W. F. Henderson to Holden, dated 9 July 1870, but he misquoted and took parts of it out of context. The letter was a joint one from William H. Howerton and Henderson, stating that Kirk's men were well-behaved. It also stated: "2 Secesh raised a disturbance but they soon saw that they would be shot if they did not retreat at once. Kirk told the citizens, if his men were fired into and killed he would burn down the town. The Ku Klux is raising a howl, but I stated to them if they misrepresented what Kirk said I would contradict it on the Stump & in the public Journals."[57]

Hamilton also misstated his facts when he wrote that Judge Robert M. Henry in his charge to the grand jury of Buncombe County denounced Holden for organizing the state troops, which were not needed.[58] On the contrary, the comments of J. C. Davidson, foreman of the grand jury, and J. E. Reed, superior court clerk of Buncombe, appeared in the *Standard*: "There is not one word of truth in the allegation that the Judge 'censured Governor Holden in strong terms for sending the infamous Kirk to domineer over our people.' On the contrary, the policy of Governor Holden, or the organization of State Troops, to be commanded by Kirk or anyone else, was not mentioned in the Judge's charge to the jury on the occasion referred to."[59]

In Salisbury, Kirk received orders from Holden to proceed to Company Shops (now Burlington), where his troops should stop and wait for instructions from Raleigh. The Kirk troops arrived there on 8 July, but it was not until 15 July that Holden's aide Douglas officially mustered them into service.[60] The United States Military Code was used for the ceremonies, with "North Carolina" being substituted for "United States." A dress parade was held, after which Colonel Kirk gave a brief talk which reiterated the intent and purpose of the military force to suppress Klan violence. He declared:

> I feel honored in presenting to you gentlemen, the commissions given you by the Governor of North Carolina. I hope you will never do anything to disgrace them. I am responsible for the conduct of every man in the regiment, and expect every officer to take upon himself his portion of the responsibility.

I will feed and clothe you well, and will do everything in my power to make you contented and happy; but remember that I command this regiment, and that I will expect strict discipline and obedience from all.

Gov. Holden has given me my instructions and I intend to carry them out. He will order nothing but is right, for he is a kind and good man, so you will never be called upon to perform any wrong action.

Obey my orders, and do nothing without orders. Interfere with no man and no man's property. Do nothing disorderly or mean. Every man will be held strictly responsible for all of his misdeeds, and will be punished as only military laws can punish.

You know me. I never forget my promise for reward or punishment. This is enough.[61]

On 8 July, Holden declared Caswell County in a state of insurrection,[62] but final plans for the utilization of the troops were not acted upon until 15 July when the infamous "Kirk-Holden War" began. The delay was due to Colonel Clarke's slow return with equipment from Fort Monroe. Meanwhile, Klan violence was occurring throughout the state, and a determined Conservative opposition to the use of troops was developing. The *Standard* announced that a Ku Klux Democratic paper published in Danbury, Stokes County, declared in its first issue that "the first and chief object to be accomplished, and the prime purpose of the paper, is to abolish the present infamous Constitution of North Carolina, and to re-establish in its stead the Old Constitution of our fathers."[63]

On Friday night, 8 July, a body of disguised klansmen entered the home of Wyatt Prince, near Buckhorn in Chatham County, and shot him five times. Later that same night, Deputy United States Marshall Bosher and a Lt. Powell led troops from the United States Eighth Infantry in a raid in Chatham, Wake, and Harnett counties, arresting nine persons for this crime and for attempting to violate the voting rights of citizens in those counties. The accused were taken to Raleigh the following day and jailed to await trial before a federal court.[64]

Meanwhile, Josiah Turner, Jr., claimed that an attack had been made on his wife's life in Hillsborough. According to a letter dated 15 July and later published in the *Sentinel*, some unknown assailant fired into the Turner residence, fortunately not harming Mrs. Turner.[65] Unknown to Holden, his secretary, W. R. Richardson, telegraphed the Turners for details regarding the incident, whereupon Turner responded in an open letter to the governor: "I received with proper loathing and profound contempt, your telegram."[66] Holden immediately instructed Clarke to station twenty men in Hillsborough and offered to provide a guard for Mrs. Turner. Turner informed Clarke, his brother-in-law, that if such a guard were posted, he would have the men arrested for forcible trespass. Turner boasted that he could not be arrested if he took such action. The *Standard* quoted Holden as responding that the firing into the Turner home might have been like the reported firing into the *Sentinel* office—"gotten-up" by Turner himself.[67]

By 15 July, Holden had completed his plans to begin an attack on the Klan. His first order was the arrest of Klan leaders in Alamance, a county in which defiance seemed most determined. The *Standard* charged that eighty unoffending persons had been scourged, six murdered, including an infant in its cradle, and Wyatt Outlaw, a civil magistrate, violently seized and hanged in the Alamance courthouse square.[68] Earlier, Lt. Paul Hambrick of the United States Army had described the situation in Alamance, saying:

> The civil authorities are helpless—Squires Harding and Albright have arrested numbers and had them sent to Court, but yet not one of them was ever punished. They are now threatened with their lives, for their action and are now afraid to take any further action. After Wyatt Outlaw was murdered Henry A. Badham expressed himself rather freely about the affair and was set upon by Adolphus Moore, who is said to be a leader, badly beaten and leg broken and yet Moore is going at large. This man Moore said openly, that he was not afraid of Gov. Holden nor the Yankees, and now boldly proclaims that the men who reported the actions of the Klan to Gov. Holden will be summarily dealt with the moment the soldiers leave. What can you do for these suffering people, a part of whom are afraid to sleep at night in their own beds. Many of whom have not slept in their homes for two months.[69]

The Outlaw murder was the precipitating reason for Governor Holden's declaring Alamance County in a state of insurrection. This incident illustrates the deceptiveness of the Conservatives. On the night of 26 February 1870 a body of robed horsemen, estimated between seventy and one hundred, rode into Graham and took over the town. Outlaw was taken from his home and hanged in the courthouse square. The next morning Outlaw's body was discovered with a note pinned on it: "Beware you guilty both white and black."[70] On that same night the klansmen broke into the house of another black leader, Henry Holt, but fortunately he escaped capture. Unable to mete punishment to Holt, they warned his wife that if her husband did not leave town within a week they would return and hang him; soon after, Holt fled the county.[71]

The Outlaw lynching was covered up, and some Conservative newspapers published reports that the murder was a fabrication of the Republican mind. Some even attributed the act to local blacks, stating that Outlaw had committed adultery with a black woman and had also stolen funds from the Union League. But the real reason for the murder was the Klan's fear of his abilities and his demonstrated leadership among both blacks and whites. An industrious mechanic, he had become the leader among blacks as early as 1866, serving as president of the local Union League, promoter in the establishment of both a school and church for blacks, and town commissioner for two terms (once appointed by Governor Holden, but elected in his own right for the second term); with William A. Albright, he had been instrumental in placing the Republican party in control of town and county governments.[72]

Shortly before Christmas 1871, after Holden's impeachment and when order had been restored to the community, Judge Tourgée, while holding superior court trials in Graham, exploited a dispute between two klansmen and secured information that led to the arrest of klansmen involved in the Outlaw murder. Two of those arrested confessed, and many other culprits fled. The state's Conservative leaders became fearful that the truth might become known; George F. Bason, a prominent attorney and confessed klansman, even confided to William A. Graham, "Our worst fears are realized." Sixty-three indictments for felony were returned by a grand jury, but before the accused could be brought to trial, Conservatives had the General Assembly repeal the law under which most of the indictments had been secured and even granted amnesty to those involved.[73] Thus, Tourgée's efforts to uncover the Klan's activities in Alamance County were largely negated. The action of the General Assembly demonstrates that the Conservatives willingly used devious means (concealment, lies, and falsehoods) to disprove the large number of crimes committed by the Klan—all in the name of "good government" and "white supremacy."[74]

Col. George B. Bergen, Kirk's second in command, arrested the most active Klan leaders, including Adolphus G. Moore, James S. Scott, James E. Boyd, James Hunter, Deputy Sheriff John R. Ireland, and H. Scott.[75] They were brought before Kirk, who refused to grant bail and ordered them to Yanceyville, where the Caswell County courthouse was used as his official headquarters and jail. He had earlier written Holden, "I find the basement of the Ct House is a perfect fort—impregnable."[76] Bergen informed his prisoners that they were to be tried by a military commission, since the county had been declared in a state of insurrection and under military rule.[77]

On 17 July, Kirk was instructed by Governor Holden to send a detachment of thirty troops to Cleveland County; there they were to "keep an eye on Plato Durham" and maintain supervision of open and fair elections in Gaston, Lincoln, and Catawba counties.[78] Professor Hamilton stated that Holden wrote in longhand the instructions for the troop action in Cleveland County and that these instructions were never recorded in the governor's letter book.[79] Kirk's version was that the troops were sent "to assist the local authorities in holding the elections and in keeping the peace. All is going well."[80]

On the day following the Alamance arrests, a petition for a writ of habeas corpus was presented to Chief Justice Richmond M. Pearson seeking the prisoners' release or for a trial by civil court procedures. The counsel for Moore and the other defendants included some of the leading Conservative-Democratic attorneys in the state, William A. Graham, Thomas Bragg, Augustus S. Merrimon, E. S. Parker, and the law firm of William H. Battle and Sons. The speed of the legal action suggests that the lawyers had already planned their course of action and were merely waiting for a favorable moment to begin their defense of the Klan. Pearson granted the writ, but Kirk refused to recognize it, even directing the process server to return it to Raleigh. His reasoning was that a military commission had been appointed to try all prisoners taken by the state troops unless there were explicit orders from the governor to do otherwise.[81] Defense counsel next sought a writ of attachment against Kirk, with a posse comitatus to be used to force him to take the prisoners to Raleigh. But before the chief justice rendered a decision on the matter, Richard C. Badger, Holden's legal adviser, suggested to him that the governor might desire to be heard. Accordingly, Pearson wrote,

> I have the honor to enclose copies of our writs of *habeas corpus*—issued by me to Col. George W. Kirk, together with affidavits, setting out that Col. Kirk refused to make returns of the writs, and stated that he made the arrests by your order. As Col. Kirk does not make returns, I do not feel at liberty to assume the fact that he acted under your order, from the conversation set out in the affidavits. Please inform me if Col. Kirk acted under orders from you in making the arrests.[82]

Holden replied immediately, seeking to explain Kirk's refusal to obey the chief justice's writ:

> Col. Geo. W. Kirk made the arrests and now detains the prisoners named by my order. He was instructed firmly, but respectfully, to decline to deliver the prisoners. No one goes before me in respect to civil law, or for those whose duty it is to enforce it; but the conditions in Alamance County and some other parts of the State have been, and is

such that though reluctant to use the strong power vested in me by law, I have been forced to declare them in a state of insurrection.

For months past there has been maturing in those localities under the guidance of bad and disloyal men, a dangerous secret insurrection. I have invoked public opinion to aid in suppressing this treason. I have issued proclamation after proclamation to the people of the State to break up these unlawful combinations. I have brought to bear every civil power to restore peace and order, but all in vain! The constitution and laws of the United States and of this State are set at naught; the civil courts are no longer a protection of life, liberty and property; assassination and outrage go unpunished and the civil magistrates are intimidated and are afraid to perform their functions. To the majority of the people of these sections the approach of night is like death; the men dare not sleep beneath their roofs at night, but abandoning their wives and little ones wander in the woods until day.

Thus civil government was crumbling around me. I determined to nip this new treason in the bud.

By virtue of the power vested in me by the constitution and the laws and by that inherent right of self-preservation, which belongs to all governments, I have proclaimed the County of Alamance in a state of insurrection. Col. Geo. W. Kirk is commanding the military forces in that County, and made the arrests referred to in the writ of *habeas corpus*, and now detains the prisoners by my orders.

At this time I am satisfied that the public interests require that these military prisoners shall not be delivered up to the civil power.

I devoutly hope that the time may be short when a restoration of peace and order may release Alamance County from the presence of military force and the enforcement of military law. When that time shall arrive I shall promptly restore the civil power.[83]

On 19 July, Justice Pearson began hearings on the habeas corpus cases, with Badger representing the governor and the entire staff of the klansmen's counsel present, including Bartholomew F. Moore. The chief justice opened the hearings by raising four questions: (1) Did Kirk have any reasonable excuse to refuse to obey the writ? (2) Was there enough evidence to show an insurrection and the need to suspend the writ of habeas corpus? (3) If the writ was not suspended, would not an attachment produce a civil war? And (4), was the law of 1868–69, providing for an attachment on failure to make proper return of a writ of habeas corpus, in effect, subservient to the militia clause of the state constitution? If so, should not the writ be directed to the governor?

The counsel for the petitioners predicated their arguments on the proposition that a state of insurrection did not exist and that the constitutional rights of the prisoners were being violated by denying them the right of trial by jury. No attempt was made to show what action Governor Holden could have taken, or should have taken, to maintain civil law; it was stated that civil courts should have been relied upon, nothing else. Incidentally, two of the counselors, Thomas Bragg and William H. Battle, had not only endorsed the suspension of the writ of habeas corpus by the Confederate government during the war but had also held that at such time defendants were not entitled to due process.[84]

Badger, speaking for Governor Holden, argued that conditions were such that the governor was justified in declaring Alamance County in insurrection; that the state constitution empowered the governor to so act; and that once martial law had been declared, the writ of habeas corpus was suspended and the petitioners were not entitled to jury trial. Ironically, had the civil court process been used, the cases would have been tried in the court of superior court judge A. W. Tourgée, the leading carpetbagger on the state bench and a strong defender of the rights of blacks. For three years he had waged relentless war on the Klan movement, and it is doubtful that the petitioners would have received the type of "justice" they were now seeking from Chief Justice Pearson. This also explains why they did not follow regular legal procedures.

Holden immediately informed President Grant of the legal battle and requested additional federal troops for the state to back the cause:

> I have declared the counties of Alamance and Caswell . . . in a state of insurrection. . . . I have embodied a considerable number of the militia, and have made a number of important arrests. Four of the persons arrested have sued out writs of *habeas corpus*, and the matter has been argued for several days before Chief Justice Pearson. . . .
>
> I have no means of knowing, with certainty, what his decision will be, but I incline to the opinion that he will substantially sustain me. There are threats of resistance, whatever his opinion may be. Colonel Kirk . . . has 350 men, . . . but the Ku Klux Klan largely outnumber them in the counties referred to, and, if they should take the field and be joined by others from other counties, the State troops would certainly be in peril.
>
> I have in Raleigh one hundred colored troops, sixty white troops, and at Hillsborough fifty white troops, and in Gaston County one company of sixty. My whole available force is not more than six hundred.
>
> I think it very important that a regiment of Federal troops be at

once sent to this State, and that the Federal troops now here be ordered to come to my aid promptly. The defeat of the State and Federal troops in any conflict at this crisis would be exceedingly disastrous. It may be that the crisis will pass, and that I may be able to punish the guilty without encountering resistance. I have deemed it my duty in this emergency to acquaint you of the expedience of ordering that we be further aided and supported by Federal troops.[85]

President Grant replied two days later from his vacation in Long Beach, New Jersey, that he would have the secretary of war dispatch additional troops to North Carolina without delay and that "they may be used to suppress violence and maintain the law, if other means should fail."[86] The troops were sent forthwith, and a temporary military district was established under the command of Col. Henry J. Hunt.[87]

Earlier Josiah Turner had consulted with a number of Conservative leaders—Matt W. Ransom, Augustus Merrimon, former governor Thomas Bragg, among them—concerning the propriety of sending representatives to consult with the president about expressing opposition to Holden's action. The move was agreed upon and Ransom, Bedford Brown, and William Graham were chosen to make the appeal. Before plans were finalized, however, the group learned of Grant's plan to be on vacation. The decision then was for Bedford Brown to go alone to the White House; as he later reported, the president listened "attentively and courteously," but said that he had made up his mind as to affairs in Caswell and Alamance and that "any effort to remove [the troops] would be unavailing. . . . There is a marked difference between my view of constitutional liberty and those of the President."[88]

On 23 July, Justice Pearson delivered his opinion endorsing Governor Holden's action, although he declared that the writ of habeas corpus had not been suspended even though Alamance and Caswell counties were in a state of insurrection as the governor had proclaimed. He further stated that under the constitution and the Shoffner Militia Act the governor had the power "to take military possession, to order the arrest of all suspected persons, and to do all things necessary to suppress the insurrection, but . . . no power to disobey the writ of *habeas corpus*, or to make the trial of any citizens, otherwise than by jury."

He ruled that he could not issue a precept to the sheriffs of either county to bring the prisoners before him by a posse comitatus, because this would cause the sheriffs to summon insurgents or insurrectionists "to join in a conflict with the military forces of the State." Also, since the executive controlled the physical power of the state, while the power of the judiciary was only of a moral character (and not of such a nature as to precipitate a bloody conflict), the issue of a call for a posse comitatus from other counties would be resorting to illegal means, and he was unwilling to be the cause of another civil war. He concluded:

> The writ will be directed to the Marshall of the Supreme Court [David A. Wicker], with instruction to exhibit it, and a copy of this opinion to his Excellency the Governor. If he orders the petitioners to be discharged to the Marshall, well; if not, following the example of Chief Justice Taney, in Merryman's case, . . . I have discharged my duty; the power of the Judiciary is exhausted, and the responsibility must rest upon the Executive.[89]

Justice Pearson expressed himself further with a sharp criticism of the tactics of the petitioners' counsel, saying that their language was as strong as that used by Kirk in refusing to obey the writ. Pearson's refusal to precipitate civil strife was, undoubtedly, the correct stand to take and was even admitted indirectly by Professor Hamilton: "Several thousand citizens, so it is said, had volunteered for service on the *posse comitatus* and Kirk's force would have been overwhelmed."[90] It should be noted, however, that on the same day, 23 July, the chief justice issued additional writs to Colonel Kirk to deliver to him the other prisoners.

Holden's refusal to obey the writs led the opposition to charge that his primary purpose was to establish a military dictatorship, and the Pearson ruling convinced others that the judiciary was cooperating by its failure to enforce orders. Former governor Vance spoke of Pearson's conduct as being "more infamous than Holden's" and suggested that an appeal be made to the Supreme Court.[91] It should be noted that while the Pearson opinion was officially his own, he had the support of the other members of the court.[92]

The *Standard* reported that the Klan had decreed Holden's death as retaliation for his efforts to suppress it and that leading Conservative editors had been so advised. Would-be assassins had been spotted lurking around the governor's residence, it reported, and "had it not been for his friends, a vigilant police and his known personal courage, he would have been in his grave today."[93]

On 26 July, Holden officially replied to Pearson's decision, and his letter was read in court the following day. It read in part:

I have declared the counties of Alamance and Caswell in a state of insurrection, and have taken military possession of them. This your Honor admits I had the power to do "under the constitution and laws." And not only this, "but to do all things necessary to suppress the insurrection," including the power to "arrest all suspected persons" in the above-mentioned counties.

Your Honor has thought proper also to declare that the citizens of Alamance and Caswell are insurgents, as a result of the constitutional and lawful action of the Executive, and that therefore, you will not issue the writ for the production of the body of Moore to any of the men of the said counties; that the "*posse comitatus* must come from the county where the writ is to be executed," and that any other means would be illegal.

. . . I have reason to believe that the governments of the said counties have been mainly if not entirely in the hands of men who belong to the Ku Klux Klan, whose members have perpetrated the atrocities referred to; and that the county governments have not merely omitted to ferret out and bring to justice those of this Klan who have thus violated the law, but that they have actually shielded them from arrest and punishment. The State judicial power in said counties, . . . has not been able to bring criminals to justice; indeed, it is my opinion, based on facts that have come to my knowledge, that the life of the Judge whose duty it is to ride the circuit to which the said counties belong, has not been safe. . . .

Under these circumstances I would have been recreant to duty and faithless to my oath, if I had not exercised the power in the several counties which your Honor has been pleased to say I have exercised constitutionally and lawfully; especially as, since October, 1868, I have repeatedly by proclamation and by letters, invoked public opinion to repress these evils, and warned criminals and offenders against the laws of the fate that must in the end overtake them, if, under the auspices of the Klan referred to, they should persist in their course.

I beg to assure your Honor that no one subscribes more thoroughly than I do to the great principles of *habeas corpus* and trial by jury. Except in extreme cases, in which beyond all question "the safety of the State is the supreme law," these privileges of *habeas corpus* and trial by jury should be maintained.

I have already declared that, in my judgment, your Honor and all the other civil and judicial authorities are unable *at this time* to deal with the insurgents. The civil and the military are alike constitutional powers—the civil to protect life and property when it can, and the military only when the former has failed. As the Chief Executive, I seek to restore, not to subvert, the judicial power. Your Honor has done your duty, and in perfect harmony with you I seek to do mine.

It is not I nor the military power that has supplanted the civil authority; that has been done by the insurrection in the counties referred to. I do not see how I can restore the civil authority until I "suppress the insurrection," which your Honor declares I have the power to do; and I do not see how I can surrender the insurgents to the civil authority until that authority has been restored. It would be a mockery in me to declare that the civil authority was unable to protect the citizens against the insurgents, and then turn the insurgents over to the civil authority. My oath to support the Constitution makes it imperative on me to "suppress the insurrection" and restore the civil authority in the counties referred to, and this I must do. In doing this I renew to your Honor, expressions of my profound respect for the civil authority, and my earnest wish that this authority may soon be restored to every county and neighborhood in the State.[94]

It is not surprising that Holden refused to surrender the prisoners for civil trial; undoubtedly an understanding had been reached between the chief justice and the governor. Even so, the entire supreme court bench supported Pearson's decision.[95] Furthermore, Pearson advised the petitioners' counsel to apply to the United States Supreme Court for redress of grievances, but they declined to act. This advice might have been given to allow the United States court to intervene in the issue, thus preventing the governor from becoming further involved with the military. At least so thought the *Wilmington Journal* on 30 July:

It may, however, be . . . that Governor Holden begins to see that he has been duped; has been made to bear more than his share of the burden of the odium attaching to this plot; that he has been not only cheated out of his expected senatorial honors at the hands of the next Legislature, but that he has also rendered himself liable to impeachment and rejection from his present position. . . . It may be that the advice of the Chief Justice . . . if acted upon, will open the door for the escape of Governor Holden from the clutches of Senator Pool.

But the petitioners' counsel did not follow the chief justice's advice; instead, they renewed their efforts to secure an attachment against the governor or Colonel Kirk, thereby forcing them to bring the prisoners before the chief justice by means of a posse comitatus. Once again Pearson denied their motion. They then turned to superior court judge Anderson Mitchell; a writ was served, but Kirk destroyed it and continued to hold the prisoners at Yanceyville.

Meanwhile, Kirk's forces had gained absolute control of the two insurrectionary counties, but continued to be confronted by a determined foe. Kirk informed the governor that he had information regarding proposed Klan attacks on his forces, including the fact that two companies of kluxers were stationed within two miles of Yanceyville. Pink Graves, one of the leaders in the Caswell organization, had been arrested coming from Danville, Virginia, "with a view of being arrested—in order to give directions to other prisoners."[96] Unfortunately for Holden, such an open confrontation never took place. Had it occurred, President Grant would have found intervention with federal troops necessary, and the issue would have become a national problem. Under these circumstances, it is doubtful that the question of Holden's impeachment would have arisen.

As the governor had stated at the beginning of the Klan problem, he hoped to turn public opinion against the group by exposing its membership and atrocities. When James E. Boyd was arrested and taken to Yanceyville, he let it be known through William R. Albright that he was ready to make a public confession of his Klan membership. Kirk then escorted him to Raleigh for several interviews with Holden, after which his release was arranged on a $50,000 personal bond so that he could return and gather the necessary evidence exposing the Klan. On 30 July the *Standard* published a lengthy confession by Boyd and fifteen others who testified concerning their Klan membership and Klan operations.[97] Consternation spread rapidly, and several hundred young men hastily fled the state for "parts unknown"—but mainly to Texas. On 1 August, Boyd wrote that the disclosure was having the desired effect. Several prominent Democrats (not members of the Klan) had informed him that they would no longer support a party which expected to succeed by violence and crime, while others who had joined the Klan not knowing of its true intent were renouncing their membership and cooperating in the efforts to dismantle the organization.[98] Boyd further warned the governor that the *Raleigh Sentinel* and its editor were attempting to stir up excitement: "A respectable colored man who came up on the train Saturday evening informed me that he heard Jo. Turner say at Durham that the Ku Klux ought to hang Jim Boyd."

John A. Moore, former member of the house of commons from Alamance and Klan member, also confessed his Klan participation and stated that the Klan planned to assassinate T. M. Shoffner for introducing the militia law used against the Klan.[99]

The majority of the eighty-two arrested by Kirk's forces were members or supporters of the Klan. Among those arrested were several prominent Caswell citizens: for example, John Kerr and Samuel P. Hill, leading Yanceyville lawyers and former legislators; Dr. N. M. Roan; Felix Roan; Sheriff Jesse C. Griffith; and former sheriff Frank A. Wiley. No doubt the John Stephens murder was the principal reason the county had been placed under martial law, but those arrested resented being held as military prisoners. Also, the klansmen's pledge of silence prevented any confessions about the Stephens affair, despite the use of force in interrogating them. The Conservative press not only denied Klan participation in the crime but placed responsibility elsewhere. Judge Tourgée complained that the murder was "fully justified by every conservative,"[100] and the *Raleigh Sentinel*, on 27 July, headlined the question "Who Killed Stephens?" and then supplied these possible answers:

1. Did an old colored man from Caswell County come to Raleigh, sometime before John W. Stephens was murdered, to see Gov. Holden, and tell him how Stephens was trying to form a coalition with Conservatives to cut Wilson Carey out of nomination to the Legislature?

2. Did not the same old colored man tell the Governor that Stephens was doing the party great harm, and would break it down in that county?

3. Did the Governor tell the old colored man that the Republicans of Caswell must kill Stephens off?

4. Did the old colored man go home and repeat the Governor's words to a number of other colored men?

5. Did these colored men misunderstand the Governor's words, and act on them literally?

6. Will anyone dare deny that the old colored man in question came to Raleigh and went back and reported to the colored people that the Governor used the expression above?

The Conservatives repeatedly tried to attribute the Stephens murder to Republicans, no doubt to remove every trace of guilt from themselves. The *Sentinel* editorialized: "Henry the Second and Holden the First, raised each his obscure man to eminence and distinction. . . . We have no idea that Henry or Holden intended harm to Becket or Stephens. . . . We can't think that the negroes murdered Stephens because of any speech from the Governor. But rulers and great men should be careful how they talk."[101] Later, when evidence did link three of the arrested klansmen to the murder, the *Sentinel* indignantly declared: "We say positively, after having known Messrs. Wiley, Mitchell, and Roan for years, that they are as innocent of the charge of murdering Stephens as their children three years old. . . . It is high time that such men . . . who are above reproach among respectable men, should be free from the censures of those whose judgments are biased by political prejudice."[102]

Rule by martial law is never popular, and such was the case with Kirk's occupation of Yanceyville. The troops were accused of roaming the country-side, pillaging and insulting the civilian population. Lacking barracks and proper water facilities, they had set up camp around the courthouse square, and they were forced to dress and bathe in public view. This violated the local citizenry's sense of decency. It was claimed that it was unsafe for women to appear upon the streets for fear of suffering indignities; yet such concerns did not deter either the women or men from strolling around the square and gawking at the soldiers. At one time the troops threatened to "shoot up" the town or burn it, and Kirk himself was quoted as saying that he would person-ally shoot prisoners if any attempt was made to free them.[103]

Such bold pronouncements led J. H. Mills, editor of the *Biblical Re-corder*, to write Governor Holden that the Beulah Baptist Association had planned to hold its convention in Yanceyville, but the moderator feared that the troops might disrupt the meeting. Holden replied immediately that while it might be unpleasant to hold the convention in an "occupied village," he felt certain that the troops would give protection to the association.[104]

Yet, despite these protests, local citizens were to retaliate. One of the more insidious forms of resistance, and one especially harmful to the black population, was the practice of the local farmers to dismiss or refuse to pay wages to workers who were sympathetic to the occupation. Violence was also threatened against those blacks who proposed to vote in the upcoming state elections. When Kirk informed the governor of such intimidation, Holden replied that he knew of no remedy except congressional enforcement of the Fifteenth Amendment. He promised that as soon as the election was over, he would request an investigation by the federal marshal, and if the accusations were true and the farmers were attempting to prevent blacks from voting, action would be taken.[105]

The worst charge lodged against Kirk's troops was that they used brutal force while interrogating prisoners for confessions. For example, a noose was placed around the neck of Lucien Murray and he was suspended until he was unconscious. Likewise, William Patton was drawn up until he fainted, then was tied up for the remainder of the night. George S. Rogers was also hanged by the neck for some time. When informed that such methods were being used, Holden wrote that such practices must be stopped immediately. "Evidence obtained in this way is worthless. All prisoners, no matter how guilty they may supposed to be, should be treated humanely."[106] The governor also sent for Patton, who reported immediately, unescorted, and, in the governor's words, "I directed him to stop at the National Hotel, which he did, remaining a day or two, I paying the bill out of my private pocket. He told me all about it. He was much frightened, but not hurt in his person."[107]

The rough tactics failed, for the klansmen either maintained silence or denied any knowledge of the crimes. They later lied under oath during the Holden impeachment trial, and leading Conservatives supported their lies. Ironically, the person most punished during the entire ordeal was not a klansman or one arrested by the state troops but Col. George Bergen. He was imprisoned for some ninety-four days for permitting such rough tactics on the prisoners, although he was later released to go to Washington, where he found safety from Democratic revenge.

The Kirk-Holden War led to many charges against Holden—brutal treatment of prisoners, militarism, humiliation of prisoners and the civilian population, and affronts to civil law and order—but in reality it was a moderate affair. There was troop misbehavior, but in light of the atrocities committed by the Klan, it is surprising that no blood was shed and not one life lost. Holden had tackled an unpopular, impossible problem while managing to keep it within bounds. The governor's mistake was in seeking legal rights and justice for *all*, while his opposition sought power and privileges for themselves only.

Holden's purpose in using military troops had been not only to suppress the Klan organization but also to ensure open elections throughout the state. The 1870 elections were vital to the contending political factions. Thus, while Kirk established military rule in Alamance and Caswell, Holden was making plans for policing other trouble spots and seeking to prevent open confrontation between the Klan and Union League. Troops were dispatched to Shelby and Asheville to circulate through the mountain counties, while Colonel Clarke sent part of his troops to Chapel Hill, Hillsborough, and Carthage.

To the credit of all, the election was conducted without violence anywhere in the state. The results, however, were not what Holden and the Republicans expected. They had entered the contest confident of victory, but the Conservatives swept the state, electing the attorney general (the only statewide race), filling five of the seven congressional seats, and gaining undisputed control of the General Assembly.[108] There is little doubt that the Conservative victory reflects determined resistance to Holden's use of troops and opposition to black suffrage, as well as the growing disclosures of legislative corruption and new tax burdens. At no time in the campaign did Democratic leaders or candidates denounce the Klan; in fact, as stated earlier, they openly abetted it. Holden, as the state's Republican leader, had to bear the blame for the unsettled conditions. The *Sentinel* commented, "As for Holden, he is simply a demagogue, trickster, and political desperado. A blatant secessionist when secession was uppermost, he is just the style of man to persecute with rabid vindictiveness not only his secession neighbors, but all Republicans who oppose his oppressive reign."[109]

On the day after the elections and before the Conservatives learned of their victory, Governor Holden made the worst blunder of his political career: he ordered the arrest of Josiah Turner, Jr., the irascible editor of the *Raleigh Sentinel.* Turner had always been sharply critical of Holden's provisional governorship and his incumbent administration, but Holden's use of the military caused Turner to decide that the only solution was to wrest political control from the Republican party and to return the state government to white supremacy rule. Turner had long been suspected of belonging to the Klan, even of being "King of the Ku Klux." Throughout the 1870 campaign he had toured the state inciting clashes between the militia and local citizens, advocating resistance to state laws, and accusing the governor, because of his use of state troops, of conspiring to overthrow the legal government.

On several occasions, Turner had openly dared the governor to arrest him. In July he violently complained,

> The devil incarnate . . . cannot and shall not threaten through his son our arrest. . . . This wicked rascal, who, through his Railroad Presidents has wronged, robbed, despoiled, and plundered the people shall be told of it. Grant and his grand army of the Potomac cannot silence us or shut the complaining mouths of the hundred thousand taxpayers of the State who are groaning under the burden, oppression, and insult that have been heaped upon them.[110]

On 2 August, Turner from his home in Hillsborough telegraphed an editorial to the *Sentinel* captioned (Holden) LIES LIKE A THIEF, and exclaiming: "The Governor has been lying on us for twelve months; his profligate son and organ lies on us to-day by calling us a Ku Klux. If we are, why don't the pumpkin-faced rascal arrest us? We defy and dare him to arrest." The following day Turner continued the attack:

TO GOVERNOR HOLDEN

Gov. Holden: You say you will handle us in due time. You white-livered miscreant, do it now. You dared me to resist you; I dare you to arrest me. I am here to protect my family; the jacobins of your club, after shooting powder in the face of Mrs. Turner, threw a five-pound rock in her window, which struck near one of my children. Your ignorant jacobins are incited to this by your lying charges against me that I am King of the Ku Klux. You villain, come and arrest a man, and order your secret clubs not to molest women and children.

Yours with contempt and defiance—*habeas corpus* or no *habeas corpus*.[111]

Such open defiance was too much, even for a former editor who had willingly taken on all opponents without flinching. The decision to order Turner's arrest was not an easy one; Holden understood that it could open the floodgate of Conservative opposition, leading to a major confrontation. After the editorials, Turner remained in Hillsborough, claiming he did so to protect his family from further assaults; but his real reason was to keep in close touch with William A. Graham, an ally in the entire affair. With luck he thought he might force the governor to place Orange County under military occupation, knowing this would lead to a legal and military confrontation. He hoped this would cause Holden's demise and also that of the Republican party.

Holden always denied giving the order for Turner's arrest. Neither his official nor his private papers, both carefully preserved, contain any such order. Yet it is highly unlikely that the arrest would have taken place without his tacit approval. Holden's defenders claimed that the arrest was made in his name, but without specific instructions from him. This version is substantiated by a fragment of a letter to Holden from Richard T. Berry, brigadier general of the Fourth Brigade of the state militia:

I was in Yanceyville the day Turner was arrested. Col. Kirk & myself were talking about the propriety of arresting Turner. [He] asked me if I had ever heard you say you would have him arrested. I told him I had not. He stated to me that if Jos. Turner was to be arrested he preferred attending to it himself—that he feared Bergin would exercise too much cruelty and to my surprise spoke of several indiscretions Bergin had been guilty of and requested me to say to you that if you wanted Turner arrested he wanted you to write to him about the matter, so that he could attend to it. On the next morning I left Col. Kirk and started for Co. Shops. You may judge of my surprise on meeting Turner a prisoner about two miles from Yanceyville. I was sure the arrest was at least with the knowledge of Kirk and of course felt some anxiety to know who ordered him arrested. Soon after my arrival that afternoon at the Co. Shops I went to see Bergin and asked him if you ordered the arrest of Turner. His reply was By God No I did it myself. I knew Holden wanted it done, and didn't have the nerve to say so. So I ordered Lt. Hunnycut & several men to go and do it, and he closed by saying tell Holden if he wants Bragg, Graham, or Vance arrested just say the word. I felt at that time a little glad to hear his statement on your account because I regretted the arrest of Turner.[112]

Regardless of who gave the order, the *Sentinel*'s editor was placed under arrest by Colonel Bergen on 5 August. He was then taken to Company Shops and later to Yanceyville, where he was confined in the same courthouse room where John W. Stephens had been murdered. During this detention, Turner thoroughly enjoyed his martyrdom. Earlier, he had written in the *Sentinel* that he intended to "preserve his personal freedom or perish with it." Now from "Holden's Basteil [*sic*]," as he called the Yanceyville jail, he wrote his wife, "I am happily situated in this fight between the Klan and League."[113] He also wrote on the prison walls: "Armed violence with lawless might around and hallowed by the name of right," and "The love of liberty with life is given, and life itself the inferior gift of Heaven." Both were signed, "Josiah Turner, Jr., Prisoner. July, 1870."[114]

Certainly not all Republicans were happy with Turner's arrest and confinement. Professor Hamilton demonstrates this displeasure by quoting an interview with Ceburn L. Harris in 1906:

> Colonel C. L. Harris . . . told [me] in 1906 that he heard on the morning of August 5 that the order had been given and, although he and Holden had not spoken for a year, he went at once to the latter's office to be greeted with the question. "What in h—l are you doing here?" Harris replied, "Governor Holden, is it true that you have ordered Turner's arrest?" Holden then said, "It is none of your d—d business, but I have ordered it." Harris said, "Governor, for God's sake, for your own sake, for the sake of the Republican party, don't do it. It will ruin everything." The interview was closed by the governor's ordering Harris to leave the office.[115]

While there can be no doubt about the agitation over the Turner arrest, Holden's words in the above interview are totally out of character. He was not one to curse or use foul language, and he was generally known for his courteous conduct. To order someone out of his office was not his style, even in dealing with political enemies.

Contrary to his claims of being maltreated during his detention, Turner received numerous privileges not usually accorded prisoners.[116] He was permitted a visit from his wife, and Kirk offered him permission to write for the *Sentinel* as long as he did not arouse further agitation against the state government. To this, Turner replied that he would not write anything, as Kirk informed the governor, "unless he got to tell how mean you [were] and how you are trying to run the country."[117]

Consternation over the Kirk-Holden War was not confined to North Carolina. The New York press devoted considerable attention to it, and as expected, the press coverage was partisan. The *New York Times*, 2 August, editorialized: "At an earlier stage they [the Conservative North Carolina newspapers] suggested a contest between the local Executive and the enemies of law in limited portions of the State. They now exhibit the Governor as the enemy of law, and as the arbitrary, unrestrained, military ruler of a State in which civil authority should be supreme." However, the *New York Herald* declared on 1 August: "If the charges set forth by these men [James E. Boyd and other Klan confessees] are true Governor Holden is right in the course he has been pursuing. When it comes to a war between the constitutional powers and an anarchical and bloody-minded mob, as this Ku Klux Klan has all along shown itself to be, there can be no question as to which is the right." On 3 August the *New York Tribune* printed a long, impassioned, but essentially accurate, letter from Judge Tourgée to Senator Abbott describing the Klan's activities within his judicial district.[118]

With the "King of the Ku Klux" Turner in the Yanceyville "Basteil" and published confessions of some klansmen, the state's Conservative leaders were forced to change their strategy if they were to secure the release of those held in detention and halt military rule. Having failed in their appeals to the superior and supreme courts of the state, the counsel turned to George Washington Brooks, judge of the United States District Court in Salisbury, petitioning him to take jurisdiction over the case on grounds that the constitutional rights of the prisoners were being violated.

There was doubt as to whether Brooks would be willing to hear their appeal, since it was considered strictly a state matter. There was also Brooks's political background. He was a former Whig, and he had been a strong Unionist and supporter of Holden during the war. Moreover, he had received his appointment to the federal bench on Holden's recommendation. After hearing the legal pleas and striking that part of the petition alluding to the state courts, however, Brooks decided that he did have jurisdiction. His reasoning was based on that portion of the Fourteenth Amendment that declares, "Nor shall any State deprive any person of life, liberty, or property, without due process of law," and the Habeas Corpus Act of 5 February 1867. The Habeas Corpus Act gave federal judges the right to issue writs of habeas corpus in cases where the constitutional liberties of persons might be restrained.[119]

Accordingly, on 6 August, Judge Brooks ordered Kirk to present the prisoners to him immediately. This ruling came like a clap of thunder, for members of the Holden administration had thought that as long as they had the support of the Grant administration, no other branch of the federal government would intervene. The governor telegraphed the president the next day.

> I deny his [Brooks's] right to interfere with the local laws in murder cases. I hold these persons under our State laws, and under the decision of our Supreme Court Judges who have jurisdiction of the whole matter, and it is known to Judge Brooks, in what manner or by what tribunal the prisoners will be examined or tried.
>
> The officer [Kirk] will be directed to reply to the writ that he holds the prisoners under my order, and that he refuses to obey the writ. If the Marshall shall then call on the *posse comitatus*, there may be a conflict; but if he should call on the federal troops it will be for you to say whether the troops shall be used to take the prisoners out of my hands.
>
> It is my purpose to detain the prisoners, unless the army of the United States, under your orders, shall demand them.
>
> An early answer is respectfully requested.[120]

Governor Holden wanted the president's authorization to refuse to surrender the prisoners to Judge Brooks. More than that, his letter suggested a way out of the dilemma of noncompliance with a federal order. If President Grant would order the intervention of federal troops, it would relieve him, while at the same time law and order could be maintained and the war against the Klan could continue. The idea was immediately endorsed by the *Standard*, saying that "the Governor will not recede until the federal army is used against him; and the federal army will not be used against him."[121]

In his role as a general, Grant might have rushed unhesitatingly to the support of Governor Holden, but as president, he felt constrained to seek legal advice from Attorney General Amos Ackerman and Secretary of War William W. Belknap as to the scope of the Habeas Corpus Act of 1867. Ackerman immediately advised Holden that Judge Brooks had the right to issue his order under the act, but should it be proved on trial that the arrests had been made under lawful state authority, the judge would have to remand the prisoners. He further stated that in determining whether or not the North Carolina laws authorized the arrests, Brooks should respect the decision of Justice Pearson of the state supreme court. Ackerman closed his opinion by saying, "I advise that the State authorities yield to the United States Judiciary."[122]

Holden was now confronted with the problem of changing strategy. He dared not ignore Attorney General Ackerman's advice and have Kirk refuse release of the prisoners, since that would have forced the president to withdraw federal support. Nor could he count on a favorable decision from Judge Brooks. If Brooks decided that the prisoners were being held illegally and released them, the entire fight against the Klan would totally collapse. Thus, after hurried consultations with his military and legal advisers, the governor decided that it would be wise to obey Justice Pearson's writ, avoiding what could be an unfavorable decision from Judge Brooks. Pearson, however, was vacationing at his home in Richmond Hill and was not available for court duty in Raleigh. There was no question about Pearson's willingness to cooperate with Holden, for he had informed James M. McCorkle, a prominent Salisbury attorney, that he did not think Judge Brooks had proper jurisdiction in the matter and that he was ready to go to Raleigh whenever requested by the governor.[123]

The administration also thought it advisable to move Kirk's headquarters from Yanceyville to Company Shops, where Holden thought a better climate for prisoner interrogation might be obtained. Kirk was ordered to parole all prisoners in whose honor he could confide and have them report to him at Company Shops at ten o'clock on the morning of 15 August. He was also instructed to leave one hundred handpicked men at Yanceyville and to take "*special care* that all prisoners are not maltreated or abused."[124] The governor continued to take precautions to see that the troops conducted themselves properly. When Thomas M. Holt, a Graham merchant, complained that he was apprehensive about his property being damaged, Holden wrote Kirk, instructing him "to be vigilant to see that no injury is done to his [Holt's] property. Those who break the law should be arrested and punished, and those who are not charged with crime should be protected in their persons and property."[125]

J. R. Bulla, a strong Unionist and Republican leader of Asheboro, and Judge Tourgée were requested to conduct the interrogations at Company Shops, thereby guaranteeing the prisoners' legal rights. Unfortunately, neither man was able to perform his assigned duty—Tourgée had official court duties elsewhere, and Bulla did not receive his letter of request because of poor mail service.[126]

On 15 August, Governor Holden dispatched John B. Neathery, his private secretary, to Richmond Hill requesting the chief justice to return to Raleigh so that Kirk might obey the order of 6 August. He wrote Pearson as follows:

> In my answer to the notices served upon me . . . in the matter of Adolphus G. Moore, and others, *ex parte*, I stated . . . at that time the public interests forbade me to permit Col. Geo. W. Kirk to bring before Your Honor the said parties; at the same time I assured Your Honor that as soon as the safety of the State should justify it, I would cheerfully restore the civil power, and cause the said parties to be brought before you. . . .
>
> That time has arrived, and I have ordered Col. Geo. W. Kirk to obey the writs of *habeas corpus* issued by Your Honor. As the number of prisoners and witnesses is considerable, I would suggest to Your Honor that it would be more convenient to make return to the writs at the Capitol in Raleigh. Col. Kirk is prepared to make such return as soon as Your Honor shall arrive in Raleigh.[127]

The chief justice gave his immediate consent to the resumption of hearings, and by 18 August he was back in his chambers in the Capitol. Pearson notified Holden that he would be in the supreme court room at the specified time, but disclaimed any responsibility for the delay in court action. "The entire responsibility rests on you. I was unwilling to plunge the State into a Civil War, upon a mere question of time."[128] Realizing that legal difficulties might arise, Pearson requested the governor to have the other supreme court justices participate in the hearings. Holden complied with this request, but they declined to intervene. Justice William B. Rodman informed Holden that "to go to Raleigh now would greatly interfere with the arrangements I have made for the next few weeks." His real reasoning, of course, was that since Pearson had acted alone in the original suit, he should continue to act alone. "It seems to me that the petitioners would have a right to complain of any interference of his associates in a jurisdiction which by their choice they have conferred on him alone."[129] By such reasoning, Rodman was showing his displeasure with the petitioners' counsel for seeking redress solely through the chief justice, and not with Holden or Pearson personally.

Meanwhile, Richard Badger had been dispatched to Salisbury to prepare for the Brooks hearing. The firm of Nathaniel Boyden and W. H. Bailey was employed to conduct the state's case, but after consultation Holden was advised that the Pearson proceedings should begin before Judge Brooks began his. In this way, the claim could be made that the petitioners were before Pearson and therefore out of Brooks's jurisdiction. W. A. Smith, North Carolina Railroad Company president, arranged a special train to take Bergen and the original defendants to Raleigh, while Kirk made plans to transport the remaining prisoners to Salisbury.

On Thursday, 18 August, A. G. Moore and the other original petitioners appeared before Justice Pearson. Attorney General Lewis P. Olds appeared for the state, while Kemp P. Battle, R. H. Battle, and Charles S. Winstead acted on behalf of the prisoners. When the chief justice opened court, Battle moved to withdraw the petitions of habeas corpus on grounds that similar writs had been obtained from Judge Brooks since Justice Pearson had declared his power "exhausted" when Holden and Colonel Kirk had refused to obey the original writs. After hearing the arguments, court was recessed, and on the following day the chief justice agreed to permit the withdrawal of the applications.[130]

Immediately, Attorney General Olds applied for bench warrants against Moore, G. T. Mitchell, Joseph R. Fowler, Samuel P. Hill, Frank A. Wiley, Felix Roan, and L. M. Totten for complicity in the Stephens murder and for conspiracy in Klan activities. The petitioners' counsel resisted this move on the grounds that insufficient evidence had been presented to the court, whereupon the chief justice delayed ruling on the issue until 22 August. All except three (Wiley, Mitchell, and Felix Roan) were immediately discharged, while the three were placed on bail. Later they too were discharged for lack of evidence, the state being unable to disprove the klansmen's alibis.

Pearson's actions changed the whole nature of the legality of the Kirk-Holden War. He would not permit the presentation of any evidence concerning the legality of Governor Holden's action against Alamance and Caswell counties or of the method by which the military forces had been organized. These two important issues were never adjudicated. More than that, Pearson's ruling that permitted the withdrawal of the defendant's applications for writs of habeas corpus was a major disappointment, seriously damaging Holden's defense later in the impeachment trial. He had expected the proceedings to provide him the opportunity of proving the need for military rule, as well as its legality; in addition, he had hoped to use the intervening time to crush the Klan movement entirely. A sympathetic court, he thought, would have enabled him to achieve both objectives. Now the state had been restricted from showing probable cause for the klansmen's participation in the Stephens murder.

Governor Holden expected the habeas corpus case to develop into a ma-

jor legal battle, with the state pitted against the best legal minds of the Conservative-Democratic ranks. Ever the wary operator and unwilling to take
chances with loose court procedures, the governor sought the services of
Rollin Stewart, a nationally known court reporter of New York City. This
decision undoubtedly was made to insure that all records were kept in strict
adherence to proper legal standards in view of a possible appeal to the United
States Supreme Court should Justice Pearson render an unfavorable decision.
Stewart, however, was unavailable, and W. H. Finch of New Bern was
employed.[131]

Judge Brooks opened court in his chambers on 18 August, but delayed
hearing arguments to give Kirk an extra day to transport the prisoners to
Salisbury. Badger, Holden's legal adviser, had been apprehensive concerning
Kirk's arrival on the appointed day, even imploring the governor to make
certain that Kirk realized the importance of this. Failure to do so, he warned,
might turn the judge's wrath against the state, thereby forfeiting any hope of
success in the trial. He also advised the governor that his private messages to
Raleigh were known within half an hour, saying, "Be cautious in the use of
language in matters important. There is a leak somewhere."[132] Even so,
Badger felt confident of the outcome of the case and the governor's chances to
continue his battle against the Klan.

Hearings began before Judge Brooks on Monday, 22 August. Attorney
General Olds, J. M. McCorkle, and W. H. Bailey appeared on behalf of the
state, while William A. Graham, Augustus S. Merrimon, and R. H. Battle,
Jr., represented the prisoners. Two days were spent arguing over the jurisdiction of the court and the merits of the case, yet not one word of testimony was
permitted to prove the guilt or innocence of those being tried; nor did the judge
make any effort to investigate the cause of their arrest. Instead, Judge Brooks
ordered the prisoners discharged immediately for "want of evidential proof."

He also refused the state's efforts to delay a final ruling in order to give
Kirk time to subpoena witnesses. The flaw in the state's case was that Kirk had
not been instructed to bring the witnesses to Salisbury. The counsel had
assumed that the trial would be of a preliminary nature to show just cause and
that the state would have sufficient time to produce witnesses. It is likely that
the only way that witnesses could have been produced would have been by
arrest by Kirk; the witnesses against the klansmen would certainly not have
cooperated voluntarily. For discharging the prisoners, Judge Brooks received
the plaudits of Conservative leaders as well as of the state's newspapers, where
he was hailed as a restorer of constitutional government. Only a few years
earlier he had been denounced as a "scalawag" because he had cooperated with

the Republican party. Moreover, he had perjured himself by subscribing to the ironclad oath of never having engaged in insurrection against the United States or given aid or comfort to the enemies thereof; actually he had served in the Confederate army. He had been permitted to subscribe to the oath in order to keep his federal judgeship.

The Conservative counsel was not content with its victory in gaining the prisoners' discharges. They wanted revenge, and they sought the arrests of Kirk, Bergen, and other officers of the state troops, whom they charged with illegal arrests, brutality to prisoners, and threats of the overthrow of civil government. Judge Brooks agreed to hear their pleas, but transferred the trial to Raleigh in order to expedite the proceedings. Oral hearings began on 25 August, with Graham and Merrimon arguing that Chief Justice Pearson's original proceedings had been highly irregular, that Kirk had refused to obey the writs of habeas corpus, and that irreparable harm had been done against those arrested. J. M. McCorkle, representing Kirk and Bergen, sufficiently proved to Judge Brooks that no lasting harm had been done to the prisoners and that civil law still prevailed, since the prisoners were no longer under military custody. The motions of Graham and Merrimon were denied.[133]

Upon release, most of the prisoners returned to their homes on the night train of the North Carolina Railroad on 19 August. Since their discharge had been given prior to the announcement by Chief Justice Pearson of his opinion, the Conservative press expressed some concern that it was done to permit the Holden administration to rearrest the former klansmen and turn them over to the chief justice to face trial for complicity in the numerous Klan outrages.[134] If true, it was quickly dropped, for Pearson released all but three of the prisoners for lack of evidence.

Josiah Turner, Jr., returned to Raleigh on Thursday, 25 August, amid a tumultuous celebration. A parade was arranged in his honor (the *Sentinel* issue of 23 August had requested the ladies of Raleigh to furnish flowers to decorate the carriages), and he was escorted from the train station to the Yarborough House, where he was serenaded. While one of the speakers was making a partisan address, a Lieutenant Deevers, one of Kirk's officers, shouted a protest, "Hurrah for Holden and Kirk," jeopardizing his own life as shots were fired at him between Salisbury and McDowell streets. Later, Turner's supporters fired into the camp of the state troopers, which the *Sentinel* explained as shots merely fired for fun or the excitement of the hour.[135] Nevertheless, evidence of such bad feelings demonstrated the need for the presence of the troops in Raleigh and elsewhere in the state.

The Conservative counsel, despite its success in the courts of both Pearson and Brooks, continued legal maneuvers in an effort to vindicate the Klan and discredit Governor Holden. R. M. Allison of Iredell County filed a petition with superior court judge Anderson Mitchell which resulted in the justice issuing an injunction against Treasurer David A. Jenkins, paymaster, that forbade him to pay the troops for their services. The governor evaded the injunction by replacing Jenkins with John B. Neathery, allowing him to withdraw sufficient funds from the treasury to make the payments. The troops were officially mustered out of the state service on 21 September, but it was not until 10 November that Holden issued a proclamation declaring the Alamance and Caswell insurrections at an end. The cost of the military action amounted to $74,367.70, divided as follows: rations, $14,409.61; transportation, $10,775.60; pay, $49,182.49.[136] This does not include $22,652.10 for clothing and equipment secured from the federal depot at Fort Monroe, which was never repaid.

On 1 September, Turner applied to supreme court justices Dick and Settle for arrest warrants against Holden, Kirk, Bergen, Lt. John Hunnicut (the officer who had actually placed Turner under arrest), and Alex Ruffin, a black member of the militia. When Dick and Settle refused to issue the warrants, Turner then appealed to justices Reade and Rodman of the supreme court and to superior court justices Watts, Thomas, Tourgée, Cloud, Henry, and Jones, who also refused to issue the warrants. He then sued the governor for $3,000 on an assault and battery charge (a grand jury in Orange County found a true bill against Holden), but when a court order was sent to Wake County Sheriff Tim Lee for the governor's arrest, Lee refused to enforce the order and the matter was dropped.[137] However, Judge Brooks did issue a bench warrant for Bergen on charges of excessive brutality, and he was required to stand trial. Later, Kirk was arrested by the United States marshal at Company Shops, and he too was imprisoned, but this was by arrangement of Governor Holden in order that he not be forced to stand trial in a state court.

Realizing that an impartial trial for the accused officers could not be held in Raleigh because of the highly emotional atmosphere, Holden appealed to Judge Hugh L. Bond, United States Circuit Court of Appeals of Maryland (but who had jurisdiction over the state), to take jurisdiction over the Bergen and Kirk cases.[138] Judge Bond had been appointed to the federal bench by President Grant because of his known opposition to the Klan. Thus it was thought that he would be inclined to look with more favor on Holden's use of troops. Bond made his appearance in Raleigh in September, staying at the National Hotel, and after hearing Holden's presentment agreed to take jurisdiction of the cases. Kirk was paroled to the United States marshal, while Bergen remained in jail, no doubt owing to the governor's unwillingness to sanction his use of force in attempting to force confessions from the klansmen.[139]

After the hearings, Bond overruled Judge Brooks and in early October ordered Bergen's release for insufficient evidence; however, to give credence to his decision, it was not announced until 24 November, when the Court of Appeals was in session in Raleigh. Both Kirk and Bergen, with the aid of Wake County Sheriff Tim Lee, secretly made their escape to Washington, D.C., where they were given protection by national authorities. Kirk found employment as a Capitol policeman, and Bergen was given an appointment as consul to Pernambuco, Brazil—an appointment later withdrawn at Holden's request. Turner followed the men to Washington and sought their arrest to stand trial in North Carolina, but this attempt was unsuccessful.[140] Thus the ill-fated Kirk-Holden War was finally ended.

NINE

Impeachment and Removal from Office

The Republican defeat in the August 1870 election came as a complete surprise to Republican and Conservative leaders alike. Few Conservatives had dared hope for victory, much less such a decided one. They were also surprised, but delighted, by the failure of President Grant and the federal army to sustain Holden's use of military troops; once the issue had been placed before the courts, Grant seemingly lost all interest and stopped further support. It did not take long for Governor Holden to realize that his personal and administrative future was his sole responsibility, that his fate rested on his own shoulders. As soon as the results of the August election were made public, the Conservative press immediately demanded the impeachment of the governor. The *Tarboro Southerner* led the drive. "He is the vilest man that ever polluted a public office and his crimes are crying in trumpet tones against him. Impeach the Traitor, the Apostate, and the Renegade, and drive him into the infamous oblivion which is so justly his due."[1] The *Hillsborough Recorder* continued the attack:

> We don't think it good policy to impeach Governor Holden. . . . [He] has been called by some of the press and the people a thief—a liar—a perjured scoundrel—a drunkard—a rioter and assassin. If two-thirds of the Legislature—yes—if a single man—believe these charges true they should "go for" Gov. Holden and move to impeach him right off— policy or no policy. If they don't do it why then they will confess to the world that they are either false or afraid and from either catagory of liars or cowards may God deliver us.[2]

There was talk also of impeaching Chief Justice Pearson and two other members of the supreme court because of their lack of support in the Conservatives' legal battles. However, this plan was dropped, since there were no grounds for conviction other than for "acts of omission." Nevertheless, Pearson employed Thomas C. Fuller to serve as his counsel in the event that impeachment charges were later drafted against him. At the January 1871 term of the supreme court he presented an elaborate defense of his actions.[3] The chief justice was likely spared this indignity because of his influence and the high regard in which he was held by members of the state bar. Also, many legislators thought it impolitic to make too clean a sweep.[4]

Senator John Pool was thoroughly denounced for his role in promoting the use of state troops, but since he was serving in the Senate and beyond the reach of the General Assembly (as far as impeachment was concerned), no serious effort was made against him. The *Wilmington Journal* wrote on 5 November 1870: "If there had been honor among villains generally, as there is said to be among thieves, Chief Justice Pearson and Senator John Pool would not have allowed Governor Holden to bear alone the brunt of the defeat of the late battle . . . in which they had made common cause."

In pressing their demand for impeachment, the Conservatives thought that if they could depose the governor, the "Captain General," the entire Republican regime would topple. They also knew the governor to be too uncompromising to avoid a fight, while too strong to be coerced into governing according to their intentions.[5] The Conservatives justified their call for impeachment by pointing out the alleged excesses of the Kirk-Holden War, along with charges of corruption, extravagance, and ignorance, but their major grievance against Holden was his and the Republican party's assault on white supremacy. While the Conservatives generally conceded that Holden's administration had not seriously threatened the whites' traditional social and economic rule, they could not accept the administration's efforts to guarantee political equality to the blacks. Even if Holden's administration had achieved success in restoring economic stability and popular self-rule, the Conservatives would never have permitted its recognition. Intolerance was the well-spring of Conservative strategy.

Once again, in autumn of 1870, Holden's political acumen alerted him to the gravity of the problem. Long before the General Assembly was scheduled to meet in regular session in November, the governor launched his counteroffensive. On 30 September he issued a general circular to all county sheriffs and other leading officials asking that they report the following information:

> 1st. How many persons have been murdered in your County during the last two years, by disguised persons or the Ku Klux?
> 2nd. How many have been shot?
> 3rd. How many have been whipped?
> 4th. How many have been mutilated, or otherwise been burned?[6]

At the same time he utilized the *Standard*, now under the ownership of W. A. Smith but temporarily edited by S. S. Ashley, in an attempt to ward off impeachment threats. No doubt the following editorial of 11 October 1870 had his approval in formulating his strategy:

> A few months ago the State was torn with internal dissensions. Bands of men, masked and armed, rose throughout fields and forests. They swept through our villages and rent the night with savage outcries. They held midnight gatherings in the woods, and pledged themselves to hostility to the colored race and to the Republican party, with blasphemous oaths, accompanied by circumstances of unutterable horror and "beyond belief."
>
> And their oaths, thus taken, they executed. No conscience, no fear of Almighty God, no human compassion, no terrors of civil law, no outraged public sentiment, not even the shrieks of unoffending womanhood nor the death agonies of innocent men withheld them from the consummation of their deeds of violence and blood. Men high in the public esteem as the standard of intelligence and honor in the Conservative party looked on and were silent, or gave a quasi approbation by styling these execrable deeds "a species of wild justice."
>
> The local authorities were also silent and powerless. The strong arm of the Federal Government failed to protect the peace. . . .
>
> One man held the power to crush these crimes, and that man was the Governor. . . . He did use the power entrusted to him by the Constitution. He proclaimed an insurrection. . . . He called out the militia by virtue of his power as Chief Executive. And where before there was terror, disorder and crime, there now is security, order and peace.
>
> . . . The more honor is due to Gov. Holden for his unflinching discharge of his duty. The more honor is due Chief Justice Pearson, who, threatened with assassination, and traduced and slandered by malicious tongues gave judgment according to law and evidence. The more honor is due to his able and upright Associates, Justices Dick and Settle.
>
> And here we are happy to do justice to the leading democratic journal in the State. It frankly acknowledged the existence of these outrages. In its issue of the 3d, it says: "It is, however, palpable, that disguised persons have gone through different sections to scare people, and in some cases it is charged, to commit crimes."
>
> Its unwillingness to have the Conservative party held responsible

for these crimes is quite natural. Candor compels us to confess that it seems to us that the Conservative party was so responsible.[7]

During this time party politics had the attention of many throughout the state because of a flurry of deaths and resignations among the state's delegation in Congress and the General Assembly. Congressman John T. Deweese resigned his Fourth District seat, and Robert B. Gilliam, succeeding him in the August election, died. In the state senate, William J. Clarke, Tenth District, resigned, and A. H. Galloway, Thirteenth District, died. In the house of representatives, Henderson A. Hodge of Wake County, Thomas R. Jernigan of Hertford County, and John H. Renfrow of Halifax County resigned. Holden made determined efforts to keep the Republican party in control of the vital posts; Samuel F. Phillips, narrowly defeated by W. M. Shipp in the race for attorney general, was nominated for the house from Wake County, while Joseph W. Holden ran for the congressional seat. Phillips defeated Dr. William B. Dunn in a special election on 26 November, but John Manning, Jr., defeated young Holden by a close vote.

The General Assembly met on 21 November; the Conservatives quickly asserted control by electing Thomas J. Jarvis of Tyrrell County speaker of the house of representatives over T. L. Hargrove of Granville. In the senate, W. L. Saunders, said to be the head of the Invisible Empire, was elected principal secretary over A. H. Dowell. Immediate objection was then raised to the seating of Republican members Robert W. Lassiter (Granville), William A. Smith (Alamance), L. C. Barnett (Person), and Wilson Carey (a black from Caswell) on grounds that free elections had been impossible during the military occupation of Alamance and Caswell counties, and in the house John White and T. J. Foster, Republican members from the two disputed counties, were not allowed to take their seats.[8] Consideration was also given to depriving John A. Gilmer, Conservative winner of the Twenty-sixth District, but since he would have secured a sufficient majority regardless of the Alamance vote, he was permitted to retain his post. Although state troops had also occupied Sampson, Cleveland, and Moore counties during the August elections, the ballot in those counties was not challenged and their elected representatives, Conservative-Democrats all, were allowed to take their seats.

Governor Holden realized that the Conservative strategy of seeking political control of the General Assembly could lead not only to the undoing of Republican policies but also to the threat of impeachment and removal from office for him. Prior to the convening of the assembly, the senate membership listed 33 Conservatives and 17 Republicans; the house had 72 Conservatives,

45 Republicans, and 3 independents. After the unseating of the six Republicans, the party membership was listed as 36 Conservatives and 14 Republicans in the senate, and 75 Conservatives, 42 Republicans, and 3 independents in the house. This meant that, should a joint ballot be required or a two-thirds vote be mandated on impeachment charges, the Conservatives would have the required majorities.

In an attempt to avoid the worst, Governor Holden made his message to the assembly a conciliatory one on 22 November and made overtures to former governor Vance. He announced his willingness to work for the removal of Vance's disabilities, thereby permitting his election to the United States Senate.[9]

Contrary to his usual practice of delivering the annual message in person, Governor Holden forwarded the message to the assembly for the house clerk to read. The governor used the occasion primarily to defend his administration in the fields of railroad construction and state debts, public education, and use of state militia—the areas that had aroused the greatest opposition. Although Holden admitted that the people had the right to expect that more progress should have been made on building the railroads, he blamed the failure on defective revenue laws that had not produced sufficient revenue to complete the construction. He also blamed the decision by the roads to issue such sizable amounts of state bonds that their value on the New York market had dropped drastically. Still, he defended the wisdom of the railroads' decisions, saying that growth of the railroads was essential to the state's economic growth, particularly in the utilization of western North Carolina's resources, and he recommended that the state continue the development of its rail lines.

Realizing that North Carolina was saddled with heavy debt and that some of the legislators were advocating repudiation of all railroad bonds, he urged a compromise solution that would scale the debts according to value received in the construction programs. By so doing he hoped that North Carolina would maintain a sound credit rating, indispensable for the state's economic growth. Holden finally expressed the hope that the state might obtain congressional aid for the Western Division of the North Carolina Road, a part of the proposed Southern Pacific Road.

Concerning education, he said:

> Up to the commencement of the late war, North Carolina had the best system of common schools of any State south of the Potomac. In former days the leading men of all parties vied with each other in caring for and promoting the education of all the children. Would that those

days return! . . . Every man and woman who loves North Carolina should lend a helping hand in this cause. It is vain to hope that the rising and coming generations will govern themselves properly, and guard and maintain their liberties, if they are deprived of the advantages of education and allowed to grow up in ignorance.

To relieve the state of the entire burden of educating its children, ne urged the state's congressmen to support the national system of public instruction being discussed in Congress at that time. Such a program, he said, would confer "immeasurable benefits on the people of the Southern States."

As for use of military troops to maintain civil government, Holden justified his actions with a full summary of the Klan's crimes and illegal activities.

It was my sworn duty, as Chief Magistrate of the State, to "execute justice and maintain truth." I was satisfied that the civil authorities in the counties referred to were not able to protect their citizens in the enjoyment of life and property; and, after much forebearance, and many remonstrances, and when patience was exhausted, I could adopt no other course which promised to restore civil law and to re-establish peace and order in those counties. . . . The majesty of the law has been vindicated.

He closed his address with a fervent plea: "It will afford me pleasure, gentlemen, to co-operate with you in such measures as may be considered best calculated to promote the prosperity and happiness of our people."[10]

Despite Holden's conciliatory tone, the assembly immediately began to undo a major portion of the Republican Reconstruction program. First, it created a commission composed of Attorney General William M. Shipp, J. G. Martin, and J. B. Batchelor to study Republican frauds. Then it began considering measures to settle state debts, either by repudiation or by scaling down according to value received. Next, it called a constitutional convention to revise the 1868 document. The Shoffner Militia Act was repealed, and the entire militia system revised. The governor's power to appoint proxies and directors in state-owned or state-controlled business enterprises was transferred to the legislature. A committee was created to investigate the activities of Senator Pool in the Kirk-Holden War, which, it was hoped, would result in his removal from the Senate. Finally, former governor Zebulon B. Vance was elected to the Senate in place of Joseph C. Abbott, whose term would expire in March 1871.

Meanwhile, a Conservative party caucus, headed by Josiah Turner and supported by the *Raleigh Sentinel*, decided to press for the impeachment of Governor Holden. Not all Conservatives or newspapers agreed with this decision. The *Salem Press* strongly opposed the move, "not because we consider it undeserved, but because it is untimely, impolitic, will take up the time of the Legislature when that body ought to be trying to do something to relieve the people, . . . will cost more money than the result whatever it may be, will justify, and it is altogether unnecessary."[11] Likewise, Vance opposed the move; shortly after his election to the Senate he urged moderation and denounced the legislature's vindictive attitude.[12] His stance is somewhat difficult to explain. One possibility is that he felt indebted to Holden for securing his release from prison in 1865 at a time when his wife was desperately ill, or perhaps Holden's offer to remove his political disabilities, thereby enabling him to take his newly acquired senatorial post, had its influence. Probably the chief reason, though, was that Vance thought that impeachment would be impolitic. Among the charges being advanced was one that implicated the governor in the railroad frauds, and Conservative leaders realized that some of their party members might be implicated if such a charge were pursued.

During the early days of the session, while Conservatives were debating impeachment, Holden and his supporters took the unqualified position that impeachment was out of the question, and therefore they were not afraid of incrimination. The *Standard* even seemed to cajole the opposition into action:

> We have had enough of this subject. . . . In the name of the people of
> North Carolina, who elected the governor and chief justice, we demand
> a trial at the bar of the Senate. Innocent or guilty, the matter has
> reached that point from which there is only one course to pursue and
> that is—give these men a trial—clear them if innocent and convict
> them if guilty. If the Democratic party will not try these men, then we
> denounce the party as being more corrupt and dishonest than has been
> charged against the Republican party.[13]

As expected, the Conservative answer was forthcoming. On 9 December 1870, Frederick N. Strudwick of Orange County, former member and leader of the Ku Klux Klan, introduced a resolution in the house of representatives: "Resolved, that William W. Holden, Governor of North Carolina, be impeached for high crimes and misdemeanors in office."[14] The resolution was adopted and referred to the judiciary committee, headed by Thomas Sparrow of Beaufort County. Five days later, 14 December, the committee reported to the house and recommended adoption of the following resolution:

That William W. Holden, Governor of North Carolina, unmindful of his oath of office, did in July last, organize, arm and equip a military force, not recognized by and in subversion to the Constitution of the State of North Carolina; which military force so unlawfully organized, was not kept under subordination to and governed by the civil power, but was, by order of said William W. Holden, Governor as aforesaid, made paramount to and subservient to the civil authority.

That the said William W. Holden, Governor as aforesaid, did in the months of July and August last, without lawful warrant and authority and in defiance and subversion of the Constitution, arrest and imprison many of the peaceable and law abiding citizens of the State, depriving them of their liberties and privileges, and did cause certain of said citizens so unlawfully arrested and imprisoned to be subjected to cruel and unusual punishment.

That the said William W. Holden, Governor aforesaid, denied to citizens unlawfully restrained of their liberty by this authority, all remedy in the lawfulness thereof; and in defiance of the Constitution, the laws, the process of the courts, he suspended the privileges of the writ of *habeas corpus*, claiming that he was Governor by "supreme law," whereby he could suspend the privileges of said writ, when in his opinion the safety of the State required it.

In view of the matters herein set forth, combining historical facts, with statements contained in public documents, and the records of the Public Departments and the Courts, the undersigned members of the committee, who are a majority thereof, are of the opinion that William W. Holden, Governor of the State of North Carolina, be impeached of high crimes and misdemeanors. They, therefore, recommend to the House the adoption of the resolution.[15]

Republican members sought its defeat in order to have the issue postponed until 16 January 1871 (after a Christmas recess), thus permitting public consideration and allowing house members to consult their constituents. In both instances the efforts failed; Representative Strudwick called for an immediate vote and the report was adopted 60 to 40. Nine Conservatives voted against impeachment, while William Cawthorne, a black Republican from Warren County, voted for the adoption of the resolution. The next day the house appointed a special committee composed of Strudwick, W. P. Welch, and Thomas Sparrow to appear before the senate and notify the body of its action; at the same time the chair appointed another committee to draft the articles of impeachment.

Faced with the impeachment resolution, Holden began to retaliate. Earlier he seemed to believe that his political strength was enough to stop the movement, or that it was impolitic for him, as governor, to give recognition to the attempt. Now he had no other choice but to throw himself into the battle. He was especially embittered over the action of Representative Strudwick, a known Ku Klux leader now leading the movement, and Thomas Sparrow's highly partisan supervision of the floor fight. Prior to the vote on the Strudwick resolution, the latter had caustically remarked that "the accredited organ of the Governor, . . . had demanded of the House that the Governor be allowed, . . . to vindicate his character against what it characterized as slanders." Immediately Holden wrote a letter of denial to the Wake County delegation: "The *Standard* is not my 'accredited organ.' I have no organ. . . . The articles in the *Standard* demanding my impeachment were not authorized by me. The only article in that paper for which I am responsible is one of recent date [28 November] headed 'Gov. Holden.' "[16] Samuel F. Phillips, spokesman for the Wake County delegation, then asked permission to read the governor's letter, but Sparrow objected on the grounds that Holden had no right to communicate with the house except in his official capacity. The house permitted Phillips to read the letter, which consequently had no effect on the vote.

On 19 December, Representative James G. Scott, Democrat of Onslow County, spoke for the special committee appointed to draft the impeachment charges and reported a total of eight articles. William P. Welch of Buncombe County then moved that the house go into a committee of the whole to consider the articles and nominate a board of seven managers. His proposal was adopted on a strictly partisan vote. The issue was not whether impeachment charges should be adopted, but rather the selection of a board of managers to prosecute the case. Governor Holden's impeachment was a foregone conclusion.

The clerk then read separately each article, and the house proceeded to vote accordingly. The first two accused the governor of unlawfully declaring Alamance and Caswell counties to be in insurrection and illegally arresting and detaining eighty-two and eighteen citizens, respectively, from the two counties. Articles three and four asserted that the governor had unlawfully arrested and imprisoned Josiah Turner, Jr., of Orange County, and John Kerr, Samuel P. Hill, William B. Bowe, and Nathaniel M. Roan of Caswell without benefit of trial. The fifth and sixth charges claimed that Holden had committed "high crimes and misdemeanors" by refusing to obey the writ of habeas corpus in the cases of Adolphus G. Moore et al. before Chief Justice Pearson. Articles seven and eight asserted that the governor had recruited unlawful troops from Tennessee, spending seventy thousand dollars or more from the state treasury for their maintenance, and had caused Treasurer David A. Jenkins to disobey a court injunction forbidding the disbursement of some eighty thousand dollars for the troops.[17]

While this action was taking place, Speaker Jarvis vacated the chair to participate in the debate, and Representative Strudwick presided over the house. Upon the adoption of the eight articles, Jarvis offered a resolution to proceed with the election of a board of managers who would conduct the trial before the senate and to confer on the board power to employ "other persons learned in the law" to assist in the prosecution. Representative Phillips questioned the latter, but Sparrow cited the Andrew Johnson trial as a precedent. Later, he was forced to admit that he had been in error—the authority to have outside counsel had existed but had not been used in President Johnson's trial. Nevertheless, his remarks persuaded the house members to give permission for selection of outside counsel. Finally, the official board of managers consisted of Thomas Sparrow, George Gregory, William P. Welch, Thomas Johnston of Buncombe, James S. Scott, C. W. Barefoot, and John W. Dunham. Strudwick was bitterly disappointed and offended that he was not selected as a manager, but his Ku Klux connections were too obvious for his inclusion. Later, former governors William A. Graham and Thomas Bragg and Augustus S. Merrimon were employed to assist with the trial.

In a special night meeting on 19 December, Representative Dunham moved that the senate be informed of the house action, his resolution being adopted by a vote strictly along party lines. Jarvis designated Strudwick, Welch, and Sparrow to perform this task. The next day the board of managers presented the impeachment articles. Lt. Governor Tod R. Caldwell accepted the articles on behalf of the senate and then retired as presiding officer, assuming the chief executive position in place of Governor Holden. Edward J. Warren of Beaufort County was then elected to succeed Caldwell. After protracted deliberations and a vote of 24 to 18, the senate requested Chief Justice Pearson to appear in the senate on 23 December to organize the court of impeachment.

Meanwhile, Holden began preparing to turn over his executive duties to Caldwell. On 20 December he wrote Attorney General Shipp asking his legal advice concerning the proper time to vacate his office, noting, "It is needless to say, that I shall be governed by your opinion." Shipp replied the same day: "When the Articles of impeachment are presented to the Senate, the 'Governor is suspended from the exercise of his office until his acquittal and that the Lieutenant Governor from that time is to act as Governor of the State.' "[18] Thus, at two o'clock, 20 December, Caldwell officially assumed the duties of governor of North Carolina.

Promptly at twelve o'clock, 23 December, Chief Justice Pearson, accompanied by senators Edmund W. Jones (Wilkes) and Lehman (Craven), entered the senate chambers and began organizing a court of impeachment.[19] Pearson then administered the following oath to each of the senators: "I swear, truly and impartially, to try and determine the charges of the Articles of Impeachment against William W. Holden, Governor of the State of North Carolina, under the Constitution and laws thereof, according to evidence. So help me God." He then announced the senate to be a court of impeachment, and the previously reported rules of procedure were formally adopted. After a short recess, promptly at one o'clock the court reconvened. The house board of managers, with Sparrow serving as spokesman, appeared and gave its formal demand that the senate consider the impeachment proceedings against Governor Holden. By a motion of Senator Lehman, the court ordered a summons immediately dispatched for Holden to appear before the senate to answer the charges against him. Justice Pearson then announced that the governor had responded to the summons and would appear through his counsel, Richard C. Badger.

Badger came forward and read Holden's response in which he asked for a thirty-day delay before filing his reply. The governor justified this request on the basis of insufficient time; since the articles of impeachment had not reached him until Tuesday night, it was impossible for him to respond by Friday, 23 December. Chief Justice Pearson then asked Badger if he would need further time for preparation. Badger assured him that additional time would not be needed, nor would the governor in any way cause a delay of a speedy trial. The respondent's request was granted and 23 January set for filing his answers, with the formal trial to proceed on 30 January 1871.

Christmas, 1870, was not the festive celebration that the Holden family usually enjoyed. It had long been the governor's custom to take a few days off from work (both when he edited the *Standard* and later as governor) to enjoy the season with his family, lavishly entertaining friends and house guests or writing poetry, which was a favorite pastime.[20] Now he was involved in preparing his defense, seeking proof on the Ku Klux Klan activities, and obtaining counsel for his trial. For the first time in his married life he faced the prospect of the holidays without his close-knit family in Raleigh. Two of the daughters were now married and moved away: Laura (Mrs. Lewis P. Olds) lived in Florida while Ida Augusta (Mrs. Calvin J. Cowles) was a resident of Charlotte. Mary Eldridge Holden (later Mrs. Claude A. Sherwood) was spending the holidays visiting with her sister Mrs. Cowles.[21]

But Holden's major family concern was the older son; Joseph W. Holden, who had demonstrated ability while serving as speaker of the house of representatives, had become something of a dandy and a fop. No doubt his excessive vanity was due to his father's position. By the summer of 1869 he had become an alcoholic, and was sent to Wentworth to Thomas Settle, a close family friend, under whose watchful eye he could begin the serious study of law and overcome his overindulgence for alcohol.[22] That experience lasted briefly, however; by 1870, Joseph had returned to work as a reporter for the *Standard* and even led a retaliatory mob demonstrating against Josiah Turner and other Conservatives. At the age of twenty-six he was unemployed, still with an alcohol problem and his father in no position to protect him. He would remain a problem for the senior Holden.[23]

Surprisingly, Holden faced the new year greatly encouraged. Friends were rallying to his cause, sending evidence of Klan activities as proof of the necessity of using troops,[24] or making financial contributions to cover the cost of employing counsel.[25] In some ways, Holden eagerly anticipated the trial, believing that if given the opportunity of presenting the truth about the Klan, he could surely convince an impartial court of his innocence. Ultimately, he hoped he could return to the governor's post and serve the interests of the people for the remainder of his term.

Holden also used the intervening time to employ some leading members of the state bar as his counsel, including J. M. McCorkle, Nathaniel Boyden, William Nathan Harrell Smith, and Edward Conigland, in addition to his former legal adviser, Richard C. Badger. Boyden and Smith later served on the state's supreme court, and Smith was named chief justice. Holden further attempted to secure the service of Bartholomew F. Moore, who was sought also by the board of managers, and former governor Vance, but both declined. Each counselor was paid $1,500 by Holden himself, although Conigland refused compensation. While there is no proof that an admonition published in the *Sentinel* forbidding any Democratic lawyer from serving the governor had any effect, the fact remains that none served. "Let Sam. Phillips, Rotating Dick, Bailey and Boyden, who have sold themselves to Holden and Pearson, and lent themselves to aid in the persecution of the honest and innocent people of the State, defend the Governor at the bar of the Senate."[26]

Holden's counsel diligently prepared themselves for the trial, and on 23 January presented the governor's answers to each of the impeachment charges. Holden sought through his answers to show the growth of Democratic opposition to his administration, from Governor Worth's protest in surrendering the executive office to the rise of the Klan movement with its defiance of law and order, even to the Klan's attempted overthrow of the state government. Holden justified his declaration of a state of insurrection in Alamance and Caswell counties, claiming that the civil authorities were either unwilling or unable to protect the welfare of their citizens and that under the Shoffner Militia Act his use of troops was legal. Further, he denied that the prisoners had been mistreated and proposed to prove that he had issued strict orders that the rights of all prisoners be protected. He denied ordering the arrest of Josiah Turner, although he admitted giving orders for his detention once he was arrested. He further admitted the suspension of the writ of habeas corpus, but claimed, as he had informed the chief justice, that it was his purpose to hold the prisoners only until civil government could be restored; then he would surrender them to the proper civil authorities. He denied that it was illegal to enroll troops, even those from Tennessee. Last, he denied that any illegality had occurred when he withdrew funds to pay the troop expenses; instead he had acted in good faith and was following proper procedures.[27]

On 30 January, the day of the trial's formal beginning, the house forwarded a resolution to the senate requesting to amend the eighth article. The request was granted, and Holden was given two days to prepare his answer. On 1 February, L. C. Edwards, a Conservative of Granville County, requested permission to take his seat in the senate after his win of a highly disputed election, unseating Republican Robert W. Lassiter. Holden's counsel challenged this move on the grounds that Edwards was not a member of the senate at the time of its organization into a court and that to seat him now would, in effect, "pack" the court. Justice Pearson, though, overruled the challenge, and arrangements were made that same day for the trial to begin.

Once under way, the trial turned into a mockery of the judicial process; in fact, use of the word *trial* in discussing it is questionable. The Democratic-controlled senate had determined the verdict before the trial began—Governor Holden was to be found guilty and removed from office. Proof of the partisanship of the court is evidenced by the fact that Holden's counsel was not permitted to introduce detailed testimony concerning the Klan's many outrages throughout the state, as well as within the counties placed under martial law. Moreover, no order was produced to prove that Holden had ordered Turner's arrest; yet he was found guilty of this charge.[28]

On 2 February, Thomas Sparrow opened the case for the board of managers. He stated that the impeachment charges had been drawn to preserve constitutional government and civil liberty in North Carolina. He charged Holden with corruption, misconduct, and committing criminal acts while in office. He further claimed that no insurrection existed in Alamance and Caswell counties; hence, placing them under martial law was illegal. Finally, he argued that even though the constitution and the Shoffner Act authorized the use of militia, Holden had exceeded his power by recruiting men who were not citizens of the state and by placing white and black soldiers in the same organization, contrary to state law.

The board then paraded some sixty-one witnesses to establish its case. Adolphus J. Rutjes and James M. Blair, proprietors of the National Hotel and Yarborough House, respectively, were called to testify that Kirk and Bergen had registered in their Raleigh hotels as Tennessee residents. Isaac E. Reeves, a Tennessee lawyer, swore as to the legal residence of Kirk, while William M. Cocke of Asheville testified to Kirk's violent character. William J. Murray, deputy sheriff of Alamance, claimed no insurrection existed in that county; nor had there been any resistance to law or to the collection of taxes. Richard Thompson testified that crimes attributed to the Klan had actually been committed by blacks disguised as klansmen, his testimony being corroborated by John A. Gilmer and John W. Graham. Other witnesses swore to the misconduct of the troops and the treatment accorded them while being held as prisoners; among them was young Patton of Alamance who, as Holden said, "denied positively that he was a ku klux, and told the story of his 'hanging' with such particularity and pathos that the hearers were moved to pity for him and indignation towards myself."[29] Henry F. Brandon, Caswell County clerk of court, swore that the laws were enforced in his county until Kirk occupied Yanceyville. Josiah Turner testified that his arrest had been specifically ordered by Holden and that he had been arrested illegally in a county not in insurrection. John W. Gorman swore that he had heard Holden make the claim that he would have Turner arrested. Several telegraphers were subpoenaed to produce orders sent by telegraph, but none could provide proof. In fact, much of such testimony was admittedly based on newspaper accounts.

During cross-examination Sheriff Murray was asked if he knew of the existence of the Ku Klux Klan, and William A. Graham immediately objected, claiming it was irrelevant to the question concerning the existence of an insurrection in Alamance. Nathaniel Boyden countered for the defense, declaring its intention to prove that the Klan's object was to prevent execution of laws in the two counties; that the members of such an organization committed crimes of violence; and that in his capacity as governor, Holden was authorized under the Shoffner Act to summon the militia. Thereupon, Merrimon challenged the constitutionality of the Shoffner Act, maintaining that the governor had no power to call out the militia at his discretion. In reply, Edward Conigland claimed that the governor did have discretionary powers in declaring counties in insurrection when the peace and safety of their citizens were in doubt. He further argued that to prove his innocence it was only necessary to prove that he had acted in good faith; it was not the governor's responsibility to inquire into the constitutionality of the Shoffner Act, but rather to enforce the law until the law had been declared invalid by the state's courts. After three days of debate the defense won its argument, and Holden was able to disprove all such allegations.

The house of representatives attempted to alter the course of proceedings while the trial was in progress. On 9 February a ninth article of impeachment was adopted by a vote of 74 to 9, charging the governor and George W. Swepson with conspiracy to defraud the state in the sale of railroad bonds. The article was prepared by Augustus S. Merrimon, member of the counsel for the board of managers, but was never presented to the senate; nor was it mentioned either in the Conservative press or in the *House Journal* thereafter. In all probability, the board of managers and Conservative leaders withdrew the article for fear that, if they pursued it, Governor Holden would be permitted to produce evidence incriminating prominent Conservatives, including Merrimon. Even so, Holden wired Swepson, "I am about to be impeached on account of issuing bonds to your Road. . . . It will be necessary, if the matter is pressed, for you to come here, and swear, as you can, that there was no 'collusion' between you and me on the subject. If this is all right, telegraph at once to C. W. Horner, Raleigh, 'All right.' "[30]

Swepson immediately replied from New York that if the matter was presented to the court, he would return to Raleigh and prove Holden's innocence.[31] Three days later, Swepson wrote from Baltimore:

> Another thing you should remember; it is this, that I will not stand still and see Littlefield and myself assailed and have all the odium of these matters put on us and allow *others* to go free. I know what members of the General Assembly have been paid; I don't pretend to know every one of them, but enough to cause dismay. I know all the Railroad Presidents who have paid to get their bills through . . . but I cannot afford to be slaughtered by myself, or have only Littlefield's company and before I submit to it, I am determined to divulge everything I know.[32]

A further consideration for dropping the proposed ninth article was that Merrimon was serving as counsel for Swepson in an 1870 Buncombe County case in which N. W. Woodfin was seeking a settlement with the Western North Carolina Railroad. It would be embarrassing and impolitic for Merrimon to be prosecuting and defending the same client.

The board of managers took more than three weeks to present its case.

The high point of the testimony came when Josiah Turner testified regarding his arrest and treatment while in Holden's "Basteil." He did not restrict his remarks to the impeachment charges, but went on to criticize Holden personally and his "demagogic" administration.

Throughout the proceedings, Chief Justice Pearson presided in a judicial manner; two of the governor's counsel, Boyden and Badger, later informed Holden, however, that the justice had advised them on matters of procedure and points of law. Boyden also told Holden that Pearson considered him innocent and thought that the board had failed to show adequate proof for conviction.[33] Nevertheless, the governor pointedly abstained from all contacts with the chief justice for fear of embarrassing Pearson by prejudicing the case against himself.

Conversely, on several occasions Pearson permitted the board much flexibility in the presentment of evidence. Defense counsel objected to the board's attempts to prove that the Klan's actions were not politically motivated by introducing so-called evidence to prove the "bad character" of the Klan's victims, but the chief justice overruled their objections. And the defense's objections were consistently overruled on the question of the admission of newspaper articles as proof of Holden's knowledge and approval of the prisoners' mistreatment; these articles had mainly appeared in Turner's *Sentinel*.

It was not until 23 February that Edward Conigland started the presentation of the defense. He began by criticizing the partisanship of the prosecution and claimed that impeachment proceedings should not have been brought without the house of representatives having first conducted a thorough investigation, based on sworn testimony, of the allegations against Holden. In fact, Representative G. L. Mabson had criticized the house judiciary committee for its failure to conduct such an investigation and for the house's failure to observe proper legal standards. The house had overridden all such protests, however.[34]

Conigland then declared that the defense would show that secret societies in Alamance and Caswell counties sought to subvert the law and that by crimes, murders, and intimidation they had exercised political control over local officials. This made it impossible for civil authorities to administer the laws, protect life and property, and preserve the peace. Replying to the prosecution's allegations that Holden had acted illegally in declaring the counties in insurrection and that the Shoffner Act was unconstitutional, Conigland based the governor's defense on six major points: (1) the term "insurrection" was not defined by the state constitution but rather was left to the discretion of the governor; (2) legislative acts are considered valid until declared unconstitutional by the courts; (3) Holden acted within the provisions of the Shoffner Act; (4) the governor was not subject to trial by any other department of state government for proclaiming an insurrection; (5) by his legal power to declare an insurrection, the governor also had the power to arrest known violators and to suspend citizen rights during such emergencies or until civil government could be restored; and (6) any maltreatment administered to the prisoners was done contrary to Holden's orders and certainly without his knowledge.[35]

The defense then proceeded to place 113 witnesses on the stand, with three weeks required for presentation of their testimony. James E. Boyd, former member of the White Brotherhood and the Constitutional Union Guard (Klan organizations), was the key witness on Ku Klux atrocities. He offered the following evidence: that James Bradshaw had admitted his participation in the hanging of Wyatt Outlaw; that he, Boyd, had met with the Klan party planning to hang Shoffner and that F. M. Strudwick, who introduced the impeachment resolution, Abel Hedgepeth, and James Bradshaw were members of the Outlaw murder party; that Caswell Holt, a black, was forced to flee the county; that some twenty of the men arrested by Kirk were active members of the Klan; that former klansmen had fled the state to escape prosecution or subpoenas to testify at the impeachment trial;[36] and that Jacob A. Long, a Klan member, admitted that the Klan had planned and carried out the murder of John W. Stephens.

The crux of Holden's defense was the Shoffner Act. Attention was called to the fact that in the trial of President Andrew Johnson, the congressional board of managers had insisted that the president had no discretionary power to judge the constitutionality of an act. Holden was charged with enforcing a law that was valid—a law passed by the General Assembly in hopes of maintaining law and order. The defense claimed that Holden had not only acted within his legal rights under the law but had also performed his authorized executive duties. For these reasons the court should give "full faith and credit" to Governor Holden for his acts, especially since he had exhausted all other means of preserving the peace.[37]

The testimony for the respondent was closed on 14 March, the thirty-seventh day of the trial. Thereupon, each side gave closing speeches. William A. Graham spoke first for the board of managers, summarizing the prosecution's testimony. He also defended the employment of outside legal counsel on grounds that legislative members were too busy in their lawmaking duties for proper presentation of a case, completely ignoring the fact that the entire legislative process stopped during the trial. Furthermore, he denied the defense allegation that Congress or the federal government might intervene and place the state of North Carolina under military rule if Governor Holden were convicted.[38]

Nathaniel Boyden spoke first on behalf of Holden. His main argument was that the governor had acted within his legal rights and therefore could not be held responsible for executing the Shoffner Act, even if it were later declared unconstitutional. He further maintained that the state had the power to declare martial law and that no civil process could function in localities placed under martial law. He also refuted the prosecution's contentions that Holden had acted illegally in refusing to obey the prisoners' petitions for writs of habeas corpus and challenged the citation by the board of managers of the *Ex parte Milligan* decision.[39] Boyden noted that the reasoning followed in the Milligan decision was not applicable to North Carolina in 1870—insurrection *did exist* in the state and civil courts *were* inoperative.[40]

William Nathan Harrell Smith presented the final arguments for Holden's defense. First, he pointed out that the prosecution had based its demands for conviction on "corruption and misconduct in his [Holden's] official capacity," thereby implying corrupt intentions on the governor's part. Smith denied this, claiming that the prosecution had failed to prove the charge. He next argued that Holden had the right and the duty to put in force the Shoffner Act, using military force in the two counties. By such action, Governor Holden had prevented similar Klan outrages across the state. As for the charge that whites and blacks had been enrolled together in militia companies, he reminded the jury that the state constitution did not prohibit voluntary association of the races and as the troops had voluntarily enlisted, no crime had been committed. Smith applied the same principle to the charge that out-of-state citizens had been enrolled in the troops, stating that the constitutional prohibition against the use of officers and privates who were not citizens did not apply to a volunteer militia. Finally, Smith addressed the consequences of declaring a county in insurrection by saying that it had been the purpose of the military authority not to bring offenders to justice but rather to break up the illegal Ku Klux Klan; the military force was, therefore, a preventive rather than a remedial force. He further justified Holden's refusal to surrender the prisoners under the writ of habeas corpus, since the governor was following the opinion of United States Attorney General Edward Bates in the case of *Ex parte Merryman*; namely, the executive branch of the government could not be made subservient to the judiciary.[41]

Former governor Thomas Bragg closed the trial for the board of managers. He denied the necessity of showing corrupt intentions or malice to warrant conviction: "It is a trial in which the principles of civil and constitutional liberty, . . . are involved, and the question whether those great principles are to be maintained or whether hereafter they are to be regarded as mere mockery." Then, after reviewing the evidence presented during the trial and maintaining that all charges had been amply proved, he concluded and asked the court for a verdict of guilty.[42]

The court agreed to vote the following day, 22 March, each senator being permitted one week to file a written opinion. Conviction was a foregone conclusion; a caucus of Conservative members had already determined the outcome. Moreover, the Conservatives were resolved not only to find Holden guilty of the impeachment charges but also to remove him from office; doing this, they would destroy forever their Republican nemesis.

Court attendance was virtually complete on 22 March, with only Senator Jesse Flythe, Republican from Northampton County, absent. The Conservatives had made certain that all of their members were present, the doorkeepers having been advised to bring senators Dargan and Murphy into the chambers even though they were too drunk to walk. Once organized, the clerk proceeded to read the impeachment articles separately, with a roll-call vote on each. Counsel for the defense was encouraged when Holden was acquitted on articles 1 and 2, the most serious charges of illegally raising troops, declaring Alamance and Caswell counties in insurrection, and unlawfully arresting and imprisoning the prisoners. The minor charges were so drawn that the senators found it easy to vote guilty; even so, it was only on the disobedience of the writs of habeas corpus (articles 5 and 6) that a decided two-thirds majority cast a vote for conviction. Had the Conservatives not replaced the three Republican members, it is doubtful that Holden would have been convicted on the other charges. After the final vote the chief justice announced the vote as follows:[43]

Guilty				Not Guilty			
Article	Dem.	Rep.	Total	Article	Dem.	Rep.	Total
1	30	0	30	1	6	13	19
2	32	0	32	2	4	13	17
3	36	1	37	3	0	12	12
4	33	0	33	4	3	13	16
5	36	4	40	5	0	9	9
6	36	5	41	6	0	8	8
7	36	0	36	7	0	13	13
8	36	0	36	8	0	13	13

At the time it was generally understood that several Conservatives had opposed conviction and expressed their intentions of voting for acquittal, but those revealing such sentiments were threatened with their lives. The power of the Klan was brought to bear on them.[44] Two prominent senators, although voting to convict Holden and remove him from office, later admitted the soundness of the defense arguments. Senator Edward Warren of Beaufort County said:

> I avail myself of the opportunity to express my abhorrence of the secret political societies which existed in Alamance. . . . They committed the most heinous crimes. They did not, so far as we know, assassinate Stephens [later confessed to by klansmen], but they murdered Outlaw and probably Puryear. They whipped and scourged many for actual or pretended offences, and some out of a spirit of wantoness or revenge. They established in Alamance a reign of terror.[45]

Senator R. M. Norment of Robeson County was even more straightforward.

> I fear, however, that when I entered the jury box as one of the triers of this case, I was not as free from prejudice against the accused as I should have been, and as I desired to be. The many reports, ex parte as they doubtless were, which came to my ears through the public press before the meeting of this general assembly, and which, without intermission, have been industriously circulated almost up to the present hour, were well calculated to warp the judgement and bias the minds of the jurors who belong to the political party of which those papers were the accredited organs. . . . My mind has been convinced beyond a shadow of doubt, that during the summer of 1870, the civil law was not adequate to the protection of life, liberty, and property in the counties of Alamance and Caswell. . . . The Sheriff of Alamance . . . was, according to his own evidence, a member of a secret association who had banded themselves together . . . and had taken the law into their own hands and whipped, scourged, maltreated and murdered citizens of the county . . . for no other reason than they had incurred the displeasure of this marauding midnight band of disguised assassins.[46]

After Justice Pearson had announced the results, Thomas Sparrow, chairman of the board of managers, arose and demanded that the court immediately proceed to the matter of punishment. Whereupon, Senator John W. Graham offered the following resolution, which was adopted without debate and strictly by a party vote:

The State of North Carolina.
The Senate of North Carolina.

March 22, 1871.

The State vs. William W. Holden.

Whereas, the house of representatives of the State of North Carolina did, on the 26th day of December, 1870, exhibit to the senate articles of impeachment against William W. Holden, governor of North Carolina, and the said senate, after a full hearing and impartial trial has, by the votes of two-thirds of the members present, this day determined that the said William W. Holden is guilty as charged in the 3rd, 4th, 5th, 6th, 7th, and 8th of such articles.

Now therefore, it is adjudged by the senate of North Carolina sitting as a court of impeachment, at their chamber in the city of Raleigh, that the said William W. Holden be removed from the office of honor, trust, or profit under the state of North Carolina.[47]

Governor Holden did not testify, although in the early stages of the trial he made daily appearances in the senate chambers and consulted freely with his counsel. He was handicapped by not having a Raleigh newspaper support his cause; the *Standard* had ceased publication on 24 December 1870. He and his counsel had been confident of winning an acquittal, especially considering that the prosecution's testimony did not prove the constitutional charges against him; they also felt that by presenting the truth about the 1870 Klan, they could convince fair-minded members not mired in prejudice. Even as late as 11 March, Holden would write to his wife, "Mr. McCorkle writes me that my acquittal is almost certain. I am glad to hear this."[48]

Still, from the beginning he had an uneasy feeling that the outcome might go against him and that the Conservatives would find a way to convict him and remove him from office. Consequently, after a consultation with his family and counsel, he decided to go to Washington until the conclusion of the trial. Contrary to the intimation of Professor Hamilton that he left Raleigh because of Josiah Turner's testimony, he needed instead to be beyond the clutches of Klan mob law.[49] Originally, he had planned to be in Washington on 20 February, as his telegram on 10 February to George W. Swepson had indicated, but he had delayed his departure to see that no new legal complications developed.[50]

Arriving in Washington on 1 March, Holden occupied a small suite at 715 Eleventh Street. Joseph Holden had preceded his father to Washington by three months and had rented a single bedroom at 602 Eleventh Street. Earlier he had been unable to find employment, but when Congress reassembled in March, he performed invaluable work for the Senate investigating committee on Ku Klux Klan activities throughout the South. Ever the proud father, Holden wrote home: "Much of the success of the Investigating Committee is due to Jo Holden. When he commenced his work three weeks ago, he was alone, with the exception of a few. Even Senators were incredulous. Now both Houses are wide awake. I have been vindicated and action of some kind will certainly be taken."[51]

Nevertheless, life in Washington had been extremely rough on the young North Carolinian. When Holden first saw his son he wrote: "Jo Holden is doing very well. He is now suffering from a hurt to one of his fingers in playing ten-pins. He *looks* like a thoroughly sober man. I think what he has seen and felt here has done him good. He told me yesterday that, having no money, he went once two days without eating, until he saw a friend who gave him his dinner. All this had done him good."[52]

Once settled into new accommodations and awaiting the verdict, Holden consulted his many friends in Congress and the administration. Intentionally, he did not seek an immediate appointment with President Grant, in spite of the fact that the president knew of his arrival and had inquired of his health and condition. Robert M. Douglas, Grant's private secretary and Holden's former aide, called at his residence on the day of his arrival and extended the president's sympathy. On 4 March Holden saw the president for a few minutes in the Senate chamber, and arrangements were made for a formal appointment the following Monday. Holden described the meeting to his wife, writing, "There was no mistaking the cordial grasp of his hand. . . . He informed me he had ordered four companies of cavalry to North Carolina. He will send infantry as soon as they can be spared. He is thoroughly with us."[53]

Holden was prompt for the appointment and visited with the president for half an hour. "I told him everything of importance. He seemed impressed and was very friendly. Three of the strongest men here are my friends, Grant, [Benjamin F.] Butler, and [Oliver P.] Morton."[54]

The suspense of waiting for the trial's conclusion was, nevertheless, vexing to Holden. Until then he had had control of his personal and public life; now he could only sit and wait impatiently, hoping that his honor and political career would be restored. Attempting to avoid his fears and impatience, he wrote frequent, almost daily, letters to his wife and family to reassure them concerning his physical and mental health. "My health is very good. I have just taken a long ride with Mr. [C. L.] Cobb to see the Secretary of State [Hamilton Fish] and Genl. Butler. We were well received."[55] Four days later he wrote: "My health is excellent. I am careful in my diet. I had for breakfast this morning a cup of coffee, two boiled eggs, hominy and milk toast. Cost, 50 cents. I expect to dine about four o'clock. . . . I have met Sion H. Rogers, Vance, and [James M.] Leach, and others of that stamp. They are very friendly. The atmosphere here is very different from that in Raleigh."[56]

In 1871 the major topic of congressional debate concerned the enactment of an anti-Ku Klux Klan law in hopes of guaranteeing free elections throughout the South, even if it meant the suspension of the writ of habeas corpus. As expected, Holden was caught up in the excitement of the debate and initially attended the congressional sessions, not only to pass the time but to offer his experience which would prove the necessity for such a law. But by March he wrote home:

> I am tired of the excitement here. It has become monotonous. The political currents change here as the weather does. If nothing is done for the South at this time it will probably be because of the purpose to fully inform the Northern public of our conditions, so as to justify military governments when Congress meets next winter. There need be no fear that Congress will not rule. However tardy it may appear to be it will hold the South with a hand of iron.[57]

The day before he had written: "I did not mean in my last letter that I was personally 'unhappy.' I meant the uncertainty of the future of the country. That concerns me, for we are all involved in it. The breach between the President and Mr. [Charles] Sumner is serious. I saw Senators [Henry] Wilson and Sumner last night. Their feelings are bitter."[58]

By the time the state senate had completed his trial, Holden had prepared himself for the bad news. "I have just heard the results. I expected it. I am calm and thoughtful. Do not be concerned on my account. Please consult friends, and determine what I shall do."[59]

Not only was he keenly disappointed in the verdict, but he was concerned about his future and his serious and growing financial problems. For the first time since his arrival in Raleigh in 1837, he was without a job and had no means of support for his family. He had an approximate indebtedness of eight thousand dollars in court costs. Moreover, he had been warned that his life would be in danger if he returned to Raleigh, which necessitated two separate family living arrangements. He had planned to relocate in the Ebbitt House Hotel, but with the news of his conviction and removal from office he decided that he should economize. Thus, on 1 April he moved into the Exchange House on Pennsylvania Avenue. "It is a little rough," he wrote his wife, "but a good house. $45 per month for board and room."[60]

He was confident that eventually financial assistance would be given by his northern Republican friends, but until that came, he remained alone in his rooms in the Exchange House desperately considering his immediate and future plans. The *Washington Chronicle*, the national Republican paper, afforded the hope that his career might not be in total ruin and expressed a view that mirrored the general feeling of the northern Republican press: "The trial was a burlesque on justice, and will be handed down to those who come after us as one of the criminal follies of the hour. The verdict will in no way affect Gov. Holden. He will be respected all the same by all, except those who hate him on political grounds. It was not for violating the law that he was impeached, but he exposed the Ku Klux organization."[61]

Still, separation from his family greatly disturbed Holden, and he began to search for ways to be reunited with his wife and children. Meanwhile, Mrs. Holden proved to be a tower of strength. She not only gave support and encouragement to her husband but also held the family together during this crisis. She took complete charge of the management of the family finances. Hardly had Holden received the news of being ousted from office when word came that Josiah Turner had instituted suit seeking to collect personal damages for the earlier arrest. Counsel advised Holden that should Turner be successful in his claims, there would probably be additional suits filed against him by other political enemies. Thus he was confronted with the concurrent problems of raising sufficient funds to pay off the trial costs, safeguarding his Raleigh property for his family's living accommodations, providing the necessary living expenses for himself in Washington and his family in North Carolina, and resisting the Turner suit and others that might arise. Also, Turner threatened to have Governor Tod Caldwell send a requisition for Holden's return to the state and set a $20,000 bail for his appearance—a sum which Holden did not have and which might be difficult to raise under the circumstances.

Moreover, Holden was greatly disheartened that more of his friends, especially northern Republicans, did not contribute more generously to his trial costs. There were many small contributions, such as $100 from J. N. Bunting,[62] $100 from Dr. William Sloan,[63] $250 from John F. Pickerell of New York City,[64] and $500 from Dr. Eugene Grissom,[65] but there is no record in any of the Holden papers of large or numerous gifts from out-of-state Republicans. His son-in-law Calvin Cowles sought without success to raise funds in New York and offered to mortgage his own property for immediate relief, but Holden refused.[66] He was determined to supply all the necessary funds himself, using the last quarter of his salary as governor amounting to $1,250, cashing in personal bonds, and calling in debts. Throughout his adult life, Holden had been generous with his money, making loans or endorsing notes for his friends; even when they failed to repay the loans, he had never sued to recover losses. He had always operated on the assumption that they would repay when financially able. Now, working through Mrs. Holden, who relied almost exclusively upon Samuel F. Phillips and son-in-law Lewis P. Olds, he sought redress, but without much success.[67]

By transferring ownership to his wife, Holden was successful in safeguarding his Raleigh property, putting it beyond the reach of Turner or other claimants. "I got the dispatch, 'All Right' [code words informing him the property transferral had been accomplished] and was much gratified. . . . If the homestead is secured I am satisfied."[68] This was verified in a letter from Holden to Cowles in 1882: "Allow me to say, in relation to this house and lot, that in 1871 Mrs. Holden paid her own money. . . . She had a separate estate of her own, and Mr. Phillips, her Counsel, advised her that she must pay her own money for the house and lot, on which only would her title be good. Her purpose then was, as it is now, on her death to devise this house and lot to me or to the seven children equally."[69] In addition, Holden had turned over approximately $30,000 in bonds from the sale of the *Standard*, which meant that Mrs. Holden had sufficient funds to lead a normal life until he could secure employment to provide for his family. He wrote his wife accordingly: "My wish is that you do not stint yourself. You have an abundance. Nothing can be recovered out of me. It is not well to be rich. A competency is all we want. Whatever may happen, or whatever Providence may direct me to do, I will be able to make a living, and we shall all be happy when most regularly employed."[70]

TEN

The Final Years: Solace and Salvation

In springtime 1871, Holden was in no mood to enjoy the beauty of his residence in exile. He was a lonely man being forced to sort out his life. Never had he felt so destitute, so desperate. Not knowing where to turn or in whom he could confide, he considered continuing a political career, returning to the field of journalism, or launching into an entirely new occupation. A short visit by Mrs. Holden in early April revived his spirits temporarily, but after her return to Raleigh he fell into melancholy. He felt unwanted, almost an intruder, yet his pride would not allow him to take a political "hand out." Worst of all, none of his former friends and supporters in the Grant administration, not even Republican congressional leaders, came forward to give him the reassurance he needed to bolster his confidence in the future. Neither a trip by steamer down the Potomac River to Mount Vernon nor regular attendance at the Mount Calvary Baptist Church altered his mood. "I was looked at and seemed to be known," he wrote his wife, "but I did not linger to make acquaintances."[1]

During this period of despondency his chief solace seemed to be the cleansing of his soul through daily letters to his wife.

Everyone treats me courteously and kindly; but what does all this mean? I can not tell. My mind is much exercised. I am no longer a citizen of the State. I am offered nothing here. I will not *ask* for anything. I have done my duty as Governor, and my conscience tells me so. The government here is a matter of commerce, and certain classes or rings govern and dispense the offices. The President, who is doing the best he can under the circumstances, no doubt feels that he ought not to tender me any subordinate position, and he has no chief position to offer. I am tired of politics and public life, and everything seems to point to a final retiring on my part from public life. "What shall it profit a man if he gains the whole world, and lose his own soul?" This thought rings through me, day and night. This City is Vanity Fair. I feel that while I am in it, I am not of it. I do not want to be of it. My Wife, and dearest and best friend, tell me what I shall do? Shall I return, and for the remnant of my days, devote my knowledge and my time to my Divine Master? My mind and my heart incline that way. If I do this I would never accept any political office, not even the Presidency. Write me on this subject. I have great confidence in your forecasts, your judgment, and your piety.[2]

Again, he lamented: "Senators Pool and Abbott . . . offered to obtain employment for me on the *Chronicle*! They regard me as defunct. If my aims were not higher, I would rattle their rickety castles about their ears."[3] Or,

Jo left yesterday for the Great West. I suffered yesterday, but I am calm to-day. He went, threadbare and poor, to Omaha. He has been tried in the fire, and if he lives he will succeed. He was too full to say all he felt. If the worst comes, and we are reduced to poverty, we can still be happy. I will not humble myself here to be recognized by any. *They say* I have saved the country in 1872, and from a terrible civil war, *but that is all.* I simply meant to do my duty to the oppressed without regard to party. Let me beg you not to be depressed. There is no reason why you should. Everything depends on you. Be mild and kind to all, but firm as a rock, and play the woman. There is light ahead.[4]

Despite such assurances to his wife, Holden continued to feel confused and depressed. His inability to help in finding employment and giving proper guidance to Joseph was especially bitter; although Jo tried to see President Grant before leaving for the West, he was unable to do so. Also, there is no question that Holden believed his experience had helped alert the nation to the necessity of taking stronger measures against the Klan in the South. As for his avoidance of war, or even saving the country by assurance of a Republican victory in the 1872 election, these are different matters. No doubt he felt that his exposure of the Klan, even the partisanship of his impeachment trial, would lead to Grant's reelection and perhaps to federal intervention in order to crush the Klan movement. Thus the Grant administration would be obliged to provide for his future. But Washington was slow to act, and he could only wait and hope. The real cause of delay was the conflict over southern legislative matters between President Grant and the two Radical leaders—Charles Sumner and Henry Wilson. This meant that both the president and Congress procrastinated in finding employment for Holden or even in extending signs of friendly recognition.[5] Holden explained the situation best in a letter to his wife: "This City is selfishness, not to say wickedness, impersonated. . . . The South is a sort of plantation. It ruled the North forty years, and now the North is ruling. This explains all. If I were to push myself I would have much consideration and notoriety, but I prefer to be quiet."[6]

By the closing days of the congressional session, with nothing positive offered him, Holden was ready to give serious consideration to returning to North Carolina despite threats of harassment and legal claims. Some of the state Republicans encouraged the move in hopes that he could bolster the Tod R. Caldwell administration and, in particular, lead the fight against the Conservative-Democratic party in its call for a constitutional convention. This he was unwilling to do, saying: "I can take no part where such men as Tim Lee [Wake County carpetbagger sheriff and leader of the local black Republican forces] or C. [Ceburn] L. Harris control, not to mention others."[7] Neither of these represented the true interests of the Republican party; they were not concerned about the betterment of "the people," as Holden always referred to the common folk. Holden was hesitant to return and face the task of wresting control from Republican leaders of that type.

On the other hand, Edward Conigland and others of his impeachment counsel recommended that he return to the state, appeal his conviction to the supreme court, and fight his legal battle "out to the end."[8] Again, Holden rationalized that such a route not only was unwise legally but could result in a long and costly legal battle, which he had neither the finances to pursue nor friends upon whom he could rely to contribute to such a trial. Holden also knew that he could never regain his right to hold political office in North Carolina without a change in public sentiment; given the strength of the Klan and deteriorating race relations, he envisioned little hope for the immediate future.

In the end, Holden wisely followed his wife's advice and remained in Washington, hoping that President Grant would soon give him a major appointment. Had there been an opening within the administrative offices, undoubtedly he would have been given serious consideration; the only other possibility was a diplomatic post, but this was an area in which Holden did not feel qualified. Furthermore, the controversial aspects of his situation precluded the State Department from seriously considering him for any of the major diplomatic posts, and he refused to accept a minor one, deeming it unacceptable for one of his position.

Meanwhile in North Carolina the Republican opposition to a new constitutional convention decisively defeated the proposition. Governor Caldwell demonstrated much leadership in his opposition to the Democratic strategy, and Samuel F. Phillips, who replaced Holden as party chairman, had reunited the party sufficiently to defeat the convention call. Yet success was not entirely due to efforts within the state. United States Attorney General Amos T. Ackerman campaigned extensively throughout North Carolina and threatened that if such a convention were called, Congress or President Grant would withdraw recognition from the state and might put it under military rule. This created sufficient fear among the Democrats to stop them from pressing their demands too vigorously.

One of the more interesting developments in the campaign was the reelection of Holden's brother-in-law William H. Harrison as mayor of Raleigh. While pleased for Harrison, Holden could not help but worry about its possible effect on his situation in Washington: "The telegraphic statement of the election in Raleigh, to wit, that the Democrats elected my brother-in-law to show a liberal feeling toward me, is calculated to do me no good with Republicans here. But I am profoundly indifferent on this respect."[9]

Holden correctly concluded that Congress would not overturn the governments in the southern states because of the Klan movement, thereby opening the way for his return as governor under military rule. It was his belief that such inaction gave the Radicals the time needed to inform the northern public regarding southern problems, thereby justifying military governments at a later date. Sion H. Rogers had reached a similar conclusion after visiting Washington and contacting congressmen of various political opinions.[10]

Accordingly, Holden began to change tactics and became more aggressive in seeking help from the Grant administration. Previously he had not pushed himself upon the president and had taken the necessary precaution of not even appearing to do so.[11] Now he arranged an interview with Grant, which he reported to his wife: "I saw the President on Saturday last [13 May] for the first time since my conviction. He was very friendly. He did not know I had been all this time in the City! I told him if I returned home I might return to 'bonds and imprisonment.' He replied, 'that is very hard.' He then said he would be glad to see me at any time, and I left."[12]

Col. Robert Douglas, Grant's private secretary, then arranged a second meeting with the president on 19 May, assuring Holden that the president was disposed to do anything he could to take care of him, but indicated that no decision had been made as to the nature of assistance.[13] When Holden called at the White House, he again found the president "very kind" and willing to be helpful. He decided that Holden should file a formal application for federal employment, which he did the following day: "Under these circumstances I respectfully ask for some employment under the government. I am not accustomed to such things, and therefore do not know what I should ask for. . . . Leaving the matter in your hands, with the assurance that, in any event, I am your unwavering friend."[14]

With this presidential promise, Holden's anxiety and fears were some-what allayed, and he expressed new hope to his wife: "I am very anxious to see you. Pray tell me when you can come to see me. You might bring one or two of the children, and if you must return and come again, then you can bring the others."[15] At the same time he wrote Laura Holden Olds: "I am unhappy at times, but not despondent. There are brighter days ahead for all of us. We must not despair. . . . I will yet triumph over all my enemies. The God of Justice will sustain me. The 'priceless love of Christ' sustains me, both for this world and the world hereafter. See your Ma, and be kind to her for *my* sake."[16] He also changed his residence to 1312 I Street opposite Franklin Square. "If I get some place here I can make arrangements by which you and all the family can live here as comfortably as at home."[17]

Still nothing was done immediately, no doubt due to Congress's adjourn-ing on 24 May and Grant's being forced to wait until political matters settled. As he wrote his wife, "There is no change in my condition or prospects. I met the President this morning on the Avenue, and he stopped to shake hands, and was very kind in his manner."[18] Yet the very next day he was uncertain whether he should return to North Carolina or remain in Washington to press for suitable employment. He summarized his prospects:

> The more I think about it the more uncertain I am whether I should re-
> turn home in the course of a week or two, or remain until September. If
> I remain you must come with the children, and this will be very expen-
> sive; if I return I will have to go to prison or give heavy bail. The latter
> could be done, and to go to jail would not hurt me. I have been away
> long enough to show that I am not disposed to play the vulgar martyr.
> The Opposition party would lose more by persecuting me than I would.
> If I should be offered a foreign mission, and should take it, I would
> leave the country under a cloud, because I could not return home be-
> fore I left any more than I can now. If I should get a place here it would
> probably be an inferior one, and friends say I ought not to accept it un-
> less I am disposed to remain here for a year or so. So you can see how
> it is. Things are drifting, and I am satisfied it is all for the best. In no
> event can my enemies now get my property. To leave the State would
> have no bearing in this respect, for there are cases already pending
> against me, in which, if pressed, they would be as apt to recover as in

new ones to be served on my return. Let me hear from you on these points. Whatever *you* say I will do.[19]

During the summer of 1871, the Republican leaders finally proposed to offer Holden the choice of diplomatic service or the opportunity to return to newspaper work. Secretary of State Hamilton Fish offered him a choice of the ambassadorship to Peru or to the Argentine Confederation, but he rejected both offers because he did not want to leave the country under questionable circumstances. Also, Democratic politicians would raise objections.[20]

The newspaper discussion involved two possibilities. At various times it was suggested that Holden take over the editorship of the *Washington Daily Chronicle*, since administrative leaders were not satisfied with the paper's support for the Grant administration. Holden was never convinced that the *Chronicle* offer was serious, since he doubted that party leaders would trust a southern Republican to speak officially for the party and the president. The National Republican Committee proposed to establish a new paper to be published jointly in Washington and Raleigh with Holden as editor. The proposed paper would represent a merger of the *Raleigh Telegram* and *Raleigh Era* and would replace the defunct *Standard* as the party's official paper in North Carolina. After prolonged discussions, Holden agreed to edit the proposed Washington edition of the paper (at that time unnamed), if granted compensation sufficient to allow his family to move to Washington and settle permanently.

He turned cool to the proposal soon afterwards, however. As he studied the matter, he realized that he would not be given a free hand in the editing: "There is little if any prospect that it will be done. The great body of the Northern Republicans, controlled by the Grand Army, hate the Southern Democrats and distrust the Southern Republicans."[21] Ultimately, this newspaper venture did not materialize because the National Republican Committee was unable to arrange adequate finances and also because of a conflict between Senator John Pool and Lewis Hanes for control.[22]

During the course of the newspaper negotiations, Holden made an interesting observation about the current political sentiment in Washington. No doubt this explains much about the difficulties of his situation. Writing to his wife, he said:

> I am writing in a third story room looking towards the Potomac, and towards my distant home. . . . The Chronicle, which, for a few days, maintained the contrary view, had been compelled to take the ground that no ex-rebel, no matter how good a Republican, should hold

office in Washington. It says Southern voters may elect them in the Southern States, that ex-rebels represent the Southern States in Congress, but that ex-rebels must not hold public office under the government. It regards us *all* as ex-rebels. Mr. Pool regards this as a good indication and thinks it will result in calling me to the Editorship of the Chronicle. I do not see it. I am to be amused until the Era is placed in new hands, the prospect of employment here will meanwhile fade, and I may be cast ashore like so much driftwood. This may or may not be so. I can not tell. I feel now that all signs are against my obtaining any employment or any position in this City. . . . I am uncertain as to the future. I am still a waif on the ocean. But everything is in the hands of Providence, and I do not despond.[23]

Holden endured the hot summer weather of Washington and the newspaper negotiations only by arranging a family reunion. Mrs. Holden, sensing her husband's loneliness, planned a leisurely visit in June. The three younger Holden children, Mary, Charles, and Beulah, accompanied their mother to Washington; first-floor rooms at the Ebbitt House Hotel were engaged so that the children could experience a stay in a first-class hotel. In his exuberance over a reunion with his family, Holden arranged a northern tour, including Niagara Falls and Saratoga. As he wrote his wife, "Five of us can go and return to Washington for $100. That is cheap. I have never seen Niagara, and it will be a great thing to the children to see it."[24] He also instructed Mrs. Holden: "Bring what summer clothing I have that will do to wear. I am still wearing thick clothing, and the weather here is at times quite hot."[25]

After the northern trip Mrs. Holden and the children returned to Raleigh, leaving Holden "somewhat lonely."[26] The months of July and early August provided no relief, this being the time when the negotiations for a diplomatic or newspaper post dragged on without producing anything. Then fortune turned in Holden's favor. In late August he began serious negotiations with Republican leaders over assuming the political editorship of the *Washington Daily and Weekly Chronicle*.[27] The National Republican Committee hoped that this paper would become the official party organ in Washington and looked to Holden as spokesman because of his experience with the *Standard*. They were also expecting Holden to unite the numerous party factions into a solid front for the upcoming presidential election. On 31 August, Holden wrote his wife: "The Chronicle matter is regarded as settled, though not so yet in form, on account of the absence of the chief proprietor [John M. Morris], who will be here on Monday."[28]

Final arrangements were not completed until 11 September, and he assumed his new duties two days later. Although he was not named editor, Holden was evidently promised enough authority and independence of action to overcome any qualms he had concerning the editorial policy. Moreover, he no longer had any fear about being able to support his family adequately. After the first day on the job, Holden wrote home: "It is a great relief to me to be employed. . . . You will see my hand in the Chronicle to-day. Everything is agreeable and pleasant. The work is easy for me."[29] Writing editorials came naturally; three days later he again wrote his wife: "I have aided on four issues, have written four columns, and have two ready for the paper of Monday next."[30] His salary was set at the rate of five thousand dollars per annum, an excellent compensation for that time, and the same as his compensation as governor. Even so, he did not regard the position as permanent because he had no intention of abandoning his beloved North Carolina. He steadily maintained the hope that popular indignation in the state would ultimately lead to his vindication. "It is only a question of time. I believe the people will, next summer, hurl them [Democratic-controlled General Assembly] from power and give us two-thirds in both houses. In that event we can rescind or expunge the whole [impeachment] proceedings. I do not believe any Legislature can be elected that would refuse to do so."[31]

Working for the *Chronicle* was a pleasant change for Holden, for he was doing what he knew best once again. He soon gained the respect of the management and staff as well as of party leaders. For his columns he consulted not only Republican leaders but also prominent citizens of Washington. For example, when the Great Chicago Fire absorbed national attention, he obtained the famed Col. Robert Green Ingersoll to write on the subject.[32] Through his energetic endeavors, the *Chronicle* prospered and its circulation increased immediately.[33]

As soon as he was settled in at his new post, Holden began making plans for his family to join him. Apparently his wife was hesitant about leaving Raleigh, however. Her health was not the best, and she also felt that she would be needed to help arrange Henrietta's (Ettie) upcoming wedding. Moreover, hatred against Holden still lingered, and she undoubtedly had second thoughts about leaving the house and property unguarded. Nevertheless, it did not take long before she gave her consent. Holden wrote to her of his happiness. "I am very glad that you are willing to live in Washington. We can obtain some pleasant place, keep house, and be happy. Come as soon as convenient. Let me know the boat by which you will arrive."[34] There was a month's delay in Mrs. Holden's departure from Raleigh because of her illness, and Holden's letters displayed his attentiveness. "I felt very much concerned about you, and was much relieved when I heard you were better. . . . Let me urge you not to exert yourself too much. It might result seriously. I am sorry I am not there to help, but it seems everything must devolve on you."[35] In the meantime, Holden rented a suitable house for his family and awaited their arrival, "lonesome but contented. . . . I shall try to have every thing in readiness when you come."[36]

By the end of 1871, life had become comfortable for Holden and his family in Washington; yet he could not rid himself of thoughts of his native state, its people, and its politics. He was constantly consulted by state leaders on major political issues. For example, W. W. Rollins sought his aid on a bill before Congress proposing a western district court,[37] while Alexander McIver wrote about the reorganization of the university and solicited Holden's support and that of the Republican party.[38] But he would not endorse a Republican proposition before the General Assembly to remove the disabling provision of his conviction:

> The conviction and removal were as unjust and iniquitous as the disabling. If we ask only for the latter, the former would seem, as it really would not, to remain with out consent. The men who performed this act will inevitably go down before popular indignation. . . .
> In that event we can rescind or expunge the whole proceedings.
> In the first place, I did my duty to the best of my knowledge and ability, in the first effort made to put down the Ku-Klux. No doubt mistakes were made, but the object was good, and was pursued unflinching and boldly. The President, all good people South and the nation generally have sustained me. I went through my trial without asking favors of the assassins or their leaders. I left the State not because I *feared* them, but for the sake of peace to a poor distracted people. I felt that I was in the way of peace, and I went into exile in the hope that good might come of it in the whole State, my enemies included. Here I am unsubdued by persecution attached to my State. . . . If my friends, of their own accord, think it best to make this movement, covering a part of the judgment, or a movement covering all of it, that is for them. But I wish it distinctly understood and announced, that I ask no favors at the hands of the present Legislature. I expect at the proper time to appeal to the people against them.[39]

No doubt Holden expected ultimate exoneration and vindication. "Judge Boyden intimated to me when here recently, that the Chief Justice had admitted that the writ of *habeas corpus* did not run to Alamance or Caswell. How is this? If this be so, then there was no shadow of ground for my conviction. Will the Chief Justice state this now, and admit that he was in error? Please show this to friends."[40] Of course, state sentiment did not turn in his favor, and he forever remained frustrated in his efforts to clear his name and restore his political rights.

Despite the unqualified success that Holden enjoyed with the *Chronicle*, he was not happy living in Washington, a city he described as a "selfish and unhappy City." He felt like an outsider in the national political arena, for he could never make it into the inner circle of the Grant administration or the National Republican Committee. While he could meet with congressional leaders and even attend congressional sessions, national events swarmed over and about him without directly or personally involving him. He missed the exhilaration and challenge of participating in the decision-making processes, although it is doubtful that he could ever have adjusted to a national role. To be sure, he had the ability and the mind needed to make a contribution to the nation, but it is doubtful if his philosophy and moral code would have permitted him to remain very long in Washington. Moreover, his genuine love for his North Carolina, coupled with his experience there and elsewhere, made him more concerned with local and state affairs.

Consequently, he resigned the editorship of the *Chronicle* on 29 February 1872 and returned to Raleigh as the newly appointed postmaster. This new position carried with it much less prestige, but it provided safety in a federal appointment beyond state harassment. It also would provide peace and happiness for his family; they could return to their residence and life without the complications of state politics. Even so, the appointment was not popularly received by Republicans or Democrats, and he was forced to return to Washington in 1873 to consult with President Grant and administration leaders about retaining his appointment. On 1 March 1873 he met with the president and then wrote his wife: "Several of us saw the President yesterday for a few minutes. He was particularly kind and polite towards me. Col. [R. M.] Douglas says that in regard to the Post Office he said I should have it any way, no matter who might oppose it."[41] Consequently, on 12 March 1873, Holden was made "regional" United States postmaster, with headquarters in Raleigh. This appointment was for four years and was renewed by President Rutherford B. Hayes in 1877 for a second four-year term.

His career as postmaster proved to be quite successful not only for him personally but for the federal government as well. It especially served to heal harsh feelings against him. Now he was free to associate with influential men of the city and state, Democrats and Republicans, friends and former enemies.

He was accepted as he really was, rather than as a "tyrant." The position also permitted him to supervise the construction of a new post office in Raleigh and to expand postal services throughout the state. In 1878 he directed the building and furnishing of a new three-story federal building, while J. G. Hill was the supervising architect.[42]

But these years were not without their problems. Opposition arose about the length of his appointment and about his employment practices—discrimination against blacks and "adopted" (carpetbagger) citizens. James H. Harris, a local leader among the blacks, was especially critical. Harris believed that the post office should be filled with patronage appointees, in contrast to Holden's policy of hiring by ability and performance, and he also resented Holden because he believed him instrumental in his earlier defeat in the congressional race. He further objected to Holden's being regarded as the Republican "boss" in the state. Another outspoken critic was Tim Lee, the carpetbagger Wake County sheriff. When Holden was informed of Lee's defeat for reelection in 1874, he expressed his sentiments simply and clearly: "Tim Lee is beaten, and all honest men are rejoiced."[43] Also, Josiah Turner and other Democratic opponents of previous years continued their vocal denunciations, making underhanded slurs, instituting legal suits against him and his estate, and seeking revocation of his post office appointment.

As postmaster, Holden set the high work standards he had followed while editing the *Standard*, which he applied both to himself and to his employees. He was always punctual, walking from his house so that he could converse with friends along the way, but once on the job he put in more than the required hours. In doing this, he seemed to be proving himself worthy of the position, just as when he was a young editor. He seldom took time off for personal vacations, although he always insisted that Mrs. Holden and the family make frequent visits to the ocean or to the mountains where they would hold family reunions and escape the heat of Raleigh. For his own relaxation, he would slip away to Kittrell Springs for a few days to renew his energies. On his free time he welcomed friends into his home, and many evenings were spent in lively discussions on countless subjects. He supervised all phases of his duties as postmaster, but he was particularly careful that federal authorities were given strict accounting of all monies expended. No doubt he wished to assure everyone that there was no taint of corruption in his post. When Maxwell Gorman, the son of a former employee and trusted friend, was suspected of robbing the mail while serving as a postal clerk, Holden considered it his duty to have him arrested: "He set a trap for himself and walked into it. I fear he is guilty."[44]

In the early years of his appointment, Holden sought to avoid active involvement in state politics, and he abstained from any engagement in party politics on government time. Realizing that he needed the job for financial security, he had no desire to further divide and alienate Republican leaders, thereby assuring the Democratic party of supremacy. Even so, he was considered an "elder statesman" and was frequently consulted by trusted friends on major issues. The fact that he never recommended anyone for a patronage job unless that person had stood resolutely by him during the years 1870-71 meant that he was not always popular with certain elements of the party.

By 1876, however, he felt more secure and began to take a more active part in Republican politics. He consented to serve on the Republican state executive committee and on the party's campaign committee as well. He declined to go to the presidential convention, but once Rutherford B. Hayes had won the nomination, he strongly endorsed his candidacy. In June 1876 he wrote to Hayes, "Put down North Carolina as a Republican State in November next. We shall be certain to give you our Electoral vote. The Republicans are jubilant, and the Democrats depressed over the news from Cincinnati."[45] Later he added: "I am of the opinion that N. Carolina with a good state ticket could be carried for you by several thousand. I have consulted Hon. Thomas Settle and others of our friends and they concur in sentiments with me."[46]

Holden steadfastly refused to campaign openly, however, for fear of being asked, "What have you to do with the question who shall hold state offices, when you yourself, like a penitentiary convict, cannot be even a constable in your own township?"[47] Nevertheless, he wrote incessantly to friends trying to persuade them to vote solidly for the Republican ticket, and in so doing, he drew fire from the Democratic opposition.[48] Despite his efforts, North Carolina voted Democratic and the popular Zeb Vance was returned to the state's gubernatorial post.

In the dispute over the outcome of the Tilden-Hayes election, Holden was convinced from the beginning that Republican Hayes would ultimately win the presidency. He reasoned, "The Democrats will bluster and threaten, but they will do nothing. It is exceedingly fortunate that Grant is in the chair. But for this fact we could have war."[49] Early in 1877, before the establishment of the special electoral commission, he advised Hayes: "What the dominant Democratic party of the South needs is to be thoroughly and finally convinced that *we have a government*; that the laws will be inflexibly maintained; that the weak will be protected against the strong; and the Reconstruction Acts are a finality. We need very great firmness, joined to kindness and justice, and honest and good men everywhere in office."[50]

Holden remained in close contact with Washington, and he promptly endorsed Hayes's policy of conciliation:

> Allow me to congratulate you on the success thus far of your policy of pacification. I am rejoiced that quiet, order and good feeling are beginning to prevail in Louisiana and South Carolina. The great body of the people will sustain you. In this State the effect of your policy is marked and gratifying. Leading men of the so-called Conservative party are openly approving your course, among them the venerable B. F. Moore, of this City, one of the expert Jurists of the South. He is a man of large means, and has, therefore, a deep stake in the public welfare. He observed, a day or two since, in private conversation, that you were keeping your pledges honestly and truly, and that the extreme men of his party in this State "did not want you to do right." Also, J. M. Leach, one of the late State Electors on the Tilden ticket, and who canvassed the State as a friend of Gov. Vance, and formerly a Whig member of Congress, is engaged in middle Western Carolina in rallying the old Whigs to your support. The people themselves are tired of strife, and they hail your policy even as "the shadow of a great rock in a weary land." . . . I believe your policy of pacification and good will, joined to healthy civil service rules, and much needed reforms in the Revenue service, will add not less than twenty thousand to our ranks during the first two years of your administration.[51]

It was not Holden's destiny to remain in the Republican party. As President Hayes and his liberal wing of the party were unable to get control of the national party, Holden realized that he could no longer wholeheartedly support party programs. Furthermore, he faced new and more determined resistance from local leaders who charged that he was no longer a "100 percent" Republican. A mass meeting assembled in Raleigh on 2 April 1881 and drafted resolutions opposing his reappointment as Raleigh postmaster. Even Judge Albion W. Tourgée used his influence with President James A. Garfield in support of the resolution.[52] Holden attempted to defend himself in a lengthy rebuttal. He claimed that during his terms as governor and postmaster he had treated all classes honestly and fairly.[53] Afterwards, Holden went to Washington to press his case, and for a time a deadlock ensued between Garfield and his patronage advisers. Holden saw Senator John Sherman and Postmaster-General Timothy O. Howe and came away with the belief that he would not lose his position. He wrote his wife: "I will be continued. . . . There is a movement on foot to dispose of [John] Nichols in some other way, and re-nominate me. The President says he owes this to Nichols, and does not want to chafe me."[54] And he wrote to Vance three days later in the same vein: "The deadlock is a good thing for me just now. I am holding over, and it is paying me $200 per month. While I would not obstruct Mr. Nichols's confirmation, still I think he might wait. . . . I have not a word to say for myself, of myself, or about myself, except that I have no objection to the deadlock. . . . I write in confidence. I have no objection to a reasonable deadlock."[55]

In the end, President Garfield refused the reappointment and retired Holden to private life. This, and his growing disenchantment with northern Republican leaders and their policies, caused him to break with the Republican party. He believed the northern advocacy of ever higher protective tariffs and black social equality, plus the failure to alleviate southern economic hardships, contradicted the original Republican philosophy. From that time on, Holden followed a completely independent political course and, characteristically, he announced his action boldly and forthrightly: "I am a 'Holden man.' The old people of the State will know what this expression means. If I shall vote at all hereafter, I will vote independently for good men and proper measures. The Union is safe. . . . *I am therefore for North Carolina and her best interests against all comers.*"[56]

With his exit from public service, Holden rearranged his life, which took on a completely new meaning. Previously his time and energies had been devoted to editorial duties, political party functions, statewide drives for peace and union, or executive responsibilities. Now he could dedicate himself to family and personal matters—some quite sad: Joseph Holden returned from Omaha still an alcoholic and died in 1875. In retirement, Holden took on a new personality, becoming a doting grandfather and a concerned neighbor who constantly performed acts of kindness for those in need. He enjoyed having the ever-growing number of grandchildren for visits and took long walks with them or enchanted them with favorite stories. He also was a friend and benefactor of the poor, concerning himself with their temporal and spiritual welfare. In 1906 the *Raleigh News and Observer* published a series of articles by the Rev. R. H. Whitaker of the Methodist *Christian Advocate* under the general heading "Reminiscences." The one entitled "William W. Holden, the Governor and the Man" cites a typical story of Holden's generosity:

> The last years of Governor Holden's life were spent in quietude, and in the bosom of his family. . . . He was a great friend of the poor, . . . and they found him a friend indeed.

No one thought that Aunt Abby House, who not only hated but openly abused and cursed him, would ever be at peace with "Bill Holden," as she derisively called him. But, strange as it may sound in the ears of those who do not know the power of the Gospel of Christ, Aunt Abby learned to love him; and when she died she carried with her . . . the recollection of the many prayers he had prayed beside her sick bed, as well as the material comforts his thoughtfulness and kindheartedness had brought to her desolate little home, in the eastern suburbs of Raleigh.[57]

In spite of these deeds, Holden was never accorded the respect or appreciation due him. Even his religiousness was a matter for confusion and misrepresentation. In early life he had been a member of the Methodist faith and an active worshiper at Edenton Street Methodist Church in Raleigh, but in 1843 he withdrew following a heated quarrel with Thomas Lemay, a former benefactor.[58] From then until impeachment he and his family declined to take an active role in church affairs, or even to join a congregation. Although he had little of the sectarian in him, his private life exemplified many Christian virtues. He was fond of quoting John Wesley: "When I was young I was sure of everything. In a few years, having been mistaken a thousand times, I was not half so sure of most things as I was before. At present I am hardly sure of anything but what God has revealed to man."[59] At the time of his death he had found complete peace with God and his fellowman. He had expressed his basic beliefs in an address in 1859 to the students of the Raleigh Female Seminary: "The source of all truth, and the best of all books, is the Bible . . . for, aside from the divine spirit which inspires it in its beauty and sublimity of style, . . . the Bible furnishes lessons in faith, fortitude, sagacity, humility, thoughtfulness, cheerfulness, courage, patience and charity, which no other book contains."[60]

During the lonely and trying days of his impeachment trial, the Holdens attended a Baptist revival in Raleigh conducted by the evangelist A. B. Earle. Holden was converted and baptized into that denomination. For the next fifteen years he was an active communicant in Washington and in Raleigh, where he attended the First Baptist Church. His political enemies, especially Josiah Turner and his *Sentinel*, ridiculed his "born-again" Christianity, claiming it was planned in an effort to gain public approbation, and for years afterwards Holden was harangued about this. One such statement was in the 20 December 1870 issue of the *New York Herald*: "Governor Holden goes to impeachment as if he were going to be hanged. On Friday he professed religion and to-day he is to be baptized." The *Nation*, 22 December 1870, said: "No record of any similar preparation for impeachment is, we believe, to be found in the books and the effect of it will be watched by jurists with deep interest."[61] The *New York World* wrote: "That nasty tenderness which fondles the poor, dear murderer, and says the ravisher has been only too acutely moved by emotion, capable of making him a grandsire in Israel if you let him go, is at work to defend Governor Holden in North Carolina."[62]

Holden's friends knew, however, that his religious experience represented a change in his personal life, for he was able to come to grips with tragedy, to find peace with God and his fellowman. Also, it provided him the strength to accept the partisan manner in which his trial was conducted. Afterwards, before finding employment in Washington, Holden wrote to his wife: "I often think what a blessed thing it was for you and I that Mr. Earle came to Raleigh. Otherwise, what would have become of us under this pressure? But the true estimate we now form of everything, and our faith, have sustained us."[63] Throughout his stay in the capital he attended Baptist services and commented, "I have heard no man like Mr. Earle."[64]

Upon his return to Raleigh he continued to be an active member of his church. His correspondence is filled with glowing accounts of Sunday school attendance, participation in the Baptist state conventions, discussions of sermons and moral issues, his work as leader of the statewide prohibition movement, and his efforts to help others find salvation. In this last work he became virtually a modern-day apostle. He wrote his friend Thomas Settle, "I have been much concerned for your salvation. I have thought and prayed for you a great deal. . . . We are saved only by grace—that is, by the favor of God, for the sake of Christ."[65]

The Salem poet John H. Boner, who had worked closely with Holden during his editorship of the *Standard* and his gubernatorial administration, left an interesting account of his experience with the former governor:

> When last I saw him, about eight years ago, his first question after we were seated in his drawing-room was: "John, what is your spiritual condition?" I confess that for several reasons I felt too embarassed to answer him. Seeing my confusion, he continued. "Tell me, would you like to see Christ reign on earth?" I quickly and honestly replied: "I would." "Then, sir," said he, slapping the arm of his chair with that emphatic gesture peculiar to him, "you are a saved man; you are saved as by fire, but you are saved." We had a long and a delightful talk, and when I left he followed me to the front door with affectionate demon-

stration, but not forgetting the dignified courteous bow which we who knew him so well remember.[66]

For many years Holden led noonday prayer services in Raleigh, holding the group together through determination and perseverance. He also attended Monday night prayer meetings. When his old friend Robert P. Dick delivered a prohibition speech in Raleigh in June 1886, he wrote a glowing account for the *News and Observer*. Whereupon Dick responded with a note of thanks:

> The people of the State—and I hope of the United States—have determined to check greatly—if not stop the terrible evil of drunkeness. Christian men have taken hold of the matter,—and Christian women are intensely interested,—and the Ministers of the Gospel now find it to be their duty to enter actively into the work. May God bless us both and spare our lives to see the manifestation of His goodness and mercy—power and glory in freeing society from the great sin and curse of intemperance.

Dick then closed by saying, "I am glad to see your days of life—as the evening comes on—so beautifully illuminated with the light of Christian faith, hope and love."[67] Holden proved himself to be a man of faith—one who lived his later years openly and performed his good deeds for the betterment of humanity.[68]

In 1887, Holden returned to the Edenton Street Methodist Church. At a special service dedicating the church's new sanctuary, he wrote a hymn rendered by the choir.[69] Holden's dissatisfaction with the Baptist church may have been due to his running dispute with the *Biblical Recorder*, the denominational paper, when it became involved in political issues. Holden was determined that his church should remain entirely free of the political arena. Too, he disagreed with the *Recorder* on the church's opposition to President Kemp P. Battle and the University of North Carolina. Writing to Battle, Holden said,

> I see with regret that the Biblical Recorder continues its unjust attacks on you.
>
> I write to express my disapproval of the course of that paper. I am a Baptist, and it has occurred to me that if you ever think of me, you may suppose that I sympathize with the Recorder in its opposition to the University. I do not so sympathize. On the contrary, I do not hesitate to denounce it for taking part in politics and for opposing the University.

I regard the University as the great hope of the State. Every true man should stand by it.[70]

It was from his family, a remarkably close-knit unit, that Holden gained his greatest pleasure in his latter years. No doubt his political adversity produced a defensive attitude in the Holden children, but Holden and his wife worked together to develop respect and self-esteem in the children. His was a three-tier family—four children from his first wife, Ann Augusta Young Holden, four by his second marriage to Louisa Harrison Holden, and the ever-growing number of grandchildren.[71] There was a close comradeship among the three levels, for each developed an almost adoring affection for their father and "Grand-pa." Whenever possible, Holden arranged for all to gather for festive occasions in Raleigh, particularly for the State Fair and the Christmas holidays. The weddings of the many daughters gave the parents additional opportunities for reunions. Like that of Ida Augusta Holden and Calvin J. Cowles in 1868, the other weddings were private affairs performed in the Holden residence; but all were proper and unobtrusive, as befitted the Holden and Harrison social position. When Beulah Williamson married Walter R. Henry, a young Raleigh attorney, on 6 October 1885, the Holdens gave a dinner for family members and close friends, including Governor Alfred M. Scales, Chief Justice William N. H. Smith, Judge Walter Clark, and Daniel G. Fowle.[72]

As the daughters married, the Holdens provided financial assistance when needed but never attempted to interfere in their family affairs. Each new member was made welcome into the family. Mary Eldridge and her husband, Claude A. Sherwood, were given a Raleigh residence that cost two thousand dollars on an adjoining lot on McDowell Street just back of the Holden residence.[73] In 1886, Mrs. Holden purchased property in Henderson at 240 Chasvasse Avenue and constructed a two-story Queen Anne–style frame house for Beulah Henry, when her husband began legal practice in partnership with W. H. Young in that city. The house still stands (known as the Holden-Edwards house) and is noted for its interesting architectural design, especially its hipped and jerkin-headed gable rooflines.[74]

The one exception in this contented family was Lewis P. Olds, Laura's husband. While he had served as the state's attorney general during Holden's governorship and had rendered legal assistance in family matters, such as raising money to cover the impeachment trial costs, the family did not regard him as totally responsible or reliable. In fact, Holden always considered him "a strange person." In later years, Olds was unable to settle on permanent employment and eventually became a restless wanderer. In 1872, the Oldses went to San Juan, Nicaragua, partly to enable Laura to recover her health. In 1876, while living in Washington, D.C., Olds threatened to move to St. Helena Island without Laura and their son Harry.[75] In 1886, Olds wrote Mrs. Holden thanking her for fifty-one dollars and deeds to property in Thomasville. All the while, Holden encouraged him to settle in Wilkesboro so that they could be under the helpful influence of Calvin and Ida Cowles.[76] Through it all, Holden wrote letters of encouragement to Laura and implored her and baby Harry "to pay us a visit."

Holden always considered Mary Holden Sherwood as the child most similar to him in temperament. It was she who patiently helped her father write his memoirs when a stroke left his right arm paralyzed. While she was still a child, he had penned the following verse for her and probably continued to think of her in this vein:

> Mirthful, graceful little Mary,
> Always happy as a fairy,
> Robed in curls which dance around her
> You would think if you had found her
> Lingering lonely near no mortal,
> Heaven an angel from its portal,
> On this earth had softly landed.
> Lips like rose buds, just expanded.
> Diamond are her eyes when lighted
> Each all soul, and so delighted,
> Never more may they be blighted.[77]

Holden never fully recovered from the shock of Joseph's death. He had held such high hopes that, because of his ability and personality, Jo would perhaps carry on the family name and succeed in state affairs where he himself had faltered. He felt the disappointment keenly and accepted some of the responsibility of Jo's failure in not supervising his son more closely. It was no wonder that he transferred his hopes to his remaining son Charles. But Charles did not have the outgoing, ambitious personality of his brother; instead, he was more academically inclined and was encouraged to follow a scholarly career. From the beginning of Charles's education, Holden made sure that he had good instructors and that the best of English and American literature was available to him; in addition there was his own vast political knowledge. Yet Charles was a frail child who suffered from asthma, and Raleigh's humid climate did not agree with him. For this reason Mrs. Holden often took him to the mountains, especially to Warm Springs (now Hot Springs), or to Kittrell Springs in Granville (now Vance) County.

In 1877 he entered Yale University, a result of his parents' determination that he receive the best education possible. There Charles proved himself to be an outstanding scholar, unlike many other southern students who were poorly prepared. Always fearful for his health and with a special fondness for her only son, Mrs. Holden was not happy in having him so far from home; so perhaps it was inevitable that he would complete his college work nearer Raleigh at the University of Virginia. No doubt Holden wholeheartedly agreed with this decision. That Charles should attend the University of North Carolina was unthinkable in view of its opposition to his father. Nevertheless, as he was a Southerner and eager that his son graduate from a southern university, the Charlottesville institution was the logical choice. Charles enrolled for the 1880 term and graduated, "doing finely," as his proud parents liked to observe. Upon graduation, he returned to Raleigh and accepted a teaching position, but his early death ended a promising career. Among Charles's pupils was David Clark, son of the supreme court justice Walter Clark; in 1890 Justice Clark wrote Charles to say: "Please examine David thoroughly. He was in same class at Graded School with Jones Fuller. I don't wish him put back unless *necessary*. He seems disposed to study but I fear he has not been taught with thoroughness."[78]

While Holden was always regarded as the head of the family, it was Louisa Holden who proved to be the real bulwark. She tied the three-tier family together during his lifetime, and when a series of paralytic strokes struck Holden, she assumed control and held the family together during his last days and after his death. Mrs. Holden had earlier demonstrated her financial acumen when she took control of the residence and family investments while her husband was governor, thereby protecting the family against lawsuits such as those under constant litigation by Josiah Turner. The relationship between husband and wife was a very close one. Although his letters to her were always signed "W. W. Holden," underneath that formality was a devoted and appreciative husband. On their thirtieth anniversary, Holden wrote: "Thirty years ago we were married. During all these years you have been a helpmate indeed. I have regretted many things, but never regretted that I made you my wife."[79] Later, Mrs. Holden returned the compliment: "No man's wife was ever treated more kindly or affectionately. My wishes were always gratified as far as he was able."[80]

As Holden made the transition from an active public life to that of a private citizen, his zeal for journalism returned.[81] He first began publishing a series of recollections of earlier days, but he was careful never to involve himself in controversial issues. He was beyond the point of further political ambition, "save only to serve and do good to others."[82] This was recognized by the *Raleigh News*, for in June 1879 he wrote a number of anonymous editorials for the paper at the request of the publisher. The next year he began publishing several biographical sketches of prominent North Carolinians for the *Charlotte Western Democrat*, a journal edited by his old friend William J. Yates. Among his published articles are the following: "Old Times in Raleigh—The Legislature—Prominent Men of 1835–'44," "Capt. John Walker of Mecklenburg—Public Affairs in N.C. from 1840 to 1860," "Gen. Alfred Dockery of Richmond County: His Public Life from 1822 to 1873," and "Henry Clay in Raleigh in 1844."

These were so well received by friend and foe that he was invited to deliver an address on the history of journalism in North Carolina before the North Carolina Press Association in Winston in June 1881. This was an ambitious undertaking for one who had been out of this business for over twelve years; yet he carried out the task in magnificent fashion. He not only traced the beginnings of the press in the state but he gave many interesting facts about the early editors who had served the state well. His address was published by the News and Observer Job Printers in Raleigh and was regarded then, as it is now, as the best source of information on the subject. Young Josephus Daniels, who was just beginning his long and illustrious career, heard the Holden address and later provided this interesting commentary:

> I had heard Governor Holden denounced as the meanest of men and worst of Governors, by stump speakers, and my mind was filled with pictures of Bluebeard and other infamous characters. I imagined him a man of powerful build, stiff grizzly beard, a stern grim visage and fearful looking eyes beneath shaggy eyebrows. I first saw him in 1881 at Winston, where by invitation he delivered an address to the editors of the State on Journalism in North Carolina. I never watched a man with so much curiosity. When he commenced to speak, I noticed that his voice was low and not at all harsh, that he spoke more kindly and warmly of the great men who in other days controlled the journalism in North Carolina; and particularly was I impressed with the thread of profound reverence for things sacred and allusions to duty to God that ran through the entire address. What thought I, can this be the man who has been such an enemy to North Carolina.[83]

The warm reception accorded his Winston address gave Holden a new lease on life and made him look forward to using his talent to write additional articles on subjects of state interest. Later that year the publication of John W. Moore's *History of North Carolina* gave Holden the opportunity to publish a series of commentaries for Samuel A. Ashe in the *Raleigh News and Observer*. In these he attempted to correct some of the errors and false assumptions perpetrated by the historian. At no time did he write from a partisan viewpoint; nor did he defend his own actions without justification. He closed his comments as follows:

> I have now done with my brief comments on Maj. Moore's history. I think I have written in a kind and considerate spirit. I have not sought to depreciate the book itself, or its gifted author. On the contrary, I would commend him for his industry and zeal, and would trust, as I do, that he will grow in knowledge and wisdom as he grows in years. I believe neither in *Union* or in *Confederate* history. True history is many-sided, but, after all, is there any history really true in all respects save the Bible?[84]

Undoubtedly Holden would have pursued such projects with keen interest had serious illness not struck him in April 1882. He suffered a stroke that left his right arm practically useless for more than a year. So serious was the paralysis that his doctor ordered complete bed rest and the house to "be kept in perfect quiet."[85] It was not until 1884 that he recovered sufficiently "to write slowly but with difficulty" and to contemplate a new project.[86] He announced in late fall that he planned to write a history of North Carolina, concentrating on the period since 1860. He anticipated that it would run between five and six hundred pages, and he thought he could "do justice to all the public men of the State, living and dead."[87] He also proposed to ask Governor Zebulon Vance, Secretary of State William L. Saunders, Duncan K. McRae, and Rufus Barringer to write sketches under their own names on the causes of the Civil War and how the state conducted itself during the war. Tragically, the project was never completed, for four such divergent viewpoints would have provided a truly unbiased account of that controversial part of the state's history.[88]

But continued ill health brought an end to Holden's project for a state history. Instead, he began writing his memoirs. Unfortunately for him, and for later generations of historians, this project did not measure up to the standards associated with Holden's name. Begun while he was still in pain and his hand paralyzed, and not always in complete control of his mental faculties, the writing became a family project with daughter Mary doing the editing. Holden dictated the memoirs between November 1889 and March 1890. The day following the completion of the manuscript, he was stricken again by paralysis, which completely shattered his speech processes. Theo. H. Hill, *New York World* editor, and John B. Neathery, longtime friend and partner in the Nichols, Gorman, and Neathery Printers of Raleigh, were both asked to edit the manuscript; but both declined. The memoirs remained, therefore, a defense of Holden's gubernatorial career, filled with religious overtones; the fire of earlier years was lacking, as well as his commanding journalistic style. Succeeding generations should not judge him by his memoirs. If it had been written in the prime of life, it surely would have given a more adequate picture of major developments in North Carolina in the nineteenth century and Holden's involvement. The manuscript was not published until 1911, long after his death; thus, for the family the memoirs created a number of problems, especially concerning whether it should be published locally or in New York. W. R. Henry, Beulah Holden's husband, gives an inkling of the family disagreements when he wrote his niece Louisa Virginia Sherwood:

> My wife and self objected simply because we did not wish them published under such conditions and by an unknown man [William K. Boyd] to be substantially buried in the archives of Trinity College.
> . . . The real reason of my objection is this—Governor Holden was and is now considered the gratest [*sic*] Editor the South ever produced, but posterity will judge him by these Memoirs if they be published, and they are written in such style—after he was paralyzed—that they reflect absolutely no proper light upon his genius.
> Besides, they are full of such Christian spirit . . . that they will be totally unappreciated, especially as a reply to the bitter partisans who crucified him politically.[89]

Holden died still barred from holding public office. His honest conviction had been that the public would turn against those who had so unfairly convicted him and that a later General Assembly would repudiate his conviction and remove the disability. But this change in public opinion never materialized. Although numerous attempts were begun to restore him to full citizenship, Holden refused to take the initiative or, in fact, to do anything in his own behalf. He was too proud to seek a legislative pardon, always insisting that such an action should come voluntarily from the people and be without friction from either of the political parties. Nevertheless, Edward Conigland took the lead in urging removal of the disabilities, and in 1875 wrote to Thomas L. Clingman asking that the 1875 constitutional convention adopt a resolution favoring such action. "Mr. Holden was rarely, if at all, the instigator of any measure for which he was impeached. . . . He often resisted their [carpetbaggers'] counsel, and the measures he adopted and which brought his difficulties upon him, were of the head and not of the heart."[90]

In 1878, when another such attempt was under way, Holden broke his silence, saying, "I think I did nothing in 1870 which deserved impeachment. I feel I was unjustly convicted, and to ask pardon would be to confess my guilt."[91] On another occasion, however, he did ask the General Assembly to restore his good name and published the following card in all of the state's papers:

> To the General Assembly of North Carolina Soon to Be in Session:
>
> Gentlemen: On the 22nd day of March, 1871, the Senate of North Carolina sitting as a Court of Impeachment, pronounced judgment against me in six out of eight articles of impeachment filed against me by the House of Representatives. I was held by this judgment as guilty of "high crimes and misdemeanors." I deny this in the most solemn manner. I do not ask you to repeal or rescind this sentence of judgment, for it is being executed, and it might not be repealed or rescinded save by the same court that passed it, but I ask you most earnestly to resolve or declare that in your opinion, I was actuated by good motives in what I did, and that I had for my object the best and highest interests of the State.
>
> I am not now a party man. Both parties have disowned me. I appeal to you solely on the ground of justice. I have never been an enemy to the State. On the contrary, I have loved her well, and do now, and am her loyal son, though proscribed and banned.
>
> The press of the State will please copy the above card as an act of kindness to a former member of the craft and send me a copy of the paper.[92]

In 1885, Senator Hezekiah A. Gudger of Buncombe County secured a pledge of a majority of the state senators to vote favorably on a removal proposal, but Holden intervened and requested that Gudger drop the effort when he learned that Henry Groves Connor, Democratic chairman of the senate judiciary committee, was opposed.[93] A similar refusal by Holden was extended to Thomas Goode Tucker in 1887, sponsor of another attempt.[94] Despite the assertion that he had overcome the stigma of the 1871 impeachment conviction and the resulting ban from holding state office, Holden always hoped that he would be vindicated and was genuinely hurt that this was never done. Holden's strict adherence to his Christian principles would not permit him to speak unkindly of those who did not support the efforts for his restoration of citizenship, yet he was still hurt. Through it all, Holden remained firm in his belief that his acts had not warranted impeachment and that his conviction was due to extreme partisanship. His hope for the restoration of citizenship was based primarily on his desire to return the Holden family name to full public acceptance. Mrs. Holden would have welcomed such an act of conscience, not only for herself and for her family members but also for her husband and his peace of mind during his last years.

Holden's health steadily deteriorated in his last year. He suffered several paralytic strokes which left him a virtual invalid. His last and fatal attack occurred a few days prior to his death, which came quietly and peacefully on Tuesday, 2 March 1892, at his residence. It is perhaps surprising that he lived so long, seventy-four years, for he was high strung and had worked at a furious pace in every undertaking.

The last rites for Holden were conducted in a simple but dignified ceremony at the Edenton Street Methodist Church at four o'clock, 3 March; he was interred in Oakwood Cemetery. The state flag flew at half mast, and among those in the overflowing congregation were such distinguished persons as Governor Thomas M. Holt and Chief Justice Augustus S. Merrimon, other state officials, longtime friends, and members of the Typographical Union, who appeared in a body to pay their respects to their former member and friend. The service was conducted by the Reverend J. N. Cole, pastor, Presiding Elder Dr. J. A. Cunninggim, and Dr. F. L. Reid, close friend and editor of the *North Carolina Christian Advocate*. It consisted of hymns, prayers, and meditation, all of which offered ample testimony to the goodness of the man. Among the hymns were Holden's favorites such as "Sleep, Warrior, Sleep," "Jerusalem, My Happy Home," and "Nearer My God to Thee." As the casket was borne from the sanctuary, the strains of "Home, Sweet Home" were played by the organ, a fitting tribute to the "voice of the people."[95]

But death did not end the Holden story. His old antagonist Josiah Turner fought for more than two years to recover damages from the Holden estate. In 1894 the Wake County Superior Court refused a judgment of approximately fifteen thousand dollars filed by Turner, and the state supreme court refused to hear his appeal. Defended by John W. Hinsdale, F. H. Busbee, and R. O. Burton, Mrs. Holden proved beyond any doubt that her husband had obtained no illegal funds while serving as governor and that his action in placing the family finances and property in her name was legal.[96] Free at last from emotional and financial harassment, Mrs. Holden could spend the remainder of her life quietly enjoying her family and friends.

Holden's fight against the Ku Klux Klan had become part of the nation's literary scene and played an increasingly greater role as the nation sought to solve its growing racial problems. Albion W. Tourgée, the carpetbagger judge from Guilford County who had so unhesitatingly fought the Klan throughout his judicial district, was defeated in 1878 by Alfred M. Scales (later elected governor) in the congressional election. After the defeat he went to Denver, Colorado, where he became the editor of the *Evening News*. At the same time he was being considered as editor for a proposed Republican paper to be published in Raleigh.

No doubt his decision to move was in part owing to fear of negative reaction to two historical novels that he had submitted for publication just prior to his departure from the state. The next year, 1879, his *Figs and Thistles* and *A Fool's Errand by One of the Fools* appeared. The latter portrayed the tragedies of Reconstruction in North Carolina and portrayed Holden in an unfair light. At the time it attracted considerable attention in the literary world. When his adventure in Colorado failed, Tourgée soon moved to New York, where he wrote four additional novels in quick succession: *Bricks without Straw* (1880); *A Royal Gentleman and Zouri's Christmas* (1882); *John Eax and Mamelon, or the South without the Shadow* (1882); and *Not Plowshares, A Novel* (1883). While none was considered great literature, those novels gained the attention of President-elect Garfield, whose inaugural address included a number of Tourgée's educational ideas.[97]

A Fool's Errand and *Bricks without Straw* remain as invaluable examples of a carpetbagger's view of northern ideas of democracy and freedom in a South bound by slavery, racism, and caste. Tourgée's biographer, Otto H. Olsen, declared that they "provide a panoramic view and an astute analysis of the Reconstruction South. The entire story is there—the postwar suffering and confusion, the issues of unionism, race, and reform, the contesting forces, the terrors of the Klan, and the final failure [of Holden and the Republicans]."[98]

It was Thomas Dixon, however, whose two vindictive novels, *The Leopard's Spots* (1902) and *The Clansman* (1905), proved most libelous to Holden. Born of poor farm parents near Shelby, Dixon attended Wake Forest College; after earning the B.A. and M.A. degrees in four years, he transferred to Johns Hopkins University to begin a doctorate in history. There he became a close friend of classmate Woodrow Wilson. After a year, however, Dixon left and went to New York to try his talent as an actor. Failing on the stage, he returned to North Carolina to study law, receiving his license in 1885. Two years later he entered the Baptist ministry, and in a Raleigh church Holden was introduced to this man who later became an admirer of the Ku Klux Klan and the spokesman for American racism. In fact, Holden went often to hear Dixon

preach, advising the young minister to stick to the Gospel and avoid sensation-
alism. This, it turned out, proved impossible.

Finding the North Carolina Baptists not always in agreement with his
radical views, Dixon moved to nondenominational Protestant congregations in
Boston and New York City. In 1899, Dixon left the pulpit to launch a new
career as lecturer and novelist. The two novels, immediate successes, were
promptly written into popular stage productions that toured the nation. In
1913, under the direction of David W. Griffith, *The Clansman* was filmed
under the title *The Birth of a Nation* and was seen on the silent screen by
millions. The National Association for the Advancement of Colored People
sought to prevent release of the movie, but Dixon had arranged for a private
showing for President Woodrow Wilson, his cabinet, members of the Supreme
Court, and congressional leaders; with their tacit approval the release could
not be prevented.[99]

In these novels, by his vilification of Holden and his portrayal of the Klan
as the savior of southern civilization, Dixon laid himself open to libel charges.
Not only did he identify Holden, using the tag "Provisional Governor" and as
the poet who wrote "Calhoun," but references throughout the books are intentionally cruel. In one of the most devastating scenes, Dixon pictures Holden as
Caliban (a cannibal, or a deformed, savage creature). Political abuse was
evident throughout the novels, with no attempt at a portrayal of the real man.
The publication of *The Clansman* was too much for W. R. Henry; he immediately wrote a most defiant letter to Dixon. "I have borne much. I cannot be
expected to remain silent and inactive, while Gov. Holden is libeled on the
stage within sight of his grave, and within the hearing of my children. To do so
would be to play the coward."[100]

The Henry letter was a masterful attempt to set Dixon and the record
straight. He first quoted one of the best-known Democratic editors of the state:
"In speaking of those times and the Legislature of '68, we do not mean to infer
that Gov. Holden himself was corrupt or dishonest, for we know his honor as a
gentleman was never assailed, nor his integrity questioned." He then quoted
from a former political enemy, and no doubt a former member of the Klan,
who wrote after Holden's death, "It is a pleasure to one who was persecuted by
the ill-advised Governor Holden, to record his testimony that Mr. Holden was
a most kindly man, upright and conscientious in all his personal relations as a
christian. The animosities once cherished had long since died out. Peace to his
ashes."

Henry then gave an illustration that best attests to Holden's character. In
1873 an indictment was brought in Alamance County Superior Court against

fifteen citizens for the murder of Wyatt Outlaw, but efforts were made to stop the prosecution in the hopes of restoring peace. Judge Thomas Ruffin, however, would not permit such action until Holden intervened. At Judge Ruffin's instructions, the district solicitor wrote to Holden and described the problem, whereupon Holden replied:

> I am decidedly of the opinion that no further action should be taken against the parties charged with these crimes. Those crimes were not committed in ordinary times. There was a formidable and for a time an all controlling insurrection. There was a government within the government. The civil magistrate was powerless. Military power was invoked. The Ku Klux organization was disbanded. Order was restored. I do not deem it advisable to deal with offenses committed under such conditions in the ordinary way. I am in favor of amnesty, oblivion, mercy to the guilty, and I know not what more to say. You are at liberty to announce the use of my opinion on this subject.

Yet these were the very klansmen whose testimony had helped to convict Holden two years earlier. As a consequence of his intervention, the men were released. This, Henry contended, read more like a passage from the Sermon on the Mount than Dixon's picture, which must have been drawn "with the devil grinning approval." In concluding, Henry suggested that if lightning had struck the Holden home in 1885, the Democratic state government would have been completely disrupted, for among those seated in the parlor were Governor Alfred M. Scales, Chief Justice W. N. H. Smith, Superintendent of Public Instruction Sidney M. Finger, Daniel G. Fowle, Col. Octavious Coke, lawyer John Gatling of Raleigh, and Thomas Settle. "Now, Mr. Dixon, 'honor bright,' do you think such a coterie of gentlemen would have been present on that occasion if Governor [Holden] was or had been the creature that you paint him in your book? Don't you see that their presence alone, proves 'The Leopard Spots' a libel?"

The Henry letter had no effect, though. North Carolina was undergoing racial and economic trials, and the general public continued to blame Holden for their troubles. The widespread circulation and popularity of *The Birth of a Nation* established this false image of Reconstruction in the minds of future generations and, furthermore, was instrumental in causing the revival of the Klan.[101] As W. J. Cash wrote in 1941, "The final great result of Reconstruction . . . is that it established what I have called the savage ideal as it had not been established in any Western people since the decay of medieval feudalism . . . and so paralyzed Southern culture at the root."[102]

Holden's controversial role in state history illustrates how he was a victim of this "savage ideal"; yet history must not overlook his contributions to society or his own ideals. More than any other North Carolinian of his era, Holden shaped the state's political, social, and economic development as he worked unceasingly for the betterment of his fellowman. Through it all he remained true to the principles he first enunciated in the *Standard* in 1843: equal justice for all, the greatest good for the greatest number, free elections, and universal suffrage. In spite of his critics' accusations and his lost administrative opportunities, William W. Holden was a man of dignity and integrity, dedicated to humanism.

NOTES

ABBREVIATIONS

CCHM Chautauqua County Historical Museum, Westfield, New York
DU Perkins Library, Duke University, Durham, North Carolina
HL Rutherford B. Hayes Library, Freemont, Ohio
LC Library of Congress, Washington, D.C.
NA National Archives, Washington, D.C.
SHC Southern Historical Collection, University of North Carolina, Chapel Hill
State Archives North Carolina Department of Archives and History, Raleigh
UCL University of Chicago Library

CHAPTER ONE

1. The major source of information on Holden's early life and family history was obtained by Edgar Estes Folk in a personal interview with Mrs. Henry Murdock, a sister, on 29 April 1930 and used in his study "W. W. Holden." The interview was transcribed, and a copy can be found in the Holden Personal Papers, State Archives. It is not known what Thomas W. Holden's middle initial stood for, but in all probability it was "William." The Holden children included Atelia (Mrs. John L. Lyon); Henry; Mary (Mrs. P. Turberville); E. Brock; Addison; Louisa (who died in infancy); Preston; Lucian; Rebecca (Mrs. John McCarroll); and Margaret (Mrs. Henry Murdock). See also *North Carolina Standard*, 2 February 1848; hereinafter cited as *Standard*.
2. Folk, "Interview," State Archives.
3. Folk, "W. W. Holden, Political Journalist," 585–86.
4. Holden described the Heartt printing techniques in *Address on the History of Journalism in North Carolina*, Winston, 21 June 1881.
5. Boyd, *William W. Holden*, 41; Folk, "W. W. Holden, Political Journalist," 8.
6. Brown, "How Billy Holden Got His First Dollar," Holden Papers, DU. Folk, "W. W. Holden, Political Journalist," 10, declared that young Holden received only silver coins amounting to a dollar rather than an actual silver dollar. Nevertheless, the money was highly prized by Holden, and he often told the story to show how he overcame his early adversities in becoming a successful editor, in contrast to John W. Syme, one of his major competitors, who failed in the publishing business despite prominent family connections, educational opportunities, and wealth.

7. Folk, "W. W. Holden, Political Journalist," 11–12; *Standard*, 5 February 1862. Holden made peace with Heartt and the older boy so that the two "had many a hearty laugh" over the incident. Holden later strongly insisted that he was never actually bound to Heartt and so he could not have broken an apprenticeship.

8. Whiteaker, "William W. Holden: The Governor and the Man," Holden Papers, DU.

9. John H. Boner to Theodore H. Hill, 10 March 1892, Holden Papers, DU.

10. *Standard*, 25 August 1868.

11. Ibid., 20 October 1858. On another occasion he told of his birth in a log cabin and to "an inheritance of ignorance and poverty" (ibid., 5 February 1862).

12. Ibid., 25 August 1868. Holden's article concerned President Andrew Jackson's demand upon France for payment of its debts to the United States.

13. Boyd, *William W. Holden*, 42.

14. Ibid., 91.

15. Holden, *Memoirs*, 150. He repaid the debt within two years.

16. For a thorough description of the Raleigh papers (the *Register*, *North Carolina Standard*, and the *Star*) and other state newspapers of that day, as well as the work of the various editors, see Holden, *Address on History of Journalism*; Folk, "W. W. Holden and the Standard," 22–47; Johnson, *Ante-Bellum North Carolina*, 764–809; Stroupe, "Beginning of Religious Journalism," 1–22, and Elliott, *Raleigh Register*.

17. Johnson, *Ante-Bellum North Carolina*, 771.

18. Amis, *Historical Raleigh*, 75. This salary was eight dollars per week in the summer months and nine dollars during the winter. He worked from sunup until sundown. During the winter months he often worked until midnight.

19. Folk, "W. W. Holden and the Standard," 25.

20. Watkins was a graduate of the University of North Carolina (A.B., 1834, and A.M., 1837) and gave the welcoming speech for Stephen A. Douglas when he campaigned in Raleigh during the 1860 national election. Amis, *Historical Raleigh*, 100.

21. Holden, *Memoirs*, 95. Included in the twenty-one graduates were Calvin Henderson Wiley and Robert W. Lassiter, who later served in the state senate, 1862–65, 1868–70. Upon Wiley's death, 15 January 1887, Holden wrote further about this experience: "The Court consisted at that time of Chief Justice [Thomas] Ruffin, Judge J[oseph] J. Daniel and Judge William Gaston. The Judges sat in Mr. Gaston's bedroom, which was then, as now, on the corner of the lot of Mrs. Taylor, on Hargett street. Mr. Gaston died in that room January 23d, 1844. The examination occupied about two hours, and was very strict. Mr. Wiley acquitted himself remarkable well" (Scrapbook, Holden Papers, DU).

22. Holden to Thomas Ruffin, 3 February 1841, Hamilton, ed., *Papers of Thomas Ruffin*, 1:192.

23. *Raleigh Star*, 22 December 1841. His first formal legal advertisement, published in the *Star*, 1 September 1841, is quite interesting because of the prominence of his

state and national references. Among those cited were Nicholas Biddle of Philadelphia, William A. Graham, and Robert B. Gilliam of Oxford, North Carolina.

24. Copy of William Peace's will, Peace College Archives, Raleigh.

25. Folk, "Interview," State Archives, but the gift was never identified, nor was it ever discussed in the Holden Papers.

26. The portrait was painted by the noted artist William Garle Brown and was presented to Peace Institute on 17 September 1885. See Holden to Rev. R. Burwell and Son, 17 September 1885, and R. Burwell to Holden, 18 September 1885, Holden Papers, DU.

27. Holden to Thomas Settle, 13 July 1852, Settle Papers, SHC; Holden to David Settle Reid, 10 August 1852, Reid Papers, State Archives.

28. Holden thought Busbee's selection would have been catastrophic. See Holden to W. A. Jeffreys, 4 April 1843, Jeffreys Papers, State Archives.

29. The story has passed down that Shepard took Holden out walking near the area that would later be the site of the Federal Cemetery and offered him the editorship. Holden was surprised and at first demurred, pointing out his ten-year record of working on Whig papers and having served as a delegate to the state Whig convention and as secretary of a Whig meeting in Raleigh on 21 February 1842. But Shepard persisted and finally gained his point as Holden returned to the city determined to reenter the journalistic field. See Ashe, ed., *Biographical History*, 3:186. Folk, "W. W. Holden, Political Journalist," 40, says that despite the popularity of the story, no documentary basis for it can be found.

30. Prior to publishing his study on Holden, W. K. Boyd contacted family members seeking verification on Holden's early life. Mary E. Sherwood responded: "I have never heard of my Father's borrowing funds from Duncan Cameron; that must be a mistake, please omit. I do know that James B. Shepard was a firm and true friend; but I have never heard before, that he was met with derision, when he suggested my Father's name as Editor. Whoever gave you these two choice (?) bits of information had heard more than did any member of the family. Please omit that" (Mary E. Sherwood to Boyd, 31 March 1898, Holden Papers, DU).

31. Folk, "W. W. Holden, Political Journalist," 46. He cites Boyd as his source, who in turn cites the *Standard*, 23 August 1868, but no copy of this issue can be found.

32. Holden, *Memoirs*, 96–97.

33. *Standard*, 7 June 1843.

34. Ibid., 28 June 1854.

35. *Leisure Hour* (Oxford), 18 November 1858. In 1854 the *Standard* was the first state, and southern, newspaper to put advertisers on a cash basis.

36. Folk, "W. W. Holden, Political Journalist," 104.

37. Ibid., 96.

38. *Standard*, 14 June 1843.

39. Holden, *Memoirs*, 97.

40. Holden later wrote: "[Clay's] appearance, his manner, his voice, his enunciation,

his action were all apparently perfect, and very impressive. I had heard Mangum, and Badger, and Henry, and Morehead, and Saunders, and Miller, and Waddell, and Graham, and Strange, but never such an orator as Clay" (*Raleigh State Chronicle*, 30 April 1886).

41. A full discussion of the issue of annexation may be found in Pegg, "Whig Party"; Norton, *Democratic Party*; Wagstaff, *States Rights and Political Parties*, 100; and Sitterson, *Secession Movement*, 36–37.

42. *Standard*, 5 March 1845.

43. Late in May 1846, when President Polk requested from North Carolina a regiment of volunteers to serve in the Mexican War, Holden arranged a public meeting in Town Hall and drafted a resolution approving the war and lauding General Zachary Taylor and Captain William J. Clarke and his Raleigh company. He then lectured Whig papers for their denunciation of the war, and especially criticized Governor Graham for appointing Whig officers exclusively in the state regiment.

44. *Standard*, 25 June 1845.

45. Walter Francis Leak, Richmond County planter and lawyer, sought the Democratic nomination, but acceded to the executive committee's decision and supported Shepard. See Holden to David S. Reid, 20 March 1846, Reid Papers, State Archives.

46. Holden to David S. Reid, 8 December 1847, ibid.

47. Holden to W. A. Jeffreys, 14 April 1843, Jeffreys Papers, State Archives.

48. Folk, "W. W. Holden, Political Journalist," 174.

49. Holden, *Memoirs*, 6.

50. *Standard*, 19 January 1848.

51. Ibid., 11 April 1848. See also Holden to David S. Reid, 19 April 1848, for his views on the participants and issues (Reid Papers, State Archives).

52. It should be noted that Reid made the decision to use "free suffrage" even though it had not been included in the Democratic platform and that this decision did not have the full approval of all party leaders. Also, the constitutional limitations on officeholding in the state were even more restrictive—members of the house of commons were required to own one hundred acres of property while state senators had to own three hundred acres. Lefler and Newsome, *North Carolina*, 377–78; Jeffrey, "'Free Suffrage' Revisited," 24–28; and "National Issues, Local Interests," 43–74.

53. *Standard*, 25 April 1848.

54. Holden, *Memoirs*, 5–6.

55. *Standard*, 7 June 1848.

56. Holden to David S. Reid, 23 June 1848, Reid Papers, State Archives.

57. Holden, *Memoirs*, 97–98. It should also be noted that by 1850 the *Standard*'s circulation and advertising patronage had more than doubled and that Holden did not subordinate journalistic ideals to mere profit making. It, along with the *Fayette-ville Observer*, was the first paper in the state to ban patent medicine advertising.

58. Folk, "W. W. Holden, Political Journalist," 224–25.
59. *Raleigh Register*, 2 August 1851. Earlier, that paper had painted a bitterly envious picture of Holden sitting in "the Vatican on Hargett Street," exercising "papal powers" as he strove to keep the party "cleansed, intact, and mobile." For Holden's response, see the *Standard*, 13 January 1864.
60. Folk, "W. W. Holden, Political Journalist," 253–54.
61. *Standard*, 26 February and 18 June 1851.
62. This proviso, first introduced by Representative David Wilmot of Pennsylvania in 1846 and declaring that slavery was to be prohibited in the whole of the territory acquired from Mexico by the United States, passed in the House of Representatives but was defeated in the Senate. For further details, see Hamilton, *Prologue to Conflict*; Morrison, *Democratic Politics and Sectionalism*; and Cooper, *South and Politics of Slavery*.
63. *Standard*, 15 September 1847.
64. Ibid., 8 December 1847.
65. Incited by John C. Calhoun, the southern extremists hoped to use the convention to stop the Wilmot Proviso sentiment in the North, or, failing in this, to bring about a secession movement. Calhoun realized that if South Carolina issued such a call, this would prejudice numerous Southerners against the movement; accordingly, he persuaded political friends in Mississippi to extend the invitation for delegates from all southern states to meet in Nashville on 1 June 1850. The meeting failed, however, to accomplish its desired purpose. The more recent study of the convention is that of Jennings, *Nashville Convention*, while the older study is that of Herndon, "Nashville Convention," 227–37.
66. *Standard*, 16 January 1850. Holden thought that he spoke for a majority of the state Democrats, but Reid, Robert Strange, and Romulus M. Saunders opposed the convention.
67. Ibid., 20 February 1850. In supporting his stand, Holden cited three major points: (1) the convention would prove to the North that the South was united on such principles, so that the North would have to change its attitude or accept responsibility for separation which would ensue; (2) the convention would preserve the Union by having the wisest and ablest southern men make common policy; and (3) the absence of North Carolina delegates would expose the state to the just suspicions of its sister states.
68. Ibid., 3 May 1851. Earlier, on 15 January 1851, Holden expressed his views on secession: "We hold the right of secession as an original preexisting, reserved sovereign right; that whenever the Constitution is palpably violated by Congress or whenever that body fails to carry out the plain provisions of that instrument when required to protect Southern rights, the Union is Dissolved, and that by a sectional majority—not until then has the State the right to look to a separate, independent existence."
69. Holden to David S. Reid, 28 December 1880, Reid Papers, State Archives. Jose-

phus Daniels gave a somewhat different version in the 29 October 1922 issue of the *Raleigh News and Observer* under the title "Where Democracy Was Born and Lives in Devotion to the Weal of the People." Daniels wrote:

After he had lost out in his first campaign for Governor, David S. Reid made a critical study of political conditions and the sentiment in the State which he had failed to reach. He saw that his party was doomed unless it truly became the sincere champion of what we now call 'the forgotten man,' the man without land, without education, without hope. Why was this forgotten man eligible to vote for Governor but not for Senator? The more Mr. Reid asked himself that question the more impossible he found it gave an answer that convinced himself. . . . After conferring with his friends Mr. Reid became convinced that he ought to come out for full manhood suffrage, putting an end to the unjust restrictions upon the landless man.

When he reached that conclusion Mr. Reid carefully wrote out his speech, packed it in his bag and set out for Beaufort where he was to make the opening speech in the campaign. He had arranged for a conference of Democratic leaders in Raleigh, to whom he wished to present the new issue and his argument in support of it. . . . Holden attended the conference in the old Guion Hotel. . . . Some of them violently opposed the new policy that Reid presented. Holden waited until most of the others had spoken. Some believed Reid might drive away more Democrats than he would gain from the opposition. Holden advised accepting and backing of Reid's issue. He could feel the resentment of the forgotten man to the discrimination against him. He advised that Reid's speech be copied and printed in the *Standard* the morning after its delivery in Beaufort. This was true journalistic enterprise as well as political acumen. Ordinarily if anything happened in Beaufort it was two weeks before it was printed in the Raleigh papers. To print the speech the next morning and spread it broadcast over the State would add to the interest in what the candidate had to say, and it was a sensational utterance that was bound to make talk.

But those who opposed the new issue were very insistent. When they could not convince Reid in Raleigh they sent a powerful Democrat to spend the night with him on the way to Beaufort to try to persuade him not to make what some leaders believed to be a blunder. But Reid said: "My speech is in type in the *Standard* office and I cannot recall it."

70. Holden, *Memoirs*, 98.
71. *Standard*, 14 September 1859.
72. Reid defeated John Kerr, Jr., of Caswell County.
73. Paul C. Cameron to Joseph B. C. Roulhac, 8 August 1850, Hamilton, ed., *Papers of Thomas Ruffin*, 2:298.
74. *Raleigh Register*, 7 May 1851. For Holden's reply see *Standard*, 14 May 1851.
75. Folk, "W. W. Holden, Political Journalist," 250–51.
76. *Standard*, 21 January 1854.

77. See the *Standard*, 23 June 1852, for a brief, formal announcement.
78. In adulthood Mary Eldridge Holden became Mrs. Claude A. Sherwood; Beulah Williamson, the wife of Walter R. Henry; and Lula Tucker, Mrs. Frank T. Ward. The Holden daughters from his first marriage married as follows: Laura, Mrs. Lewis P. Olds; Ida Augusta, Mrs. Calvin J. Cowles; and Henrietta (Ettie), Mrs. Fritz Mahler.
79. At the outbreak of the Civil War, Joseph William Holden enlisted in the state troops prior to his seventeenth birthday and was stationed on Roanoke Island. He distinguished himself with gallantry in service, but was captured by Union troops and confined as a prisoner of war for a year. Released on parole, he returned to Raleigh, and then attended the University of North Carolina for one year, 1862–63, until a strong desire to return to military service caused him to give up his formal education. His father persuaded him, however, to work for the *Standard*, which he did until 1868, when he was elected as a Republican member of the state house of representatives from Wake County and then as speaker of the house. In 1870 he was defeated in a bid for Congress, and after his father's impeachment trial went west and worked for the *Leavenworth* (Kansas) *Times*. Ill health made him return to Raleigh, where he was elected mayor in 1874. He died the following year before completing his term of office.

    Young Holden should probably best be remembered for his poetry. He began writing verse as a young boy, often publishing in the *Standard*; his poem "Hatteras," written when he first saw the whitecaps of Hatteras while on board ship as a prisoner of war, probably was his best. It was later included in Henry Wadsworth Longfellow's collection of writings entitled *Poems of Places*. Walter Hines Page once described it as being the "best in sentiment and tone written in the South." Had his life and times been different, the young poet might have achieved national recognition. For further information see Ashe, ed., *Biographical History*, 6:320–26.
80. Holden to wife, 8 November 1857, Holden Papers, DU.
81. Holden to Laura Holden, 6 August 1858, ibid.
82. Ibid., 4 April 1858.
83. In 1852 he had employed Wilson to report the house of commons activities while he covered the senate.
84. *Standard*, 17 May 1854.
85. Ibid., 16 May 1855.
86. Ibid., 1 August 1855.
87. Anthony Burns, originally owned by a Richmond, Virginia, master, was captured in Boston and returned by Judge Loring. Later, he was sold to D. McDaniel of Nash County, North Carolina, for $900, who, in turn, sold him for about $1,800. *Standard*, 14 March 1855; Pease and Pease, *Fugitive Slave Law*, 28–53. See also the *Standard*, 21 February 1855, for an account of Harvard University's refusal to elect Judge Loring to its law faculty.

88. *Standard*, 21 March 1855.

89. The *Register* insinuated that Holden was unhappy for not being appointed a delegate to the convention, but he replied that he had told friends who had offered to vote for him that he could not attend even if selected. See *Standard*, 30 April 1856.

90. Holden's speech was printed in its entirety, *Standard*, 12 July 1856, but for a description of the entire celebration proceedings see the issue of 9 July 1856.

91. Ibid., 12 September 1856.

92. Millard Fillmore to William A. Graham, 9 August 1856, Hamilton, ed., *Papers of William A. Graham*, 4:643–44. Preston Smith Brooks, congressman from South Carolina, assaulted Senator Charles Sumner of Massachusetts because of the latter's intemperate remarks concerning the "Bleeding Kansas" affair and his uncle A. P. Butler. Sumner's vitriolic speech, entitled "The Crime against Kansas," spoke of the "rape" of Kansas, and while he insulted several southern senators, he called Butler a "Don Quixote who had chosen a mistress," slavery.

93. Hamilton, *Benjamin Sherwood Hedrick*; Cox, "Freedom during the Fremont Campaign," 357–83.

94. *Standard*, 17 September 1856.

95. Ibid., 1 October 1856.

96. Ibid., 8 October 1856. Thus began the feud between Hedrick and Holden that continued throughout Holden's later political career. When Hedrick returned to the state in 1865, Holden apologized for the 1856 incident: "I met Holden yesterday. He expressed himself sorry for his past course towards me" (Hedrick to wife, 12 May 1865, Hedrick Papers, SHC). However, when Holden did not utilize Hedrick's services during his provisional governorship, the feud was renewed, and Hedrick was instrumental in getting Jonathan Worth elected to the governorship in 1865 instead of Holden. Also, the Hedrick case brought charges that Holden was opposed to the university, and even though he was elected to the board of trustees in 1857 and generally supported the institution through the *Standard*, he was never able to gain the full support and confidence of the administration.

97. Proceedings of the 6 October faculty meeting were published in the *Standard*, 15 October 1856. Henri Harrise, a young French professor at the university, was associated with Hedrick and dissented against the faculty's demand that Hedrick submit his resignation. Harrise's stand drew immediate insults from the students, and he submitted his own letter of resignation in December 1856. He returned to his native France and became a well-known French historian and authority on Napoleon.

98. Cox, "Freedom during the Fremont Campaign," 381.

99. For further information, see Hamilton, *Party Politics*, 180, or Cowper, "A Sketch of the Life of Governor Thomas Bragg," 132. Pulaski Cowper was Governor Bragg's personal secretary, but his account of the meeting was written many years afterward. It is generally considered accurate, but it does contain errors of fact.

CHAPTER TWO

1. Although this issue was never discussed by Holden, either in the *Standard* or in his correspondence, it was widely known and recognized throughout the state. As it did for President Andrew Johnson, this desire for recognition and acceptance played a major part in Holden's character. At the same time it explains his determination to seek reforms, especially to industrialize the state and to change the status of human labor.

2. The *Standard*, 27 March 1850, reprinted a table (originally published in the *Raleigh Times*) listing the number of slaves owned by the various state editors, and it showed Holden owning 190, the second largest number. Nowhere in the entire Holden correspondence, however, does he ever discuss any aspect of his personal slave ownership except for mentioning houseservants in letters to members of his own family. The Holden slaves belonged to Mrs. Holden. According to his granddaughter Mary Sherwood, he personally owned but one slave, and that through his kindness of reuniting a slave family. She was affectionately known as "Aunt Katie" and lived on the Holden property in an old smokehouse which had been converted into a home for her by Holden's daughter Mrs. Claude Sherwood. Fritz Mahler, another grandson, however, said that Holden owned three slaves at various times: Aunt Tempy Webb, cook; Calvin Strickland, whom Holden bought to prevent his being sold and sent to New Orleans; and Calvin's wife, who was taken in payment of a debt. See "History Was Made about Ancient Holden Mansion in Stirring War Period," *Raleigh Times*, 19 December 1925, and Folk, "W. W. Holden, Political Journalist," 320.

3. Most of this description was given by one of Holden's daughters, probably Mary Sherwood, to Claude G. Bowers and may be found in his *Tragic Era*, 313–14.

4. As early as 1852, Holden held consultations with Stephen A. Douglas and former governor John M. Morehead upon the subject of constructing the shortest railroad system from Morehead City across the state in conjunction with the North Carolina Railroad (Raleigh to Charlotte) to Memphis, Tennessee, and then on to the Pacific Coast. The project was strongly endorsed by the *Standard*, and progress was made until Duff Green took over, only to see it ultimately fail because of the Panic of 1857 and the loss of adequate capitalization. For further information, see Brown, *State Movement in Railroad Development*.

5. The question of a state penitentiary owned and operated by the state had been an issue since 1800, when the proposal was defeated by the state legislature. In 1816 sectional prejudices over the location (Raleigh versus Fayetteville) led to a second defeat. Popular support was not again raised until the 1844–45 legislature voted to submit the issue to a vote of the people in 1846. Although supporting the project personally and through his editorial columns in the *Standard*, Holden correctly predicted its defeat at the polls. The need still existed in the 1850s, but it was not

until his Republican administration of 1868–70 that Holden was able to bring to fruition this much-needed reform. See chapter 6 for details on how the project was completed.

6. *Standard*, 1 October 1845.
7. His education address was printed in the *Standard*, 5 July 1857, and it compared the status of education in North Carolina with that of both northern and southern states. He demonstrated that the state was ahead of all other slaveholding states and that it compared favorably with northern systems on matters of number of children in attendance, length of school term, and teacher pay; however, between 50,000 to 60,000 white children in the state never attended any school. For further analysis, see the *North Carolina Journal of Education*, 1:22.
8. In October the *Greensborough Patriot* reported, "Either Holden or Branch will be put on the track as the candidate for Governorship," but in December it offered the following: "It was Holden the aristocrats were trying to stop and they were grooming Judge S. J. Person for the task." Folk, "W. W. Holden, Political Journalist," 335, analyzed the candidates as follows: "W. W. Avery was unpopular in the east because of certain internal improvements of his, Ellis was unpopular in the mountains and not particularly popular anywhere, and Judge Person and D. W. Courts, state treasurer, were not available."
9. *Fayetteville Observer*, 4 January 1858.
10. Folk, "W. W. Holden, Political Journalist," 333, quoting J. B. Godwin, editor of the *Democratic Pioneer*.
11. The *Standard* did print the various proceedings, and the following counties endorsed the Holden nomination: Wake, Chatham, Surry, Guilford, Orange, Johnston, Alexander, Gates, Duplin, Alamance, Stokes, and Randolph. Seven counties endorsed Ellis, ten for Avery, three for Person, one for Thomas Settle, while the others pledged themselves to support whomever the party named.
12. Other committee members included William K. Lane, Wayne; James H. White, Gaston; R. S. French, Robeson; R. P. Waring, Mecklenburg; and James Fulton, New Hanover.
13. *Standard*, 17 February 1858.
14. *Greensborough Patriot*, 12 February 1858.
15. *Raleigh Register*, 14 April 1858.
16. It was generally understood that Ellis had a majority of support of the convention but he would be unable to obtain a two-thirds majority. By imposing the latter requirement the Holden forces hoped he could stop Ellis and ultimately win the nomination. It is interesting to note that Holden was singularly silent in his *Memoirs* about his convention defeat, but a thorough account may be found in the *Raleigh Register*, 21 April 1858, and an article entitled "The Democratic Convention of 1858" in the *Charlotte Observer*, 3 May 1908.
17. *Wilmington Journal*, 26 February 1858.
18. The western section of the state had never had its fair representation in the Demo-

cratic party, just as it had always been underrepresented in the state legislature. Population was not a basis for representation; instead, a county system was used. Accordingly, the eastern counties held an approximate 3–2 majority in the number of legislators, despite the western counties having 4–3 population majority.

19. *Standard*, 21 April 1858.
20. Ibid. Holden, though, was less than enthusiastic in his support of Ellis over the ad valorem taxation issue. The state's slaveholders wanted their slaves taxed as persons, while the nonslaveholders wanted them taxed according to their value as property. As a supporter of the lower classes, Holden favored ad valorem, while Ellis did not. See Butts, "The Irrepressible Conflict," 44–66.
21. *Standard*, 21 April 1858.
22. Ibid., 20 October 1858.
23. Ibid., 3 November 1858; Folk, "W. W. Holden, Political Journalist," 368.
24. *Fayetteville Observer*, 25 November 1858.
25. In April 1859, the *Standard* failed to carry the news of a Democratic meeting in Raleigh. That he did not attend is significant. The proceedings were published by R. Harper Whitaker in the *Live Giraffe*, a literary paper, and the *Raleigh Register*, a Know-Nothing paper. See Folk, "W. W. Holden, Political Journalist," 382–86.
26. *Standard*, 25 June 1859.
27. Ibid., 5 December 1860.
28. Ibid., 8 June 1859.
29. Folk, "W. W. Holden, Political Journalist," 392.
30. Holden's vacillation cost him the services of Frank I. Wilson, who supported the ad valorem principle and who had presided at a meeting of the Raleigh Working Men's Association in October 1859 which endorsed the idea. About the same time, Holden lost the service of another reporter, John Spelman, but for a different reason. Spelman became the editor of the *Salisbury Banner*. Later, in 1860, Holden nominated Bledsoe for the state senate in a county Democratic meeting, only to have him defeated by George W. Thompson. Bledsoe ran as an independent and defeated Thompson, 1,613 to 1,467.
31. To cover the episode, Holden dispatched Wilson (accompanied by T. H. Utley and W. H. Finch) who, after Brown was hanged, rushed back to Raleigh to give a firsthand account. The *Standard* was thus the first paper in the state to have special reporting of a nonpolitical news story. See *Standard*, 14 December 1859.
32. *Standard*, 28 December 1859. Although Helper was a native of Rowan County, he and his book were generally denounced throughout the state, and to read or own a copy almost always meant social ostracism.
33. Ibid.
34. Ibid., 14 January 1860.
35. Holden, *Memoirs*, 13–14. He also related that Brown was ridiculed by the other convention delegates for a pro-Union speech. "Colonel Brown then turned to me and said, 'Mr. Holden, let us shake off the dust from our feet, of this dis-union

conventicle, and retire.' " They returned to the Charleston Hotel amidst the shout "Damn the star-spangled banner; tear it down!" A few days afterwards, R. C. Pearson of Burke County approached Holden and said most earnestly,

"You must make a speech and hold our delegation against going out." He had come for me through the Virginia delegation who sat in the rear, "for," said he, "from what I have heard, if our delegates go out, Virginia will go out also, and the convention will be broken up."

I said, "Mr. Pearson, I am not in the habit of speaking very often—there are 600 delegates here and a vast audience—besides, it would be a piece of assurance on my part to attempt to address this body at this time, especially amid this excitement, with Mr. Cushing, the President of the body, hostile to Mr. Douglas and his friends. I can't get a hearing." "Yes, you can," said he, "I will go around and speak to the Indiana, the Illinois, and the Ohio delegations, and ask them when you arise to speak, to insist on North Carolina being heard." I then told him I would try. . . . I arose and said: "Mr. President, Mr. Holden of North Carolina." Mr. Cushing sat for twenty seconds and did not recognize me. Then the States mentioned arose and demanded in a voice of thunder that North Carolina be heard. Mr. Cushing arose and bowed and gave me the floor. I spoke for ten minutes.

36. *Standard*, 16 May 1860. The North Carolina delegation as listed in the 11 April 1860 edition of the *Standard* consisted of Bedford Brown, William S. Ashe, W. W. Avery, and Holden as "state delegates at large"; N. M. Long and W. A. Moore, 1st District; R. R. Bridgers, L. W. Humphrey, 2nd District; James Fulton and W. L. Steele, 3rd District; J. W. B. Watson, T. J. Greene, 4th District; Robert P. Dick, C. S. Winstead, 5th District; Samuel Hargrave, 6th District; William Lander, H. B. Hammond, 7th District; and Columbus Mills and H. T. Farmer, 8th District. During the convention Holden wrote to his wife: "I incline to think our delegation will vote the first time for Hunter, though I would prefer Lane or Breckenridge. Douglas may, after all, be nominated" (Holden to wife, 22 April 1860, Holden Papers, DU).

37. During this time serious consideration was given to nominating Thomas L. Clingman to run as a compromise candidate for the presidency. Holden wrote in the *Standard*, 5 May 1860: "We hail with pleasure the prospect of Mr. Clingman's nomination, and hope before we go to press to receive another dispatch announcing that he has been nominated. With Clingman and some good Northern Democrat, we believe that victory will again perch upon the banner of the great national Democratic party."

38. *Standard*, 9 June 1860.

39. Holden to Stephen A. Douglas, 1 June 1860, Douglas Papers, UCL. When Douglas spoke in Raleigh at a late August statewide campaign (100 delegates representing 33 counties), however, Holden thought the visit had a divisive effect on the state's Democratic voters. He did give full coverage to the Douglas speech. See *Standard*, 5 September, 10 October 1860.

40. Ibid., 15 August 1860. Holden thought that John Bell, the Constitutional Union party candidate, had no chance of winning election and advocated no support be given him. Even so, Holden was punished by the state Democratic leaders for not fully supporting the Breckenridge-Lane ticket by not being reelected state printer.

41. Ibid., 11 June 1860.

42. See Hamilton, ed., *Correspondence of Jonathan Worth*, 1:125–26. This is an undated fragment of a letter written by Worth probably to J. J. Jackson. He also listed some of the prominent state Democrats interested in joining a "Southern League" as W. W. Avery; Eli W. Hall of New Hanover; Marcus Erwin, Buncombe; Nathaniel H. Street, Craven; Samuel J. Person, New Hanover; John F. Hoke, Lincoln; Joseph B. Batchelor, Warren; and Robert R. Bridgers of Edgecombe. See also the *Standard*, 28 November, 1 December, 5 December 1860, 9 January and 5 February 1861. Especially interesting is the *Standard* account of a "Constitutional Union Meeting" held in Raleigh, 20 November, 1 December 1860, at which time Zeb Vance spoke and resolutions drafted by Holden were adopted.

43. Spelman was elected state printer mainly owing to the influence of Governor Bragg, causing a breach between the two men that never healed over.

44. *Standard*, 24 November 1860. In one sense, the break between Holden and party leaders was looked upon as a matter of relief to both sides. Holden was now free candidly to criticize party and administrative policy.

45. Ibid., 23 January 1861.

46. Ibid., 9 January 1861.

47. Ibid., 6 February 1861.

48. Ibid., 20 March 1861. See also Holden, *Memoirs*, 14–15. Holden, George E. Badger, and Quentin Busbee were elected as Wake County delegates to the proposed convention. Holden had endorsed the proposed convention, for as he wrote in his *Memoirs*, "Mr. Badger, today the people of the State will elect 80 union and 40 secession delegates, and if the convention carries and is assembled, we can take steps to prevent secession, and save the union."

49. *Raleigh Register*, 6 February 1861; see also Folk, "W. W. Holden, Political Journalist," 456–57.

50. *Standard*, 9 December 1863.

51. Ibid., 18 May 1861. In the next issue, 22 May, Holden admitted that he had previously been challenged by Col. Richard I. Wynne, Spelman, and another young man, but that he had given the same answer to each.

52. On 15 April, Secretary of War Simon Cameron telegraphed Governor Ellis: "Call made upon you by tonight's mail for two regiments of military for immediate service." Ellis replied: "*You can get no troops from North Carolina*" (Tolbert, ed., *Papers of John Ellis*, 2:612).

53. See the *Standard*, 29 May 1861, for a complete listing of the delegates. For biographical sketches, see McCormick, *Personnel of the Convention*, and Schenck, *Personal Sketches*. In his *Memoirs*, Holden said the convention consisted of 70 Democrats and 50 Conservatives, while Lefler and Newsome, *North Caro-*

lina, 449, said it consisted of 42 secessionists, 28 "conditional unionists," and 50 "unconditional unionists." Surprisingly, Holden voted for William A. Graham for president of the convention rather than Weldon N. Edwards (who was elected) despite his previous opposition to Graham. He did so because he knew Edwards to be a secessionist, while Graham had been and was a Union man.

54. Holden, *Memoirs*, 16–17, 41–42. It was at this time that a reconciliation was worked out between Holden and Graham. As Holden wrote:

> Governor Graham the next day sent me word by Mr. Ben Kitrell of Davidson County, . . . that he proposed that we should be reconciled and on speaking terms, "for," said Mr. Kitrell, "Mr. Graham has just said to me, he believes you are a true man." I replied to Mr. Kitrell, "Please say to Mr. Graham, I would like to be on speaking terms with him, but how shall it be effected?" He said, "Mr. Graham has arranged all that. He says you are the youngest man, and should approach him first. You have both about equally offended each other. He says when the Convention adjourns today, he will stand in his place near his seat, and as you approach him he will extend his hand and shake hands." . . . Afterwards, I conferred with him freely and profited by his advice.

55. The story of the gold pen and his statement "the greatest act of my life" is from the pen of Ashe, *Biographical History*, 3:198. Boyd, *William W. Holden*, 66, declared that Holden actually said his signing was "the proudest moment of my life" and that he planned to bequeath the pen "as an heir loom to his posterity." Folk, "W. W. Holden, Political Journalist," 475, claims that there is no evidence to support the above story—that it was simply apocryphal. Holden was one of those men in history about whom legends easily sprang up. He later repudiated the secession doctrine, and this brought about his final break with the Democratic party. At the time, however, he and the other Unionist leaders were forced to go along with secession because of the overwhelming pressure of southern opinion. No one dared to act in disobedience to the inflexible will of the prevailing ruling class.

56. *Standard*, 3 July 1861. In an editorial entitled "Plain Facts," Holden explained his reasons for changing his position: "When Mr. Lincoln issued his proclamation, making an unjust and unconstitutional war upon the South, . . . the *Standard* denounced it, and declared that the time had arrived when North Carolina should make common cause with the South." He then concluded, "We affirm, that all we have said or done, has been with a single eye to the good of the State, which we prefer above self—above party."

57. Holden was not alone in his support of the Union. Jonathan Worth concurred: "In N.C. the Union sentiment was largely in the ascendant and gaining strength until Lincoln prostrated us. . . . He did more than all the secessionists to break up the Union, but whether he did this, not being statesman enough to comprehend the effect of his measures; or whether his purpose was to drive all the slave states into rebellion, . . . Gov. Graham . . . was as strong for the Union as Edward Everett till

Lincoln's proclamation" (Hamilton, ed., *Correspondence of Jonathan Worth*, 1:150–51).

58. For a fuller analysis of Holden's Civil War career, see Raper, "William W. Holden and the Peace Movement," 493–516.

59. Holden even volunteered to organize a military company of 60 men, who were either household heads or too old for active combat service, but who would be used to defend Raleigh in time of need. Governor Bragg was elected captain, while Holden was listed as a private. *Standard*, 24 April 1861.

60. Ibid., 12 June 1861.

61. Ibid., 5 June 1861.

62. Ibid., 7, 27 August 1862.

63. Ibid., 11 September, 2 October 1861. It should be noted that because of inflation Holden was forced to raise the subscription price for the *Standard* from $2 to $3 for the weekly and from $4 to $5 for the semiweekly, while reducing the page size. However, circulation trebled—going to 7,000 for the weekly edition and 1,500 for the semiweekly. See *Standard*, 13 May 1863.

64. Ibid., 11 December 1861.

65. John H. Boner to Theo. Hill, 10 March 1892, Holden Papers, DU.

66. See *Standard*, 18 June 1862, for a list of despotic acts he held against the Davis administration; also, on 22 April 1863 he published a three-column letter to Confederate Secretary of War James A. Seddon decrying the Davis "despotism" and encroachment on states' rights.

67. *Raleigh State Journal*, 2 February 1862; see also Yates, "Zebulon B. Vance as War Governor," 46–47.

68. The convention passed an ordinance on Saturday, 26 April 1862, providing the exact procedures for the election.

69. For additional information, see Johnston, ed., *Papers of Zebulon B. Vance*, 1:242n.

70. Holden had his assistant editor, William E. Pell, contact Graham and urge him to accept the nomination. When Graham declined, he then urged George E. Badger to consult Graham, but he refused to do so. Thus, Holden determined that Vance was the next best candidate, but since he was a Democrat and Vance a Whig, he felt that his nomination should proceed from a Whig press, for example, the *Fayetteville Observer*. He contacted Merrimon to come to Raleigh, where plans were finalized. Merrimon proceeded to Fayetteville and secured Edward Hale's (*Observer*) approval, wrote a brief article under the editorial lead of the *Observer* entitled "Communicated," and then traveled to Kinston and got Vance's letter of acceptance and returned to Raleigh. A meeting was next held in the law office of Daniel G. Fowle (with Holden, Merrimon, W. H. Harrison, and James F. Taylor present), where final plans were adopted. On 4 June, Holden officially endorsed the Vance nomination in the *Standard*.

71. Dowd, *Life of Zebulon B. Vance*, 68. Vance stated his case in a public letter

addressed to Holden (and to Hale's *Fayetteville Observer*) dated 15 June 1862 and published in the *Standard* on 21 June 1862.

72. *Standard*, 7 June 1862.

73. Ibid., 24 May 1862.

74. State troops were also sent to Wilkes and Yadkin counties to prevent deserters from interfering at the election polls. See Hamilton, *Reconstruction in North Carolina*, 45.

75. Tatum, *Disloyalty in the Confederacy*, 111. See also Dowd, *Life of Zebulon B. Vance*, 447–48, for Vance's reactions to such issues.

CHAPTER THREE

1. Vance did not always listen to Holden's advice. In November 1862, prior to his taking office, J. G. Martin, the adjutant general, formulated a plan to send state agents abroad to buy needed supplies for both the army and civilian population and to purchase an interest in several vessels sailing to Europe from various Confederate ports or from the West Indies to the state ports. Martin had presented his recommendations to Governor Clark, but as his term of office was about to expire, Clark thought it unwise for him to undertake the initiative in such a bold plan and suggested that Martin present it to Governor-elect Vance instead. This he did, but as the plan bristled with financial difficulties and international complications, Vance discussed it with Holden and Bartholomew F. Moore. Both men urged the rejection of the Martin plan, and Moore pointed out that Vance would be subjecting himself to impeachment if he undertook to commit the state to so costly, so venturesome, and so unconstitutional an enterprise. Nevertheless, Vance assumed the responsibility and sent agents to Europe to buy those items which kept the troops well clothed throughout the war and most of the state's industries from being forced to close. This endeared the governor to the people for the remainder of the war.

2. Vance admitted as much in a letter to Edward J. Hale, 21 November 1862, Hale Papers, State Archives.

3. The governor was also empowered to investigate the causes of the arrest of state citizens held by the Confederate authorities in their military prison at Salisbury. As Holden saw it, the program was designed to oppose the growing centralization of power by the Confederate government at Richmond. Vance was very assertive on the matter of states' rights, no doubt influenced by the infamous Laurel Valley incident in Madison County. In December 1862 a body of men and boys from that region made a raid to Marshall to get "their share" of salt, and in the process committed outrages on local citizens by taking property illegally. Following this action, Colonel J. A. Keith of the Sixty-fourth North Carolina Troops arrested a

group of suspects and shot them on the spot. Some women accompanying the party were whipped, and one boy of about fifteen was wounded. His mother begged for his life, but Keith killed him by shooting him in the head. Upon hearing of the tragedy, Vance had Secretary of War Seddon court-martial Keith; as Vance said to Holden, "I will follow him [Keith] to the gates of hell or hang him" (Holden, *Memoirs*, 27–29). Ironically, it fell to Holden, as provisional governor in 1865, to arrange safe conduct through Tennessee so that Keith could be transported to Madison County to stand trial for the crime, only to have him escape from the Madison County jail and flee the state, probably to California. See also Paludan, *Victims*.

4. U.S., Official Records, Series I, LI, 807.

5. Bardolph, "Inconsistent Rebels," 163–89, gives a complete explanation for the many causes of desertion among state troops, while Reid, "A Test Case of the 'Crying Evil,'" 234–55, presents a statistical analysis of the extent of desertion. Reid also reprints a portion of the *Report of the United States Provost Marshall General* (1866) which listed 23,694 desertions from the enlisted men's ranks (23 percent) and 428 officers (6 percent). The standard account of desertion in both the Confederate and Union armies is Lonn, *Desertion during the Civil War*. Also useful sources are Tatum, *Disloyalty in the Confederacy*, and Moore, *Conscription and Conflict*.

6. See the *Standard*, 5 August 1863.

7. Ibid., 12 August 1863 and 19 February 1864; however, the Holden critics saw him as the major cause for the growing defection from the Confederate cause. Gen. Daniel H. Hill repeatedly wrote to the Richmond government that state newspapers induced troops to desert. Gen. Stephen D. Ramseur wrote his wife, "W. W. Holden is responsible in great measure for the desertions among North Carolina troops." Even Gen. Robert E. Lee placed the blame on "that disgraceful 'peace' sentiment spoken of by the *Standard*." See Bardolph, "Inconsistent Rebels," 184.

8. *American Annual Cyclopedia* (1863), 691. Part of the explanation of Vance's and the state's opposition was that an outsider, a Major Bradford of Virginia, was appointed to collect the tithes. Another irritant was the John W. Irvin case, in which Secretary of War Seddon ordered that a decision of Chief Justice Richmond M. Pearson be ignored. The chief justice believed that the Confederate conscription law was unconstitutional and granted writs of habeas corpus to secure the release of anyone arrested for desertion or disloyalty to the Confederacy. Also, in December the General Assembly instructed Governor Vance to secure the release of an Orange County minister, the Reverend J. R. Graves, who had been arrested as a spy and imprisoned in Richmond. For further information on the Graves case, see U.S., *Official Records*, Series II, V, 794–95. See also Yates, "Zebulon B. Vance as War Governor," 61.

9. Charles Dana to Secretary of War Edwin M. Stanton, 8 September 1863, U.S., *Official Records*, Series I, XXX, 182–83.

10. General John G. Foster to Secretary of War Stanton, 22 July 1863, ibid., Series I, XXVII, 751.
11. Vance to James A. Seddon, 5 January 1863, ibid., Series IV, Pt. II, 298–99; Seddon to Vance, 5 May 1863, ibid., Series I, LI, Pt. II, 702.
12. Holden, *Memoirs*, 43. See also Hamilton, *Reconstruction in North Carolina*, 58n. Prior to his trip to Richmond, Vance asked Holden publicly to state that the *Standard* was not "my [Vance's] organ." Holden replied, "The *Standard* is an independent Conservative paper, and is not the organ of either Presidents, Governors, or Generals" (*Standard*, 15 July 1863).
13. Davis to Vance, 24 July 1863, U.S., *Official Records*, Series I, LI, Pt. II, 739; Vance to Davis, 26 July 1863, ibid., 740.
14. Vance to Edward J. Hale, 11 August 1863, Hale Papers, State Archives.
15. John A. Gilmer should be credited with originating the motto. Holden to Samuel A. Ashe, 28 November 1881, Holden Papers, DU. Upon his return from Richmond, Vance conversed with Holden and told how he had defended him from the complaints of treason by Confederate authorities. This led Holden to believe that Vance still supported the peace movement, but evidently Vance held back certain ideas from Holden, which caused the *Standard* to charge that Vance had gone to Richmond as an anti-Davis man but returned as a red-hot war man. *Standard*, 4 January 1865.
16. Hamilton, "Heroes of America," 10–19.
17. Holden published a full account of the Orange Court House Meeting, together with the adopted resolutions, in the *Standard*, 21 August 1863, but noted that it was an "officer" affair because the common soldier was not represented and had no voice in the proceedings.
18. For further information on the subject, see Samuel F. Phillips to David L. Swain, n.d., Swain Papers, SHC.
19. In addition, had not Governor Vance taken strong preventive measures the *Raleigh Progress* would have also been destroyed. For further information, see Amis, *Historical Raleigh*, 139. See also Hamilton, *Reconstruction in North Carolina*, 54–55. There is disagreement over the route used by Holden to reach the Governor's Mansion and his later actions. In the 1864 campaign, Vance claimed that Holden had traveled via a back street, entered the empty house, and gone directly to the bedroom, where he turned down the gaslight and sat in the dark until the governor's return. He also stated that Holden was so badly shaken that he asked for a glass of brandy to calm his nerves. The *Salisbury Watchman*, edited by J. J. Bruner, even implied that Holden had been so scared that he dived under the governor's bed to await his return. However, Holden gave his own version in the *Standard*, 13 May 1864, and then answered the *Watchman*: "The editor of the *Watchman* is, we believe, a member of the church, but this does not prevent him from uttering a wilful and deliberate falsehood. . . . Every word in the article is grossly false" (*Standard*, 18 May 1864).

20. *Standard*, 2 October 1863. See also Holden to Edward J. Hale, 11 September 1863, and Vance to Edward J. Hale, 11 September 1863, Hale Papers, State Archives.
21. The five successful peace congressmen were James T. Leach, Josiah Turner, Jr., Samuel Christian, Dr. J. G. Ramsey, and George W. Logan. Not all the enmity against the state peace movement was found in North Carolina. John Syme of Virginia, a former editor of the *Raleigh Register*, advocated mob action against the *Standard*. Through his Petersburg, Virginia, paper he persuaded one Taylor of Montgomery County to introduce a resolution in the Virginia senate to stop, by law, the circulation of the *Standard* in that state. The resolution was defeated, but the Order of the Knights of the Golden Circle persuaded John Wooten, the commonwealth attorney general, to forbid its circulation. Army postmasters were also commanded to prevent the paper from being distributed to soldiers in Virginia. *Standard*, 16, 30 October 1863.
22. Vance to Davis, 30 December 1863, and Davis to Vance, 8 January 1864, U.S., *Official Records*, Series I, LI, 808–10.
23. Leach was an Old Line Whig who opposed secession in 1861, but was elected to the Confederate House of Representatives in 1863 pledged to see "a just, honorable and lasting peace." In Congress he voted to override every presidential veto and impugned the competence of every cabinet member. When Richmond editors criticized his position, Leach wanted them "Dead, Dead, Dead!" (Warner and Yearns, *Biographical Register*, 148–49). See the *Standard*, 9 September 1863, for an account of the Granville County meeting.
24. Jonathan Worth to Daniel L. Russell, 16 February 1864, Hamilton, ed., *Correspondence of Jonathan Worth*, 1:296–98.
25. Vance to William A. Graham, 1 January 1864, Graham Papers, State Archives.
26. Holden to Calvin J. Cowles, 18 March 1864, Holden Papers, State Archives. Prior to making his decision, Holden called a meeting of close friends to discuss the probable effect suspension would have on free speech in the state. Among those attending were B. F. Moore, W. R. Richardson, and Jonathan Worth. For further discussion of the meeting, see Samuel F. Phillips to William A. Graham, 26 February 1864, *Papers of William A. Graham*, 6:31–36.
27. A term used by the Conservatives and peace advocates to denote those who gave 100 percent support to the Confederate cause. At times the term was also used interchangeably with "war party" supporters.
28. *Standard*, 3 May 1864. President Tyler had virtually been read out of the Whig party because of his vetoing the Whig legislation that would have created a Third United States Bank and returned the nation to a high protective tariff policy. Chitwood, *John Tyler*; Van Deusen, *Life of Henry Clay*; Eaton, *Henry Clay*.
29. Vance to Edward J. Hale, 30 December 1863, Hale Papers, State Archives.
30. Holden further stated that he hoped to resume regular publication of the *Standard* in either May or June, but that he would keep his readers posted by special editions,

especially during the upcoming meeting of the General Assembly. In the meantime, he urged his Conservative friends to hold meetings and nominate legislative candidates. "Be prudent, firm, and united, and *vote* when the time comes," he counseled.

31. Vance to Edward J. Hale, 30 December 1863, Hale Papers, State Archives.
32. Duncan K. McRae to Edward J. Hale, 26 April 1864, ibid.
33. See Holden's statement, "To the Conservatives of North Carolina," dated 19 May 1864, and published in the *Standard*, 20 May 1864.
34. Holden to Calvin J. Cowles, 19 July 1864, Holden Papers, State Archives.
35. *Greensborough Patriot*, 21 July 1864.
36. After the Churchill disclosure other confessions were published, resulting in a large loss of membership. See Hamilton, *Reconstruction in North Carolina*, 64. Four legislators (W. W. Hampton, William Horton, James M. Gentry, and Elisha M. Welborn) stated that it was Holden's intention to take the state out of the Confederacy (see ibid., 64).
37. Concurrent with the introduction of the resolutions in the General Assembly, Congressman James T. Leach of the Third North Carolina District introduced similar resolutions in the Confederate Congress, but they were tabled without consideration. All but two of the North Carolina delegation voted against their being tabled, however.
38. Holden to Calvin J. Cowles, 29 July 1864, Holden Papers, State Archives. See also the *Standard*, 2 August 1864.
39. U.S., *Official Records*, Series I, XL, Pt. III, 598. The 9 August 1864 issue of the *Standard* cited other examples of fraud and intimidation. In Warren County, "no man could vote for Holden except under a threat that he would be hung." In Wilkesboro, "two companies of infantry of the 68th N.C. regiment . . . had the effect to keep many from the polls. . . . The soldiers were in squads at the election grounds." In Wayne County, William T. Dortch, Confederate senator, "stumped the County of Wayne, told the people that every man who voted for Holden would be marked as a traitor; that the government had the power to put all detailed men in the army, and would put all in who might vote against Vance."
40. Yates, "Governor Vance and the Peace Movement," 112.
41. *Standard*, 17 August 1864.
42. Holden's defeat was primarily due to three reasons: (1) he had relied upon the popular cause of the peace movement to win election, but the popular strength was not nearly so effective as it had appeared in newspaper accounts; (2) Vance's administration had won the affection and gratitude of the people because of his measures to relieve the suffering of the poor while maintaining ample supplies and equipment for the armed forces; and (3) the disclosure of the secret society, "The Heroes of America" or "Red Strings," had created an unfavorable reaction to the Holden campaign.
43. Holden's major consolation was in the continued support given him by such

supporters as Robert P. Dick, who wrote: "I was so perfectly astonished by the result of the recent election that I have not yet recovered from the shock. I can not account for so universal and so sudden a change in public sentiment" (Dick to Holden, 20 August 1864, Holden Papers, State Archives).

44. *Standard*, 12 August 1864.

45. On 11 October 1864, Governor Vance wrote the following to Gen. Braxton Bragg: "There is a meeting of Governors at Augusta on Monday the 17th, to consult about how to spare more men from the service. I am very anxious to know what North Carolina has done in comparison with the other States. Can you furnish the information from the Adjutant General's office?" The conference met on 17 October, with Virginia, North Carolina, South Carolina, Georgia, Alabama, and Mississippi represented. Governor William Smith of Virginia presided. Eight resolutions were adopted, the most important being as follows: (1) Confederate authorities were requested to send into the field every able-bodied man, without exception, and that disabled officers and soldiers should replace those sent; (2) state authorities should arrest all deserters and stragglers; (3) slaveowners should remove all slaves from the line of the enemy's (Sherman) approach, so as to keep them from joining the Union army; (4) the Confederate Congress should remove all export restrictions; and (5) it is "our firm and unalterable purpose, . . . to maintain our right of self-government, to establish our independence, and to uphold the rights and sovereignty of the States or perish in the attempt" (U.S., *Official Records*, Series I, XLII, 1145, 1149–50).

46. The Pool resolutions were introduced on 24 November and read as follows:
   Resolved, That five commissioners be elected by this General Assembly, to act with commissioners from the other States of the Confederacy, as a medium for negotiating a peace with the United States.
   Resolved, That each of the other States of the Confederacy be respectfully requested to create a similar commission, with as little delay as practicable and to cooperate with North Carolina in requesting President Davis, in the name of these sovereign States, that he tender to the United States a conference for negotiating a peace through the medium of these commissioners.
   Resolved, That the Governor make known to each of the other States of the Confederacy this action of the General Assembly of North Carolina, and endeavor to secure their cooperation.
   Resolved, That whenever five of the States shall have responded by the appointment of commissioners, the Governor communicate the proceedings, officially, to President Davis, and request his prompt action upon the proposition. (*Standard*, 29 November 1864).

47. For a full wording of the Leach proposal, offered 25 November, see the *Standard*, 2 December 1864. Later, John Pool (Bertie County), Samuel T. Carson (Beaufort County), Edward D. Hall (New Hanover County), and Samuel J. Person (New Hanover County) were appointed as commissioners by the General Assembly to

visit Richmond and consult with President Davis and the state's congressmen about peace prospects. As Holden commented, "It was not to be expected that this commission would secure peace, or even make any important approaches to it. But it was a step in the right direction" (*Standard*, 7 February 1865).

48. *Standard*, 8 April 1865. Governor Vance left Raleigh an open city, with former governor David L. Swain standing alone in front of the state capitol and surrendering the keys of the entire city to the advance guard of Gen. William T. Sherman. Later, when news of the Lincoln assassination reached Raleigh, rumors circulated freely that the occupying Union troops would wreak vengeance upon the city by mob violence, and most of the citizens were so terrified that they sat up during the entire night. About nine o'clock the alarm of "fire" was heard, and many thought the destruction had begun. Hundreds rushed to the scene of the flames, but happily discovered only the accidental burning of an abandoned workshop. It was authoritatively stated, however, that the city would have been sacked save for the prompt action of Maj. Gen. John A. Logan. For further information, see Amis, *Historical Raleigh*, 145, and Spencer, *Last Ninety Days of the War*, 162.

CHAPTER FOUR

1. *Standard*, 20 April 1865.
2. Ibid., 24 April 1865.
3. Ibid.
4. Beale, *Critical Year*, 35. This varies with the opinion of Hugh McCulloch in his *Men and Measures of Half a Century*, 378, that Secretary of War Edwin M. Stanton presented at the first Johnson cabinet meeting "the very same instrument for restoring the national authority over North Carolina, and placing her where she stood before her attempted secession, which had been approved by Mr. Lincoln."
5. Holden, *Memoirs*, 45.
6. Swain later commented: "He [Johnson] heard us patiently and unyieldingly, insisted that as the General Government was called to guarantee to each state a republican form of government that his purpose could only be effected in the existing state of things, by a reconstruction of the whole fabric of government, by the hands of loyal men" (David L. Swain to Thomas Ruffin, 15 September 1865, Hamilton, ed., *Papers of Thomas Ruffin*, 4:28).
7. Holden to Andrew Johnson, 6 December 1865, Andrew Johnson Papers, LC.
8. Holden, *Memoirs*, 47. For a more detailed discussion of the Washington meeting and analysis of Holden's provisional administration, see Raper, "Political Career of William Woods Holden."
9. Prior to publishing the final version, President Johnson had his secretary read the document paragraph by paragraph to Holden and Dick. At times the president indicated that he expected to confiscate the estates of the large slaveholders,

whereupon Holden and Dick remonstrated against this idea and begged him to be as "forebearing" and as generous as possible. B. F. Moore also was candid with Johnson in opposing the idea (Holden, *Memoirs*, 55–56). For a copy of the president's proclamation, see U.S., *Messages and Papers of the Presidents*, 6:310ff. It was also reprinted in the *Standard*, 10 June 1865, and other papers throughout the state.

10. Holden began his duties 5 June. He never took an official oath of office for the provisional governorship, and no oath was ever tendered him. He did subscribe, however, to the amnesty oath of future loyalty to become a voter. Holden to Andrew Johnson, 4 March 1866, Johnson Papers, LC. See also Holden, *Memoirs*, 48n.

11. U.S., *Messages and Papers of the Presidents*, 6:310ff.

12. William H. Seward to Holden, 29 May 1865, Johnson Papers, LC. This sum was based on the previous rate of compensation for state governors, but did not include house rental. During the provisional governorship, Holden lived in his own residence.

13. Two days prior to his assumption of office, Holden turned over the editorial, but not financial, control of the *Standard* to Joseph S. Cannon, a longtime associate, and his son Joseph W. Holden. It is interesting to note that the new editors did not comment on Holden's new role or even give an account of his taking over the executive control of the state.

14. *Standard*, 13 June 1865.

15. Jonathan Worth to John M. Worth, 9 August 1863, Hamilton, ed., *Correspondence of Jonathan Worth*, 1:253–54.

16. St. Clair, "Judicial Machinery in North Carolina," 428. Copies of such communications can be found in the Holden Governor's Papers, State Archives.

17. See Holden to Robert M. Henry, 26 June 1865, Holden Governor's Papers, State Archives, for such directions and also for a complete listing of other such commissioners.

18. Typical of the latter was a statement by Bartholomew F. Moore: "A large portion of the gentlemen in North Carolina who had been in office in former times, who had taken just such a part in the rebellion, against their will and wishes, as to make them obnoxious to the provisions of reconstruction, were kept out of office. . . . A great many of the new appointments were men of known bad character, men convicted of theft, and men who could not read or write" (Fleming, *Documentary History of Reconstruction*, 2:43–44). This is in complete variance with the present author's findings, however. For some years I have been engaged in the process of editing the Holden papers, and from my study of the appointments, based on a comparison of the 1860 and 1870 censuses, an overwhelming majority were men of wealth and social standing comparable to those who served in similar positions prior to the Civil War. They were not, to be sure, of the former aristocratic families, nor had they been formally educated at the University of North Carolina.

19. Holden to Sheriff Richard J. Jones, 14 July 1865, Governor's Papers, State Archives.
20. Andrews, *South since the War*, 117–18.
21. Holden's official staff was as follows: aides, Joseph S. Cannon, Eugene Grissom, and Tod R. Caldwell; private secretaries, Lewis Hanes, Richard Badger, and William H. Bagley; clerks, S. M. Parrish and J. D. Pullem; treasurer, Jonathan Worth; attorney general, Sion H. Rogers; secretary of state, Charles R. Thomas; superintendent of Institute for Deaf and Dumb, William J. Palmer; and superintendent of Institute for Insane, Dr. Edward Fisher.
22. Holden also named the following solicitors: Jesse Y. Yeates, David M. Carter, John A. Stanly, Thomas Battle, Archibald R. McDonald, David M. Furchess, William P. Bynum, and Robert M. Henry.
23. Holden to Andrew Johnson, 18 August 1865, Johnson Papers, LC.
24. George G. Meade to Holden, 22 September 1865, Governor's Letter Book, State Archives.
25. See letter of instruction, Holden to Judge Anderson Mitchell, 14 September 1865, Governor's Papers, State Archives.
26. Kenneth Rayner to President Johnson, 8 July 1865, Johnson Papers, LC.
27. Henry Watterson to Andrew Johnson, 29 June 1865, Johnson Papers, LC.
28. To further aid the economic recovery in the state, Holden reorganized the State Bank and the various railroads in which the state held major financial interests; in fact the latter were able to resume normal operation within two months after the state's restoration.
29. Governor's Proclamation, 29 July 1865, Governor's Papers, State Archives.
30. Powell (usually called Dr. Powell) was a native of Richmond County, but had left the state in 1840 to work for the federal government, and prior to 1860 was serving in the Treasury Department. During the war he continued to serve the Union cause, but did work in behalf of state prisoners of war confined in the North. One of his first missions was to check on the status of Governor Vance, then in prison in Washington, D.C. He informed Holden that he feared the southern governors might be hanged, whereupon Holden replied, "Dr. Powell, that will never do. . . . If there is danger of what you say, I will return here at once and appeal to the President." He continued, "I would not, of course, have served if the President had allowed these things to be done" (Holden, *Memoirs*, 45–46).
31. Robert Powell to Holden, 6 September 1865, Governor's Papers, State Archives.
32. Two such cases especially infuriated Holden. George Mordecai and Dr. W. J. Hawkins of Raleigh had submitted their applications prior to 1 August, but Holden had recommended temporary suspension of their applications. The two men went to Washington, however, and through the use of a professional pardon broker (a cousin of Attorney General James Speed) obtained their pardons despite the governor's recommendation. When informed of the situation, President Johnson advised

Holden he could tax the two for getting their pardons illegally, but that he would not revoke them. See the *Standard*, 7 September 1865.

33. A ledger was maintained in the governor's office, listing all applicants, date of request, Holden's recommendation, and in most instances the final action and date of granting the pardons. The ledger is among Holden's Governor's Papers, State Archives.

34. Holden, *Memoirs*, 58–59.

35. Ibid., 59–60.

36. Josiah Turner, Jr., had written his father's application and had included a rather defiant statement that if the senior Turner had been younger he would have shouldered a musket and fought for the South. Holden was afraid such an expression might move the president to refuse the pardon, and so in his endorsement had suggested that Turner was "an old man, a Henry Clay Whig, and deserving of pardon." The president granted the pardon immediately, and Holden forwarded it to Hillsborough (ibid.).

37. Ibid., 61.

38. Ibid., 62–63.

39. Holden to Robert Powell, 5 October 1865, Johnson Papers, LC. He had earlier written President Johnson: "Many of the oligarchs are still unsubdued. I think it a good plan to hold their pardons in suspense, and whether their estates are to be confiscated or not, they ought not to be allowed to vote for twelve months. But I find, what is a little singular, that the ultra original secessionists who profess to have repented, appear to be really more penitent than the ultra partisans of Vance who were once Union men. . . . A firm, discreet use of pardoning power and the patronage of the government will contribute greatly to keep them down, and thus preserve tranquility and order in the state" (Holden to Andrew Johnson, 26 July 1865, Johnson Papers, LC).

40. The *Raleigh Progress* spoke of the governor's having an attack of jaundice; the *Wilmington Journal* called it neuralgia; Holden himself called it "my old headache." He later recalled, "I was robust and in good health when I entered on my duties, but at the end . . . I was thin and shallow and weak" (Boyd, *William W. Holden*, 106).

41. Holden to Andrew Johnson, 26 August 1865, Governor's Papers, State Archives. See also Johnson's telegram to Holden, 22 August 1865, Johnson Papers, LC.

42. General Orders No. 31, General Orders, War Department, Adjutant General's Office, 1865–66. It was printed in the *Standard*, 2 May 1865. For further information on Schofield, see Schofield, *Forty-Six Years in the Army*, and St. Clair, "Judicial Machinery in North Carolina," 415–22.

43. Holden, *Memoirs*, 52.

44. Quoted in the *Wilmington Herald*, 24 June 1865.

45. *Raleigh Sentinel*, 2 September 1865.

46. Ibid., 1, 11 September 1865. These articles were unsigned, but according to Professor Hamilton they were written by Victor Barringer. His views were absorbed from his brother, Rufus Barringer, who as a prisoner of war at Fort Delaware had been able to ascertain the northern viewpoint. See Hamilton, *Reconstruction in North Carolina*, 150–52.

47. J. W. Hood, a free Negro Methodist minister from Connecticut, who came to the state soon after the Union forces occupied New Bern, was elected president; the other officers were J. P. Shanks (Charlotte), James H. Harris (Raleigh), John P. Sampson (Wilmington), Isham Sweat (Fayetteville), William Smith (Wilmington), Stewart Ellison (Raleigh), and Sgt. Littleton of the First North Carolina Heavy Artillery, vice presidents; John Randolph (Greensboro), secretary; William Cawthorne (Warren County), assistant secretary; and J. R. Caswell, treasurer.

48. The convention was ignored by the state press at first. The *Standard* ran only a brief account of the first day's proceedings on 30 September, while the *Raleigh Sentinel* published the address in its 4 October issue with the comment: "It is admirable in temper, felicitous in its style, and modest in the tone of its demand." *Convention of the Freedmen of North Carolina. Official Proceedings* [Raleigh, 1865]. The best source of information is Andrews, *South since the War*, 120–51.

49. See "A Proclamation to the People of North Carolina," *Standard*, 9 August 1865.

50. Holden to Andrew Johnson, 21 September, Governor's Papers, State Archives. Johnson to Holden, 21 September 1865, Johnson Papers, LC.

51. As the election turned out, eleven delegates did require special presidential pardons, but as all were Holden or Union supporters, no difficulties arose in securing them speedily. These included John Pool, Daniel L. Russell, Sr., Matthias E. Manly, A. B. Barnes, Duncan K. McRae, John B. Odom, Churchill Perkins, Alfred Dockery, Ceburn L. Harris, Calvin J. Cowles, and A. A. McKay.

52. The agenda was prepared by a committee of nine headed by B. F. Moore, and included most of the outstanding leaders of the convention: Patrick Winston, William Eaton, Jr., Samuel F. Phillips, Matthias E. Manly, William P. Bynum, William A. Wright, Alfred Dockery, and Dennis Ferrebee. The problem of congressional redistricting arose over the fact that in 1861 the state held eight congressional seats, but the convention was informed that there would be one less. Under the direction of Chairman William Sloan, however, the districts were redrawn into fairly equal units. *American Annual Cyclopedia* (1865), 627.

53. N.C., *Ordinances of the 1865–1866 Convention*, 3; Andrews, *South since the War*, 144–51. See also *Standard* for a running account of all sessions, as well as the Ferrebee proposal.

54. In commenting on the black demands, Chairman Pool declared: "We deplore the premature introduction of any schemes that may disturb the operation of the kindly feelings, or influence the inherent social prejudice that exists against the colored race. The necessary legislation should be conceived in a spirit of perfect fairness and justice, and in full and unreserved conformity to existing relations; but it

should be suited to the actual conditions of the parties, and aimed to their material and moral welfare, and to the general peace and prosperity of the State, than to any theoretical scheme of social and political equality" (N.C., *Ordinances of the 1865–1866 Convention*, 44–45; see also Andrews, *South since the War*, 159–61).

55. N.C., *Ordinances of the 1865–1866 Convention*, 4.
56. *Raleigh Sentinel*, 10 October 1865. No such letter can be found in the Governor's Papers, State Archives.
57. N.C., *Ordinances of the 1865–1866 Convention*, 6.
58. The *Raleigh Sentinel* had advocated such an official so as to have an elected officer in case the governor left office. Only three times previously had the problem arisen: (1) in 1776 when Governor Thomas Burke was captured by British forces; (2) in 1854 when Governor David S. Reid was elected to the United States Senate; and (3) in 1861 upon the death of Governor John W. Ellis.
59. N.C., *Ordinances of the 1865–1866 Convention*, 9.
60. *Raleigh Sentinel*, 25 October 1865; see also Hamilton, *Reconstruction in North Carolina*, 125–26.
61. Andrews, *South since the War*, 136.
62. N.C., *Ordinances of the 1865–1866 Convention*, 19. This ordinance was modified later to read that all state offices held by those who took an oath to support the Confederacy were vacant and that persons so removed could not regain office until reappointed or reelected.
63. Ibid., 26.
64. Ibid., 17, 29.
65. Ibid., 23.
66. The new taxes consisted of the following: a tax of 1 percent on every surgeon, dentist, physician, lawyer, painter or artist, merchant, actor, broker, auctioneer, and factory owner whose total receipts from practices, fees, or commissions exceeded $1,000; (2) a fee of $.25 on each gallon of whiskey or brandy distilled for personal use; and $.50 per gallon imported into the state for sale; (3) a fee of $15 on every company of circus riders or exhibitors of animals for each county exhibited; (4) a tax of 5 percent of total gross profits on insurance companies; (5) a tax of 6 percent on profits of bond holders, private bankers, or agents of banks from other states; (6) a fee of $100 on every public billiard table and $25 on each private one; (7) a fee of $50 on every livery stable; (8) a fee of $75 for every retail establishment of spiritous liquors; (9) a tax of 2 percent on all purchases of spiritous liquors made in the state or elsewhere; (10) a tax of $50 on every peddler in the state for each county visited; (11) a 5 percent levy on the gross amount received by all express companies; (12) a tax of $2 on each bale of cotton, hogshead of tobacco, and on $200 of manufactured tobacco, held or owned by anyone other than the producer; (13) a tax of $1 on each bale of cotton, hogshead of tobacco grown in 1865 and on each lot of manufactured tobacco products worth $200; (14) a tax of $.5 on each barrel of tar, turpentine, and rosin held by the producer while a tax of $.10 on each

barrel for other than the producer; and (15) a tax of .5 percent on all purchases (cotton, tobacco, turpentine, rosin, and liquor excluded), in and out of the state, for each or credit, by any merchant, tailor, jeweler, druggist, apothecary, factor, and every other trader (N.C., *Ordinances of the 1865–1866 Convention*, 11).

67. *Wilmington Herald*, 7 September 1865.
68. According to Treasurer Worth's report, the state debt as of 3 September 1865, stood at $30,215,985.61, with $13,619,500 being the bonded debt, plus interest, of the debts contracted prior to 20 May 1861.
69. On the second day of the convention, Edward Conigland of Halifax County asked that Governor Holden be required to furnish information concerning the special value and time of issuance of all state bonds and treasury notes during the war years. This was put in the form of an inquiry or request for information and was intended to create a debate. The convention tabled the resolution immediately, for it wanted no part of the issue.
70. Holden to President Johnson, 17 October 1865, Governor's Papers, State Archives. He had informed the president earlier that the convention would ignore the issue.
71. Andrew Johnson to Holden, 18 October 1865, Johnson Papers, LC. His complete reply was as follows:

> Every dollar of the debt created to aid the rebellion against the United States should be repudiated finally and forever. The great mass of the people should not be taxed to pay a debt to aid in carrying on a rebellion which they in fact, if left to themselves, were opposed to. Let those who have given their means for the obligations of the State look to that power they tried to establish in violation of law, Constitution, and the will of the people. They must meet their fate. It is their misfortune, and they cannot be recognized by the people of any State professing themselves loyal to the United States in the Union. I repeat, that the loyal people of North Carolina should be exonerated from the payment of every dollar of indebtedness created to aid in carrying on the rebellion. I trust and hope that the people of North Carolina will wash their hands of everything that partakes in the slightest degree of the rebellion which has been so recently crushed by the strong arm of the government in carrying out the obligations imposed by the Constitution of the Union.

72. It read: "That all debts and obligations created or incurred by the State in aid of the late rebellion, directly or indirectly, are void, and no General Assembly of this State shall have power to assume or provide for the payment of the same or any portion thereof; nor shall any General Assembly of this State have power to assume or provide for the payment of any portion of the debts or obligations created or incurred, directly or indirectly, by the late so-called Confederate States, or by its agents or under its authority" (N.C., *Ordinances of the 1865–1866 Convention*, 31).
73. *Standard*, 18 July 1865.

74. While written at an earlier date, the comments of William George Thomas of New Hanover County present an interesting viewpoint on why it would have been in the state's best interest to have accepted Holden's bid for the governor's chair without opposition:

> Before the War, Mr. [Curtis H.] Brogden of Edgecombe told me that Mr. H[olden] had said to him in the confidence of private consultation, that he had labored and toiled all his life for social position. He wanted it for his children and that the talents he knew he possessed might be used for the best interest of *society* and the State,—that the Gubernatorial Chair could alone give it to him & that sooner or later he would have it. I have heard other prominent men in the State say the same thing of him, and that social position was the first of all considerations with him. Now take the fact and connect it with the present facts—that Pres. Johnson has made him Prov. Governor, with the avowed purpose to make him the Gov. elect hereafter, with the threat that if that is not so done, woe betide the aristocracy of N.C. Kemp Battle, Wm. H. Jones and Dr. [William H.] McKee say that Holden has good qualities—socially & mentally, and all [agreed] to expect the state of things threatened if he is not properly sustained. . . . These gentlemen . . . say that Mr. Holden is determined to pursue a conciliatory course and struggle to lift the State out of its present degradation and ardently claims the support and confidence of the good people.
>
> Now what I want to say, and what I propose will astonish you as much as it has myself, is this: will it not be better for the leading and influential men in every county & section of the State to let Mr. Holden know, in some way they may deem most suitable, that they are ready and willing to give him true and active support in his laudable effort to disenthral the state of the chains which now bind her hand & foot, that they know he has the position and power to do this to the extent that no other man ever had, and that he may safely trust them for support in all proper exertions to better our present forlorn conditions, and will it not be better part of wisdom for those who can to extend to him that social rank & position we have reason to know he desires so much. Is not this the wisest policy and the most sensible course? (William G. Thomas to Jones Fuller, 9 June 1865, Jones Fuller Papers, DU.)

    The tragedy, however, was that the wisdom of such a policy was not recognized.
75. "In this connection it may not be improper for me to say that I was offered a Senatorship 'by authority' of Ex-Governor Graham, but I emphatically declared that I felt I owed it to you to remain where I am, and that in no event could I accept it." Holden to President Johnson, 6 December 1865, Johnson Papers, LC. See also *Standard*, 18 October 1865; Holden, *Memoirs*, 64–65.
76. Worth had advocated postponement of the war debt consideration, and no doubt Holden's appeal to the president and the latter's telegram demanding immediate repudiation was designed to "smoke out" the Worth forces and place Holden on the proper Union side in the election.

77. Worth to John Pool and Lewis Thompson, 16 October 1865, Hamilton, ed., *Correspondence of Jonathan Worth*, 1:429.

78. *Standard*, 20 June 1866.

79. Holden to Andrew Johnson, 6 December 1865, Johnson Papers, LC. No such letter is found in the published papers of either Worth or Graham.

80. Chamberlain, *Old Days in Chapel Hill*, 118.

81. *Standard*, 23 October 1865. The paper accused Worth of being the candidate of secessionists, "not that they love him, but they hate Holden." Andrews, *South since the War*, 173–74.

82. To counter the Holden charge that a Worth vote would amount to disloyalty to the national government, the *Sentinel* replied, on authority "little less than coming from the President himself," that the government would in no way interfere in the state election (*Raleigh Sentinel*, 30 October 1865). However, Worth appealed to friends in Washington to do something that would counteract such impressions in the North. See Worth to Benjamin S. Hedrick, 8 October 1865, Hamilton, ed., *Correspondence of Jonathan Worth*, 1:433. The *Charlotte Times* gave one of the sharpest attacks against Holden by saying: "Vote for Holden and be loyal, and vote against him and be a traitor. That is the English of it. And if that is to be the test, then we are a traitor and glory in the treason" (reprinted in the *Raleigh Sentinel*, 22 November 1865).

83. *Standard*, 27 October 1865. Holden had far greater newspaper support, as well as from individual state leaders, than he did in 1864. The *Wilmington Herald*, 28 October 1865, cited eight of the state's leading papers as supporting Holden, three favoring Worth, while four were noncommittal.

84. *Standard*, 15 December 1865. The congressional elections primarily involved Union men, most of whom had opposed secession, and their campaigns did not attract too much newspaper comment. The one exception was Turner's bid for Congress. The two ordinances up for ratification (repudiation of slavery and secession) won overwhelming approval.

85. The four Holden men elected were T. C. Fuller, Third District, over George Little; Bedford Brown, Fifth District, over Lewis Hanes; S. H. Walkup, Sixth District, over J. G. Ramsey; and A. H. Jones, Seventh District. The three Worth supporters were Jesse R. Stubbs, Charles C. Clark, and Josiah Turner, Jr., in the First, Second, and Fourth Districts, respectively.

86. Joseph S. Cannon to President Johnson, 13 November 1865, Johnson Papers, LC.

87. Jonathan Worth to A. B. Hill, 6 December 1865, Hamilton, ed., *Correspondence of Jonathan Worth*, 1:455–56.

88. Secretary of State William H. Seward to Holden, 21 November 1865, Johnson Papers, LC.

89. Andrew Johnson to Holden, 27 November 1865, Johnson Papers, LC. This message was copied verbatim from the text sent him by agent Robert Powell. Powell had written, "Our leading friends are of opinion that it is of the greatest importance that your wishes be made known in such manner that they can't be misunderstood

by anyone. I think if you send or telegraph something as following it will do great good."

90. Holden to President Johnson, 6 December 1865, Johnson Papers, LC.

91. North Carolina, *Journal of the North Carolina Senate* (1865), 24; *Raleigh Sentinel*, 2 December 1865.

92. Sion Hart Rogers was elected attorney general (he had been appointed by Holden to fill the same post during the provisional government); Kemp Plummer Battle, treasurer; Curtis H. Brogden, comptroller; and Robert W. Best, secretary of state.

93. Two of the state supreme court members (Richmond M. Pearson and William H. Battle) were reelected from the provisional government court, while Edwin G. Reade became the third member, replacing Matthias E. Manly, an open Holden opponent; five of the eight superior court judges were also reelected (David A. Barnes, Daniel G. Fowle, Robert B. Gilliam, Ralph P. Buxton, and Anderson Mitchell), while Edward J. Warren, William M. Shipp, and Augustus S. Merrimon were newly elected justices; while most of the solicitors were newly elected, the final selections included M. L. Eure, W. T. Faircloth, Sion H. Rogers, Thomas Settle, Neill McKay, L. Q. Sharpe, William P. Bynum, and David Coleman.

94. The problem over the short-term post arose because of a legal question involving Thomas L. Clingman. In 1860, Clingman had been elected to the Senate seat, but entered the Confederate army rather than fill the position. After the war he claimed the seat and even proceeded to Washington and tried to present himself as an elected member of Congress. Of course, he was not recognized by the Senate. In the meantime, the state senate judiciary committee reported that while the state was without authority to declare the Senate seat vacant, it could assume that the seat was vacant, since Congress had expelled all southern members at the beginning of the war. It concluded, therefore, that it was the duty of the General Assembly to fill the vacancy (North Carolina, *Journal of the North Carolina Senate* [1865], 56).

95. *Raleigh Sentinel*, 15 December 1865. According to Holden, after he refused the nomination, John Pool, Bedford Brown, Thomas S. Ashe, Nathaniel Boyden, William N. H. Smith, Robert M. Henry, and William Eaton, Jr., were nominated, with Pool winning the post as a concession to the Holden forces (*Standard*, 20 June 1866).

96. Holden to President Johnson, 6 December 1865, Johnson Papers, LC.

97. Worth's speech was printed in the *Raleigh Sentinel*, 16 December 1865.

98. Hamilton, ed., *Correspondence of Jonathan Worth*, 1:457–58.

99. Holden to President Johnson, 6 December 1865, Johnson Papers, LC.

100. Professor Hamilton makes such an assertion in his *Reconstruction in North Carolina*, 145, and cites as his authority a letter of Benjamin S. Hedrick. It should be remembered, however, that this was the same B. S. Hedrick who was "run out" of the university in 1856 by Holden and who, in the summer of 1866, represented Worth's administration in Washington as state agent. See Hedrick to Worth, 8 July 1866, Hamilton, ed., *Correspondence of Jonathan Worth*, 2:674–76.

101. *Wilmington Herald*, 23 November 1865.

102. Holden to President Johnson, 6 December 1865, Johnson Papers, LC.
103. Secretary of State William H. Seward to Holden, 23 December 1865, Governor's Papers, State Archives.

CHAPTER FIVE

1. *Standard*, 17 January 1865; see also Holden to Andrew Johnson, 4 July 1865, Johnson Papers, LC. In his *Memoirs*, 45–46, Holden wrote:
     I did not when in Washington [1865] call to see Governor Vance. I thought if I did it might look as assumption of superiority over him. . . . But I sent word by Mr. [B. F.] Moore and Colonel [John H.] Wheeler who called upon him, that I sympathized with him, and [I] would be glad to loan him funds if he needed them. . . . I asked [Robert J.] Powell what he thought would be the fate of Governor Vance (and Southern Governors then in the old Capitol Prison). He said he thought they would all be hanged. I replied: "Dr. Powell, this will never do. If this is done we cannot reconstruct nor restore North Carolina. Vance stood and stands for our people as Davis did for the entire South. Please keep me informed on these matters constantly. If there is any danger of what you say, I will return here at once and appeal to the President!" I would not, of course, have served if the President had allowed these things to be done.
2. *Standard*, 6 March 1866. Holden later accused Worth of repudiating the president's restoration plans by replacing true Unionists with secessionists and "rebels." B. F. Moore was removed from the presidency of the Bank of North Carolina and replaced by George W. Mordecai; Charles R. Thomas was removed from the Atlantic Railroad by Nathaniel Whitford; Robert W. Lassiter was replaced by William J. Hawkins in the Raleigh and Gaston Railroad; and Tod R. Caldwell was removed from the presidency of the Western Railroad by Samuel McDowell Tate. See *Standard*, 13 September 1866.
3. Congress had refused to seat the newly elected southern members in December 1865, partly because the congressmen-elect were not representative of President Johnson's hopes of establishing a more democratic society in the South and because of the southern states' enactment of the Black Codes, which were interpreted in the North as an attempt to "reenslave" the blacks.
4. William E. Pell, editor of the *Raleigh Sentinel*, accused the *Standard* of reading like the *New York Tribune* (Pell to William A. Graham, 15 March 1866, Graham Papers, State Archives). In April, Holden declared that he favored allowing Congress to act in reconstruction matters without opposition. See *Standard*, 25 April 1866.
5. For Benjamin S. Hedrick's commentary on the appointment, see his letter to Jonathan Worth, 20 June 1866, Hamilton, ed., *Correspondence of Jonathan Worth*, 1:638–39.

6. Hamilton, *Reconstruction in North Carolina*, 177. See Commager, *Documents*, 30–31, 38–39, 49, for the 2 March 1867 Reconstruction Act and later supplementary legislation which established Test Oath requirements. Earlier, Holden had advocated the state's adoption of the proposed fourteenth amendment as a means of restoring political control to "loyal" men. See *Standard*, 6, 13 June 1866.

7. Both the Holden evaluation and Johnson's intended statement can be found in the Andrew Johnson Papers, LC. See Holden to Johnson, 11 July 1866, ibid.

8. The North Carolina Constitutional Convention, 1865–66, met upon two separate occasions. The 1865 session adopted ordinances that were specifically designed to meet President Johnson's terms for the state's readmission to the Union. It adjourned in December 1865, to meet again in May 1866 to consider additional changes in the state constitution. For further information on the latter changes, see Hamilton, *Reconstruction in North Carolina*, 172–75.

9. Holden to President Johnson, 1 August 1866, Johnson Papers, LC.

10. A similar meeting was held in Guilford County under the control of Albion W. Tourgée and George E. Welker, both Northerners, and resolutions calling for a statewide convention were adopted. The major difference between the two meetings was that black suffrage was recommended at the Guilford meeting.

11. For an account of the convention activities, see the *Standard*, 22 September 1866, and also for Holden's speech entitled "The President's Plan Considered."

12. Holden thought that Matt W. Ransom of Northampton County would have been a more suitable candidate to oppose Worth, but he declined to run, being opposed to having any contest at that time. The names of James T. Leach and W. R. Cox were next considered, but they were dropped when they failed to pursue the matter. See the *Standard*, 1 August 1866; also, Hamilton, *Reconstruction in North Carolina*, 177.

13. As appointed by Holden, the steering committee consisted of David M. Carter (Beaufort); Eugene Grissom (Granville); Charles R. Thomas (Craven); Oliver H. Dockery (Richmond); E. L. Pemberton (Cumberland); Thomas Settle (Rockingham); Robert P. Dick (Guilford); Calvin J. Cowles (Wilkes); Tod R. Caldwell (Burke); Robert M. Henry (Macon); Alexander H. Jones (Henderson); L. L. Steward (Buncombe); George W. Logan (Rutherford); and William Sloan (Mecklenburg).

14. *Standard*, 25 December 1866; see also ibid., 30 January 1867.

15. Reprinted from the *Troy* (New York) *Daily News*, 18 February 1867, in the *Standard*, 27 February 1867. North Carolina was not the only southern state to reject the amendment.

16. The bill was framed primarily by Holden, John Pool, Thaddeus Stevens, and Congressman Nelson T. Taylor of New York. Professor Hamilton in his *Reconstruction in North Carolina*, 187, claimed that it was James F. Taylor of North Carolina instead of Nelson T. Taylor who was one of the authors of the bill, but this is refuted by James A. Padgett. See Alexander H. Jones to Thaddeus Stevens, 4 January 1867, Padgett, ed., "Reconstruction Letters," 191–92.

17. Miller, *Thaddeus Stevens*, 301–2. In a later biographical study of Stevens, Ralph Korngold points out that he preferred that the right of suffrage of whites, as well as blacks, be restricted to those who could read and write or owned real estate assessed at one hundred dollars or more. Actually he wanted to place the southern states under territorial government so that, if necessary, federal authorities would have been able to intervene whenever necessary to maintain order, establish public schools, and gradually introduce Negro suffrage. See his *Thaddeus Stevens*, 381.

18. Perman, *Reunion without Compromise*, 259–65; Zuber, *Jonathan Worth*, 246–47; Hamilton, *Reconstruction in North Carolina*, 190.

19. Under the terms of the act of 2 March 1867, the South was placed under military rule, with North Carolina joined with South Carolina to form the Second Military District under the command of General Daniel E. Sickles. Upon his assumption of duties, 21 March 1867, Sickles placed the state on a provisional basis, subject to the rule of Congress. Local laws were permitted to stand in effect only when not in conflict with those of the federal government.

20. This conversation was repeated by Holden to Randolph A. Shotwell in 1880 and is reprinted by Hamilton, ed., in *Papers of Randolph Abbott Shotwell*, 2:230–31.

21. *Standard*, 2, 9 January, 13 March 1867.

22. Holden to Senator John Sherman, 23 February 1867, Padgett, ed., "Reconstruction Letters," 292–93.

23. *Standard*, 9 March 1867. For the exact wording of the 2 March act, see Commager, *Documents*, 30–31.

24. Ibid.

25. Quoted in the *Standard*, 26 March 1867.

26. Ibid.

27. See ibid., 7 March 1867, for the list of names included in the general invitation.

28. See ibid., 26 March 1867, for an account of the Raleigh and Fayetteville meetings together with Holden's invitation.

29. Ibid., 28 March 1867. An account of the convention's activities was published by the *Standard*, 30 March 1867.

30. Jones was one of the strongest Unionists in the western part of the state and had taken a leading role in Radical activities from the beginning. Long an advocate of Negro suffrage, he wrote a congratulatory note to Thaddeus Stevens on his reconstruction bill. In it he said: "This proposition is much more preferable than the one introduced at the instance of Messrs. Holden, Pool, and Taylor [North Carolina Enabling Act] from the fact that it allowed the freedmen to vote without qualifications, and because it disqualifies all who held office, civil or military, under the Confederate authorities" (Jones to Stevens, 4 January 1867, Padgett, ed., "Reconstruction Letters," 191–92).

31. Daniel Reaves Goodloe was a native of Louisburg, North Carolina, who after an unsuccessful legal practice moved to Washington, D.C., in 1844 and worked on several newspapers. In 1852 he became assistant editor of the *National Era*, an

antislavery paper, and later its editor until the outbreak of the Civil War. Next he was a correspondent for the *New York Times* until 1862, when President Lincoln appointed him chairman of a commission to carry out the compensation provision of the act emancipating slaves in the District of Columbia; from 1863 to 1865 he did editorial work for the *Washington Chronicle*. In 1865, President Johnson appointed him U.S. marshall for North Carolina, and he was still employed in that capacity when he joined in the movement to form the Republican party. See *Dictionary of American Biography*, 7:390–91. Benjamin S. Hedrick returned to the state after suffering a severe illness in the summer of 1867. Governor Worth arranged complimentary tickets for his entire family "on account of your service to the State." See Worth to Hedrick, 24 August 1867, Hamilton, ed., *Correspondence of Jonathan Worth*, 2:1042.

32. *Standard*, 30 March 1867.
33. For a listing of the executive committee members appointed by President Jones see the *Standard*, 2 April 1867.
34. *Raleigh Sentinel*, 28 March 1867.
35. Reprinted in ibid., 8 May 1867.
36. Reprinted in the *Standard*, 3 April 1867.
37. *Nation*, 4 April 1867.
38. *Standard*, 9 July 1867. Black organizations that marched included the Benevolent Society, the Union Brotherhood True American, and the Equal Rights League.
39. *Nation*, 18 July 1867.
40. Albion Winegar Tourgée, a native of Ohio and Union army veteran, settled in Greensboro in 1865, where he practiced law, especially in suits filed by southern Unionists against the United States for damages inflicted by Sherman's army. Through his Union League activities he became an early advocate for the formation of a state Republican party. During Holden's administration he served on the superior court bench, and since many of the Ku Klux Klan activities occurred in his district he made a valiant attempt to flush out and suppress the movement. After Holden's removal from office in 1871 Tourgée found himself increasingly at odds with the state government, finally fleeing west to Denver, Colorado. He is best known for his later career as a novelist, especially for his books about his Reconstruction experiences (*A Fool's Errand by One of the Fools*, 1879, is the most noted), and for his legal brief in the segregation case of *Plessy v. Ferguson*, 1896. The best and most definitive study of Tourgée is Olsen's *Carpetbagger's Crusade*. A full coverage of the Union League's activities in the state is found in Hamilton, *Reconstruction in North Carolina*, 327–42.
41. Reverdy Johnson was considered one of the nation's leading constitutional lawyers. He served as senator from Maryland, 1845–48 and 1863–69, and as attorney general, 1849–50. From 1868 to 1869 he served as United States minister to England, beginning negotiations over the disputed *Alabama* claims.
42. *Standard*, 20 February 1867.

43. Holden to Edward McPherson, Clerk of the United States House of Representatives, 6 July 1867, Padgett, ed., "Reconstruction Letters," 196.
44. Worth to Walter F. Leak, 5 January 1867, Hamilton, ed., *Correspondence of Jonathan Worth*, 2:859–60.
45. Reprinted in the *Raleigh Sentinel*, 31 August 1867.
46. *New York Herald* Supplement, 13 December 1866.
47. In this proposal, Stevens was supported by Charles Sumner, Wendell Phillips, and the American Anti-Slavery Society.
48. *Standard*, 1 August 1867.
49. Ibid., 24, 31 July 1867.
50. Joseph Carter Abbott was born in New Hampshire but moved to Massachusetts, where he edited the *Manchester Daily American* and the *Boston Atlas*. During the war he served as lt. colonel, Seventh Regt., New Hampshire Volunteers; in 1865 he was made brev. general for "gallant and meritorious service in the capture of Fort Fisher, N.C." After the war, he settled in Wilmington and for a time was commandant of the city; later he became involved in business developments, especially internal improvements and lumber manufacturing. A United States senator from 1868 to 1871, he served as collector of port of Wilmington under Grant and inspector of eastern ports under Hayes, and as special agent for the United States Treasury until his death in 1881. See *Dictionary of American Biography*, 1:23–24, and *Biographical Congressional Directory* (1913), 427.
51. For a complete account of the convention, see *Standard*, 11 September 1867.
52. For a full description of the Sickles administration in the state and the reasons for his removal, see Hamilton, *Reconstruction in North Carolina*, 227–33.
53. Worth to D. G. Worth, 24 October 1867, Hamilton, ed., *Correspondence of Jonathan Worth*, 2:1058–59; Worth to W. G. Moore, 31 December 1867, ibid., 1098–99.
54. U.S., Senate, *Senate Executive Documents*, 40th Congress, 2nd Session, No. 53. As reported by General Canby, the election vote was as follows:

Registered voters	179,653
White voters	106,721
Colored voters	72,932
Votes cast	126,130
For convention	93,006
Against convention	32,961
Vote by race—for convention	
White	31,284
Colored	61,722
Vote against convention	
White	32,961
Colored	———

Persons not voting	53,686
White	42,476
Colored	11,210
Number of persons disfranchised	12,179
White	11,686
Colored	493
Number failing to register	23,766
White	19,477
Colored	3,289

55. Worth's major complaints concerned Canby's removal of Conservative civil officers and replacement of them with Republicans, conflict of jurisdiction between the civil courts and military authorities, rise of Negro crime, and the Canby attempt to appoint Albion W. Tourgée as superior court judge upon the resignation of Daniel G. Fowle. See Worth to W. G. Moore, 31 December 1867 and 4 January 1868, Hamilton, ed., *Correspondence of Jonathan Worth*, 2:1098–99, 1107–10, and Worth to Benjamin S. Hedrick, 8 January 1868, ibid., 1120–23.

56. On 23 July 1868, Cowles married Holden's twenty-two-year-old daughter, Ida Augusta, in a private ceremony in the Holden residence. Typical of the Holden's lack of ostentatiousness, the announcement was made by the *Standard* the next day in a brief, five-line account.

57. David Heaton, a native of Ohio, played the major role in the writing of the "Canby Constitution," as it was deviously called by the Conservatives. Nevertheless, Heaton had much legislative experience, having served in the Ohio Senate in 1855 and the Minnesota Senate from 1858 to 1863. In that year he moved to New Bern as a special agent for the United States Treasury. Later he served North Carolina in the United States House of Representatives from 1867 until his death in 1870. *Biographical Congressional Directory* (1913), 717.

58. Under the direction of Calvin H. Wiley, North Carolina had started a good system of schools in the 1850s, and by 1860 it was not only the best in the South but it compared most favorably with many in the northern states. Now, however, it became a definite part of the state constitution. See Knight, *Public School Education*.

59. Lefler and Newsome, *North Carolina*, 489–90. For a critical analysis of the convention, see Hamilton, *Reconstruction in North Carolina*, 253–78.

60. The slate of candidates for the two parties read:

Republicans		*Conservative-Unionists*
William W. Holden	Governor	Thomas Samuel Ashe
Tod R. Caldwell	Lieutenant Governor	Edward D. Hall
Henry J. Menninger	Secretary of State	Robert W. Best
David A. Jenkins	Treasurer	Kemp P. Battle
Henderson Adams	Auditor	S. W. Burgin

Ceburn L. Harris	Supt. of Public Works	Samuel F. Patterson
Samuel S. Ashley	Supt. of Public Instruction	Braxton Craven
William M. Coleman	Attorney General	Sion H. Rogers
Richmond M. Pearson	Supreme Court	Richmond M. Pearson
William B. Rodman	Supreme Court	William H. Battle
Robert P. Dick	Supreme Court	Edwin G. Reade
Thomas Settle	Supreme Court	Matthias E. Manly
Edwin G. Reade	Supreme Court	Augustus S. Merrimon
	Congressmen	
John R. French	First District	Henry A. Gilliam
David Heaton	Second District	Thomas S. Kenan
Oliver H. Dockery	Third District	Thomas C. Fuller
John T. Deweese	Fourth District	Samuel Williams
Israel G. Lash	Fifth District	David P. Caldwell
Calvin J. Cowles	Sixth District	Nathaniel Boyden
Alexander H. Jones	Seventh District	Burgess Gaither

Two interesting facts should be noted about the above slate. First, two supreme court candidates, Pearson and Reade, were endorsed by both parties and both remained close friends with Holden throughout his political and later career. Second, Ceburn L. Harris of Rutherford County was persuaded by Holden to accept the nomination as superintendent of public works instead of the presidency of the North Carolina Railroad Company, which had previously been promised him. This was the beginning of the feud that developed in their relationship, especially as to which one would control the state's railroads during Holden's administration.

61. See the *Raleigh Sentinel*, 9 March and 1 April 1868, for a general review of the Conservative arguments.

62. The *Standard* replied to the charges by labeling each as "Rebel Lie No. 1, No. 2, No. 3, and No. 4" (26 March 1868).

63. Hamilton, *Reconstruction in North Carolina*, 284. Lefler and Newsome, *North Carolina History*, 491, quoted it as "spectre."

64. *Standard*, 16 March 1868.

65. Robert C. Schenck to Holden, 13 April 1868, Governor's Papers, State Archives.

66. Connor, *Manual of North Carolina*, 1001–2, 1016–18.

67. The exception in the congressional race was Calvin J. Cowles's defeat by Nathaniel Boyden. The superior court judges elected included Charles Pool, Edmund W. Jones, Charles R. Thomas, Daniel L. Russell, Jr., Ralph P. Buxton, Samuel W. Watts, A. W. Tourgée, Darius H. Starbuck, George W. Logan, Anderson Mitchell, James L. Henry, and Riley H. Cannon. Solicitors elected were Jonathan W. Albertson, Joseph J. Martin, John V. Sherard, John A. Richardson, Neil McKay, William R. Cox, J. R. Bulla, A. H. Joyce, William P. Bynum, W. P. Caldwell,

Virgil S. Lusk, and William L. Tate. See General Order No. 83, Headquarters Second Military District, Charleston, S.C., 12 May 1868, as reprinted in the *Standard*, 21 May 1868.

68. Ibid. The general order listed all county winners in addition to the state's executive, legislative, and judicial officials, including those who ran for the posts of sheriff, coroner, treasurer, county clerk of superior court, register of deeds, surveyor, and commissioners.

69. James A. Rawlings was a Galena, Illinois, neighbor of U. S. Grant and served as his secretary of war in 1869. Laflin to Holden, 15 June 1868, Governor's Papers, State Archives.

70. Canby to Holden, 15 June 1868, Governor's Papers, State Archives.

71. *Standard*, 15 April 1868.

72. Reprinted in the *Raleigh Sentinel*, 20 May 1868.

73. John Pool to Holden, 9 May 1868, Governor's Papers, State Archives.

74. Worth to William A. Graham, 16 June 1868, Hamilton, ed., *Correspondence of Jonathan Worth*, 2:1222–23.

75. Holden issued his proclamation when he received word that Congress had passed the legislation for the state's readmission, for he knew that it had the necessary votes to override a possible presidential veto.

76. Worth to Holden, 1 July 1868, Governor's Papers, State Archives.

77. Holden, *Memoirs*, 113–14.

78. North Carolina, *Executive and Legislative Documents*, Nos. 1, 2.

CHAPTER SIX

1. After Mrs. Holden's death, the house passed out of the Holden family possession, and in 1925 it was torn down and replaced by the Professional Office Building. See the *Raleigh News and Observer*, 18 January 1925, and the *Raleigh Times*, 19 January 1925, for a complete description of the house and grounds.

2. In returning the mansion furniture to Governor Vance, Holden listed the pieces, times received, and his accountability. From R. H. Bradley he received the following pieces in 1865: one large mahogany bedstand, one marble slab round table, two marble slab side tables, one sideboard, one iron hat rack, two Lambrequines [*sic*], two plated candlesticks, one tea set, some pieces of china, plated spoons, a few pieces of glassware, and one large punch bowl. The above items were sent to Gov. Worth in the latter part of 1865 and returned to Holden by Worth in 1868, except the hat rack and the Lambrequines. In addition, he received from Worth the following: one rosewood bedstand, with spring mattresses, one mantel mirror, one clock, two turkish chairs, four silver spoons, eight small silver spoons. In 1868 he recovered from the Governor's Mansion the upper part of the above-mentioned sideboard, part of a rosewood wardrobe, two mantel mirrors, one mahogany

wardrobe, and some gas fixtures. The clock and two large chandeliers were sent north for repairs. As had Worth earlier, Holden also received one carpet which he did not return since it was "worn out." In fact, Worth got other pieces of mansion furniture that he did not turn over to Holden, and some old and useless pieces were either left in the mansion or sold to pay for the repairs. See Holden to Vance, 17 April 1877, Zebulon B. Vance Papers, State Archives.

3. Dated receipts of 27 February 1869 and 8 June 1869, Holden Papers, State Archives.

4. See Holden to R. James Powell of the Public Grounds Committee of the House of Representatives, 8 December 1876, Plato Durham Papers, a copy of which is in the Holden Papers, DU.

5. Holden sold the *Standard* in 1868 to N. Paige and Company, but this was merely a front for Gen. Milton Littlefield, the state's chief carpetbagger. Fred G. Mahler, a Holden grandson, wrote the author on 4 July 1956 that he always understood the sale price to be $25,000, while Professor Hamilton set it at $40,000.

6. On 10 April 1875, Josiah Turner, Jr., entered suit against Holden for his 1870 "assault, arrest & false imprisonment" in Orange County. The case was tried in the state superior court, Judge Ralph P. Buxton presiding, and Turner was awarded $8,000. Holden then appealed to the state supreme court, and the judgment was rescinded. After Holden's death in 1892, Turner, long since repudiated by his own Conservative-Democratic friends and in a deplorably demented condition, sued Mrs. Holden for $15,000 (to be collected from Holden's estate) for "defamation of character" and attempted to prove that Holden had been guilty of corruption during his term of office, such as receiving a $30,000 "bribe" from Swepson in the North Carolina Bank case. Again, Turner lost his case. For further information, see transcript of the *Turner* v. *Holden* suit, State Archives, and correspondence between Mrs. Holden and John W. Hinsdale, her attorney, in the Holden Papers, DU.

7. Holden to Canby, 16 July 1868, Governor's Letter Book, State Archives.

8. Holden met with some resistance to filling the offices; for instance, Raleigh officials at first refused to turn over their offices to a new administration headed by Mayor Robert Harrison, Holden's brother-in-law, while the sheriffs of New Hanover and Granville counties had to be forcibly removed by military troops.

9. North Carolina, *Journal of the House* (1868), 154–55; North Carolina, *Journal of the Senate* (1868), 181.

10. On 16 October, Adjutant General Fisher wrote Holden from Vermont that he could secure three thousand Springfield rifles, and Governor Page, after consultation with his advisers, pushed through the Vermont legislature a resolution authorizing him "to collect the arms, ammunition and quarter-master stores belonging to the State and make such deposit and disposition of the same as he shall deem advisable; provided, this authority shall not be construed to authorize the sale of such arms, ammunition and stores" (*Journal of the* [Vermont] *House of Representatives . . . Annual Session, 1868, Wednesday, 21 October*, 75). Absolute verification of

the "loan" is impossible to ascertain, owing to the burning of the records of the Vermont Arsenal in 1945, but evidently it was handled through one of the Vermont colleges, for several such loans were mentioned in the Vermont Quartermaster General's Reports for 1868 and 1869, although no specific reference was made of loans to North Carolina (Clara E. Follette, Assistant Director, Vermont Historical Society, Montpelier, Vermont, to author, 14 February 1949). Furthermore, ten companies of federal troops were stationed in the state, and they helped to maintain law and order.

11. William M. Coleman of Cabarrus County was first named attorney general, but when he proved incompetent Holden persuaded President Grant to appoint him as the U.S. consul at Stettin, Prussia, in April 1869 rather than fire him. He then selected Olds to fill the post. In other examples of nepotism, Henry J. Menninger, son-in-law of Congressman David Heaton, was named secretary of state; Senator John Pool secured offices for six members of his family, including Solomon Pool, brother, president of the university, and Charles Carroll Pool, nephew, superior court judge; when Fayette Eaves, son-in-law of superior court justice George W. Logan, resigned from the state legislature, he was promptly replaced by Logan's son, Robert Logan; Samuel S. Ashley had one of his relatives working in the office of superintendent of public instruction, while Fiske P. Brewer, a brother-in-law, was appointed to a professorship at the university; and the prominent Cobb family of Pasquotank County had Clinton Levering Cobb in the United States House of Representatives, William L. Cobb, brother, a chaplain in the United States Navy, and G. W. Cobb, mayor and United States collector for the port of Elizabeth City.

12. Hamilton, *Reconstruction in North Carolina*, 348.

13. The following lawyers were employed for extra-legal services: V. C. Barringer, $100; J. R. Bulla, $100; A. S. Seymour, $100; William J. Clarke, $350; R. F. Lehman, $100; W. L. Ball, $200; Richard C. Badger, $700; Boyden and Bailey, $2,000; Blackner and McCorkle, $1,000; L. P. Olds, $500; and James E. Boyd, $250 (Governor Tod R. Caldwell to Speaker of House, 21 December 1870, Caldwell Papers, State Archives). See also Treasurer Jenkins's "Reply to the House Resolution on State Payment of Monies," in North Carolina, *Executive and Legislative Documents* (1870–71), no. 13.

14. Ibid.

15. Menninger was also involved in a swindle in purchasing new carpet for the Capitol. In October 1869 he visited the Raleigh firm of E. Via and Company and asked for carpet price quotations. He was informed that the desired quality would cost $2.25 a yard, but since he wanted 500 yards he might have it for $1.93 per yard. At the same time Menninger purchased two sets of china and a bedroom set of furniture for himself and had his purchases delivered to his residence. The following day, Menninger returned to the store and asked the manager if he knew the difference between "tweedle dee and tweedle dum." He then wrote out $2.19 x 500 and showed it to the manager. The latter understood it to mean that Menninger pro-

posed to pay for his personal purchases out of the Capitol carpet purchase, and indicated he did not care how the money was paid so long as the store was paid for all the purchases. Menninger then drew a warrant on the state for 500 yards of carpet at $2.19 (testimony of J. G. Hester, manager of the E. Via Company, before the Shipp Fraud Commission, in North Carolina, *Report of the Commission to Investigate the Charges of Fraud and Corruption*, 498–576).

16. John H. Renfrow of Halifax County had proposed to give free franking privileges to all members of the General Assembly.

17. Pearson to William L. Scott, 16 July 1868, Scott Papers, DU.

18. Pearson's address was printed in the *Standard*, 11 August 1868, and in *A Full Report of the Proceedings in the Matter of the Bench and Bar of North Carolina*, a copy of which is found in the State Archives. Conservative criticism was widespread, with the *Wilmington Journal*, 28 August 1868, giving a typical reaction: ". . . cannot recall another instance in the history of North Carolina, as a State, when her highest judicial dignitary so far forgot the propriety of his position as to descend into the political arena—a partisan champion, stripped and girded for the fight. . . . The position of the Chief Justice proves he has entirely misconceived the character of the issues joined in the present political contest. Whether the negro shall, or shall not, be deprived of the franchise, does not enter into it at all."

19. Ceburn L. Harris to W. E. Chandler, 17 October 1868, Padgett, ed., "Reconstruction Letters," 65–67; see also C. L. Harris to Thomas S. Tullock, 4 September 1868, and n.d., 1869, in the Correspondence of Superintendent of Public Works (1868–69), 7, 11–13, State Archives.

20. Hamilton, *Reconstruction in North Carolina*, 362. Congressman John T. Deweese had his franking privilege taken from him for sending campaign documents to blacks throughout the state, and was indicted by a federal court, tried, but found not guilty. Postmaster General Alexander W. Randall then returned the privilege to Deweese. See *Raleigh Sentinel*, 30 September 1868.

21. *New York Evening Post*, 30 September 1868. Further complicating the issue was the news received by Holden that guns and ammunition had been secreted in the state by the opposition and distributed among people in Charlotte and points west. "I have received reliable reports," he wrote to Gen. Nelson A. Miles, "legally substantiated, that several hundreds of Henry and Spencer rifles (many of them sixteen shooters) with accouterments &e., complete, have been received in Wilmington and thence distributed to organizations in the State, styling themselves 'Seymour and Blair Clubs' and K.K.K.'s . . . " (Holden to Miles, 7 October 1868, and published in the *Standard*, 9 October 1868). See also Holden's "Proclamation" issued on 12 October 1868, in which he declared the illegality of such actions while, at the same time, guaranteeing state protection of black citizens. A copy of this proclamation can be found in the Governor's Letter Book, State Archives.

22. Jonathan Worth to Montgomery Blair, 24 August 1868, Hamilton, ed., *Correspondence of Jonathan Worth*, 2:1242–43.

23. In an effort to offset the Conservative strategy, General Littlefield and Attorney General Coleman went to Washington just prior to the election and attempted to persuade President Grant and the secretary of war to send federal troops to the state to quell a "rebel" uprising by the Conservatives. See Hamilton, *Reconstruction in North Carolina*, 372.

24. The five lawyers were Edward Graham Haywood, Daniel G. Fowle, Samuel F. Phillips, Bartholomew F. Moore, and Thomas Bragg. See *Wilmington Journal*, 24 October 1868.

25. William M. Coleman to Holden, 20 October 1868, *Standard*, 21 October 1868.

26. See *Standard*, 27 October, 5 November 1868.

27. According to the *Standard*, 9 November 1868, the "fracas" occurred when a black man attempted to vote but was denied the right because he had been "whipped at the post." Words passed between the black and the clerk, and this led to a fight in which the black was knocked down. This led to the "riot" which left one dead and five or six others wounded. For the Conservative version, see the *Raleigh Sentinel*, 18 November 1868.

28. In the 1st District, Republican C. L. Cobb defeated D. A. Barnes, Democrat; 2nd District, David Heaton, Republican, defeated T. S. Kenan, Democrat; 3rd District, O. H. Dockery, Republican, won over A. A. McKay; 4th District, John T. Deweese, Republican, defeated Sion H. Rogers, Democrat; 5th District, I. G. Lash, Republican, defeated Livingston Brown, Democrat; 6th District, Francis E. Shober, Democrat, won over Nathaniel Boyden, Republican; and, 7th District, A. H. Jones, Republican, ultimately was declared victor over Plato Durham.

29. John R. French ran in opposition to C. L. Cobb in the 1st District; James H. Harris and John A. Hyman, both blacks, opposed Deweese in the 3rd District but were "bought off," with Harris receiving $4,000 and Hyman $500; W. F. Henderson and Judge Albion W. Tourgée conducted heated campaigns against each other before withdrawing in favor of the incumbent, Lash. See Hamilton, *Reconstruction in North Carolina*, 367–68, 375.

30. *Standard*, 9 November 1868.

31. John Pool to Holden, 13 December 1868, Governor's Papers, State Archives; see also *Charlotte Western Democrat*, 15 December 1868.

32. North Carolina, *Executive and Legislative Documents* (1868–69), no. 1. The 1868 Convention (as had earlier legislatures) passed a stay law to provide relief to debtors, saying that civil proceedings founded on causes of action prior to May 1865 should be suspended until 1 January 1869, or until the new constitution went into effect. Holden was in complete agreement with the homestead exemption in the 1868 constitution, however, since it would "secure a home for the family" in cases of nonpayment of debts.

33. Rufus Yancy McAden was president of the First National Bank of Charlotte. He was born in Caswell County, graduated from Wake Forest College, studied law and began practice in Graham, Alamance County. He was a cousin, but raised as a

brother, of Virginia Yancey, the future wife of George W. Swepson, and through her formed a close business relationship with Swepson. In 1861 he was elected to the 1861 "Secession" Convention and served in the house of commons from 1862 to 1867, being elected speaker for one term. In addition to his banking interests he was involved in the construction of the Atlantic and Charlotte Railroad and the Spartanburg, S.C., to Asheville Railroad, both of which later became part of the Southern line. In 1881 he went into the textile field, building a large mill in Gaston County. See Ashe, ed., *Biographical History*, 5:198–202.

George W. Swepson was born in Virginia, but moved to Caswell County at the age of twenty-three. He married Virginia Yancey, daughter of Bartlett Yancey, and through her formed a business relationship with R. Y. McAden. Before the war, Swepson amassed a fortune in cotton mills in Swepsonville and was a partner in the New York City brokerage firm of Swepson, Mendenhall and Company. During the war he became a leading banker in Raleigh and financier in the state's railroads. In 1868 he bought interest in the Deep River Manufacturing Company, especially in the Chatham Railroad Company and the proposed Deep River penitentiary site. With Gen. Milton Littlefield, he was involved in the railroad scandals of the Western Division of the Western North Carolina Railroad and two Florida roads, resulting in the loss of most of his fortune. At the time of the bank episode, however, he was one of the most highly respected financial leaders in the entire state. For the best account of his financial involvement, see Daniels, *Milton S. Littlefield*.

34. See McAden's "Card," dated 19 November 1868, and published in the *Standard*, 25 November 1868, in the *Charlotte Western Democrat*, 24 November 1868, and in the *Raleigh Sentinel*, 19 November 1868.

35. North Carolina, *Executive and Legislative Documents* (1868–69), no. 19. The author was unable to uncover bankruptcy records of the Bank of North Carolina; hence it was impossible to learn the exact manipulations that benefited the directors. However, George W. Mordecai, William R. Pool, John Bryan, Sr., Bartholomew F. Moore, J. W. B. Watson, Charles Manly, Kemp P. Battle, D. M. Barringer, and George E. Badger served as directors before the war, and the investigating committee mentioned Moore, Bragg, Pool, and Barringer in its 1869 report, and each of the above represented a different social and economic element from Holden. This remains one of the unsolved mysteries in the state's Reconstruction history, but the author is convinced that enough is known to show that graft and malfeasance must be shared by the Conservative-Democratic leadership along with Republicans.

36. Jonathan M. Heck was born in Virginia, now West Virginia, and was a large land speculator before the Civil War. During the war he served in the Confederate Quartermaster Department until captured. He was paroled by Gen. George B. McClellan and permitted to take his family to North Carolina, where he became "a Baptist, a Confederate, and promoter." He acquired financial control of the White

Sulphur Springs in Warren County and operated a major resort center throughout the war. He was instrumental in unveiling a monument for Mary Lee, daughter of Robert E. Lee, who died at the springs. After the war he was active in promoting land sales in the state and attracting northern investments, as well as inducing northern migration. See Daniels, *Milton S. Littlefield*, 7.

37. Such allegations were never proved. See North Carolina, *Executive and Legislative Documents* (1868–69), no. 14.
38. Ibid.
39. Prior to this time each county had been responsible for incarcerating its own convicted criminals, often resulting in inhuman treatment of the felons.
40. Committee members included Ceburn L. Harris, Robert Lassiter, John Hyman, Hugh Downing, J. H. Renfrow, James H. Harris, and William Robbins.
41. North Carolina, *Executive and Legislative Documents* (1868–69), no. 7. See also *Standard*, 24 November 1868.
42. Robert W. Lassiter of Granville County supposedly sold a tract of land to General Littlefield for $3,000, sight unseen. The *Raleigh Sentinel*, 1 January 1869, put the figure at $7,000 for "land so poor that the squirrels go about crying all the fall, because of the scarcity of food." The state purchased 125 acres on the Deep River for a penitentiary site and paid $100,000, with $56,000 going to Jonathan M. Heck of the Deep River Manufacturing Company and $44,000 to D. J. Pruyn. Prior to the sale, the Deep River Company (Heck, Swepson, and A. B. Andrews being the principal stockholders) had purchased 8,000 acres from the original owners for approximately $11,600. One of the owners had deemed the land worthless and was glad to rid himself of paying taxes on it. The Heck outfit then sold the state 100 acres at $1,000 an acre, or $100,000, with an additional 25 acres "thrown in" as an inducement. The contract was drawn up by Kemp P. Battle and Richard S. Tucker, both leading Conservative lawyers.
43. "Report of the Investigation Commission on the Penitentiary Site," printed in the *Standard*, 18 January 1869.
44. Salmon Adams to Silas Burns, 12 November 1868, printed in the "Report of the Joint Committee on Location of the Penitentiary," North Carolina, *Executive and Legislative Documents* (1868–69), no. 7.
45. Salmon Adams to Ceburn L. Harris, 11 January 1869, ibid., no. 20.
46. *Charlotte Western Democrat*, 26 April 1870; see also *Raleigh Sentinel*, 23 April 1870.
47. The antebellum school program had been financed largely by the Literary Fund of about $3,000,000, but without state tax support. Superintendent Wiley refused to allow this fund to be invested in Confederate securities during the war but thought it safely invested in state bank notes, internal improvement projects, and $650,000 in state bonds. Later all was lost. The state bonds were repudiated; the railroad and navigation company stocks were without value, for in 1866 they produced income of only $776; the six thousand shares of the Wilmington and Manchester Railroad

and the Wilmington and Weldon Road, valued at $600,000, were sold in 1869 for $148,000 and reinvested in tax bonds that were later repudiated; the stock in the Cape Fear Navigation Company, valued at $32,500, was sold for $3,250; and the stock in the Bank of North Carolina and the Bank of Cape Fear became worthless when the two banks went into bankruptcy.

48. The 1865 constitution had declared all incumbents who had taken oaths of allegiance to the Confederacy to be ineligible to hold office. Furthermore, there was some Conservative objection to Wiley's reappointment because of rumors of gross negligence in the administration of swamp lands owned by the Literary Fund, although this was never proved. Actually, members of the legislative finance committee probably wished to convert the Literary Fund to purposes other than education, for in 1863 the state had borrowed $128,000 from the fund. The bankrupt condition of the state in 1866 may have presented to some a ready use for the remainder of the fund. See Jonathan Worth to Calvin H. Wiley, 31 March 1866, Hamilton, ed., *Correspondence of Jonathan Worth*, 1:522–23; see also Knight, *Public Education*, 223–24.

49. North Carolina, *Public Laws of North Carolina* (1866–67), chaps. 14 and 15. In addition, the two acts provided for the creation of local boards of education with the authority of financing local schools from funds from the town treasuries, plus a poll tax of two dollars. Primary schools were to be established first, with higher grades not to be started unless additional funds were available.

50. *Standard*, 12 June 1869.

51. Samuel Standford Ashley (1819–87) was a native of Rhode Island and attended public schools in Ashford, Conn., and Providence, R.I. He attended Oberlin College, Ohio, but ill health forced him to withdraw halfway through his junior year. He returned to Providence to organize temperance societies, edit a newspaper, the *Samaritan*, and serve as principal of the Meeting Street School, 1843–46. He reenrolled in Oberlin in its theological department and graduated in 1849. He then became a congregational minister, holding pastorates in Wakeman, Ohio, and Fall River and Northborough, Mass.

In 1864 he entered into evangelical service with the United States Christian Commission at City Point and Fortress Monroe, Virginia. Toward the end of the war, Ashley became greatly interested in the welfare of the freedmen, and in May 1865 he was appointed by the American Missionary Association (AMA) as a missionary to evangelize and educate the freedmen in and around Wilmington, while simultaneously serving as assistant superintendent of education for the Wilmington District for the Freedmen's Bureau. In this capacity he helped establish ten freedmen's schools in Wilmington, Fayetteville, Bladenboro, Goldsboro, and Brunswick County and to establish the Brewer Orphan Asylum near Wilmington. He next joined the state Republican party, helped in the establishment of the *Wilmington Post*, and was elected to the 1868 constitutional convention. He chaired the committee on education and helped draft the article that for the first time provided for the public education of blacks.

During Holden's administration he served as superintendent of public instruction, and under his leadership the public school system, which had ceased during the war, was revived. In 1870 the Conservatives gained legislative control and began to cut his program, whereupon he resigned, believing the cuts were aimed at him personally, rather than see the whole system destroyed. Ashley next served as professor and acting president of Straight University, New Orleans, under the auspices of the AMA. Ill health forced his temporary retirement, but in 1874 he headed a Congregational mission in Atlanta, Ga., where he served as pastor of the First Congregational Church, and in Marietta, as well as promoting the establishment of Atlanta University. In 1878 he returned to Northborough, where he farmed and served as the local postmaster until his death (Powell, ed., *Dictionary* 1:58–59).

52. Article 9, North Carolina, *Constitution of 1868.*

53. Article 5, Section 2, ibid.

54. Typical of the Conservative efforts is the following resolution introduced by Plato Durham: "The General Assembly shall provide separate and distinct schools for the black children of the state, from those provided for white children." It failed adoption, but it brought forth this reply from Ashley: "It being understood that this section is not offered in sincerity, or because there is any necessity for it, and that it is proposed for the sole purpose of breeding prejudice and bringing about a political re-enslavement of the colored race" (North Carolina, *Journal of the Constitutional Convention of 1868*, 338, 342).

55. In their efforts to defeat ratification of the 1868 constitution, the Conservatives stressed two main points: first, that the taxes for such a program would be prohibitively high on white property holders, while the colored parents, without property, would pay little or no taxes; and second, that under the compulsory attendance clause the poor man, unable to educate his children by "other means," would be compelled to send them to integrated schools. Holden and the Republican newspapers branded such arguments, especially the charge that white children would be forced to attend mixed schools, as "Rebel Lie No. 2" (*Standard*, 28 March 1868). It should be noted that when the General Assembly met in its regular session in November 1868, separate schools were authorized, thus definitely refuting the Conservative charges that the Republicans were intent on school integration.

56. North Carolina, *Executive and Legislative Documents* (1868–69), no. 2.

57. Ibid., no. 1.

58. North Carolina, *Public Laws of North Carolina* (1868–69), chap. 184. The state supreme court, in *Lane v. Stanly*, later invalidated the section that authorized local school committeemen to levy taxes to finance their schools if the town trustees failed to do so, on the ground that a school tax for the support of a four-month term was not a necessary expense and could not, therefore, be imposed except by the consent of the people. Nevertheless, Whitener, in his monograph "Public Education in North Carolina during Reconstruction, 1865–1876," 79–82, says that the 1869 school law contemplated a "general and uniform system of state schools . . .

and make[s] it the foundation statute upon which the school system during three quarters of a century have been built." This study does much to revise the previous interpretations of North Carolina education by professors Hamilton and Knight.

59. The Board of Education attempted to raise money by selling stock owned by the Literary Fund in the Wilmington and Manchester Railroad for $10,000 (original investment being $200,000) and the Wilmington and Weldon Road for $148,000 (original investment of $400,000) and the Cape Fear Navigation stock for $3,250 (original investment of $32,500)—in all, receiving $172,648.25. From this amount, however, the schools received only $5,490.07, since $3,000 was lent to the university and $158,000 to the state on a short-term basis. In 1869 the state repaid the $158,000, but the board invested $150,000 of the total in special tax bonds of the Wilmington, Charlotte, and Rutherford Railroad, buying $450,000 worth at the rate of 33⅓ cents on the dollar. It was expected the bonds would return $27,000 in interest per year, which would have relieved the people from taxation; however, as noted elsewhere, the bonds depreciated completely in value and were later defaulted by the state.

60. North Carolina, *Public Laws of North Carolina* (1869–70), chap. 229. At the end of that school year, Supt. Ashley reported that 1,415 schools were in operation with approximately 49,000 students. He also estimated that 270 of the state's 800 townships had functioning schools, and these were spread over 74 of the 90 counties in the state. The total number of schoolhouses was 709; the number of teachers, 1,400; the average teacher monthly pay was $20.21. North Carolina, *Executive and Legislative Documents* (1870–71), no. 6; see also *American Annual Cyclopedia* (1870), 553–54. By comparison, the American Missionary Association conducted 136 black schools (158 teachers and 10,971 pupils) in the state in May 1866 and 156 schools (173 teachers and 13,039 pupils) in March 1867. See Alexander, "Hostility and Hope: Black Education in North Carolina," 125.

61. Knight, *Public Education*, 243.

62. General Sherman is reported having remarked that his cavalry mounts were the best-educated horses in the entire Union army, as they were stabled in the university library (Henderson, *First State University*, 84; see also Chamberlain, *Old Days in Chapel Hill*, 86–89).

63. Chamberlain, *Old Days in Chapel Hill*, 99.

64. Mrs. Spencer, in her self-assured manner, stated it bluntly: "Ellie Swain's marriage had helped this along, no doubt" (Russell, *Woman Who Rang the Bell*, 76–77).

65. Ibid., 86–87. Bishop Green mentioned that several parties favored the selection of Joseph Eggleston Johnston, former Confederate general, as the new president.

66. Battle, *History of the University of North Carolina*, 2:9.

67. Russell, *Woman Who Rang the Bell*, 102–3, 108.

68. Ironically, Swain's fall was from a horse given him in 1865 by General Sherman. The board of trustees selected an executive committee composed of Judge William B. Rodman, James F. Taylor, Thomas Settle, plus the following state officials: Governor Holden, Tod R. Caldwell, Henry J. Menninger, David A. Jenkins,

Henderson Adams, Samuel S. Ashley, Ceburn L. Harris, and William M. Coleman. See Battle, *History of the University of North Carolina*, 2:4–5.

69. Solomon Pool to Holden, 15 August 1868, Governor's Papers, State Archives.
70. *Standard*, 16 December 1868.
71. *Raleigh Sentinel*, 23 November 1868. The paper further claimed that Judge Rodman, Superintendent Ashley, and James Taylor had actually introduced a proposal calling for the admission of blacks to the university.
72. Henderson, *First State University*, 194.
73. Pool's selection was undoubtedly due to his brother's (Senator John Pool) influence. He was a native of Elizabeth City and graduated from the university in 1853 as a second-honor graduate. He remained in Chapel Hill, serving first as a tutor, 1853–60, and then as professor of mathematics, 1860–66. He had the reputation of being an able and competent instructor and outstanding speaker, but lacking a commanding personality. He was elected professor of mathematics at Trinity College, January 1866, but chose to accept a position with the Internal Revenue Service instead. Always a strong Unionist, he became a prominent and active member of the state's Republican party and a personal adviser to Holden. He served as president of the university from 1868 to 1875, although the institution was not in actual operation for the entire period. He resigned the presidency in 1875 and taught school in Cary; later he filled pastorates in Methodist churches in Raleigh, Winston, and Greensboro.
74. Brewer, professor of Greek, was a Yale graduate, a man of scholarly attainments, and strongly recommended by President Theodore D. Woolsey of Yale. A brother, David Joseph Brewer, had a distinguished career on the United States Supreme Court. Brewer's professional ability was never questioned, but his belief in racial equality caused him to be ostracized while living in Chapel Hill. Before his appointment he taught in a school for black children in Raleigh and had entertained Negroes in his home. In Chapel Hill he boarded with a black family, and his sister taught in a black school. Needless to say, Professor Brewer was the "stormy petrel" of the new faculty. McIver was also a university graduate of the class of 1853; he was professor of mathematics at Davidson College until forced out because of Union sympathies and his insistence on voting for Grant in the 1868 national election. He became professor of mathematics at the university and exchanged residences with Dr. Charles Phillips, who succeeded him at Davidson. Probably this accounts for the fact that he was better received by the Chapel Hill citizens. David Patrick, professor of Latin, was a university graduate of 1856; he served as principal of an Arkansas school until his uncle Judge Thomas Settle interceded on his behalf and secured his election to the university. James A. Martling, professor of belles lettres, was a native of Missouri and the brother-in-law of Superintendent of Public Instruction Samuel S. Ashley. George Dixon, professor of agriculture, was a native of England and English trained, but since he had not stayed long at the university, very little is known about his background or his work at the university.
75. Chamberlain, *Old Days in Chapel Hill*, 161–62.

76. Holden to General Assembly, 20 November 1870, Governor's Papers, State Archives.
77. Included were such Republican notables as supreme court justices Robert P. Dick, Thomas Settle, and William B. Rodman; superior court justices Charles R. Thomas and Samuel W. Watts; Congressmen John T. Deweese and Nathaniel Boyden; Superintendent Samuel S. Ashley; Willie D. Jones; and other lesser-known political figures. For a complete account of the commencement exercises, see *Standard*, 12 June 1869.
78. Holden's address was reprinted in the *Standard*, 12 June 1869. For the Conservative reaction, see Russell, *Woman Who Rang the Bell*, 132. To them the samll turnout represented a grand victory, as Mrs. Spencer reported: "There never was such a grand (and to our side, delightful) fizzle as Commencement has been. . . . Nobody came" (Cornelia Phillips Spencer to Mrs. Laura [Charles] Phillips, 14 June 1869, quoted by Chamberlain, *Old Days in Chapel Hill*, 164).
79. Holden to Solomon Pool, 31 August 1869, and Pool to Holden, 31 August 1869, Governor's Papers, State Archives.
80. Holden to General Assembly, 21 January 1870, Governor's Papers, State Archives.
81. See the *Standard*, 14 June 1870, for an account of the 1870 commencement exercises.

CHAPTER SEVEN

1. Hamilton, *Reconstruction in North Carolina*, 71.
2. North Carolina, *Executive and Legislative Documents* (1871–72), no. 1.
3. North Carolina, *Constitution of 1868*, chaps. 3, 17, 19, 20, 30, and 48. The convention also adopted two measures affecting state debts that concerned railroad legislation and which caused much legal debate in later years: first, the legislature was forbidden to contract any new debt until the state bonds should reach par value unless it included, within the same bill, the levying of a special tax to pay the interest on the new debt; and, second, the legislature was forbidden to give or lend the credit of the state to any person, association, or corporation, except for the completion of railroads unfinished at the time of the adoption of the 1868 constitution or those roads in which the state had a direct financial interest, unless the matter was submitted to a vote of the people and received favorable ratification.
4. North Carolina, *Executive and Legislative Documents* (1868), no. 2.
5. Testimony of Swepson, North Carolina, *Report of the Commission to Investigate the Charges of Fraud and Corruption* (hereafter cited as *Shipp Fraud Commission Report*), 201–4; testimony of W. J. Hawkins, ibid., 538. The Salem Railroad Company and the Edenton and Suffolk Company were the only roads receiving aid from the state that did not pay tribute to the Ring.

6. Soutter and Company of New York City paid $5,000 to L. G. Estes, John T. Deweese, and Joseph C. Abbott to procure passage of an ordinance authorizing the state to endorse $1,000,000 of the Wilmington, Charlotte, and Rutherford Railroad Company bonds, ostensibly to protect the state's interest in a $2,000,000 second mortgage which it held on the road. At the close of the convention, the following members were paid money by Swepson on Littlefield's order: James H. Harris, John Hyman, Henry Eppes, J. C. Abbott, Bryon Laflin, and Albion W. Tourgée. Although the last considered it a "loan," he never repaid it. John A. McDonald later testified that Littlefield lent him $500, for which payment was never requested, and Swepson an additional $200. See North Carolina, *Report of the Railroad Investigation Commission* (hereafter cited as the *Bragg Fraud Commission Report*), 17, 78–80; *Shipp Fraud Commission Report*, 316–20, 540; Olsen, *Carpetbagger's Crusade*, 143–44.

7. Hamilton, *Reconstruction in North Carolina*, 389. Turner was particularly caustic when writing of administration leaders, dubbing them the "Governor's hands." He labeled them as "Pilgrim [S.S.] Ashley," "Windy Billy [W. F.] Henderson," "Kildee [Robert W.] Lassiter," "Chicken [John W.] Stephens," "Greasy Sam [S. W.] Watts," "Blow your Horn [Billy] Smith," "Ipecas [Henry J.] Menninger," "Parson [James] Sinclair," and "Captain [Thomas] Settle." Typical Turner remarks were: "Looking for a dog, . . . I found the Governor." "We have been frequently asked if the Governor was drunk. . . . Now we say he was not drunk, but only filled with meaness, malice, and poison." See *Raleigh Sentinel*, 13 January, 26 March 1869.

8. After repeated attacks from Turner's pen, Republican leaders decided to silence him. Thus, upon his return to Raleigh from a speaking engagement in Smithfield he was met at the railroad station by Joseph W. Holden, William Sloan, D. J. Pruyn, Henry J. Menninger, and Ceburn L. Harris, among others, and they threatened his life. Turner drew a "six-shooter" and warned his attackers that if they advanced closer, he would fire. About that time, two policemen arrived at the scene and ordered Turner to hand over his gun to them. He refused to obey the order until Mayor Robert Harrison, Holden's brother-in-law, compelled the surrender. Turner was marched to the mayor's office and was met there by Governor Holden. Turner was later released, and nothing serious developed out of the incident. Another attempt was made against Turner on 6 April when several shots were fired through the *Sentinel*'s windows. Holden ordered his adjutant general, A. W. Fisher, to assign two detectives to the case and offered to post a $500 reward for the criminal if Turner would state on his honor that he believed an attempt had been made to assassinate him. Turner declined. For an account of the latter episode, see Turner to A. W. Fisher, 7 April 1869, *Raleigh Sentinel*, 8 April 1869.

9. The *Raleigh Daily News*, 9 December 1873, also charged that Turner had been instrumental in defeating former governor Vance in his candidacy for the Senate in 1872 and that Turner had written a threatening letter, the "J. S. Anderson" letter, to Representative John W. Norwood of Orange County that unless Norwood changed

his vote to make Turner state printer, no support would be given to the William Allen proposal of giving amnesty and pardons for all offenses committed by members of the Union League and Ku Klux Klan prior to 1 September 1871.

10. William Yates, editor of the Conservative *Charlotte Western Democrat*, wrote in 1870: "How ridiculous and inconsistent it is for newspapers to abuse and denounce one man [General Littlefield] who has been swindling the State in the matter of Railroad appropriations, and then praise and eulogize another [Swepson] who has cooperated with him in the schemes." Yates then explained the inconsistency by the fact that Swepson had advanced Turner the money to purchase the *Sentinel* and that Swepson continued to hold a mortgage on the paper. Turner denied this, but in 1873 he admitted he had told half-truths in his 1870 statements, and that $5,000 had been borrowed from Swepson, who made the loan as president of the Raleigh National Bank. See *Charlotte Western Democrat*, 8 March 1870; *Raleigh Sentinel*, 26 March, 6 April 1870, and 5 December 1873.

11. North Carolina, *Private Laws of North Carolina* (1868), chaps. 14, 15, and 24; North Carolina, *Public Laws of North Carolina* (1868–69), chaps. 17 and 28. When the Western North Carolina Railroad Company was divided into the Western and Eastern divisions, on 19 August 1868, state bonds were not selling at par value on the New York Stock Exchange, and as the act did not provide for a special tax to pay the annual interest on the bonds, the bonds were actually unconstitutional. This was rectified, however, on 12 November, when the regular session of the General Assembly levied a special tax of one-thirtieth of 1 percent on the taxable property of the state.

12. Samuel McD. Tate, to George W. Swepson, 21 September 1868, Swepson Papers, State Archives. Earlier, on 2 August, Tate wrote Swepson: "Everything works well and Littlefield says all will go as arranged before you left. The Funding Bill will pass" (ibid.).

13. *Shipp Fraud Commission Report*, 14–16.

14. In July and August 1868, some of the legislators found themselves without funds and unable to pay their room and board bills while in attendance in the General Assembly. Treasurer Jenkins advanced $100 to each member, since the assembly was slow in fixing the per diem and mileage rates. Later, some members drew drafts on the Treasury for additional payments, and these were discounted by D. J. Pruyn and the Raleigh National Bank, controlled by Swepson, at 5 percent. After the legislature fixed the rates, Jenkins paid the members the remaining sums due them and, at the same time, paid Pruyn $1,419.25 for the drafts he had discounted.

15. North Carolina, *Executive and Legislative Documents* (1868–69), no. 21. The Robbins charges reacted against the Conservatives, however, for it was disclosed that Senator Robbins had himself accepted a $20 "fee" from John W. Stephens to obtain per diem and mileage while contesting the senatorial seat of Bedford Brown in 1868. For further details, see *Standard*, 25 January 1869.

16. See "Report of the Joint Select Committee to Investigate the Operations of the

Public Treasurer," North Carolina, *Executive and Legislative Documents* (1868–69), no. 28, and "Reply of D. A. Jenkins to the Sweet Charges of Fraud," *Standard*, 25 February 1869.

17. *Standard*, 3 February 1869. For a thorough account of this and other affairs involving General Littlefield see Daniels, *Prince of Carpetbaggers*.

18. North Carolina, *Public Laws of North Carolina* (1868–69), chaps. 22, 29, 30, and 92.

19. Governor Holden appointed native North Carolinians rather than carpetbaggers: William Sloan, Wilmington, Charlotte, and Rutherford Road, although Senator Joseph C. Abbott had strongly urged John R. French, a native of New Hampshire, for the post; William A. Smith, North Carolina Road; George W. Swepson, Western Division of the Western North Carolina Road; John J. Mott, but later replaced by Samuel McD. Tate, Eastern Division; Edward R. Stanly, Atlantic and North Carolina Road; Robert R. Bridgers, Wilmington and Weldon Road; Edward Belo, Northwestern Road; and William Johnston, Atlantic, Tennessee, and Ohio Railroad.

20. Serving with Swepson as directors were highly respectable men, such as A. T. Davidson, Augustus S. Merrimon, Thomas L. Clingman, Joseph C. Abbott, Alexander H. Jones, W. W. Rollins, George W. Gahagan, J. R. Ammons, Robert M. Henry, and George W. Dickey.

21. Thomas Lanier Clingman, a native of Surry (now Yadkin) County spent his adult life in Buncombe County. He served in the state senate, 1841–43, House of Representatives, 1843–45, 1847–58, and Senate, 1858–61. He served as colonel, Twenty-fifth North Carolina Regt., 1861–62, and then was made brigadier general, serving in Eastern North Carolina and Virginia until the end of the war. After the war he was prohibited from returning to politics by the amnesty provisions, and so resumed his careers as a lawyer and a propagandist for Western North Carolina. Powell, *Dictionary*, 1:387–88.

22. The Ring was able to fool both the railroad directors and general public by the following typical resolution passed by the Western North Carolina Railroad: "Resolved, That the Board of Directors of the Western Division be and they are hereby requested and urged to place under contract at the earliest day possible, and push rapidly to completion, the branch road down the French Broad River to Paint Rock, and that the officers of the Company use their influence to attain this object without delay." The directors included former governor Vance, Hugh Reynolds, Dr. J. C. McDowell, Augustus S. Merrimon, Francis Shober, G. F. Davidson, Dr. A. M. Powell, Robert L. Patterson, A. M. Erwin, A. C. Cowles, and Montgomery Patton. Major stockholders included Tod R. Caldwell, Burton Craige, and Nathaniel Boyden (*Annual Proceedings of the Western North Carolina Railroad*).

23. One should note the similarity of financial arrangements used by the Credit Mobilier Company in its construction of the Union Pacific Railroad.

24. North Carolina, *Executive and Legislative Documents* (1869–70), no. 30.

25. Henry E. Colton to George W. Swepson, 16 November 1868, Swepson Papers, State Archives. Colton later asked Holden to use his influence and secure his appointment to the presidency of the Western North Carolina Railroad. See Colton to Holden, 3 February 1870, Governor's Papers, State Archives.

26. Coleman concluded: "If then there is no such corporation as the University Railroad Company there is manifestly no president of said company entitled to even claim the bonds" (Coleman to Holden, 1 April 1869, Governor's Papers, State Archives). Originally, Holden had appointed Henry C. Thompson, T. M. Argo, Solomon Pool, E. A. Woods, and his son Joseph W. Holden as directors on the University Road.

27. While unanimous in their conclusion that the University Railroad was unconstitutional, court members differed on whether the principles of the case extended to all legislation passed by the General Assembly in the issuance of special tax bonds. See *University Railroad Company* v. *Holden*, 63 N.C., 410.

28. Battle received $250 from Porter just for sending the telegraph alerting him on Judge Pearson's decision.

29. The Western North Carolina Railroad Company's Western and Eastern Divisions were supposed to share in the expenses, but the latter refused. Furthermore, nearly $6,250 was unaccounted for, according to the claims of Swepson. It probably went to T. H. Porter, the Soutter and Company representative. *Shipp Fraud Commission Report*, 463.

30. Three examples of intentional fraud in construction work involved the Western North Carolina Road, the Western Division of the Western North Carolina Road, and the Wilmington, Charlotte, and Rutherford Road. In the Western Division fraud, a general contract was let to General Littlefield, a director of the road and not in the contracting business, who relet the job to H. M. Drane and W. H. McDowell, bona fide contractors, without a competitive bid, and some $400,000 of work was actually performed. However, Swepson ordered the contract drawn so that one-third of the whole amount of the construction costs could be paid in company stock. In the Western Railroad action, the John A. Hunt Company was given the construction contract despite the fact that its bid was $170,000 higher than other submitted bids, and it was later disclosed that Swepson and President A. H. Jones were financially benefited by the contract. With the Wilmington, Charlotte, and Rutherford road, V. A. McBee, treasurer, and M. S. Sumner and B. S. Guion, directors, received "kick-backs" from the construction contracts. William Sloan, president, probably was not involved in such transactions, for when he learned of the frauds, he refused to pay off the contractors. For the testimony in the Western Division case, see the *Bragg Fraud Commission Report*, 12–14, 78–80, 155–95; for the Western North Carolina Road, see *Shipp Fraud Commission Report*, 196–340; for the Wilmington, Charlotte, and Rutherford Road, see ibid., 367–440.

31. *Raleigh Sentinel*, 9 July 1869.

32. In 1876 Holden wrote a lengthy statement, which he evidently intended to have published, in regard to Bryon Laflin, but for some unexplained reason he never did so. W. K. Boyd, however, copied the statement, and it is to be found among the Holden Papers, DU. The author considers it the best defense of Holden's railroad transactions, and it should go a long way in exonerating him from the false charges of profiting from any of the frauds. It reads as follows:

The [*Raleigh*] *News* of the 19th copies from the Jan. 19, 1876 *Philadelphia Times* an article in which it is charged that I "joined a gang of thieves" when Governor. The *Times* is, I believe, [Samuel S.] McClure's paper. This is doubtless the McClure who came to Raleigh in 1869 to lease the Central Road. Bryon Laflin had been State proxy in 1868, but I removed him in 1869, and appointed R. C. Badger. Laflin traveled here in company with McClure. When I told Laflin I had removed him, he complained bitterly, and told me there were five hundred thousand dollars in the City *extra* for the lease, to be paid to three persons, if the lease should be made to McClure for $2,000,000. I went right to my office and wrote peremptory instructions to Mr. Badger to *vote against the lease*. I did not join McClure, and hence he dislikes me.

The last batch of bonds to Mr. Swepson was issued in accordance with the last amended charter, by the Treasurer, Mr. Jenkins. I simply signed them, and had the Great Seal attached, and Mr. Jenkins delivered them. Mr. Jenkins will state to any one, as he has to me repeatedly, that he hesitated some two or three weeks to issue them by an argument made to him by Judge Merrimon, Counsel to Mr. Swepson.

Mr. Swepson swore, before the Fraud Commission, that there was no corrupt complicity between him and myself in any of these matters; and when Judge Merrimon prepared the 9th Article against me in regard to corruption in issuing bonds, he informed the Judge that he would go before the Court of Impeachment and swear the charge was false; whereupon the 9th Article was dropped.

Maj. W. W. Rollins informed me that he paid the State Counsel $2,000 and took their receipts to Mr. Swepson's friends, and that the State's Counsel settled with Mr. Swepson at *six cents on the dollar*. All these Counsels were Democrats, and distinguished men. I have never used this, and do not wish to. But it seems they took fees from both sides, and let Mr. S[wepson] off very lightly.

I did not appoint Littlefield. I positively refused him any place on the Western Road. But I appointed Geo. W. Gahagan, an honest man, State proxy, and he overreached, and General Littlefield was elected President of the Road. I would have removed him, if I had had the power. Mr. Jenkins repeatedly warned Mr. Swepson against Littlefield, and I apprehend Mr. S[wepson] owes nearly all his troubles to Littlefield.

I never had any "margins". I did not speculate in State bonds. A Supreme

Court Judge [William B. Rodman] had a "margin", and admitted it before the Fraud Commission; yet I am assailed, and he is spared. I do not say that he ought to be assailed, for he thought at the time he was raising the State credit, and that the act was not dishonest.

I might say a great deal more. It is hard for me to be held up as a friend to thieves, while the Treasurer is complimented in your columns. If you doubt me, consult him. He will tell you that I was as careful and as honest as he was. But I had no veto power, and we were all overwhelmed at the time by the demand for bonds. What could one man, without the veto, do against the great pressure? Remember, the *News* is a respectable paper, and what it says affects the present and goes to posterity.

W. W. Holden

I performed no official act during my administration for any consideration, fee or reward. I did all according to law, as far as I knew how, and was not influenced by bribes of any kind. I was so careful about these things, that I would not purchase any stock in the N.C. Railroad, though I could have made money by it, because I appointed Directors on that Road.

Oct. 7, 1876 W. W. Holden

33. North Carolina, *Public Laws of North Carolina* (1868–69), chap. 31.
34. Haywood attempted to employ Augustus S. Merrimon and Matt W. Ransom to collect a lobbyist commission for Deweese.
35. *Galloway v. Jenkins*, 64 N.C., 147; see also Hamilton, *Reconstruction in North Carolina*, 436. In this case, A. J. Galloway of Wayne County applied to Judge Watts for an injunction to restrain the treasurer from issuing the Chatham Railroad bonds on the ground that the act authorizing them was invalid. The injunction was granted, but the case was later appealed to the supreme court, which ruled the Chatham Road legislation unconstitutional because it had not been submitted to a vote of approval in a general election, hence the bonds were void.
36. *Shipp Fraud Commission Report*, 158; see also Hamilton, *Reconstruction in North Carolina*, 446.
37. Of the seventy-seven bonds, eight each were delivered to Fowle and Badger, five to Judge Watts, four to Kehoe, ten to W. F. Askew, who had been approached by McAden to learn the identity of the originator and purpose of the injunction and who later was asked by Haywood to write McAden and suggest a settlement of the case, and the remaining forty-six were divided between Haywood and Deweese. Littlefield received forty-six, ten of which he gave to Sheriff Tim H. Lee of Wake County for expediting the matter. Few of the recipients were able to convert their bonds into cash. Fowle and Badger sent their bonds to New York for resale but, upon hearing the true intentions of Deweese and Haywood, recalled the bonds and later turned them over to the company. Kehoe hypothecated his bonds to the National Bank of New Bern for $1,000 but later redeemed them and sold them for $800 cash. Judge Watts lost his entire holding when he sent them to the New York

banking house of Fuller, Treat, and Cox and the bank went into bankruptcy before paying off. Sheriff Lee sent his bonds also to Fuller and received $1,500 before the outfit failed. W. F. Askew turned his share over to the State National Bank, but it failed to dispose of them, and later his bonds were bought by McAden for ten cents on the dollar. Haywood, Deweese, and Littlefield were able to sell their shares for approximately thirty-five to forty cents on the dollar. *Shipp Fraud Commission Report*, 158, 178, 464, and 466; see also Hamilton, *Reconstruction in North Carolina*, 446.

38. For a detailed account of the railroad frauds and the Democratic involvement see the *Bragg Fraud Commission Report*, 196–340, the *Shipp Fraud Commission Report*, 205–466, and North Carolina, *Executive and Legislative Documents* (1870–71), no. 33.

39. Those participating included Swepson; Littlefield; Andrew J. Jones of the Western North Carolina Railroad; William Sloan of the Wilmington, Charlotte, and Rutherford Railroad; T. P. Branch, a Richmond, Virginia, broker; Samuel McD. Tate; Thomas W. Dewey, a Charlotte banker; and Robert Y. McAden.

40. William R. Utley to George W. Swepson, 10 September 1869, Swepson Papers, State Archives. Utley was a New York broker connected with Utley and Dougherty; he was involved by Swepson in the pool arrangement. By April 1870 state bonds sold as low as $21 per $100. For a complete listing of state bond pricing, 1869–70, see Hamilton, *Reconstruction in North Carolina*, 449.

41. *University Railroad Company* v. *Holden*, 63 N.C., 410. This decision, when broadly interpreted, applied to all special tax bonds not submitted to a vote of approval in a general election. All would have to be considered unconstitutional.

42. Clingman to Henry Clews, 6 October 1869, printed in the *Standard*, 13 October 1869.

43. See letter of confirmation, Henry Clews to Holden, 2 November 1869, Governor's Papers, State Archives. Treasurer Jenkins was in New York at the time the pool arrangements were consummated and no doubt participated in the decisions. See Holden's telegram to Swepson, 4 November 1869: "Mr. Jenkins had discretion in the matter & if he agreed to anything certain before he got specific instructions he is bound by the agreement." Holden's Letter Book, State Archives.

44. The land-script monies came from the state's sale of public lands received from the Morrill Land Grant Act. See Samuel A. Ashe, "Reply of North Carolinians to the Committee of Bondholders," September 1910, Ashe Papers, State Archives.

45. This was the attempt, which came to a climax 20–24 September 1869, of Jay Gould and "Diamond Jim" Fisk to corner the gold market. Beginning in June, when assured the Grant administration would not intervene, Gould began buying up the precious metal, forcing its price up to 140. By 24 September the price had risen to 163, and Gould began selling, causing Wall Street to panic and sending the price down to 135. Fisk repudiated his purchases and informed his partner that "nothing is lost save honor." The episode is generally referred to as "Black Friday."

46. Hamilton, *Reconstruction in North Carolina*, 444.
47. Holden to George W. Swepson, 1 November 1869, Swepson Papers, State Archives. Swepson had decided to resign his directorship on the Western Division Road because of the speculation, but Holden was hesitant to accept it. In his letter, Holden asked Swepson to reconsider his resignation, but, at the same time, inquired whether Kemp P. Battle would be a good replacement should he follow through with the resignation.
48. The Lassiter proposal was supposedly written by Victor C. Barringer, with prior approval by the Ring, and handed to Lassiter by the three "visitors" during the conference in the Capitol lobby. Under the proposal the commission was to have had a paid clerk with a salary of $6,500 and was to report to the assembly in 1870. In introducing his measure, Lassiter explained that the other three proposals were not sufficiently comprehensive, while his proposed commission could conduct a thorough investigation that would be satisfactory to all concerned.
49. For Holden's version of how Littlefield was elected president of the Western Division Railroad, see note 32.
50. *Standard*, 10 March 1870. For earlier house action see the *Raleigh Sentinel*, 6, 19 January 1870; also see Ashe, "Reply to Bondholders."
51. North Carolina, *Public Laws of North Carolina* (1869–70), chap. 58.
52. Holden officially notified the railroad presidents of the act, and to demand compliance, wrote to the sheriffs of the counties in which the railroad home offices were located requiring them to serve notice and return a duplicate copy with the day on which it had been served. See Governor's Letter Book, 10 February 1870, State Archives.
53. Holden to Swepson and Littlefield, 9 February 1870, Governor's Papers, State Archives. This action indicates Holden's unwillingness to participate in a "cover-up" and his own law-abiding tendencies. Later, the assembly passed a resolution forbidding the sale of state bonds thereafter, with the introduction of the measure being declared sufficient notice to the general public. Also, a subsequent act, passed on 8 March 1870, repealed all appropriations in aid of the state's railroads in 1868 and 1869. North Carolina, *Public Laws of North Carolina* (1869–70), chap. 71.
54. Robert W. Pulliam was president of the Raleigh National Bank controlled by Swepson, while Goodson M. Roberts was secretary-treasurer of the Raleigh National Bank and treasurer of the Western Division Road.
55. Timothy F. Lee, a native of Ireland, was a carpetbagger and a close associate of Littlefield and the Ring. Holden never trusted him, and as a result Lee sided with James H. Harris, a leading black Republican in Raleigh, and helped to cause a breach in Republican party unity in the 1880s and the ousting of Holden as party leader in the state.
56. *Raleigh Sentinel*, 6 April 1870.
57. *Standard*, 10 March 1870.

58. Ashe, "Reply to Bondholders."
59. The general conclusion was that Littlefield had been too smart to be caught by the Bragg Commission. See John McLean Harrington to his son Sion Harrington, 7 March 1870, Harrington Papers, DU.
60. William L. Scott to H. M. Miller, 24 March 1870, Scott Papers, DU. It should be noted, however, that the General Assembly continued to promote railroad construction and the improvement of the transportation system in the state. It realized that the public wanted, and needed, improved transportation despite the evil practices of some manipulators. Consequently, the assembly adopted legislation providing for sixteen railroad projects and incorporating fourteen turnpikes, canals, and other means of transportation. North Carolina, *Public Laws of North Carolina* (1869–70), chaps. 22, 45, 67, 68, 69, 83, 86, 92, 126, 145, 152 and 221.
61. *Raleigh Sentinel*, 10 March 1870.
62. Ibid., 11 March 1870; see also *Shipp Fraud Commission Report*, 269–72.
63. The Woodfin Commission, so called because its chairman was Nicholas W. Woodfin, Henderson County lawyer, consisted of the following members: Judge J. L. Henry, W. W. Rollins, W. G. Candler, and W. P. Welch.
64. Before fleeing the state, Littlefield sold his financial interest in the *Standard* to W. A. Smith and Co., and Joseph W. Holden resigned his speakership of the house of representatives and assumed its editorship.
65. North Carolina, *Executive and Legislative Documents* (1872–73), no. 6. See also Thomas L. Clingman's testimony before the Shipp Commission, *Shipp Fraud Commission Report*, 196–340. For accounts of Swepson and Littlefield's activities, see Daniels, *Prince of Carpetbaggers*; Brown, "Florida Investments of George W. Swepson," 275–78, and Davis, *Civil War and Reconstruction in Florida*, 655–63.
66. North Carolina, *Executive and Legislative Documents* (1872–73), no. 6.
67. Augustus S. Merrimon and Matt Ransom.
68. Littlefield lived in Morristown, New Jersey, but maintained an office in New York City, where he continued to operate as a "promoter of business enterprises." In later years he supposedly agreed to return and stand trial if North Carolina would guarantee that all others involved in the railroad manipulations would be brought to trial at the same time. Of course, the Democratic leadership would not consent to involve their own membership; consequently, nothing was ever done to bring him "to justice."
69. Marmaduke Swaim Robbins, former member of the house of commons and state senate from Randolph County, and Superior Court Judge George Howard, Jr., of Edgecombe County were originally appointed to the commission, but each declined to serve.
70. For Holden's denial of ever benefiting financially from any of the railroad frauds, see his statement in note 32.
71. As late as 1901 Schafer Brothers, a New York City brokerage firm that owned a

large number of state bonds, gave ten of them to the state of South Dakota, which then brought suit in the United States Supreme Court for recovery (*South Dakota* v. *North Carolina*, 192 U.S., 286). The Supreme Court also upheld the validity of the 1880 constitutional provision of repudiation (*Baltzer* v. *North Carolina*, 161 U.S., 240). For further information, see Hamilton, *Reconstruction in North Carolina*, 659–62; Ratchford, "North Carolina Public Debt, 1870–1883," 1–20, 157–67; and Newsome, "Report of an Investigation on the Passage of the Reconstruction Bond Ordinances."

72. North Carolina, *Executive and Legislative Documents* (1870–71), no. 1.

CHAPTER EIGHT

1. Holden to S. A. Ashe, 6 December 1881, Holden Papers, DU.
2. Nathaniel Boyden (1796–1873) was one of five outstanding barristers employed by Holden in his impeachment trial. Born in Conway, Mass., Boyden attended Williams College and Union College of Schenectady, N.Y., graduating in 1821. He studied law under his uncle Moses Hayden, a New York congressman, but moved to Guilford County in 1822. Later, he moved to Salisbury, where he gained success as a lawyer. He served in the house of commons, 1838–41; state senate, 1844–45, 1862–64; United States House of Representatives, 1847–49, 1868–69; and as associate justice of the North Carolina Supreme Court, 1871–73. Family tradition suggests that President Lincoln had decided to name Boyden provisional governor of the state shortly before his assassination. For additional information, see Powell, *Dictionary*, 1:204–5.
3. North Carolina, *Impeachment Trial*, 1:316.
4. Brevard, *Reminiscences*, 109.
5. For a comprehensive study of the formation and activities of the Klan in North Carolina, see the chapter "The Ku Klux Klan Movement" in Hamilton's *Reconstruction in North Carolina*, 452–81; but for a completely different viewpoint, see Olsen, *Carpetbagger's Crusade*, 156–69. See also Olsen's study, "The Ku Klux Klan," 340–62. The two most reliable studies of the Klan generally are Allen W. Trelease's *White Terror* and Stanley Horn's *Invisible Empire*.
6. Olsen, *Carpetbagger's Crusade*, 156–57.
7. Holden to General Nelson A. Miles, 24 October 1868; Holden to Mayor T. A. Brynes of Fayetteville, 23 October 1868; Holden to Charles R. Thomas, 4 January 1869; Holden to Mrs. H. J. Moore, 4 January 1869, Governor's Papers, State Archives. See also O. H. Bidwell to Holden, 27 February 1869, ibid.
8. The authorship of the address, unknown at the time, later proved attributable to John Pool and Judge Edwin Reade. It was reprinted in Cox, *Three Decades of Federal Legislation*, 462–63. W. F. Henderson issued a similar address to the Heroes of America, and it was reprinted in the *Standard*, 26 August 1868.

9. Holden to James Moore, 14 October 1868, Governor's Papers, State Archives.
10. Appendix to North Carolina, *Executive and Legislative Documents* (1870–71), 1–5.
11. "An Act to prescribe the powers and duty of the Governor in respect to Fugitives from Justice," was enacted on 19 February 1869, and published in the *Standard*, 23 February 1869.
12. Proclamation issued by Holden on 16 April 1869, Governor's Papers, State Archives.
13. For Holden's advice, see the *Standard*, 23 September 1869; for Pool, see his *Speech of John Pool before the United States Senate*, 31 March 1871.
14. A. W. Tourgée to Holden, 3 July 1869, Governor's Papers, State Archives.
15. Andrew Tarpley, a fifteen-year-old black youth, was convicted and sentenced to death for ravishing an eleven-year-old black girl. See petition of E. S. Parker, Graham attorney, to Attorney General L. P. Olds, 17 August 1870, Governor's Papers, State Archives.
16. U.S., *Senate Ku Klux Report*, 42nd Congress, 1st Session, no. 1, p. xiv.
17. H. C. Vogel to General Oliver O. Howard, 14 December 1869, Governor's Papers, State Archives; Eliphalet Whittlesey to Holden, 18 December 1869, ibid.
18. *Rutherford Vindicator*, 1 November 1869.
19. Proclamation issued by Holden on 20 October 1869, Governor's Papers, State Archives.
20. Hamilton, *Reconstruction in North Carolina*, 402, 470. Because he had introduced the anti-Klan legislation, Shoffner's death was voted by the Orange County Ku Klux, who prepared to kill him and ship the body to Governor Holden. Fortunately, Shoffner was alerted in time to make his escape to Greensboro, and then to Indiana. See also *Impeachment Trial*, 1526, 1975–96, and U.S., *Senate Ku Klux Report*, 35.
21. North Carolina, *Public Laws of the State of North Carolina* (1869–70), chap. 27.
22. *Raleigh Sentinel*, 6 January 1870.
23. *Standard*, 22 January 1870.
24. U.S., *Senate Ku Klux Report*, 224.
25. The Norwood conversation was described in a letter from Pride Jones to Holden, 4 March 1870, Holden Papers, DU.
26. The petition requesting Jones's appointment was signed by John W. Norwood, George Laws, James Webb, Henry K. Nash, Henry N. Brown, and A. Hooker, dated 5 March 1870, ibid. See also Holden's letter of appointment to Jones, 7 March 1870, and Holden to Ramsey, 7 May 1870, Governor's Papers, State Archives.
27. Pride Jones to Holden, 19 April 1870; Holden to Jones, 22 April 1870; Ramsay to Holden, 23 May 1870, Governor's Papers, State Archives.
28. Holden to Thomas A. Donaho, 22 April 1870; Donaho to Holden, 16 May 1870, ibid.

29. Holden to President Grant, 10 March 1870, Holden to the North Carolina Congressmen, same date, ibid.
30. Holden to Joseph C. Abbott, 17 March 1870, ibid.
31. Thomas A. Donaho to Holden, 16 May 1870, ibid.
32. Olsen, *Carpetbagger's Crusade*, 162–63.
33. It was later learned that Wiley was definitely a Klan member.
34. Wilkerson, "Caswell County and the Kirk-Holden War." In his account of the Stephens murder, Professor Hamilton inferred that the killing was committed not by the Klan but by disgruntled black Republicans (see *Reconstruction in North Carolina*, 473–75), and in so doing, he followed the line of Josiah Turner's *Sentinel*, 27, 31 June 1870. For a Republican account, see letter of "Caswell" to *Standard*, 23 May 1870, and reprinted on 26 May 1870. See also Holden's Proclamation of 6 June 1870, in which he offered a $500 reward for the arrest of the perpetrators of Stephens's murder and that of Wyatt Outlaw of Alamance County, Robin Jacobs of Caswell County, the drowning of one Puryear in Alamance County, the murder of Neil and Daniel McLeod of Cumberland County, and the forcing of Senator T. M. Shoffner to flee the state in fear of his life (Governor's Papers, State Archives).
35. *Tarboro North Carolinian*, 10 June 1870.
36. *Raleigh Sentinel*, 3 August 1870; see also *Raleigh Daily News*, 6 December 1873.
37. Appendix to Holden's *Memoirs*, 187–99.
38. *Raleigh Sentinel*, 15 July 1870.
39. Holden, *Memoirs*, 81–82.
40. Holden to S. A. Ashe, 6 December 1881, Holden Papers, DU.
41. Crow, "North Carolina Planter Women."
42. *Raleigh Weekly Constitution*, 26 October 1876.
43. For more detailed information on Kirk's career, see U.S., *Official Records*, ser. 1, 39:232–34; Arthur, *Western North Carolina*, 605–8. Also, for an interesting comparison of how Kirk treated Confederate mountain supporters and how Confederate officials maltreated Union mountain men upon their return from the war, see Gutrage Garland, Clerk of the Superior Court located in Bakersville, N.C., to Joseph W. Holden, 10 July 1870, and reprinted in the *Standard*, 20 July 1870. The *Rutherford Star* wrote the following about Kirk: "Soon after the surrender Col. Kirk came to this place and set up a small store, and carried on business for a few months. While here his conduct was unexceptionable, he showed himself to be firm and determined in anything he undertook, and we can say without fear of contradiction, that no one can lay a charge against him while in our midst. The hue and cry that he is a bad man, is for political effect. He is the right man in the right place. Honest men need not, do not fear him" (reprinted in the *Standard*, 4 August 1870).
44. W. J. Clarke to Holden, 18 June 1870, Governor's Papers, State Archives.
45. Clarke to M. C. Meigs, 17 June 1870, and Meigs to Holden, 21 June 1870, ibid. For a complete listing of all supplies furnished, see C. A. Alligood to Charles W. Thomas, Deputy Quartermaster, Fort Monroe, 14 July 1870, ibid.

46. North Carolina, *Impeachment Trial*, 1:282–83.
47. Kirk to Holden, 22 June 1870, Governor's Papers, State Archives.
48. The official appointments announced by Fisher (General Order no. 6) on 22 June and published in the *Standard* on 6 July read as follows:

Aide-de-camp to Commander-in-Chief, with rank of Colonel, Isaac J. Young, of Granville County, A. D. Jenkins, of Gaston.

Major Generals.	
1st Division,	William J. Clarke, Craven.
2nd Division,	Curtis H. Brogden, Wayne.
3rd Division,	William H. Harrison, Wake.
4th Division,	Andrew J. Jones, Columbus.
6th Division,	Jerry Smith, Alexander.
7th Division,	J. C. Duckworth, Transylvania.

Brigadier Generals.	
1st Brigade,	Clinton L. Cobb, Pasquotank.
2nd Brigade,	William A. Moore, Chowan.
3rd Brigade,	Joseph J. Martin, Martin.
4th Brigade,	Richard T. Berry, Craven.
5th Brigade,	William F. Loftin, Lenoir.
6th Brigade,	Edwin R. Brink, New Hanover.
7th Brigade,	H. L. Grant, Wayne.
8th Brigade,	John Norfleet, Edgecombe.
9th Brigade,	Peter R. Davie, Warren.
10th Brigade,	John C. Gorman, Wake.
11th Brigade,	Edward B. Lyon, Granville.
13th Brigade,	John McL. Harrington, Harnett.
14th Brigade,	James E. Eldridge, Bladen.
15th Brigade,	Oliver H. Dockery, Richmond.
16th Brigade,	William F. Henderson, Davidson.
17th Brigade,	Stephen A. Douglas, Rockingham.
18th Brigade,	J. Julius Martin, Stokes.
19th Brigade,	C. S. Moring, Rowan.
20th Brigade,	G. W. Flow, Union.
21st Brigade,	David A. Jenkins, Gaston.
22nd Brigade,	J. J. Mott, Catawba.
23rd Brigade,	A. C. Bryan, Wilkes.
24th Brigade,	Jacob W. Bowman, Mitchell.
25th Brigade,	C. L. S. Corpening, McDowell.
26th Brigade,	Nathan Scoggin, Henderson.
27th Brigade,	W. W. Rollins, Madison.
28th Brigade,	E. R. Hampton, Jackson.

49. *New York Tribune*, 22 June 1870.
50. Pool to Holden, 22 June 1870, Holden Papers, DU.
51. Quoted by Stephen A. Douglas, Jr., to William R. Richardson, Holden's Private

Secretary, 1 July 1870, and printed in the *Standard*, 2 July 1870. See also the *Standard*, 7 July 1870, for a report of the first strategy meeting of the Holden-Republican forces.

52. President Grant to Holden, 22 July 1870, Governor's Papers, State Archives.
53. *Standard*, 26 July 1870.
54. The Douglas speech was printed in full in the *Standard*, 16 July 1870.
55. An analysis of the Kirk muster roll shows several departures from strict legality. The use of "North Carolina State Troops" instead of state militia was contrary to the state constitution. Of the 670 men enrolled, 399 were under twenty-one years of age and 40 were over forty years of age, although the militia law set the age limits at twenty-one to forty. Over 200, and all field-grade officers, came from East Tennessee, even though the militia law required all officers and enlisted men to be electors of the state. Kirk also enrolled white and colored troops in the same outfit, contrary to the militia requirement that the two races be registered separately. The administration denied any wrongdoing in this matter, violating neither the state constitution nor militia law, since the governor had called up "volunteer troops" rather than utilize regular state militia forces. See North Carolina, *Impeachment Trial*, 3:2306. J. C. Bowman, United States assessor in Bakersville, however, was more concerned over the fact that nearly 300 of the troopers came from Mitchell County alone, with an overwhelming majority of all others coming from the Seventh District. His problem was that unless the men would vote "absentee" while out of their counties, the Republicans might not be able to maintain political control of the counties in the August election. See Bowman to Holden, 7 July 1870, Governor's Papers, State Archives.
56. Hamilton, *Reconstruction in North Carolina*, 504.
57. W. F. Henderson and William H. Howerton to Holden, 9 July 1870, Governor's Papers, State Archives.
58. Hamilton, *Reconstruction in North Carolina*, 501.
59. *Standard*, 6 July 1870.
60. Douglas, son of the famous Illinois Democratic senator Stephen A. Douglas, was serving on Holden's administrative staff and as brigadier general of the Seventeenth Brigade in the state troops.
61. North Carolina, *Impeachment Trial*, 3:2306; *Standard*, 16 July 1870.
62. See Proclamation by Governor Holden, 8 July 1870, Letter Book, State Archives.
63. *Standard*, 12 July 1870.
64. *Standard*, 11 July 1870. Colonel A. W. Shaffer, United States commissioner, committed the men to jail in Raleigh. See his letter, dated 16 July 1870, to the *Sentinel* refuting Turner's charges of prisoner maltreatment. His letter was reprinted in the *Standard*, 19 July 1870.
65. *Raleigh Sentinel*, 18 July 1870.
66. *Standard*, 20 July 1870. No copy of the letter can be found in either the official or private collections of the Holden papers. It should be noted, however, that Turner

was traveling throughout the state making abusive speeches against Holden. See W. F. Henderson to Holden, 19 July 1870, describing a Salisbury speech, Governor's Papers, State Archives.

67. Ibid.
68. Ibid.
69. Hambrick probably referred to John W. Hardin, a Graham merchant, and W. A. Albright, clerk of superior court. Hambrick to Holden, 12 March 1870, Governor's Papers, State Archives.
70. H. A. Badham, John W. Hardin, P. R. Hardin, Henry M. Ray, and W. A. Albright to Holden, 28 February 1870, ibid.
71. Olsen, *Carpetbagger's Crusade*, 161.
72. Ibid.
73. Interestingly, Holden actively participated in the amnesty movement, since his natural feelings of humanity caused him to forgive others even though they might have wronged him. He explained his reasoning in a moving letter to S. A. Ashe, 6 December 1881:

   In the autumn of 1873 I was in Hillsborough, and united with the Hon. Thomas Ruffin, now of the Supreme Court, and James E. Boyd, Esq., in a correspondence, which was published in the newspapers, and led to the amnesty act soon after passed by the Legislature. One of the grounds of the appeal to me to join in the correspondence was, that the father of this young man [Patton, who had testified against Holden in his Impeachment Trial by denying that he was ever a member of the Klan and who had fled to Tennessee to escape indictment in the Outlaw murder] was on his death-bed, and desired to see his son before he died. The young man returned, and may be now a citizen of Alamance. (Holden Papers, DU.)

74. For a thorough description of the Outlaw murder and Judge Tourgée's exposure of Klan activities in his judicial district, see Olsen's *Carpetbagger's Crusade*, 160–62, 184–86. The Bason letters to Graham, 18, 19 December 1871, are found in the Graham Papers, State Archives. See also Bason's letter confessing that he had belonged to the Klan and had refused to support James E. Boyd's attempt to expose the secrets of the Klan organization, Bason to Holden, 30 July 1870, Governor's Papers, State Archives.
75. A. G. Moore was a Graham merchant; James S. Scott was also a Graham merchant; James E. Boyd was a Graham attorney and, at the time, a Conservative candidate for the state house of representatives; James Hunter was a Graham merchant; H. Scott was a Graham merchant.
76. Kirk to Holden, 24 July 1870, Governor's Papers, State Archives.
77. The military commission, as finally constituted, consisted of Kirk's regimental officers, Willie D. Jones, C. S. Moring, W. A. Albright, H. M. Ray, J. W. Hardin, and R. W. Hancock. Dr. J. J. Mott had been requested to serve, but declined. It was planned for the commission to meet on 25 July, just prior to the state election (no

doubt for the proper political effect), but the time was set back to the second week in August.

78. North Carolina, *Impeachment Trial*, 3:2318.

79. Hamilton, *Reconstruction in North Carolina*, 506n.

80. Kirk to Holden, 1 August 1870, Governor's Papers, State Archives.

81. Hamilton, *Reconstruction in North Carolina*, 508. Hamilton's version was based upon North Carolina, *Report of the Proceedings in the Habeas Corpus Cases*.

82. Pearson to Holden, 18 July 1870, Governor's Letter Book, State Archives.

83. Holden to Pearson, 19 July 1870, ibid.

84. Bragg, as President Davis's commissioner, had prosecuted W. N. Bragg (a relative) and James Everitt, a Goldsboro minister, for evading draft laws. Battle, as an associate justice of the state supreme court, had similarly ruled in two cases.

85. Holden to President Grant, 20 July 1870, ibid.

86. President Grant to Holden, 22 July 1870, ibid.

87. Brig. Genl. R. C. Drum to Brig. Genl. Irwin McDowell, 11 September 1870, ibid.

88. *Raleigh Sentinel*, 9 September 1870.

89. "Opinion of Chief Justice Pearson in the Habeas Corpus Case of A. G. Moore," North Carolina, *Executive and Legislative Documents* (1870–71), 64–72.

90. Hamilton, *Reconstruction in North Carolina*, 515.

91. Zebulon B. Vance to William A. Graham, 28 July, 6 August 1870, Graham Papers, State Archives. Vance declared that H. W. Guion thought such action was possible under section 27 of the Habeas Corpus Act, chapter 110, of the 1868–69 state law.

92. This support of the other justices was universally accepted by leading Conservative-Democrats. See Thomas B. Keogh to William L. Scott, 27 July 1870, Scott Papers, DU.

93. *Standard*, 25 July 1870.

94. Holden to Pearson, 26 July 1870, Governor's Papers, State Archives. Once again Professor Hamilton must be faulted for his interpretation of the issue. He wrote: "Few official communications in the history of North Carolina contain so large a proportion of falsehood as to be found in this letter, particularly to this point (the state judiciary being unable to bring the criminals to justice). The statements were untrue and Governor Holden knew them to be so." See his *Reconstruction in North Carolina*, 513n. In fact, undeniable proof shows that the statements about the Klan's outrages and the court's inability to guarantee the criminals would receive a true and fair trial were true, and Professor Hamilton must have known them to be so, but chose to write otherwise. Furthermore, Judge Tourgée was subjected to a variety of threats and death notices. So perturbed was he that he seriously considered leaving the state permanently for a foreign post, "where the Judge wouldn't mind yellow fever, cholera, fleas, earthquakes, vertigo, smallpox, cannibalism, icebergs, sharks, or any other name or shape of horror—provided always there are no K.K.K." (Olsen, *Carpetbagger's Crusade*, 167–68).

95. The chief justice later wrote: "It is gratifying to be able to say that the other Justices

have been unreserved in conference with me, and all concur in the habeas corpus proceedings" (*Standard*, 4 August 1870).

96. Kirk to Holden, 24 July 1870, Governor's Papers, State Archives.

97. Copies of Boyd's and other Klansmen's confessions are to be found in the Governor's Papers, State Archives, and were also published in the *Standard*.

98. James E. Boyd to Holden, 1 August 1870, Governor's Papers, State Archives.

99. Moore's confession was published in the *Standard*, 18 August 1870.

100. Olsen, *Carpetbagger's Crusade*, 165.

101. *Raleigh Sentinel*, 31 July 1870.

102. Ibid., 21 October 1870.

103. North Carolina, *Impeachment Trial*, 1:759; Hamilton, *Reconstruction in North Carolina*, 516–20.

104. J. H. Mills to Holden, 9 August 1870, Governor's Letter Book, State Archives; Holden to Mills, 9 August 1870, ibid.

105. Holden to Kirk, 3 August 1870, Governor's Papers, State Archives.

106. Ibid. See also North Carolina, *Impeachment Trial*, 1:660, 701.

107. Holden to S. A. Ashe, 6 December 1881, Holden Papers, DU.

108. William M. Shipp defeated Samuel F. Phillips for attorney general, while the congressional returns were as follows: 1st District, Clinton L. Cobb (R) won over Morgan (Ind.); 2nd District, Charles R. Thomas (R) won over Humphrey (D); 3rd District, Alfred M. Waddell (D) won over Oliver H. Dockery (R); 4th District, Sion H. Rogers (D) won over Madison Hawkins (R) and James H. Harris (R), although Harris contested the Rogers victory; 5th District, James M. Leach (D) defeated William L. Scott (R); 6th District, Francis E. Shober (D) won over Alexander H. Jones (R).

109. *Washington* (D.C.) *Star*, as quoted in the *Raleigh Sentinel*, 1 August 1870.

110. *Raleigh Sentinel*, 28 July 1870.

111. Ibid., 3 August 1870.

112. Richard T. Berry to Holden, 28 November 1870, Holden Papers, DU.

113. Josiah Turner, Jr., to wife, 8 August 1870, Josiah Turner Papers, DU.

114. Hamilton, *Reconstruction in North Carolina*, 525. Either Hamilton erred in recording Turner's imprisonment date as "July," or this is another example of inaccurate reporting by the *Sentinel* editor.

115. It should be remembered, however, that at the time of the supposed conversation, Harris was openly feuding with Holden because he had been denied the presidency of the Western North Carolina Railroad.

116. Turner, according to Professor Hamilton, was "refused all comforts even such as soap and towels. Part of the time he was locked in a cell with a negro under sentence of death and was not even given a seat of any sort. The cell was full of vermin and was altogether loathsome" (Hamilton, *Reconstruction in North Carolina*, 524–25).

117. Kirk to Holden, 7 August 1870, Holden Papers, DU. Kirk characterized Mrs.

Turner as being "very impertinent and scornfully defiant." In this same letter, Kirk informed the governor that his brother E. Brock Holden and other delegates from all sections of Caswell County called upon Kirk trying to get the troops removed. Brother Brock Holden refused to admit that the Klan existed in Caswell or that it had committed any outrages. There is no question that the Klan-Negro issue produced a split in Holden's family relationships which were never healed.

118. A controversy developed over this letter. Abbott had sent a copy to Holden, who, unbeknownst to Tourgée, gave it to the Raleigh correspondent of the *New York Tribune*, who sent it to his paper for publication. In the process of transferral, Tourgée's figures on Klan outrages were incorrectly increased. Professor Hamilton inferred that Holden had falsely altered the figures for his own political benefit. See Hamilton, *Reconstruction in North Carolina*, 528n. In his later study, Olsen proves Hamilton was in error and that Tourgée did not believe Holden was responsible for the inaccuracy. Furthermore, Olsen points out that the *Sentinel*, 29 September 1870, garbled the letter even further (*Carpetbagger's Crusade*, 167n). Editor Turner was not above misquoting when it served his purpose.

119. Ironically, the state leaders who had so adamantly opposed the adoption of the Fourteenth Amendment and Radical Reconstruction legislation generally were now using both to oppose Governor Holden, the early advocate of each in North Carolina.

120. Holden to President Grant, 7 August 1870, Governor's Letter Book, State Archives.

121. *Standard*, 12 August 1870. It further asked: "Is Judge Brooks ready to involve the people . . . in civil war? Does he suppose Governor Holden will recede before him? . . . We are on the eve of civil war, and when it begins all the blood and all the horrors of it will be on the skirts of Judge Brooks."

122. The Ackerman opinion was forwarded to Holden by telegraph, Belknap to Holden, 8 August 1870, Letter Book, State Archives.

123. Telegram of J. M. McCorkle to R. C. Badger, Holden's legal counsel, 15 August 1870, Governor's Papers, State Archives.

124. Special Order no. 14, A. W. Fisher, Adjutant General, 11 August 1870, Governor's Letter Book, State Archives.

125. Holden to Kirk, 22 August 1870, ibid.

126. A. W. Tourgée to Holden, 12 August 1870, Holden Papers, DU; J. R. Bulla to Holden, 16 August 1870, Governor's Papers, State Archives.

127. Holden to Pearson, 15 August 1870, Governor's Letter Book, State Archives.

128. Pearson to Holden, 18 August 1870, ibid.

129. Holden to Rodman, 16 August 1870, ibid.; Rodman to Holden, 21 August 1870, Governor's Papers, State Archives.

130. Pearson's ruling of 19 August was reprinted in full by the *Standard*, 20 August 1870. It can also be found in North Carolina, *Report of Proceedings in Habeas Corpus Cases*, 59–66.

131. Telegram, Holden to Stewart, 18 August 1870, Governor's Papers, State Archives; Finch to Holden, 19 August 1870, ibid.
132. Telegram, Badger to Holden, 18 August 1870, ibid. There is no evidence that any official staff member was disloyal to Holden. The "leak," therefore, must have been through telegraph operators.
133. *Standard*, 26 August 1870.
134. Kirk to Holden, 19 August 1870, Governor's Papers, State Archives.
135. *Standard*, 27 August 1870.
136. Hamilton, *Reconstruction in North Carolina*, 532. Hamilton's figures are not quite accurate, since his totals amounted to $74,267.70.
137. Turner continued to seek financial redress from Holden, not only for his arrests but also for many other "trumped up" charges of fraudulent mismanagement of state financial affairs. Even as late as 1891 he was still trying, but without success. See Judge Tourgée's ruling of 12 October 1870, Holden Papers, DU. Deposition of Mrs. Holden in the case of *Turner* v. *Holden*, 1891, ibid., and the Turner Papers, SHC, give ample testimony to Turner's continued failures.
138. Holden to H. L. Bond, 29 August 1870, Letter Book, State Archives.
139. Holden later described his action against Bergen:
      And what of the officer who did this "hanging" without a shadow of authority from me? I ordered him to report to me at my office in Raleigh on the 6th August, 1870. I had meanwhile stationed Capt. Hancock, of New Bern, with a file of men in an adjoining room, and, as soon as the officer referred to was seated, I called for Capt. Hancock and said to him, "This man has violated my orders. Take him to camp, confine him in a tent under guard, and deny him the privileges usually accorded to officers." And then, addressing the officer myself, I said: "There are grave charges against you. I have directed the Adjutant-General to prefer charges. You will be tried, and cashiered from the service." A few days afterwards the Marshall of the United States demanded him on a civil writ. I yielded to the civil power, and he was taken and confined in Wake County Jail until released by Judge Bond. (Holden to S. A. Ashe, 6 December 1881, Holden Papers, DU.)
140. Josiah Turner, Jr., to wife, 4 March 1871, Turner Papers, SHC.

CHAPTER NINE

1. *Tarboro Southerner*, 11 August 1870.
2. Reprinted in the *Standard*, 11 November 1870.
3. Hamilton, *Reconstruction in North Carolina*, 541.
4. For a discussion of the *Sentinel*'s charges against Pearson that he had accepted a $2,500 bribe and formulated his decisions by guilty connivance with Holden, see the *Standard*, 9 November 1870, and a defense in his behalf reprinted from the

Salisbury Old North State; see also Hamilton, *Reconstruction in North Carolina*, 541.

5. *Standard*, 11,15 October 1870. The Conservatives were accused of proposing a call for another constitutional convention to revise the 1868 document, impeach Governor Holden, revolutionize the public school system by a return to the "old field school houses" for the poor and a university exclusively for the rich, abolish the homestead law, nullify the Fourteenth and Fifteenth amendments, and inaugurate the Invisible Empire "to put down the Republican party and to keep down the nigger."

6. Governor's Papers, State Archives.

7. *Standard*, 11 October 1870.

8. Lassiter and Barnett were permitted to take their seats temporarily, but in January, Lassiter was unseated and replaced by L. C. Edwards, a Conservative. Smith and Carey were replaced by James A. Graham and Livingston Brown, both Conservatives.

9. *Charlotte Western Democrat*, 24 November 1870; see also *Raleigh Sentinel*, 29 November 1870.

10. North Carolina, *Executive and Legislative Documents* (1870–71), no. 1. A copy is also to be found in the Governor's Letter Book, State Archives.

11. Reprinted in the *Standard*, 19 December 1870.

12. *Charlotte Western Democrat*, 17 January 1871.

13. *Standard*, 19 November 1870.

14. North Carolina, *Impeachment Trial*, 1:1.

15. Ibid.

16. Holden to Samuel F. Phillips, Steward Ellison, R. W. Morgan, and T. W. Young, 15 December 1870, reprinted in the *Standard*, 15 December 1870. In the 28 November issue, Holden had authorized the *Standard* to give his views on "universal amnesty" and to deny that he had appointed Dr. C. Tate Murphy, state senator from the 16th District, supervisor of the State Insane Asylum in an attempt to influence his future political course of action. Murphy declined the appointment. As for "amnesty," it was being rumored that Holden had expressed willingness to have former governor Vance's disabilities removed so that he could assume his seat in the United States Senate, thereby securing Conservative support and stopping any impeachment movement.

17. The complete articles of impeachment may be found in North Carolina, *Impeachment Trial*, 1:9–18. In 1881, Holden wrote a series of letters to S. A. Ashe for publication in the *Raleigh News and Observer* reviewing John W. Moore's *History of North Carolina*. In his 29 November 1881 letter, Holden commented on evidence that was not permitted to be introduced in his trial, which prevented him from getting a fair and impartial hearing:

I am obliged to the historian for these statements [Klan outrages in 1870], because they enable me to state a fact heretofore unknown to the people of the

State. Governor Graham dwelt much in the impeachment on the fact that I began my military movement only a month before the August election; and he thence drew the inference that my purpose was to influence the election thus near at hand. The Senate or impeachment court had ruled no witnesses outside the two counties in insurrection could be heard in evidence. The Legislature had appropriated seventy thousand dollars to be used by me in enforcing the law. If the Hon. David A. Jenkins, the State Treasurer, could have been heard as a witness, he would have sworn that it was my wish to begin the movement at least two months before the election; that he had no funds in hand at that time that I could use; and that he notified me on the first of July that he was in receipt of ninety thousand dollars, dividends from the North Carolina Railroad, and that I could have the seventy thousand from the amount thus received. I think this explains the matter to the satisfaction of every fair-minded man. My recollection is that W. R. Albright, Esq., of Alamance, swore before the impeachment court, or before the court in chambers, that he had told me a week or two before the election that while he approved of my course, yet the shock to the people of the State was so great as the result of my course that he feared that the result would lose the State; and that I replied in these words: "I do not care how the State goes, if by what I am doing I shall save one human life." I declared that all I desired at the time was a free ballot and a fair count; and that I was moved solely in what I did by a wish to protect life and property; to protect the poor and the humble as well as the rich, and that, too, without regard to race or party.

18. Holden to W. M. Shipp, 20 December 1870, Governor's Letter Book, State Archives; Shipp to Holden, 20 December 1870, ibid.
19. In assuming his role as presiding officer of the court, Pearson announced that, contrary to Chief Justice Chase's taking a special oath in the Andrew Johnson trial, he would regard his own oath of office as sufficient in view of its requirement that he "do his duty impartially and according to law."
20. Throughout the trial, Holden was referred to as "Governor Holden."
21. Mary Holden to Holden, 30 December 1870, Holden Papers, DU.
22. Thomas Settle to Holden, 28 July 1869, ibid. Settle wrote: "I am happy to inform you that Jo. is well and doing well. He has not touched a drop of whiskey or brandy since his arrival at my house on Saturday last—only a little wine. He has sworn off and don't desire it. He seems perfectly contented and has commenced reading Blackstone."
23. Young Holden did later redeem himself. After losing his job as a reporter for the *Standard* when it ceased publication in December 1870, he went to Washington and worked briefly for the Senate investigating committee on Klan activities. Failing to secure permanent employment, however, he migrated to Leavenworth, Kansas, where he worked for the *Times*, edited by the brother of Susan B. Anthony. He achieved immediate success, being promoted to the post of managing editor. Ill

health forced him to return to Raleigh, where he was elected mayor in 1874, but he died before completing his term of office.

24. A summary of thirty acts of Klan atrocities in Orange County was submitted by James B. Mason, Andrew W. King, and Turner King to Holden, 10 January 1871, Holden Papers, DU. See also John W. Hardin to Holden, 1 February 1871, and A. J. King to Henry C. Thompson, 4 February 1871, ibid.

25. John N. Bunting to Holden, 4 January 1871, ibid.

26. *Raleigh Sentinel*, 20 December 1870. Professor Hamilton, *Reconstruction in North Carolina*, 547n, states that Holden also sought to employ the notorious Benjamin F. Butler of Massachusetts, but there is no evidence in any of the Holden Papers that substantiates such a claim.

27. North Carolina, *Impeachment Trial*, vol. 1, includes a verbatim copy of the Holden answers to the charges and the replies of the board of managers.

28. Curtis H. Brogden to Holden, 12 February 1890, Brogden Papers, DU; Holden, *Memoirs*, 172.

29. Holden to S. A. Ashe, 6 December 1881, Holden Papers, DU. It should be noted, also, that while Holden's political enemies denied during the trial, and even afterwards, that the Ku Klux Klan ever existed in North Carolina, many of them confessed their participation, and begged for mercy in a letter to Judge H. L. Bond. It read:

Raleigh, September 30, 1871.

Sir: We have the honor, in the interest of the peace of the people of North Carolina, to address you this note.

The fact that a secret, unlawful organization, called the Ku Klux or Invisible Empire, exists in certain parts of the State has been manifested in the recent trials before the Court in which you preside. We condemn without reservation all such organizations. We denounce them as dangerous to all good government, and we regard it as the eminent duty of all good citizens to suppress them. No right-minded man in North Carolina can palliate or deny the crimes committed by these organizations; but we think if the further prosecution of the persons charged with these offences were continued until November term, it would enable us to enlist all law-loving citizens of the State to make an energetic and effectual effort for the restoration of good order. We assure you that we believe that before the November term of the Circuit Court that this unlawful organization will be effectually suppressed.

In the name of a just and honorable people and by all the considerations which appeal to good men, we solemnly protest that these violations of law and public justice must and shall cease. . . .

[Signed]Thomas Bragg
Geo. V. Strong
Daniel G. Fowle
Jos. B. Batchelor

B. F. Moore
Wm. M. Shipp
M. W. Ransom
Will. H. Battle
R. H. Battle, Jr.
D. M. Barringer

Former governor Vance and Alfred M. Scales, who was later to be governor of the state, would have signed the letter had they been in Raleigh at the time. A copy of the letter may be found included in Curtis H. Brogden to William K. Boyd, 18 May 1898, Holden Papers, DU. Brogden further wrote:

These inveterate enemies of Gov. Holden frankly confessed the wicked and abominable crimes of their associates and called the Ku Klux "an evil which could bring nothing but calamity to the State." So those great democratic leaders and traducers of Gov. Holden gave the strongest and most conclusive proof in vindication and defense of Gov. Holden, for trying to preserve peace and order and to stop the outrages of the Ku Klux. He was impeached for that, and after it was done, his enemies were forced to admit that he acted right in trying to put them down.

Brogden concluded his letter to Professor Boyd by citing how in 1877 the governors of several northern and western states had called out the militia to subdue riots and labor strikes, but nothing was said or done about impeaching any of them. "It seemed that Gov. Holden's unpardonable offense was in trying to discharge his duty faithfully while acting under the constitution and the laws. The whole history of his administration as Gov. shows that he done all he could to maintain and preserve peace and good order among the people."

30. Holden to George W. Swepson, 10 February 1871, Swepson Papers, State Archives.
31. Boyd, *William W. Holden*, 124.
32. Swepson to A. J. Jones, 12 February 1871, Swepson Papers, State Archives.
33. Holden, *Memoirs*, 150–51. According to Boyden and Badger, Pearson gave his advice to the defense counsel individually and without the other counsel knowing that such advice was being given.
34. *Standard*, 14 December 1870.
35. North Carolina, *Impeachment Trial*, 2:1039–89.
36. John W. Long, for example, was living in Huntsville, Alabama, and had changed his initials from John W. to W. A. Long.
37. Throughout the trial, Badger and Merrimon conducted the cross-examination of the witnesses for their respective sides.
38. North Carolina, *Impeachment Trial*, 3:2270–2311.
39. By an act of 3 March 1863, Congress authorized the president to suspend the writ of habeas corpus, and under this authority President Lincoln, 15 September 1863, suspended the writ in cases where army officers held persons for offenses against

the military forces. Milligan, a civilian, was arrested, tried by a military commission, found guilty of fomenting insurrection, and sentenced to be hanged. He petitioned the U.S. circuit court for a writ of habeas corpus, claiming that he should have been tried by a civil court since civil courts existed in the locality and at the time of his arrest. The Supreme Court agreed with his plea and freed him. See Commager, *Documents of American History* (1958), 2:22–26.

40. North Carolina, *Impeachment Trial*, 3:2270–2311.

41. Ibid., 3:2367–2438. For an analysis of the Merryman decision, see Commager, *Documents of American History*, 1:398–401.

42. North Carolina, *Impeachment Trial*, 3:2439–2532.

43. Cook, Cowles, Flemming, Gilmer, Norment, and Speed were the six Democrats who voted not guilty on article 1; Cook, Cowles, Flemming, and Norment voted not guilty on article 2; Cook, Cowles, and Flemming voted not guilty on article 4; Hawkins, Lehman, McCotter, and Moore were the Republicans who voted guilty on article 5; while Barnett, Hawkins, Lehman, McCotter, and Moore voted guilty on article 6.

44. Pool, *Speech of Senator John Pool before the United States Senate*, 31 March 1871.

45. North Carolina, *Impeachment Trial*, appendix, 100–108.

46. Ibid., appendix, 9–11.

47. Ibid., 3:2564. Under said terms, it also disqualified and prohibited Governor Holden from ever holding state office thereafter unless the disability was removed by legislative action.

48. Holden to wife, 11 March 1871, Holden Papers, DU.

49. Hamilton, *Reconstruction in North Carolina*, 552.

50. Holden to George W. Swepson, 10 February 1871, Swepson Papers, State Archives.

51. Ibid., 11 March 1871.

52. Ibid., 2 March 1871.

53. Ibid., 4 March 1871.

54. Ibid., 11 March 1871.

55. Ibid.

56. Ibid., 15 March 1871. He had seen, but did not talk with, Josiah Turner, who was in Washington seeking to have Kirk and Bergen arrested and returned to North Carolina.

57. Ibid., 16 March 1871.

58. Ibid., 15 March 1871.

59. Ibid., 22 March 1871. Earlier, on the 18th, he had written: "I have taken it for granted all along that I would be convicted. The chances are and have been against me. Whatever may happen to me will be for the best. I will hear the result, no matter which way it may be, with but little emotion. . . . Let me beg you all not to be concerned about me. Let us trust in Providence, and submit humbly to His will."

60. Holden to wife, 1 April 1871, Holden Papers, DU.
61. *Washington Chronicle*, 23 March 1871.
62. J. N. Bunting to Holden, 4 January 1871, Holden Papers, DU.
63. Holden to wife, 1, 9, 11 April 1871, ibid.
64. Holden to wife, 11 April 1871, ibid.
65. Ibid.
66. Ibid., 1, 9 April 1871.
67. Mrs. Holden visited Washington early in April where, undoubtedly, financial matters were discussed. She also contracted a bad cold. See Holden to wife, 9, 11, 12 April 1871, ibid. For a general review of Phillips's career, see Miller, "Samuel Field Phillips," 263–80.
68. Holden to wife, 11 April 1871, ibid. See also deposition of Mrs. Louisa Holden in 1891 in the case of *Turner* v. *Holden*, Holden Papers, DU, and Mrs. Holden to John W. Hinsdale (her attorney), 30 May 1893, ibid.
69. Holden to Calvin J. Cowles, 3 August 1882, ibid.
70. Holden to wife, 30 April 1871, ibid.

CHAPTER TEN

1. Holden to wife, 30 April 1871, Holden Papers, DU.
2. Ibid., n.d., but later April 1871.
3. Ibid., 3 May 1871.
4. Ibid., 6 May 1871.
5. Ibid., 15 March 1871.
6. Ibid., 30 April 1871.
7. Ibid.
8. Edward Conigland to Holden, 2 May 1871, ibid.
9. Holden to wife, 3 May 1871, ibid.
10. Ibid., 16 March 1871.
11. Ibid., 3 May 1871; however, Holden was trying to get senators Pool and Abbott to find employment for his son-in-law L. P. Olds.
12. Ibid., 15 May 1871.
13. Ibid., 17 May 1871.
14. Holden to President Grant, 20 May 1871, ibid.
15. Holden to wife, 20 May 1871, ibid.
16. Holden to Laura Holden Olds, 20 May 1871, ibid.
17. Holden to wife, 21 May 1871, ibid.
18. Ibid., 25 May 1871.
19. Ibid., 26 May 1871.
20. Ibid, Holden, *Memoirs*, 48–49.
21. Holden to Joseph W. Holden, 16 August 1871, Holden Papers, DU.

22. Holden to wife, 7, 10, 15 August 1871, ibid. Holden often expressed doubts about the negotiations: "I am not sanguine as to success."
23. Ibid., 10 August 1871.
24. Ibid., 5, 10, 16 June 1871; for Joseph Holden's reaction to the family trip, see his letter to Mary Holden, 12 August 1871, ibid.: "And at Saratoga—well, I never see the enjoyment there, as long as they sold bottled water at Pescud's [Raleigh] drug store. But take it all in all, the North is rich and powerful while the South is poor and unhappy."
25. Ibid., 10 June 1871.
26. Holden to Mary Holden, 21 August 1871, ibid. Holden's problem was further complicated by breaking his glasses; he could not see well enough to write without them. He bought "a dollar pair of excellent plain glasses" as replacements, but he dropped and broke them on a Sunday, leaving him helpless and despondent over a weekend (Holden to wife, 27 August 1871, ibid.).
27. Holden had hoped to have complete control (editorial policy and business management) of the paper, but he was forced to accept editorial control only.
28. Holden to wife, 31 August 1871, Holden Papers, DU.
29. Ibid., 13 September 1871.
30. Ibid., 16 September 1871; he referred to himself as "Editor of the *Chronicle*"; see Holden to George W. Swepson, 25 September 1871, ibid.
31. Holden to L. P. Olds, 1 December 1871, ibid.
32. Holden to wife, 12 October 1871, ibid.; Ingersoll had served in the Union army during the Civil War and as attorney general of Illinois, 1867–69, but was currently a practicing attorney in Washington. He was best known as an agnostic and attacker of popular Christian beliefs.
33. On 13 November 1871, the *Chronicle* announced that new presses had been purchased and that the paper was "expending more money upon our journal than is devoted to by any other journal of the city."
34. Holden to wife, 13 September 1871, Holden Papers, DU.
35. Ibid., 12 October 1871.
36. Ibid.
37. W. W. Rollins to Holden, 9 December 1871, ibid. Rollins wrote: "This bill was prepared by Judge Henry . . . with the understanding that we should have Western men to control the [courts] that the loyal people of the West might be protected. Now we learn that Eastern men are trying to push themselves to get all the offices and thereby control the Courts. All we ask is Justice at the hands of the powers that be and in as much as this idea was originated in the West we demand that the West be heard."
38. Alexander McIver to Holden, 17 November 1871, ibid.
39. Holden to L. P. Olds, 1 December 1871, ibid. This letter was copied later by Mary Holden, and this explains, no doubt, the several punctuation mistakes in the text.
40. Ibid.

41. Holden to wife, 2 March 1873, ibid.
42. Holden to Postmaster-General David McKendree Key, 17 September 1878, ibid. As the designated custodian for the new building, he ran into difficulties in assigning office space because of petty disagreements between the federal officials, but these he settled—if not amicably, at least satisfactorily. In addition to the postal facilities on the first floor, the other offices included the collector of internal revenue and his agents for the 2nd, 4th, and 5th districts; the U.S. marshall; clerk of the U.S. district court; U.S. district attorney; U.S. commissioner; register of bankruptcy; and the superior in chief of federal elections for the Eastern District of North Carolina.
43. Holden to Mary Holden, 6 August 1874, ibid.
44. Holden to Ettie Holden, 27 July 1874, ibid.
45. Holden to Rutherford B. Hayes, 16 June 1876, Hayes Papers, HL.
46. John A. McDonald to Rutherford B. Hayes, 4 August 1876, ibid. Holden had added the following endorsement: "I am well acquainted with Mr. McDonald. He is a man of character and a good Republican."
47. Copy of a petition from Holden to President James A. Garfield, 2 April 1881, Holden Papers, DU.
48. Ibid. By 1880, however, Holden refrained from active participation in national issues upon the request of the state Republican party chairman, who feared the Democrats would retaliate by arousing the passions of the people, or even revive the Ku Klux Klan.
49. Holden to Calvin J. Cowles, 14 December 1876, Holden Papers, State Archives.
50. Holden to Rutherford B. Hayes, 1 January 1877, Hayes Papers, HL. Woodward's two monographs, *The Compromise of 1877* and *Origins of the New South*, are still considered the best studies on the subject.
51. Ibid., 25 April 1877. On 15 May he again wrote to the president, enclosing a letter from J. M. Leach, who also endorsed the presidential policies. Holden also suggested that Leach would make a good U.S. attorney for the Western District of North Carolina.
52. Olsen, *Carpetbagger's Crusade*, 246–47. Olsen maintains that "almost a third of Garfield's [inaugural] address was devoted to the need for Federal aid to education, and it closely resembled, almost directly repeated, the general analysis that Tourgée had been championing. Subsequently, the Judge held two or more conferences with the President and showed the extent of his influence by securing the withdrawal of an appointment to the post of postmaster at Raleigh of William W. Holden, that long suffering, but longer-suspect, Reconstruction ally."
53. See Holden's petition to President Garfield, 2 April 1881, Holden Papers, DU.
54. Holden to wife, 25 April 1881, Holden Papers, DU, said, "I have never written so strong a paper as the letter I wrote to the President. It is obliged to have weight with him." John Nichols did replace Holden as postmaster, and served until 1885. Earlier he had served as principal of the State Institute for the Deaf and Dumb and

the Blind, 1873–77, and as senior member of the Nichols, Gorman, and Neathery Printing House in Raleigh. In 1886 he was elected to and served one term in the House of Representatives, 1887–89. He served as the chief of the division of mail files and records of the Treasury Department during the Harrison administration, but returned to Raleigh in 1893 and worked in the Internal Revenue Office there.

55. Holden to Zebulon B. Vance, 28 April 1881, ibid.

56. For a complete explanation for Holden breaking with the Republican party, see his card in the *Raleigh News and Observer*, 31 August 1883. At the same time he denied rumors that he contemplated rejoining the Democratic party or editing a Democratic paper.

57. Undated copy, Holden Papers, DU.

58. Ewing, "Two Reconstruction Impeachments," 204–25; see also, *Raleigh State Chronicle*, 9 September 1886, and the *Christian Advocate*, 25 May 1887.

59. Address delivered to the Raleigh Female Seminary, 7 June 1859, Holden Papers, DU.

60. Ibid.

61. Both quotations were cited by Hamilton, *Reconstruction in North Carolina*, 545.

62. Ibid.

63. Holden to wife, 27 May 1871, Holden Papers, DU.

64. Ibid., 15 May 1871. Holden also attended services at the Young Men's Christian Association.

65. Holden to Thomas Settle, 12 May 1886, Settle Papers, SHC.

66. John H. Boner to Theo. H. Hill, 10 March 1892, Holden Papers, DU.

67. Robert P. Dick to Holden, 12 June 1886, ibid.

68. J. S. Hampton, Greensboro printer, to Holden, 24 September 1884, ibid.

69. Holden had written a similar hymn for the First Baptist Church at the time of President Garfield's death, and copies of both hymns are to be found in the Holden Papers, ibid.

70. Holden to Kemp P. Battle, 29 January 1886, Battle Family Papers, SHC. See also Battle to Holden, 30 January 1886, Holden Papers, DU.

71. The Holden children were as follows: Laura Holden Olds; Joseph William; Ida Augusta Cowles; Henrietta (Ettie) Mahler; Mary Eldridge Sherwood; Beulah Holden Henry; Charles C. Holden; and Lula Holden Ward, who was born after the Holdens' return to Raleigh in 1872.

72. Unidentified newspaper clippings, Holden Papers, DU.

73. For verification of the Sherwood property, see Holden to Calvin J. Cowles, 3 August 1882, Holden Papers, DU.

74. The deed, dated April, 1895, reads: "For $10.00 and for the natural love and affection which she bears to her daughter." See also Henderson *Guide to Historic Buildings*. The Henrys lived only ten years in the house, returning to Raleigh to make their residence. A daughter, Beulah Louisa Henry, was often referred to as the "Lady Edison" of Raleigh, as she had more than eighty inventions put on the market. Included among the items were an umbrella whose top could be changed to

match various colored dresses, a sewing machine device, a talking doll, a toy cow, "Milky Moo," that could be milked, and a typewriter attachment that eliminated the use of carbon paper. For further information on Miss Henry, see *Raleigh News and Observer*, 26 June 1935.

75. Writing to Ida Holden Cowles, 5 August 1872, Holden commented: "We have heard from Mr. Olds. They reached San Juan, Nicaragua, in due time. They are much pleased, and Laura's health has improved" (Cowles Papers, SHC). In 1876, Holden wrote that Olds had actually departed for St. Helena after he had forwarded funds to him. Holden to Calvin J. Cowles, 14 December 1876, ibid.

76. L. P. Olds to Mrs. Holden, 18 June 1886, ibid.; Holden to Calvin J. Cowles, 10 February 1887, Cowles Papers, SHC.

77. Undated, but a copy of the poem is among the Holden Papers, DU.

78. Walter Clark to Charles Holden, 30 January 1890, ibid.

79. Holden to wife, 7 March 1884, ibid.

80. Deposition of Mrs. Holden in 1891 in the case of *Turner* v. *Holden*, ibid.

81. Holden always had a special fondness for poetry and spent countless hours in composing for his own pleasure. He was once described as "the most finished rhetorician" of his day. There has never been a complete compilation of his poetry, and the author is convinced that he published much of his work anonymously in the *Standard*, but the following are to be found among his collected papers: "I Am Passing Away" (1838); "To the Rev. C. F. Deems" (1842); "A Christmas Hymn" (1875); "Christmas" (1876); "Marvin" (1877); "De Profundis" (1880); "Procession or March of the International Lessons" (1880); "Song of the Telegraph" (1880); "Christmas Address of the Biblical Recorder" (1883); "Lines to Rev. A. B. Earle & Wife on the Occasion of Their Golden Wedding Reception" (1886); "Ode to Henry Clay" (n.d.).

82. Holden to David S. Reid, 27 March 1880, Reid Papers, State Archives.

83. Written by Daniels in 1886 and quoted by W. R. Henry to Thomas Dixon, 12 September 1905, Holden Papers, DU.

84. Holden to Samuel A. Ashe, 6 December 1881, ibid. Earlier commentaries to Ashe were letters dated 24, 29 November 1881, ibid.

85. John P. Devereux to Holden, 3 April 1882, ibid.; see also W. W. Smith to Holden, 13 April 1882, ibid.

86. Holden to Thomas Settle, 4 October 1884, Settle Papers, SHC.

87. Holden to Zebulon B. Vance, 26 November 1884, Holden Papers, DU. This official "announcement" read: "If my health will permit I propose to write a history or sketch of North Carolina, from 1860 to 1885. I will be greatly obliged to persons who will send me documents or facts in relation to men and events in the State for the last thirty years. I feel deeply the responsibility I assume in attempting such a work, and shall need all the encouragement that may be kindly offered."

88. Holden to Zebulon Vance, 11 December 1884, ibid. In this letter Holden told Vance that Saunders "warmly approved the project."

89. W. R. Henry to Louisa Sherwood, 20 January 1911, ibid.

90. Edward Conigland to Thomas L. Clingman, 21 September 1875, copy of which is found in the Holden Papers, ibid.
91. *Raleigh News*, 4 October 1878.
92. Undated "Card," Holden Papers, DU.
93. Holden, *Memoirs*, 181.
94. Ibid., 180–81.
95. The above account was drawn from a composite of obituaries in the state newspapers, copies of which are found in the Holden Papers, DU.
96. John W. Hinsdale to Mrs. Holden, 22 January, 8 February, 8 March, 21 April and 17 November 1894, ibid.; see also Mrs. Holden to Hinsdale, 17 November 1894, ibid.
97. Olsen, *Carpetbagger's Crusade*, 247.
98. Ibid., 223–41. Tourgée's major achievement was his preparation of the legal brief in behalf of Negro civil rights in the famous case of *Plessy* v. *Ferguson*. It is interesting that another brief was submitted and argued orally before the United States Supreme Court in the same case by Samuel F. Phillips, Holden's longtime friend. While the *Plessy* decision established the principle of "separate but equal," Tourgée and Justice John Marshall Harlan, the one-time Whig and slaveholder from Kentucky, provided the arguments that foreshadowed the reversal of *Plessy* and the end of segregation in the modern case of *Brown* v. *Board of Education of Topeka* (1954).
99. Davenport, "Thomas Dixon's Mythology," 351–67; Cook, "Man behind 'The Birth of a Nation,'" 519–23.
100. W. R. Henry to Thomas Dixon, 12 September 1905, Holden Papers, DU.
101. Tindall, *Emergence of the New South*, 186.
102. Cash, *Mind of the South*, 137; see also Tindall's chapter "The South and the Savage Ideal," from his definitive study, *Emergence of the New South*, 184–218.

SELECTED BIBLIOGRAPHY

A NOTE ON SOURCES

This study of William Woods Holden has endeavored to portray the many phases of his life and work, from editor to public official as provisional governor and governor, and return to private citizenship. It also attempts an interpretative explanation for his actions and contributions to the history of North Carolina. Since Holden was noted for his precise articulation in expressing thoughts or justifying decisions on public issues, the author has used his own words whenever possible. His pre–Civil War correspondence was destroyed by fire, but by searching through the *North Carolina Standard* and all known collections, a complete file of his papers has been obtained. Accordingly, the narrative is based almost entirely on his personal and administrative papers and the *Standard*.

Holden's Governor's Papers, 1865 and 1868–70, have been researched by scholars writing about the state's Reconstruction history, but the personal papers have not been objectively scrutinized until recently. The Duke University collection contains materials primarily concerned with his defense in his impeachment trial and later career, but they provided significantly new insights for a better understanding of his personality and family relationships. His *Memoirs*, published posthumously by his family in 1911, do not conform to the high standards or use the pungent style that characterized his editorial days.

Special recognition should be given to the late William K. Boyd, who was responsible for persuading the Holden family to donate their voluminous collections of papers to Trinity College, now Duke University, and to Edgar E. Folk for interviewing Holden relatives in the 1920s and depositing those materials with the Department of Archives and History. Certainly no Holden biography would be complete without their important contributions. Also, it should be noted that Professor Boyd's biographical study and Folk's doctoral dissertation, "W. W. Holden, Political Journalist" (finally published in collaboration with Bynum Shaw under the title *W. W. Holden: A Political Biography*), and his two articles in the *North Carolina Historical Review*, "W. W. Holden and the North Carolina Standard, 1843–1848," and "W. W. Holden and the Election of 1858," provide an excellent review of Holden's editorial career.

Biographical data (other than for Holden) was obtained from three major sources: U.S. Census Reports for 1860 and 1870, sketches in North Carolina biographies, and local and county histories. The census reports were helpful in identifying the Holden correspondents, especially blacks and poor whites whose names were seldom recorded in local histories, and the thousands of his political appointees who filled local and county offices. They also proved indispensable in checking the approximately two thousand pardon requests transmitted through his office to President Johnson in 1865. The author found no great difference in reliability between Democratic poll takers of 1860 and the Republican pollsters of 1870.

For generations, Samuel A'Court Ashe's *Biographical History of North Carolina*, together with an unpublished manuscript for an additional volume in the Van Noppen Papers, Duke University, has furnished most biographical data, but many of its sketches were too eulogistic for complete credibility. When completed, William S. Powell's *Dictionary of North Carolina Biography* promises to be the most comprehensive and reliable of all such sources. Volume 1, A–C, the first of eight proposed volumes, was published in 1979. Another valuable resource is Robert Diggs Wimberly Connor's *Manual of North Carolina*, although many errors were corrected in an updated publication, *North Carolina Government, 1584–1974*. Also, William S. Powell's *North Carolina Gazetteer* provides a complete dictionary of tar heel places. Local and county histories were consulted, but, with few exceptions, they were not highly analytical in their discussions.

The standard work on Reconstruction history in the state has long been Joseph Gregoire de Roulhac Hamilton's *Reconstruction in North Carolina*, but as Olsen observed, it is "a reliable and mainly political history which is marred by a hostility toward Republicans and a readiness to accept political slander as fact" (*Carpetbagger's Crusade*, 374). It should also be noted that Professor Hamilton demonstrated a distinct bias against blacks, the Freedmen's Bureau, and Northerners, and generally agreed with Josiah Turner, Jr.'s antagonistic views toward Holden. In all fairness to Hamilton, however, he wrote when racial attitudes and political feelings were basically different from those of today. For these reasons the author attempted to set the record straight whenever possible by correcting faulty allegations about Holden.

Among the special studies, monographs, and biographies, three recent works have done much in repudiating the myths of Radical Reconstruction as being completely harmful to North Carolina and the South. The first, Carl N. Degler's *The Other South*, discloses that there were Southerners who opposed slavery, supported the Union during and after the Civil War, and, moreover, rejected the white aristocratic rule that controlled southern politics. Second, Michael Perman's *Reunion without Compromise: The South and Reconstruction* traces the maneuvers of southern leaders during the time Washington (Radical Republicans) was devising the terms for state readmission and asserts that the Democratic leadership was ill advised in its opposition to Union politics. But the most important, considering North Carolina politics, is Otto H. Olsen's *Carpetbagger's Crusade: The Life of Albion Winegar Tourgée*. This study sheds new insights on Republicanism, anti–Ku Klux Klanism, black equality, free public school education, and penal reform.

The author consulted all of the manuscript collections in their original form, as well as the North Carolina Historical Commission's publications (see listing in bibliography). The Andrew Johnson publications have not reached the Holden correspondence, while the Ulysses S. Grant Papers, now being published by the Southern Illinois University Press, were not made available. However, Holden's Governor Papers include most of the essentially important correspondence of the two presidents. A few editorial errors were found in McPherson's "Letters from North Carolina to Andrew Johnson" and Padgett's "Reconstruction Letters from North Carolina." The Second Military District Records and the North Carolina Records of the Bureau of Freedmen and Abandoned Lands were indispensable in this study of Holden and for the state's Reconstruction history generally. Also helpful has been the compilation of all North Carolinians who served in the Civil War. John W. Moore's *Roster of North Carolina Troops in the War between the States* (1882) proved incomplete, so the Department of Archives and History began a new twelve-volume project in 1965 entitled *North Carolina Troops, 1861–1865*, under the editorship of Louis H. Manarin. To date, volumes 1–7, covering artillery, cavalry, and initial infantry units, have been published.

During Holden's lifetime the state press was highly partisan, with the newspapers serving primarily as organs of the political parties; nevertheless, they furnish proof of the vitality of the political process at work throughout the state in the nineteenth century. Holden's own *North Carolina Standard* is a storehouse of factual and philosophical data on the three parties (Democratic, Conservative, and Republican) he led to political power. It also gives the reader an idea of state sentiment on national issues, as well as an indication of economic growth, educational development, and cultural trends. For additional perspectives, and because of their different viewpoints, the author consulted Edward J. Hale's *Fayetteville Observer*, Josiah Turner, Jr.'s *Raleigh Sentinel* (although this paper must be carefully studied because of its highly biased versions of events and sometimes completely inaccurate reporting), and William J. Yates's *Charlotte Western Democrat*. A geographical sampling of other state papers verified Holden's influence on the state's pulse and the success and failure of his administrative policies.

PUBLISHED MANUSCRIPT COLLECTIONS

Graf, Leroy P., Haskins, Ralph W., and Clark, Patricia P., eds. *The Papers of Andrew Johnson*. 6 vols. Knoxville: University of Tennessee Press, 1967–83.

Hamilton, Joseph Gregoire de Roulhac, ed. *The Correspondence of Jonathan Worth*. 2 vols. Raleigh: N.C. Historical Commission, 1909.

———, ed. *The Papers of Thomas Ruffin*. 4 vols. Raleigh: N.C. Historical Commission, 1920.

———, ed. *The Papers of Randolph Shotwell Abbott*. 3 vols. Raleigh: N.C. Historical Commission, 1929–36.

———, and Williams, Max R., eds. *The Papers of William Alexander Graham*. 6 vols. Raleigh: N.C. Historical Commission, 1957–76.

Johnston, Frontis W., ed. *The Papers of Zebulon Baird Vance*. Raleigh: N.C. Historical Commission, 1963.

McPherson, Elizabeth Gregory, ed. "Letters from North Carolina to Andrew Johnson." *North Carolina Historical Review* 27 (July 1950): 336–63, and 29 (October 1952): 569–78.

Olsen, Otto H., and McGrew, Ellen Z., eds. "Prelude to Reconstruction: The Correspondence of State Senator Leander Sams Gash, 1866–1877." *North Carolina Historical Review* 60 (January 1983): 37–88; 60 (April 1983): 206–38; and 60 (July 1983): 333–66.

Padgett, James A., ed. "Reconstruction Letters from North Carolina." *North Carolina Historical Review* 18 (April 1941): 171–95; 18 (June 1941): 278–300; 18 (October 1941): 373–97; 21 (January 1944): 46–71; 21 (April 1944): 139–57; and 21 (July 1944): 232–47.

Tolbert, Noble J., ed. *The Papers of John Willis Ellis*. 2 vols. Raleigh: N.C. Historical Commission, 1964.

Yearns, W. Buck, ed. *The Papers of Thomas Jordan Jarvis*. Raleigh: N.C. Historical Commission, 1969.

MANUSCRIPT COLLECTIONS

Chautauqua County Historical Museum, Westfield, New York
    Albion Winegar Tourgée Papers
Library of Congress, Washington, D.C.
    William E. Chandler Papers
    Andrew Johnson Papers
    John Sherman Papers
    Elihu B. Washburne Papers
National Archives, Washington, D.C.
    North Carolina Records of the Bureau of Freedmen and Abandoned Lands
    Second Military District Papers, War Department Records, 1867–68, Office of the Secretary of War
    War Department Collection of Confederate Records, Office of the Secretary of War
North Carolina Department of Archives and History, Raleigh
    Samuel A'Court Ashe Papers
    George Edmund Badger Papers
    Tod Robinson Caldwell Governor Papers
    Calvin Josiah Cowles Papers
    John Willis Ellis Governor Papers
    William Alexander Graham Papers
    Edward Joseph Hale Papers

William Woods Holden Personal Papers
    Provisional Governor and Governor Papers
Thomas Jordan Jarvis Governor Papers
William Andrew Jeffreys Papers
Bartholomew Figures Moore Papers
David Settle Reid Governor Papers
David Lowry Swain Papers
George William Swepson Papers
Zebulon Baird Vance Governor Papers
Jonathan Worth Personal Papers
    Governor Papers
Perkins Library, Duke University, Durham, North Carolina
    Curtis Hooks Brogden Papers
    John Heritage Bryan Papers
    Lawrence Bryan Papers
    Tod Robinson Caldwell Papers
    Henry Toole Clark Papers
    Plato Durham Papers
    Jones and Edwin W. Fuller Papers
    John McClain Harrington Papers
    Benjamin Sherwood Hedrick Papers
    William Woods Holden Papers
    William Lafayette Scott Papers
Rutherford B. Hayes Library, Freemont, Ohio
    Rutherford Birchard Hayes Papers
Southern Historical Collection, University of North Carolina, Chapel Hill
    Bedford Brown Papers
    James Augustus and John Heritage Bryan Papers
    Ralph Potts Buxton Papers
    David Franklin Caldwell Papers
    Tod Robinson Caldwell Papers
    William John Clarke Papers
    Calvin Josiah Cowles Papers
    John Wilson Cunningham Papers
    John Willis Ellis Papers
    John Thomas Gatling–Bartholomew Figures Moore Papers
    Daniel Reaves Goodloe Papers
    William Alexander Graham Papers
    Edward Jones Hale Papers
    Benjamin Sherwood Hedrick Papers
    William Woods Holden Papers
    George W. Mordecai Papers

Richmond Mumford Pearson Papers
Matt Whitaker Ransom Papers
Daniel Lindsay Russell Papers
David Schenck Papers
Thomas Settle Papers
Cornelia Phillips Spencer Papers
David Lowry Swain Papers
Samuel McDowell Tate Papers
Josiah Turner, Jr. Papers
Calvin Henderson Wiley Papers
University of Chicago Library, Chicago, Illinois
Stephen Arnold Douglas Papers

OFFICIAL DOCUMENTS

North Carolina. *Answer to the Articles of Impeachment*. William Woods Holden. Raleigh: James H. Moore, State Printer, 1871.
_____. *Articles against William W. Holden*. Document No. 18, Session 1870–71. Raleigh: James H. Moore, State Printer, 1871.
_____. *Argument in the Impeachment Trial of W. W. Holden*. Raleigh: James H. Moore, State Printer, 1871.
_____. *Code of Civil Procedure of North Carolina, Prepared by Code Commission of V. C. Barringer, Judge Rodman, and Albion W. Tourgée*. Raleigh: N. Paige, 1868.
_____. *Constitution of the State of North Carolina together with the Ordinances and Resolutions of the Constitutional Convention, Assembled in the City of Raleigh, Jan. 14, 1868*. Raleigh: W. W. Holden, 1868.
_____. *Executive and Legislative Documents of the North Carolina General Assembly, 1868–72*.
_____. *Impeachment Trial of William W. Holden*. 3 vols. Raleigh: Sentinel Printing Office, 1871.
_____. *Journals of the North Carolina Senate and House of Commons, 1851–71*.
_____. *Journal of the North Carolina Convention, 1865–1866*. Raleigh: Cannon and Holden, 1866.
_____. *Journal of the Constitutional Convention of the State of North Carolina at Its Session, 1868*. Raleigh: W. W. Holden, 1868.
_____. *Ordinances of the North Carolina Convention, 1865–1866*. Raleigh: William E. Pell, 1867.
_____. *Ordinances and Resolutions of the Constitutional Convention Assembled in the City of Raleigh, January 4, 1868*. W. W. Holden, 1865.
_____. *Private Laws of the State of North Carolina, 1868–70*.
_____. *Proclamations by the Governor of North Carolina: Together with the Opinion*

of Chief Justice Pearson and the Reply of the Governor. Raleigh: Standard Book and Job Printers, 1870.

————. *Public Laws of the State of North Carolina*, 1865–72.

————. *Report of the Commission to Investigate the Charges of Fraud and Corruption.* Raleigh: James H. Moore, State Printer, 1872.

————. *Report of the Proceedings in the Habeas Corpus Cases.* By William Horn Battle. Raleigh: Nichols and Gorman, 1870.

————. *Report of the Railroad Investigation Commission.* Raleigh: James H. Moore, State Printer, 1871.

————. *Revenue Acts of North Carolina with Instructions to Officers*, 1868. Raleigh: William E. Pell, 1868.

United States. *A Compendium of the Ninth Census* (1870). Washington: Government Printing Office, 1872.

————. *A Compilation of the Messages and Papers of the Presidents, 1789–1897.* Edited by James Richardson. 10 vols. Washington: Government Printing Office, 1896–99.

————. *Executive Documents*, 40th Congress, 2nd Session. Document 276, "Second Military District," and Document 342, "General Orders—Reconstruction."

————. *Executive Documents*, 40th Congress, 3rd Session. Document 102, "Persons Turned Over for Trial to Civil Authorities."

————. *Report of the Joint Committee on Reconstruction.* Washington: Government Printing Office, 1872.

————. *Report of the Joint Select Committee to Inquire into the Condition of Affairs in the Late Insurrectionary States.* Vols. 1 and 2. Washington: Government Printing Office, 1872.

————. *Senate Executive Documents*, 39th Congress, 1st Session. Document 2, "Carl Schurz Report," Document 26, "Provisional Governors of States," Document 27, "Freedmen Bureau Report."

————. *Senate Executive Documents*, 40th Congress, 2nd Session, vol. 2. Document 53, "Letters of Registered Voters in Rebel States."

————. *Senate Executive Documents*, 42nd Congress, 1st Session. Document 1, "Ku Klux Report."

————. *The War of the Rebellion. A Compilation of the Official Records of the Union and Confederate Armies in the War of the Rebellion.* 128 vols. Washington: Government Printing Office, 1880–1901.

COLLECTED DOCUMENTS

Cheney, John L., comp. *North Carolina Government, 1584–1974.* Raleigh: North Carolina Department of Archives and History, 1975.

Commager, Henry Steele. *Documents of American History.* New York: Appleton-Century-Crofts, 1958.

Connor, Robert Diggs Wimberly, comp. *A Manual of North Carolina Issued by the North Carolina Historical Commission for the Use of Members of the General Assembly, Session 1913.* Raleigh: 1913.

Dumond, Dwight Lowell. *Southern Editorials on Secession.* New York: Century Company, 1931.

Fleming, Walter Lynwood. *Documentary History of Reconstruction, Political, Military, Social, Religious, Educational and Industrial, 1865 to the Present Time.* 2 vols. Cleveland: Arthur H. Clark, 1906–7.

Moore, Frank, comp. *The Rebellion Record: A Diary of American Events, with Documents, Narratives, Illustrative Incidents, Poetry, etc..* 11 vols. New York: Putnam, 1861–63, Van Nostrand, 1864–68.

Powell, William S. *The North Carolina Gazetteer: A Dictionary of Tar Heel Places.* Chapel Hill: University of North Carolina Press, 1968.

CONTEMPORARY PAMPHLETS

Address to the Colored People of North Carolina; Signed by Members of the State House of Representatives. Raleigh: n.p., 1870.

Annual Proceedings of the Western North Carolina Railroad, with Reports of Officers for 1868. Statesville: Eugene B. Drake and Sons, 1868.

Badger, Richard Cogsdell. *Removal of the Disabilities of Governor W. W. Holden.* Raleigh: John Nichols, 1883.

Brogden, Curtis Hooks. *Opinion on the Impeachment Trial.* Raleigh: Sentinel Book Company, 1871.

Convention of the Freedmen of North Carolina. Official Proceedings. Raleigh: 1865.

DeBow, James Dunwoody Brownson. *The Interest in Slavery of the Southern Non-Slaveholder.* Charleston: Presses of Evans and Cogswell, 1860.

Ellis, John Willis. *Speech Delivered before the Democratic State Convention, March 9, 1860.* Raleigh: W. W. Holden, 1860.

Full Report of the Proceedings in the Matter of the Bench and Bar. Raleigh: Nichols and Gorman, 1869.

Goodloe, Daniel Reaves. *The Marshalship in North Carolina, being a Reply to Charges Made by Messrs. Abbott, Pool, Heaton, Deweese, Dockery, Jones, Lash, and Cobb, Senators and Representatives of the State.* N.p., 1869.

Green, John Patterson. *Recollections of the Inhabitants, Localities, Superstitions and Ku Klux Outrages of the Carolinas.* N.p., n.d.

Holden, William Woods. *Address Delivered before the Duplin County Agricultural Society, November 6, 1857.* Raleigh: Standard Printing Company, 1857.

_____. *Address Delivered before the State Educational Association of North Carolina.* Raleigh: Standard Printing Company, 1857.

_____. *Address on the History of Journalism in North Carolina at the Ninth Annual*

Meeting of the Press Association of North Carolina. Winston, 21 June 1881. Raleigh: News and Observer Book and Job Printers, 1881.

Moore, Bartholomew Figures. *Constitutionality of the Convention Acts.* Raleigh: n.p., 1868.

Moore, William Armistead. *Law and Order vs. Ku Klux Violence.* Raleigh: Standard Printing Company, 1870.

Pool, John. *Address to the People of North Carolina.* Raleigh: Standard Printing Company, 1867.

––––––. *Speech of John Pool before the United States Senate, March 31, 1871.* Washington: Government Printing Office, 1871.

Shepard, William Biddle. *Speech upon the Right of Secession, Revolution, etc.* Raleigh: n.p., 1851.

Vance, Zebulon Baird. *The Political and Social South During the War.* Washington: Government Printing Office, 1886.

Warren, Edward Jenner. *Speech upon Resolution Concerning the Recent Action of the Governor.* Raleigh: n.p., 1871.

Wilson, Frank I. *Address Delivered before the Wake County Workingmen's Association.* Raleigh: Standard Printing Company, 1860.

NEWSPAPERS AND PERIODICALS

American Annual Cyclopedia and Register of Important Events. New York: A. Appleton and Company, 1861–72.

Charlotte North Carolina Whig, 1852–61.

Charlotte Western Democrat, 1856–61, 1868–72.

Fayetteville Observer, 1858–64.

Greensborough North State, 1872–78.

Greensborough Register, 1868–70.

Hillsborough Recorder, 1847–61.

New Bern Progress, 1858–60.

New York Times, 1865–71.

Raleigh Daily News, 1872–75.

Raleigh News and Observer, 1875–95.

Raleigh North Carolina Advertiser, 1865.

Raleigh North Carolina Standard, 1843–70.

Raleigh Progress, 1865.

Raleigh Register, 1847–61.

Raleigh Sentinel, 1865–73.

Raleigh Star, 1841, 1854–56.

Raleigh State Chronicle, 1873.

Raleigh Weekly Constitution, 1865.

Roanoke News, 1868–70.
Rutherford Star, 1868–71.
Rutherford Vindicatory, 1868–70.
Salisbury Carolina Watchman, 1854–56.
Salisbury Republican Banner, 1854–61.
Tarboro Southerner, 1868–70.
Washington (D.C.) *Daily and Weekly Chronicle*, 1870–71.
Wilmington Daily Journal, 1865–71.
Wilmington Daily Post, 1868–70.
Wilmington Herald, 1865.
Wilmington Star, 1868–70.

MEMOIRS AND CONTEMPORARY WRITINGS

Alderman, John T. "Memories of 1865–1871." *North Carolina Booklet* 13 (1914): 199–214.

Andrews, Sidney. *The South since the War: As Shown by Fourteen Weeks of Travel and Observation in Georgia and the Carolinas*. Boston: Ticknor and Fields, 1866.

————. "Three Months among the Reconstructionists." *Atlantic Monthly* 17 (February 1866): 237–45.

Battle, William James, ed. *Memoirs of an Old Time Tar Heel by Kemp Plummer Battle, President of the University of North Carolina, 1876–1891*. Chapel Hill: University of North Carolina Press, 1945.

Biggs, Asa. *Autobiography of Asa Biggs*. Edited by Robert Diggs Wimberly Connor. North Carolina Historical Commission Publication no. 19. Raleigh, 1915.

Blaine, James Gillespie. *Twenty Years of Congress*. 2 vols. Norwich, Conn.: Henry Bill, 1884.

Boutwell, George Sewall. "The Usurpations." *Atlantic Monthly* 17 (October 1866): 506–13.

Brevard, John Alexander. *Reminiscences of the Past Sixty Years*. Charlotte: Ray Printing, 1906.

Cheshire, Joseph Blunt. *Nonulla: Memoirs, Stories, Traditions, More or Less Authentic*. Chapel Hill: University of North Carolina Press, 1930.

Cox, Samuel Sullivan. *Three Decades of Federal Legislation*. Providence, R.I.: Reid Company, 1894.

Cralle, Richard, ed. *Works of John C. Calhoun*. 6 vols. New York: Appleton, 1854–57.

Dixon, Thomas. *The Clansman: An Historical Romance of the Ku Klux Klan*. New York: Grossett and Dunlap, 1902.

————. *The Leopard's Spots*. New York: Doubleday, Page, 1902.

Holden, William Woods. *The Memoirs of W. W. Holden.* Durham: Seeman Printery, 1911.

Jarvis, Thomas Jordan. "The Conditions That Led to the Ku Klux Klan." *North Carolina Booklet* 1 (1902): 1–24.

Long, Mary Alves. *High Time to Tell It.* Durham: Duke University Press, 1950.

McCulloch, Hugh. *Men and Measures of Half a Century.* New York: Scribners, 1889.

Moore, Bartholomew Figures. "Bartholomew F. Moore on Secession and Reconstruction." Trinity College Historical Society Publications no. 2, 1898, pp. 75–82.

Porter, Robert H. "State Debts and Repudiations." *International Review* 9 (November 1880): 556–604.

Reid, Whitelaw. *After the War: A Southern Tour, May 1, 1865 to May 1, 1866.* Cincinnati: Moore, Wilstack and Baldwin, 1866.

Schurz, Carl. "The True Problem." *Atlantic Monthly* 19 (March 1867): 371–78.

Sherman, William Tecumseh. *Memoirs of General William T. Sherman.* 2 vols. New York: Appleton, 1875.

Somers, Robert. *The Southern States since the War, 1870–71.* Southern Historical Publications no. 1. University: University of Alabama Press, 1965.

Spencer, Cornelia Phillips. *Last Ninety Days of the War in North Carolina.* New York: Watchman, 1866.

Tourgée, Albion Winegar. *A Fool's Errand, by One of the Fools.* New York: Fords, Howard and Holbert, 1879.

Wheeler, John Hill. *Reminiscences and Memoirs of North Carolina and Eminent North Carolinians.* Columbus, Ohio: Columbus Printing Works, 1884.

Whipple, E. P. "The Johnson Party." *Atlantic Monthly* 18 (September 1866): 374–81.

BIOGRAPHIES

Ashe, Samuel A'Court, ed. *Biographical History of North Carolina From Colonial Times to the Present.* 8 vols. Greensboro: Van Noppen, 1905–7.

Bancroft, Frederick. *The Life of William H. Seward.* 2 vols. Harper, 1900.

Bassett, John Spencer. *Anti-Slavery Leaders in North Carolina.* Baltimore: Johns Hopkins University Press, 1898.

A Biographical Congressional Directory with an Outline History of the National Congress, 1774–1911. Washington: Government Printing Office, 1913.

Boyd, William Kenneth. *William W. Holden.* Trinity College Historical Publications no. 3. 1899.

Caldwell, Bettie D. *Founders and Builders of Greensboro, 1808–1908.* Greensboro: J. J. Stone, 1925.

Chamberlain, Hope Summerell. *Old Days in Chapel Hill: Being the Life and Letters of Cornelia Phillips Spencer.* Chapel Hill: University of North Carolina Press, 1926.

Chitwood, Oliver Perry. *John Tyler: Champion of the Old South*. New York: Appleton-Century-Croft, 1939.

Cowper, Pulaski. "A Sketch of the Life of Governor Thomas Bragg." *North Carolina University Magazine*, new series, 10 (February 1891): 123–34.

Daniels, Jonathan. *Milton S. Littlefield: Prince of Carpetbaggers*. Philadelphia: Lippincott, 1958.

Dodd, William Edward. *Jefferson Davis*. Philadelphia: George W. Jacobs, 1907.

Dowd, Clement. *Life of Zebulon B. Vance*. Charlotte: North Carolina Observer Printing and Publishing Company, 1897.

Dowd, Jerome. *Sketches of Prominent Living North Carolinians*. Raleigh: Edwards and Broughton, 1888.

Eaton, Clement. *Henry Clay and the Art of American Politics*. Boston: Little, Brown, 1956.

Folk, Edgar Estes, and Shaw, Bynum. *W. W. Holden: A Political Biography*. Winston-Salem: John F. Blair, 1982.

Grant, Daniel L. *Alumni History of the University of North Carolina*. Chapel Hill: University of North Carolina Press, 1924.

Griffin, Clarence W. *Western North Carolina Sketches*. Forest City: Forest City Courier, 1941.

Hamilton, Joseph Gregoire de Roulhac. *Benjamin Sherwood Hedrick*. James Sprunt Historical Studies in History and Political Science no. 10. Chapel Hill: University of North Carolina, 1910.

Korngold, Ralph. *Thaddeus Stevens: A Being Darkly Wise and Rudely Great*. New York: Harcourt, Brace, 1955.

McCormick, Gilchrist. *Personnel of the Convention of 1861*. Chapel Hill: University of North Carolina, 1908.

Miller, Alphonse B. *Thaddeus Stevens*. New York: Harper, 1939.

Milton, George Fort. *The Age of Hate: Andrew Johnson and the Radicals*. New York: Coward-McCann, 1930.

Olsen, Otto H. *Carpetbagger's Crusade: The Life of Albion Winegar Tourgée*. Baltimore: Johns Hopkins University Press, 1965.

Peale, William Joseph, ed. *Lives of Distinguished North Carolinians*. Raleigh: North Carolina Publishing Society, 1898.

Powell, William Henry. *List of Officers of the Army of the United States from 1779 to 1900*. Detroit: Gale Research, 1967.

Powell, William S., ed. *Dictionary of North Carolina Biography*. Vol. 1, A–C. Chapel Hill: University of North Carolina Press, 1979.

Russell, Phillips. *The Woman Who Rang the Bell: The Story of Cornelia Phillips Spencer*. Chapel Hill: University of North Carolina Press, 1949.

Schenck, David. *Personal Sketches of Distinguished Delegates of the State Convention, 1861–1862*. Raleigh: n.p., 1865.

Schofield, John McAllister. *Forty-Six Years in the Army*. New York: Century, 1897.

Van Deusen, Glyndon S. *The Life of Henry Clay.* Boston: Little, Brown, 1937.

Villard, Oswald Garrison. *John Brown, 1800–1859: A Biography of Fifty Years After.* Boston: Houghton Mifflin, 1911.

Warner, Ezra, and Yearns, W. Buck. *Biographical Register of the Confederate Congress.* Baton Rouge: Louisiana State University Press, 1975.

White, Laura Amanda. *Robert Barnwell Rhett: Father of Secession.* New York: Century, 1931.

Zuber, Richard L. *Jonathan Worth: A Biography of a Southern Unionist.* Chapel Hill: University of North Carolina Press, 1965.

GENERAL, STATE, AND LOCAL HISTORIES

Allen, James Stewart. *Reconstruction: The Battle for Democracy, 1865–1876.* New York: International Publishers, 1937.

Allen, William C. *Centennial of Haywood County and Its County Seat Waynesville, N.C., 1808–1908.* Waynesville: Courier Printing Company, 1908.

Amis, Moses Neal. *Historical Raleigh from Its Foundation in 1792.* Raleigh: Commercial Printing Company, 1902.

Arthur, John Preston. *Western North Carolina: A History from 1713–1913.* Raleigh: Edwards and Broughton, 1914.

Ashe, Samuel A'Court. *History of North Carolina.* 2 vols. Greensboro and Raleigh: Van Noppen, 1908 and 1925.

Burgess, John W. *Reconstruction and the Constitution, 1866–1876.* New York: Scribners, 1903.

Chamberlain, Hope Summerell. *History of Wake County.* Raleigh: Edwards and Broughton, 1922.

Connor, Robert Diggs Wimberly. *North Carolina: Rebuilding an Ancient Commonwealth, 1584–1925.* Chicago: American Historical Society, 1929.

Cooper, Horton. *History of Avery County.* Asheville: Biltmore Press, 1964.

Coulter, E. Merton. *The Confederate States of America, 1861–1865.* Baton Rouge: Louisiana State University Press, 1950.

————. *The South During Reconstruction, 1865–1877.* Baton Rouge: Louisiana State University Press, 1947.

Davis, William Watson. *The Civil War and Reconstruction in Florida.* New York: Columbia University Press, 1913.

Eaton, Clement. *A History of the Southern Confederacy.* New York: Macmillan, 1954.

Fleming, Walter Lynwood. *The Reconstruction of the Seceded States.* New York: New York State Educational Department, 1905.

Fletcher, Arthur. *Ashe County: A History.* Jefferson: Ashe County Research Association, 1963.

Franklin, John Hope. *Reconstruction after the Civil War*. Chicago: University of Chicago Press, 1961.

Freel, Margaret Walter. *Our Heritage: The People of Cherokee County, North Carolina*. Asheville: Miller Printing Company, 1956.

Fries, Adelaide L. *Forsyth County*. Winston: Stewart's Printing House, 1898.

_____. *Forsyth County: A County on the March*. Chapel Hill: University of North Carolina Press, 1949.

Griffin, Clarence W. *History of Old Tryon and Rutherford Counties, North Carolina*. Asheville: Miller Printing Company, 1937.

_____. *History of Rutherford County*. Asheville: Inland Press, 1952.

Hamilton, Joseph Gregoire de Roulhac. *Reconstruction in North Carolina*. New York: Columbia University Press, 1914.

Hamilton, Peter Joseph. *The Reconstruction Period*. Philadelphia: printed for subscribers only by G. B. Barrie and Sons, 1906.

Hill, David Harvey. *North Carolina in the War between the States*. 2 vols. Raleigh: Edwards and Broughton, 1926.

Hollingsworth, Jesse G. *History of Surry County or Annals of Northwest North Carolina*. Greensboro: W. H. Fisher, 1935.

Johnson, Guion Griffis. *Ante-Bellum North Carolina: A Social History*. Chapel Hill: University of North Carolina Press, 1937.

Lefler, Hugh Talmage. *North Carolina History Told by Contemporaries*. Chapel Hill: University of North Carolina Press, 1965.

_____, and Newsome, Albert Ray. *North Carolina: The History of a Southern State*. Chapel Hill: University of North Carolina Press, 1973.

Leonard, Jacob C. *Centennial History of Davidson County*. Raleigh: Edwards and Broughton, 1927.

Montgomery, Lizzie Wilson. *Sketches of Old Warrenton, North Carolina*. Raleigh: Edwards and Broughton, 1924.

Moore, John Wheeler. *History of North Carolina*. 2 vols. Raleigh: A. Williams, 1884.

Oberholtzer, Ellis Paxton. *A History of the United States since the Civil War*. 5 vols. New York: Macmillan, 1917–37.

Powell, William S. *When the Past Refused to Die: A History of Caswell County, North Carolina, 1777–1977*. Durham: Moore, 1977.

Randall, James Garfield, and Donald, David Herbert. *The Civil War and Reconstruction*. Boston: D. C. Heath, 1961.

Rhodes, James Ford. *History of the United States from the Compromise of 1850, to the Final Restoration of Home Rule at the South in 1877*. 7 vols. New York: Macmillan, 1896–1906.

Rumple, Jethro. *A History of Rowan County, North Carolina*. Salisbury: J. J. Bruner, 1881.

Schouler, James. *History of the Reconstruction Period, 1865–1877*. 7 vols. New York: Dodd, Mead, 1894–1913.

Schwab, John Christopher. *The Confederate States of America, 1861–1865: A Finan-*

cial and Industrial History of the South during the Civil War. New Haven: Yale University Press, 1901.

Sondley, F. A. *History of Buncombe County, North Carolina.* 2 vols. Asheville: Advocate Printing Company, 1930.

Stockard, Sallie Walter. *History of Alamance County, North Carolina.* Raleigh: Capital Publishing Company, 1900.

Tompkins, Daniel A. *History of Mecklenburg County and the City of Charlotte from 1740 to 1903.* Charlotte: Observer Publishing House, 1903.

Turner, Joseph K., and Bridgers, John L. *History of Edgecombe County, North Carolina.* Raleigh: Edwards and Broughton, 1920.

Wall, James W. *History of Davie County: In the Forks of the Yadkin.* Mocksville: Davie County Historical Publishing Association, 1969.

Weathers, Lee B. *The Living Past of Cleveland County.* Shelby: Star Publishing Company, 1956.

Whitaker, Walter. *Centennial History of Alamance County, 1849–1949.* Charlotte: Dowd Press, 1949.

Whitener, Daniel J. *A History of Watauga County.* Kingsport, Tenn.: Franklin Printing Company, 1949.

Yates, Richard Erwin. *The Confederacy and Zeb Vance.* Tuscaloosa, Ala.: Confederate Printing Company, 1958.

ARTICLES

Alexander, Roberta Sue. "Hostility and Hope: Black Education in North Carolina during Presidential Reconstruction, 1865–1867." *North Carolina Historical Review* 53 (April 1976): 113–32.

Allen, Jeffrey Brook. "The Racial Thought of White North Carolina Opponents of Slavery, 1789–1876." *North Carolina Historical Review* 54 (January 1982): 1–23.

Auman, William T., and Scarboro, David D. "The Heroes of America in Civil War North Carolina." *North Carolina Historical Review* 58 (October 1981): 327–63.

Bardolph, Richard. "Inconsistent Rebels: Desertion of North Carolina Troops in the Civil War." *North Carolina Historical Review* 41 (April 1964): 163–89.

Barnes, Johnny W. "The Political Activities of the Union League of America in North Carolina." *Quarterly Review of Higher Education among Negroes* 18 (1952): 141–50.

Battle, Kemp Plummer. "The Secession Convention of 1861." *North Carolina Booklet* 15, no. 4 (April 1916).

Bernstein, Leonard. "The Participation of Negro Delegates in the Constitutional Convention of 1868 in North Carolina." *Journal of Negro History* 34 (1949): 391–409.

Boyd, William Kenneth. "North Carolina on the Eve of Secession." *Annual Report of the American Historical Association* 3 (1910): 165–79.

Brabham, Robin. "Defending the American University: The University of North Carolina, 1865–1875." *North Carolina Historical Review* 57 (October 1980): 427–55.

Brown, Cecil Kenneth. "The Florida Investments of George W. Swepson." *North Carolina Historical Review* 5 (October 1928): 275–88.

Browning, James Blackwell. "North Carolina Black Codes." *Journal of Negro History* 15 (1930): 461–73.

Butts, Donald C. "The Irrepressible Conflict: Slave Taxation and North Carolina's Gubernatorial Election of 1860." *North Carolina Historical Review* 58 (January 1981): 44–66.

Connor, Robert Diggs Wimberly. "The Rehabilitation of a Rural Commonwealth." *American Historical Review* 36 (October 1930): 44–62.

Cook, Raymond A. "The Man behind 'The Birth of a Nation.'" *North Carolina Historical Review* 34 (October 1962): 519–40.

Cox, Monty Woodall. "Freedom during the Fremont Campaign: The Fate of One North Carolina Republican in 1856." *North Carolina Historical Review* 45 (October 1968): 357–83.

Crow, Terrell Armistead. "As Thy Days, So Shall Thy Strength Be: North Carolina Planter Women in War and Peace." *Carolina Comments* (bimonthly publication of the North Carolina Division of Archives and History) 28, no. 1 (January 1980).

Dailey, Douglas C. "The Elections of 1872 in North Carolina." *North Carolina Historical Review* 40 (July 1963): 338–60.

Davenport, F. Garvin, Jr. "Thomas Dixon's Mythology of Southern History." *Journal of Southern History* 36 (November 1970): 350–71.

Dorris, Jonathan Truman. "Pardon Seekers and Brokers: A Sequel of Appomattox." *Journal of Southern History* 1 (August 1935): 1–17.

———. "Pardoning North Carolinians." *North Carolina Historical Review* 23 (July 1946): 360–401.

———. "Pardoning the Leaders of the Confederacy." *Mississippi Valley Historical Review* 15 (June 1928): 3–21.

Ewing, Cortez Arthur Milton. "Two Reconstruction Impeachments." *North Carolina Historical Review* 15 (July 1938): 197–230.

Felon, Paul E. "The Notorious Swepson-Littlefield Frauds." *Florida Historical Quarterly* 32 (1954): 231–61.

Folk, Edgar Estes. "W. W. Holden and the North Carolina Standard, 1843–1848." *North Carolina Historical Review* 19 (January 1942): 22–47.

———. "W. W. Holden and the Election of 1858." *North Carolina Historical Review* 21 (October 1944): 294–318.

Hamilton, Joseph Gregoire de Roulhac. "Heroes of America." *Publications of the Southern History Association* 11 (January 1907): 10–19.

———. "The North Carolina Convention of 1865–1866." *Proceedings and Addresses of the Fourteenth Annual Session of the State Literary and Historical Association of North Carolina. Publication of the North Carolina Historical Commission*, 1913, 56–68.

Harris, William C. "William Woods Holden: In Search of Vindication." *North Carolina Historical Review* 59 (October 1982): 354–72.

Herndon, Dallas T. "The Nashville Convention of 1850." *Alabama Historical Society Transactions*, no. 5, (1905): 227–37.

Heyman, Max L. " 'The Great Reconstructor': General E. R. S. Canby and the Second Military District." *North Carolina Historical Review* 32 (January 1955): 52–80.

Jeffrey, Thomas E. " 'Free Suffrage' Revisited: Party Politics and Constitutional Reform in Antebellum North Carolina." *North Carolina Historical Review* 54 (January 1982): 24–48.

_____. "National Issues, Local Interests, and the Transformation of Antebellum North Carolina Politics." *Journal of Southern History* 50 (February 1984): 43–74.

Mabry, William Alexander. "The Negro in North Carolina Politics since Reconstruction." Trinity College Historical Society Publications no. 23, 1940, 1–87.

Miller, Robert D. "Samuel Field Phillips: The Odyssey of a Southern Dissenter." *North Carolina Historical Review* 58 (July 1981): 263–80.

Olsen, Otto H. "The Ku Klux Klan: A Study in Reconstruction Politics and Propaganda." *North Carolina Historical Review* 34 (July 1962): 340–63.

_____. "Albion W. Tourgée: Carpetbagger." *North Carolina Historical Review* 40 (October 1963): 434–54.

Price, Charles Lewis. "The Railroad Schemes of George W. Swepson." East Carolina Publications in History no. 1, 1964.

Raper, Horace W. "William W. Holden and the Peace Movement in North Carolina." *North Carolina Historical Review* 31 (October 1954): 493–516.

Ratchford, Benjamin Ulysses. "North Carolina Public Debt, 1870–1883." *North Carolina Historical Review* 10 (January 1933): 1–20; 10 (July 1933): 157–67.

Reid, Richard. "A Test Case of the 'Crying Evil': Desertion among North Carolina Troops During the Civil War." *North Carolina Historical Review* 58 (July 1981): 234–62.

Russ, William A. "Radical Disfranchisement in North Carolina." *North Carolina Historical Review* 11 (July 1934): 271–83.

St. Clair, Kenneth Edson. "Debtor Relief in North Carolina During Reconstruction." *North Carolina Historical Review* 18 (July 1941): 215–35.

_____. "Judicial Machinery in North Carolina in 1865." *North Carolina Historical Review* 30 (October 1953): 415–39.

Snow, Richard F. "Thomas Dixon." *American Heritage* 31, no. 6 (1980): 80–81.

Stroupe, Henry S. "The Beginning of Religious Journalism in North Carolina, 1823–1865." *North Carolina Historical Review* 30 (January 1953): 1–22.

Sutherland, Daniel E. "Charles Force Deems and 'The Watchman': An Early Attempt at Post–Civil War Sectional Reconciliation." *North Carolina Historical Review* 58 (October 1980): 410–26.

Trelease, Allen W. "Republican Reconstruction in North Carolina: A Roll-Call Analysis of the State House of Representatives, 1868–1870." *Journal of Southern History* 42 (August 1976): 319–44.

Whitener, Daniel Jay. "Public Education During Reconstruction." In *Essays in Southern History Presented to Joseph Gregoire de Roulhac Hamilton by His Former Students*, edited by Fletcher M. Green, 67–90. Chapel Hill: University of North Carolina Press, 1949.

──────. "The Republican Party and Public Education in North Carolina, 1867–1900." *North Carolina Historical Review* 37 (July 1960): 382–96.

Wilkerson, A. A. "Caswell County and the Kirk-Holden War." *Durham Sun*, 14 July 1946.

Work, Monroe Nathan. "Some Negro Members of the Reconstruction Conventions and Legislatures and of Congress." *Journal of Negro History* 5 (January 1920): 60–120.

Yates, Richard Edwin. "Zebulon B. Vance as War Governor of North Carolina." *Journal of Southern History* 3 (February 1937): 43–75.

──────. "Governor Vance and the Peace Movement." *North Carolina Historical Review* 17 (January 1940): 1–25.

MONOGRAPHS AND SPECIAL STUDIES

Barrett, John C. *Sherman's March through the Carolinas*. Chapel Hill: University of North Carolina Press, 1956.

──────. *The Civil War in North Carolina*. Chapel Hill: University of North Carolina Press, 1963.

Battle, Kemp Plummer. *Legislation of the Convention of 1861*. James Sprunt Historical Studies in History and Political Science no. 1. Chapel Hill: University of North Carolina, 1900.

──────. *History of the University of North Carolina*. 2 vols. Raleigh: Edwards and Broughton, 1907–12.

Beale, Howard Kennedy. *The Critical Year: A Study of Andrew Johnson and Reconstruction*. New York: Harcourt, Brace, 1930.

Bowers, Claude Gernade. *The Tragic Era: The Revolution after Lincoln*. Cambridge: Houghton Mifflin, 1929.

Boyd, William Kenneth. *The Story of Durham: City of the New South*. Durham: Duke University Press, 1927.

Brown, Cecil Kenneth. *A State Movement in Railroad Development: The Story of North Carolina's First Effort to Establish an East and West Trunk Line Railroad*. Chapel Hill: University of North Carolina Press, 1928.

Carr, John Winder. *The Manhood Suffrage Movement in North Carolina*. Trinity College Historical Society Publication no. 11, (Durham). 1915.

Cash, Wilbur J. *The Mind of the South*. New York: Knopf, 1941.

Cole, Arthur Charles. *Whig Party in the South*. Washington: American Historical Association, 1913.

Coleman, Charles Herbert. *The Election of 1868: The Democratic Effort to Regain Control*. New York: Columbia University Press, 1933.

Cooper, William J. *The South and the Politics of Slavery*. Baton Rouge: Louisiana State University Press, 1978.

Craven, Avery Odelle. *The Coming of the Civil War*. New York: Scribners, 1942.

Curry, Richard O. *Radicalism, Racism, and Party Realignment: The Border States during Reconstruction*. Baltimore: Johns Hopkins University Press, 1969.

Davis, Susan Lawrence. *Authentic History: Ku Klux Klan, 1865–1877*. New York: Susan Lawrence Davis, 1924.

Degler, Carl N. *The Other South: Southern Dissenters in the Nineteenth Century*. New York: Harper & Row, 1974.

Dorris, Jonathan Truman. *Pardon and Amnesty under Lincoln and Johnson: The Restoration of the Confederates to Their Rights and Privileges, 1861–1898*. Chapel Hill: University of North Carolina Press, 1953.

Dumond, Dwight Lowell. *The Secession Movement, 1860–1861*. New York: Macmillan, 1931.

Elliott, Robert N. *The Raleigh Register, 1799–1863*. Chapel Hill: University of North Carolina Press, 1955.

Fite, Emerson Davis. *The Presidential Campaign of 1860*. New York: Macmillan, 1911.

Gillette, William. *Retreat from Reconstruction: A Political History, 1867–1878*. Baton Rouge: Louisiana State University Press, 1979.

Gray, Wood. *The Hidden Civil War: The Story of the Copperheads*. New York: Viking Press, 1942.

Green, Fletcher M. *Constitutional Development in the South Atlantic States, 1776–1860: A Study in the Evolution of Democracy*. Chapel Hill: University of North Carolina Press, 1930.

Hamilton, Holman. *Prologue to Conflict: The Crisis and Compromise of 1850*. Lexington: University of Kentucky Press, 1964.

Hamilton, Joseph Gregoire de Roulhac. *Party Politics in North Carolina, 1835–1860*. James Sprunt Studies in History and Political Science no. 15. Durham: Seeman Printery, 1916.

Henderson, Archibald. *The Campus of the First State University*. Chapel Hill: University of North Carolina Press, 1949.

Horn, Stanley. *The Invisible Empire: The Story of the Ku Klux Klan, 1866–1871*. Boston: Houghton Mifflin, 1939.

Jennings, Thelma. *The Nashville Convention: Southern Movement for Unity*. Memphis: Memphis State University Press, 1980.

Johnson, Gerald White. *The Secession Movement of the Southern States*. New York: Putnam, 1933.

Knight, Edgar Wallace. *The Influence of Reconstruction on Education in the South*. New York: Columbia University Press, 1913.

————. *Public School Education in North Carolina.* Boston: Houghton Mifflin, 1916.

Lonn, Ella. *Desertion during the Civil War.* New York: Century, 1928.

McKitrick, Eric L. *Andrew Johnson and Reconstruction.* Chicago: University of Chicago Press, 1960.

Moore, Albert Burton. *Conscription and Conflict in the Confederacy.* New York: Macmillan, 1924.

Morrison, C. W. *Democratic Politics and Sectionalism: The Wilmot Proviso.* Baton Rouge: Louisiana State University Press, 1967.

Noble, Marcus Cicero Stephens. *A History of the Public Schools of North Carolina.* Chapel Hill: University of North Carolina Press, 1930.

Norton, Clarence Clifford. *The Democratic Party in Ante-Bellum North Carolina, 1835–1861.* James Sprunt Studies in History and Political Science no. 21. Chapel Hill: University of North Carolina Press, 1930.

Paludan, Phillip Shaw. *Victims: A True Story of the Civil War.* Knoxville: University of Tennessee Press, 1981.

Pease, Jane H., and Pease, William H. *The Fugitive Slave Law and Anthony Burns: A Problem in Law Enforcement.* Philadelphia: Lippincott, 1975.

Perman, Michael. *Reunion without Compromise: The South and Reconstruction.* London: Cambridge University Press, 1973.

Russel, Robert Royal. *Economic Aspects of Southern Sectionalism, 1840–1861.* Urbana: University of Illinois Press, 1923.

Scott, William Amasa. *The Repudiation of State Debts.* New York: Thomas Y. Crowell, 1923.

Sefton, James E. *The United States Army and Reconstruction, 1865–1877.* Baton Rouge: Louisiana State University Press, 1967.

Sitterson, Joseph Carlyle. *The Secession Movement in North Carolina.* James Sprunt Studies in History and Political Science no. 23. Chapel Hill: University of North Carolina Press, 1939.

Tatum, Georgia Lee. *Disloyalty in the Confederacy.* Chapel Hill: University of North Carolina Press, 1934.

Taylor, Rosser Howard. *Slaveholding in North Carolina: An Economic View.* James Sprunt Studies in History and Political Science no. 18. Chapel Hill: University of North Carolina Press, 1926.

Tindall, George B. *The Emergence of the New South, 1913–1945.* Baton Rouge: Louisiana State University Press, 1967.

Trelease, Allen W. *White Terror: The Ku Klux Klan Conspiracy and Southern Reconstruction.* New York: Harper and Row, 1971.

Wagstaff, Henry McGilbert. *States Rights and Political Parties in North Carolina, 1776–1861.* Baltimore: Johns Hopkins University Press, 1906.

Wellman, Manly Wade. *Dead and Gone: Classic Crimes of North Carolina.* Chapel Hill: University of North Carolina Press, 1954.

Woodward, Comer Vann. *Origins of the New South, 1877–1913.* Baton Rouge: Louisiana State University Press, 1951.

———. *Reunion and Reaction: The Compromise of 1877 and the End of Reconstruction*. Boston: Little, Brown, 1951.
Yearns, W. Buck. *The Confederate Congress*. Athens: University of Georgia Press, 1960.

THESES AND OTHER PAPERS

Cotton, William Donaldson. "Appalachian North Carolina: A Political Study, 1860–1896." Ph.D. dissertation, University of North Carolina, 1956.
Drumm, Austin Marcus. "The Union League in the Carolinas." Ph.D. dissertation, University of North Carolina, 1955.
Folk, Edgar Estes. "W. W. Holden, Political Journalist." Ph.D. dissertation, George Peabody College, 1934.
Harris, William Durham. "The Movement for Constitutional Change in North Carolina, 1863–1876." M.A. thesis, University of North Carolina, 1932.
Hoffman, Richard Lee. "The Republican Party in North Carolina, 1865–1870." M.A. thesis, University of North Carolina, 1960.
Holder, Branston Beeson. "The Three Banks of the State of North Carolina, 1810–1872." Ph.D. dissertation, University of North Carolina, 1937.
Lacy, Dan Mabry. "The Beginnings of Industrialization in North Carolina, 1865–1900." M.A. thesis, University of North Carolina, 1935.
London, Lawrence Foushee. "The Public Career of George Edmund Badger." Ph.D. dissertation, University of North Carolina, 1936.
McFayden, Henry C. "The Administration of Governor Jonathan Worth." M.A. thesis, University of North Carolina, 1942.
McLeod, John Blount. "The Development of North Carolina Election Laws, 1865 to 1894." M.A. thesis, University of North Carolina, 1947.
Macon, Hershal Luther. "A Fiscal History of North Carolina, 1776–1860." Ph.D. dissertation, University of North Carolina, 1932.
Newsome, Albert Ray. "Report of an Investigation of the Passage of the Reconstruction Bond Ordinances and Acts of North Carolina in 1868–1869." Manuscript in hands of author.
Nowaczyk, Elaine Joane. "The North Carolina Negro in Politics, 1865–1876." M.A. thesis, University of North Carolina, 1957.
O'Quinn, Marion Nolan. "Carpetbagger Samuel S. Ashley and His Role in North Carolina Education, 1865–1871." M.A. thesis, University of North Carolina, 1975.
Pegg, Herbert Dale. "The Whig Party in North Carolina, 1834–1861." Ph.D. dissertation, University of North Carolina, 1933.
Price, Charles Lewis. "Railroads and Reconstruction in North Carolina, 1865–1871." Ph.D. dissertation, University of North Carolina, 1959.
Raper, Horace W. "The Political Career of William Woods Holden with Special Refer-

ence to His Provisional Governorship." M.A. thesis, University of North Carolina, 1948.

——. "William W. Holden: A Political Biography." Ph.D. dissertation, University of North Carolina, 1951.

St. Clair, Kenneth Edson. "The Administration of Justice in North Carolina." Ph.D. dissertation, Ohio State University, 1939.

Scroggs, Jack Benton. "Carpetbagger Influence on the Political Reconstruction of the South Atlantic States, 1865–1876." Ph.D. dissertation, University of North Carolina, 1952.

Thompson, Samuel Horton. "The Legislative Development of Public School Support in North Carolina." Ph.D. dissertation, University of North Carolina, 1936.

Wooten, Samuel R. "A History of Richmond Hill Law School." M.A. thesis, University of North Carolina, 1963.

INDEX

Public Works, 116, 135, 139, 290 (n. 60), 297 (n. 40); on Turner's arrest, 189, 319 (n. 115)

Harris, James F., 285 (n. 16)

Harris, James H.: Republican party leader, 93, 116, 297 (n. 40); petitions Worth's removal, 95; railroad scandals, 128, 303 (n. 6); opposes Holden, 234, 310 (n. 55); 1865 Freedmen's convention, 287 (n. 47); 1868 Congressional candidate, 295 (n. 29), 319 (n. 108)

Harris, James T., 95

Harris, Nelson T., 285 (n. 16)

Harrise, Henri, 260 (n. 97)

Harrison, Robert, 21, 107, 292 (n. 8), 303 (n. 8)

Harrison, William H., 21, 227, 267 (n. 70), 315 (n. 48)

Hawkins, Madison, 319 (n. 108)

Hawkins, Philemon B., 326 (n. 43)

Hawkins, William J., 130, 133, 276 (n. 32), 284 (n. 2)

Hayes, O. S., 114

Hayes, President Rutherford B., 233, 235–36

Haywood, Edward Graham, 128, 134, 136–37, 156, 295 (n. 24), 308 (n. 34), 309 (n. 37)

Hearne, William A., 166

Heartt, Dennis, 4–7, 8, 10, 254 (n. 7)

Heaton, David, 94, 95, 97, 104, 290 (n. 60), 293 (n. 11), 295 (n. 28); sketch, 289 (n. 57)

Heck, Jonathan M., 115; sketch, 296–97 (n. 36), 297 (n. 42)

Hedgepeth, Abel, 215

Hedrick, Benjamin Sherwood, 25–26, 54, 93, 99, 260 (n. 96), 283 (n. 100), 287 (n. 31)

Helper, Hardie H., 100

Helper, Hinton Rowan, 34, 100, 263 (n. 32)

Henderson, William F., 166, 172, 295 (n. 29), 303 (n. 7), 312 (n. 8), 315 (n. 48)

Henry, Beulah Louisa, 330–31 (n. 74)

Henry, James Love, 290 (n. 67), 311 (n. 63), 328 (n. 37)

Henry, Robert M., 172, 197, 276 (n. 22), 283 (n. 95), 285 (n. 13), 305 (n. 20)

Henry, Walter R., 246, 250–51, 331 (n. 83)

Henry, Mrs. Walter R. (Beulah Williamson Holden), 21, 230, 241, 259 (n. 78), 330 (nn. 71, 74)

Heroes of America (Red Strings), 48, 54, 272 (n. 42)

Hill, General Daniel H., 269 (n. 7)

Hill, J. G., 234

Hill, Samuel P., 184, 194, 207

Hill, Theophilus H., 246

Hillsborough Recorder, 4, 6, 7, 199

Hinsdale, John W., 248

Hodge, Henderson A., 202

Hodgin, David, 139

Hoke, John F., 265 (n. 42)

Hoke, Michael, 13, 14

Holden, Addison, 253 (n. 1)

Holden, Anne Augusta Young, 9, 241

Holden, Atelia. *See* Lyon, Mrs. John L.

Holden, Beulah Williamson. *See* Henry, Mrs. Walter R.

Holden, Charles Collier, 21, 230, 242–43, 330 (n. 71)

Holden, E. Brock, 3–4, 253 (n. 1), 320 (n. 117)

Holden, Henrietta (Ettie) Reid. *See* Mahler, Mrs. Fred

Holden, Henry, 253 (n. 1)

Holden, Ida Augusta. *See* Cowles, Mrs. Calvin J.

Holden, Joseph W., 9, 22, 306 (n. 24), 328 (n. 24), 330 (n. 71); military service, 42, 259 (n. 79); co-editor of